1988
14th EDITION
THE COMPLETE HANDBOOK OF
PRO BASKETBALL

D1600338

EXCITING SPORTS ACTION

1988
14th EDITION
THE COMPLETE HANDBOOK OF
PRO BASKETBALL

EDITED BY ZANDER HOLLANDER

A SIGNET BOOK
NEW AMERICAN LIBRARY

ACKNOWLEDGMENTS

Whatever else the new season may bring, it promises a large dose of excitement in the presence of the smallest man ever to play in the NBA—5-foot-3 Tyrone (Muggsy) Bogues. May the Wake Forest pepperpot make it big as a Bullet.

We acknowledge the many hands who contributed to the 14th edition of *The Complete Handbook of Pro Basketball:* contributing editor David Kaplan, the writers listed on the contents page and Lee Stowbridge, Howard Blatt, Fred Cantey, Steve Wisniewski, Richard Rossiter, Bob Rosen, Seymour Siwoff, Alex Sachare, Brian McIntyre, Terry Lyons, Matt Winick, Marty Blake, the NBA team publicity directors, Dot Gordineer, Beri Greenwald, Barbara Berger and Chris Swirnoff of Libra Graphics and the folks at Westchester Book Composition.

Zander Hollander

PHOTO CREDITS: Front cover: Focus on Sports; back cover —Noren Trotman; inside photos—George Gojkovich, Ira Golden, Vic Milton, Kevin Reece, Richard Reiss, CBS-TV, Wide World, UPI and the NBA team photographers.

SIGNET TRADEMARK REG. U.S. PAT. OFF. AND FOREIGN COUNTRIES REGISTERED TRADEMARK—MARCA REGISTRADA
HECHO EN CHICAGO, U.S.A.

SIGNET, SIGNET CLASSIC, MENTOR, ONYX, PLUME, MERIDIAN AND NAL BOOKS are published by NAL PENGUIN, 1633 Broadway, New York, New York 10019

First Printing, November, 1987

1 2 3 4 5 6 7 8 9

PRINTED IN THE UNITED STATES OF AMERICA

CONTENTS

Editor's Note: The material herein includes trades and rosters up to final printing deadline.

THE WORLD
OF
MAGIC

By GORDON EDES

Just like the man who won the award, the trophy honoring the NBA's Most Valuable Player belongs to the neighborhood. The House that Magic Built may be a mansion in exclusive Bel-Air, where Hollywood stars like Richard Pryor live around the block, but Earvin Johnson, heart and soul, still resides in Lansing, Mich., on whose playgrounds he was made.

Even as he was having his finest season, one that culminated in a world championship for the Lakers, his first regular-season MVP award and third playoff MVP trophy, Johnson still could hear the voice of Reggie Chastine, his 5-foot-3 Everett High School teammate and friend.

"Take it to 'em, Earvin. Bring it on. C'mon. Don't take no stuff."

All Earvin Johnson had wanted, ever since he'd first looked at the pictures in the newspaper, was to be named All-City in Lansing. Reggie was always the one pushing him to bigger dreams.

"On the playground, see, they want you," Magic Johnson said. "If you're the best player, they want you. So it takes not only being good, you have to have that drive. You have to say, 'I'm going to take all your best shots. I'm not looking to fight, but I'm looking to dominate you.' Reggie taught me that.

"He was the first one who really believed in me. I doubted myself, but he was looking to big things. To have that sense of the big dream and that strongness . . . I needed that."

So, even as Johnson stood on the steps of City Hall and invited Los Angeles to party the day after the Lakers had beaten the Boston Celtics for their fourth world title in the Magic era, there

---

Gordon Edes of the Los Angeles Times *regularly views and reviews the legend and legerdemain of Magic Johnson.*

Magic Johnson skyhooks in 1987 NBA finale.

was a part of him that wished Chastine could have been there, too. The years have long since dried the tears Magic shed after Chastine was killed when someone ran a stop sign and struck his car the summer before the two friends were to be high-school seniors together. The debt, however, will never be forgotten.

For the same reason, Magic's MVP trophy is proudly displayed in the living room of Earvin Johnson Sr.—Big E, as his son calls him. When Big E would come home after working his two full-time jobs, there were times he'd fall asleep right in the middle of that same living-room floor.

"I feel so much for him now," Johnson says of his father. "When I was young, I didn't really think about what he was doing, but now I understand how much he did for me and my brothers and sisters.

"When a game would come on TV, he'd tell me, 'Wake me up.' He taught me so much, watching those games. We'd watch, and then he'd go back to sleep, and I'd go back on the court working on those things we talked about."

Now, when Big E wakes up and flips on his TV, he can watch his son at the top of his game and profession. There are those who would argue—recalling that electrifying night in his rookie season of 1979-80 when Magic filled in at center for an injured Kareem Abdul-Jabbar and scored 42 points in a title-clinching win over the 76ers—that Magic's act could never get better.

It did, however, last season, when Johnson added scoring to his repertoire and the Lakers made the dramatic transition from being a team that revolved around Abdul-Jabbar to one that relied on Magic.

"He came back from losing to Houston [in the playoffs the previous year] with fire in his eyes," said Laker teammate Mychal Thompson. "You could tell he was on a mission, that he wasn't going to let this team fail."

How was that mission—which culminated in a six-game conquest of the Boston Celtics in the finals—accomplished? All Magic did was become the first guard since Oscar Robertson in 1963-64 to win the regular-season MVP award, and the first player ever to become a three-time playoff MVP. Not even Bill Russell was able to pull that off, not to mention Magic's archrival, Larry Bird.

"Michael Jordan is a hell of a basketball player, he scored a lot of points, but I believe in the total game," Bird said. "When you look at the total game, nobody's close to Magic."

The numbers can only suggest the totality of Magic's game. They cannot capture the keen intelligence, breathtaking improvisation and unyielding heart that separate him from others with perhaps as much natural ability. Those intangibles can only be captured in the mind's snapshot of a scene—as in the closing seconds of Game 4 in Boston—when Magic threw in what he called his "junior, junior, junior skyhook." It's fashioned after the weapon made famous by Kareem and it crushed the Celtics on their own Boston Garden parquet.

The numbers, however, deserve a recitation, if only to understand what Magic demanded of himself after the Lakers' shocking loss to the Rockets in the Western Conference finals in the spring of 1986.

He led the team in scoring with a career-high average of 23.9 points a game, six points higher than he'd averaged the season before. He scored 40 or more points three times last season, a total he'd exceeded only twice before in regular-season play. Yet he still led the NBA in assists for the fourth time in the last five seasons, averaging 12.2 a game and setting a club record with a total of 977.

He had 11 triple-doubles (double figures in rebounds, assists and points), five in the last 11 games of the season, and three more in the playoffs. And he threw in a 78-foot shot against the Denver Nuggets in the first round of the playoffs.

"His willingness to score made everyone else better," Riley said.

Johnson knew there would be changes before training camp began last season. He knew he would be asked to do more. "I knew it had to start with me," he said. "I had to show everybody I was ready. I had to be an example that I would do whatever it takes to be a winner."

Riley, too, had come to similar conclusions. He recognized that it would no longer be enough for Abdul-Jabbar—who would turn 40 before the playoffs began—to be the focal point of the offense. The ball, which had always been in Magic's hands, was now his to shoot.

But would Abdul-Jabbar understand? It had taken nearly five years, Johnson said, for the two men to warm to each other. Without that breakthrough, he said, the torch could not have been passed last fall.

"I always thought this would happen," Johnson said, "but I always thought it would be after he was gone . . . In his own way, he pushed me to step forward. When you get the eye and the confidence from him, it's like, 'Go for it, man.' He told me, 'You've got to average over 20 points a game.'"

In December, Abdul-Jabbar missed three games with an eye infection. The Lakers lost the first, to the Mavericks in Dallas. The next night, in Houston, Magic scored 38 points and had 16 assists in a 103-96 Laker win. The third game, he scored a career-high 46 in a 127-117 overtime win against Sacramento.

"After those three games, I told myself, 'Okay, I can go out and do it every night,'" Johnson said.

And the Lakers were never the same. The wraps had come off, and no one was happier than Riley. When asked how he planned to keep Magic humble in the future, Riley jokingly said he'd have to slap him around in practice. Then he turned serious.

"He's not only humble, but you have to be humbled to be humble," Riley said. "If any person on this team has experienced humiliation a number of times, it's been Magic . . . In 1980-81, he was blamed for us losing [to Houston, when he put up an airball with the game on the line]. In 1981-82, he was blamed [for coach Paul Westhead being fired]. In 1984, he was blamed for choking against the Celtics. He's always been blamed.

"That goes with the territory, but he feels it. He gives so much, he puts himself in the middle of everything to win, then when he doesn't win, people say, 'Well, that's the way it goes for you.'

"But he's a winner, an MVP, and the award is long overdue."

Johnson, told of Riley's comments, nodded his head in agreement.

"This eases the pain of everything that ever went bad," he said. "It also enhances everything in the game that has been good. This takes it to a new level. This is a higher fun than I've ever had."

And Magic likes to have his fun, even though his idea of celebrating the Lakers' championship was to go home to his mansion and cry.

"A cry of happiness," he said in the crush of the Laker locker room after the clinching game. "I'll be alone, I'll think about all that we've accomplished. That's the best time for me . . . It's nice, it's just my way. It's different, maybe, but that's what I do."

The solitude never lasts too long, however. He loves playing DJ in a recording studio built into his home, or shooting a few baskets on his racquetball-court-sized gym, but Magic loves steppin' out, too. He'll go to a movie in nearby Westwood, standing in line with everybody else, take in a Dodger or Raider game, show up backstage at a concert, pop up at a black-tie dinner, or invite two dozen or so friends over for a barbecue—and do the grilling himself.

"I get out a lot," he said. "I have to. I like talking to people, seeing what's going on. I like to see it live instead of on TV."

His schedule last summer left little time for relaxation. In the first month after the season's end, Magic made an anti-drug pitch at a 4-H rally in his home state of Michigan, appeared at a friend's basketball camp in Kentucky and a clinic in Indiana, where he also attended the wedding of Pacer center Herb Williams. He also ran his own basketball camps in Los Angeles and San Diego, as well as sponsored a benefit all-star game for the United Negro College Fund.

"I can go on little vacations," said Johnson, who often seeks out the company of best friends Isiah Thomas and Mark Aguirre when he does, "but then I get antsy. The camps are fun for me."

His idea of kicking back, he said, is to head for a local park, buy an ice cream and watch friends play softball. Some of those friends include the brothers of pop star Michael Jackson.

"I know Michael," Magic said. "He wants to have that, too, but he knows that he can't. That's why you see him now going to

Michigan State's Magic: No. 1 in 1979 draft.

Disneyland and stuff, just to relax...He can't go out like he wants to, and I feel sorry for him."

But just once, Magic said, he'd love to be Jackson on stage.

"The energy, the stage presence, the way he makes people feel," Johnson said wistfully. "He has that aura about him that makes him stand out."

Somehow, Johnson doesn't grasp that on his own personal stage, he has a similar aura.

"What amazes me most about Magic is how well he handles

Magic acknowledges fans after 1979 NCAA title win.

his position, his stature," said Mitch Kupchak, a one-time team-mate who is now the Lakers' assistant general manager. "He is a genuinely nice guy to people—kids and adults. At airports, he signs autographs and talks to kids.

"He could be aloof and arrogant, but he isn't. He has gotten better about that over the years, and normally the opposite is the way it happens. The more famous a guy is, the more unap-proachable he is."

The stars—Jack Nicholson, Dyan Cannon, Bruce Willis, Don Johnson—come out to see Magic play, but he still acts like a tourist with a camera around his neck when he's around them—as when he visited the set of "Dynasty."

"There I am, acting like a kid. There's Joan Collins, there's so-and-so, but what blew me away was that they were going crazy over me," Johnson said, giggling. "It's nice to see people respond."

So far, Johnson hasn't gone Hollywood. But he believes the time has come.

"I've turned down a lot of roles, but I'm going to start doing a little acting," he said. "That's the fun of playing here."

Lights, camera, Magic.

And so far, at age 28, Johnson has remained single. A year ago last August, he called off an engagement. Her name was Cookie, and they had met as freshmen at Michigan State. His eyes still soften when he speaks of her.

"She was . . . ooomm," he said softly. "It was nice."

Yet, he decided it couldn't work.

"I'm so into this—basketball—that I felt it would be better if I got married after I'm done. Because I think I can be just as good a husband during that time as I am in basketball," Magic said. "I'd hate to send a lady through what I go through now. It would be unfair and I realize that."

He also realizes how insanely high the demands of a game can get.

"I love it that much, and I will pay the price, but it makes you lonely, too," he said. "It takes a lot out of you. But I have to do whatever it takes to win."

For Magic, Larry Bird always has provided tremendous incentive, from the time Magic's Michigan State vanquished Bird's Indiana State for the NCAA title in 1979. Magic says his future in the game—his contract expires in 1994, but he says he'll be gone by then—may be predicated on how much longer Bird plays.

"I think what's going to happen is Larry's going to go first, and I'm going to go right after him," Magic said. "We feed off one another, that's why we go on. That's why we always want to top each other . . . It's an exclusive club. There's just something about guys that can make a team win and make players respond."

How long can the Magic-Bird rivalry last?

"I think I'll be done, and then I'll want to come back," said Johnson, smiling his trademark smile. "I think I'll call Larry and say, 'Let's go to the NBA All-Star Game and have some fun.'

"And then I think we'll bring a team out and play in some summer leagues on the playground. That would be wild. We'll give all the fans a chance to see us."

BILL RUSSELL'S NEWEST CHALLENGE

By DON DRYSDALE

Bill Russell is an old hand at mountain climbing. He got one of his clearest views of the world, and of himself, early one morning 12,000 feet up Mt. Raineer in Washington. He turned back before reaching the summit.

There was no disappointment. He had seen all he wanted to see that particular day. And, of course, Russell has scaled numerous mountains in the course of a career that includes 11 NBA championships in 13 seasons, two as player/coach of the Celtics; five Most Valuable Player Awards; a 1980 designation as "The Greatest Player in the History of the NBA, and the pride of watching a daughter, Karen, graduate from the Harvard Law School last spring.

In front of Russell now, however, stands the NBA's equivalent to Mt. Everest. Russell is the new head coach of the Sacramento Kings, sometimes known as the "Sad Sack-ramento" Kings. And Bill Russell could be facing his greatest challenge.

There is some talent on the club—guard Reggie Theus is an established star, power forward Otis Thorpe is on the rise, and swingman Derek Smith can be great when healthy—but over the past five years, the Kings have compiled a 180-230 record. They have bettered the .500 mark only once in this decade. The Kings were 29-53 last season, their worst record since 1959-60, when they were the Cincinnati Royals. They allowed 114.1 points a game on defense; only four teams were worse.

All the negative numbers do not depress Russell, who does not describe his new undertaking as a challenge—even though many view it as such.

"I can't say that I've ever had a challenge," Russell said. "I go

Don Drysdale covers the Kings for the Sacramento Union *and looks forward to the Bill Russell era.*

Bill Russell returns as a King.

into a job or situation and do the best I can. I don't look at this as being a challenge. I look at it as something I know how to do and I'm going to try to do it. I look forward to it. It will be something that's a lot of fun."

At last year's All-Star Game break, the Kings were more laughable than fun. Phil Johnson, in his second tenure as Kings' coach, was fired with a 14-32 record. His top assistant, Frank Hamblen, was out, too, leaving second assistant Jerry Reynolds as interim head coach.

Reynolds, a former head coach at Pittsburg State (Kan.) and Rockhurst College (Mo.), said from the start he was in over his head. Kings president/general manager Joe Axelson said Reynolds might finish the season or be replaced by a "permanent" head coach.

Axelson made a list of 42 candidates for the job. Russell was NOT on it. For all anyone knew at the time, James Naismith's name belonged on the wish list before Russell's.

"I did not dream that Bill would want to coach again," Axelson said.

Russell was doing NBA commentary for superstation WTBS

and had not coached for 10 years.

Could any amount of money or a job title bring him back to coaching? Probably not. The desire had to come from within and the position had to be just right. "I've been offered some jobs before, but they were always on the East Coast," Russell said. "I'd never live on the East Coast."

After success in college, in the Olympics and as a player and coach with the Celtics, Russell had walked away from his job as coach/general manager of the Seattle SuperSonics with a year remaining on his contract. That was after the 1976-77 season. He was sick of fat, long-term player contracts and half-hearted efforts and, maybe, a bit tired of being held up to his own standards.

Two years ago, however, then-Portland Trail Blazers' coach Jack Ramsay was looking for a tutor for his promising young center, Sam Bowie. Russell obliged, and he later worked with the Clippers' Benoit Benjamin.

"I thoroughly enjoyed being around the players again," Russell said. "It kind of got me thinking I wanted to get back into it."

Russell and Axelson had been friends for a decade. Russell had been offered the general managership of another club and asked Axelson for an opinion. "I told him I didn't think it was right for him," Axelson recalled. "I said, 'Do you want to get back into it?' He said he did and I said, 'What about here?'"

Russell came to Sacramento for top-secret meetings with Axelson and Kings managing general partner Gregg Lukenbill. When news of those meetings was leaked, it was practically ignored by a skeptical press. Why would Russell come to Sacramento when he probably could have his pick of locales? Why would he risk his reputation working with a proven loser? Why, at 53 years old and after leaving his last coaching job in disgust, would he want to jump back into the fire?

"I was stunned when I heard Russ took the job," said former teammate Bob Cousy. "I thought that Bill was interested in enjoying the good life, and going back into coaching doesn't constitute the good life, in my opinion. I might do it myself if I needed the work. I assume that Bill isn't hurting for money. He's been working all along and doing well for himself."

"My first reaction was: 'Why does Bill want to come back to the NBA at this time, and why Sacramento?'" Lukenbill wondered.

Axelson and Lukenbill spent nine hours at Russell's home on Mercer Island, near Seattle (his next-door neighbor is Rick Barry) in late April.

"I told Gregg, 'If you want a team that just goes to the

playoffs, I'm not the guy to coach them. If you want a team that contends for the championship, I'm the guy,' " Russell said.

Those were the words that Lukenbill wanted to hear. He, like Russell, is a doer. The young construction magnate—who almost single-handedly has pushed Sacramento into the big-time in sports—strives for naught but the grand prize.

"I don't see any risk," Russell said. "I may be overbearing when I say it, but I know as much as anyone about basketball. I think I have an understanding of people, I respect people . . . I know how to motivate players and myself. I think a lot of good things are going to happen with the Kings."

If you can imagine turning on the TV to hear the bulletin, "Christ returns, film at 11," you can understand the shock Sacramentans felt at Russell's hiring. Fans and players alike were unanimous in their approval.

"I'm ecstatic about the news," guard Franklin Edwards said at the time. "It's a very strong statement from the club in terms of the direction we're going."

"I think it's good for the organization," forward Mark Olberding said. "He's a winner and hopefully he'll be able to instill that attitude in the players."

"I think we raised a lot of eyebrows," Jerry Reynolds said. "Teams across the country who are looking for coaches are saying: 'Why didn't we think of that?' I think this puts us a giant step ahead."

If anyone was supposed to feel sad over the move, it was Reynolds. Unproven and overwhelmed, he nonetheless guided the Kings to a 15-21 finish. He gained remarkable popularity through his performance, self-effacing manner and wry wit, and would have been the Kings' choice had Russell not been hooked.

"How can I complain?" Reynolds said. "I've got a full-time job [as an assistant, along with Willis Reed] and my wife's got a new vacuum cleaner. Life is great. I'm certainly not ready to be a winning head coach in the NBA. And I don't know if I ever will be, but being around Bill Russell for awhile certainly is going to give me a lot better chance at that."

Russell will indeed be around awhile. He signed a seven-year contract that will make him general manager and president when Axelson gives up those jobs. Russell also will have the opportunity to become a part owner.

Frustrated by what he called "the most disappointing season of my career," Axelson had been mulling retirement. Buoyed by his coup, Axelson signed a three-year extension.

"I have been fascinated by Bill Russell's awesome playing ability and by his immense intelligence for a long time," Axelson

Russell led San Francisco to 55 consecutive wins.

said in announcing Russell's signing.

Both men pride themselves on intellect and basketball insight, and it is said the pre-draft skull sessions were sometimes spirited. While ultimate authority rests in Axelson's hands, Russell had made a mark on the club less than a month after officially taking over on June 1.

On June 20, about half an hour before the temporary trading moratorium that preceeds the college draft, the Kings sent forward Eddie Johnson to the Phoenix Suns for Ed Pinckney and a 1988 No. 2 draft choice. Johnson had led the Kings in scoring three straight seasons until the last one. But he does not play defense hard enough for Russell's taste.

"We wouldn't have made that trade a year ago," Axelson said.

Players who are strictly jump-shooters are dinosaurs in the Russell regime. He envisions length-of-the-court defense and cheap baskets.

He has a great view of the future from atop his 6-foot-9 peak. Russell encountered his first mountain early in life. He was born in Monroe, La., where the mayor was Jim Crow.

In his autobiography *Second Wind: The Memoirs of an Opinionated Man*, Russell refers to his father as "Mister Charlie." He was 6-foot-2 and built like a heavyweight boxer. Katie Russell was a match for her husband via spiritual strength. Russell's grandfather, the "Old Man," was smaller than Bill's father, but the strongest man in town. They were poor but tight-knit.

The Ku Klux Klan once came after the "Old Man," who fended them off with shotgun blasts.

"Mister Charlie" and the "Old Man" were as well educated as most blacks in Louisiana in their time. The family patriarch refused to work for a boss. He was a farmer who went broke, then did odd jobs with his mule team. "Mister Charlie" worked in a bag factory, in what was known as a "Negro job."

Education was important to the Russell family. Bill's middle name, Felton, came from Felton Clark, the president of Southern University at the time. Charlie and Katie decided to have only two children so there would be money to get them through school. They began saving for Bill's education when he was a one-year-old.

School was a shack with walls propped up by poles. White kids went to another school, to be sure, and threw rocks at the black kids. Russell knew little of the white world as a youngster.

Partly to get his youngsters a better education, partly to escape racial tensions in the South, Charlie Russell decided to move his family. He went alone to Detroit and got a job at a Ford plant. But he could not stand the cold. He then headed for Oakland and sent for his family.

Bill was 12 when his mother passed away. The family tried to convince Charlie to move his family back to Louisiana, to no avail.

Bill's older brother, Charlie, was an outstanding athlete. Bill, tall but ungainly, was slow to develop. Perhaps the most amazing aspect of his career is that he ever became a basketball player at all.

He attended Oakland's McClymonds High School, but as a 6-foot-2 sophomore weighing only 128 pounds he constantly tripped over his own feet. In his junior year he was only a third-string center. But by the end of the season he had grown three inches and was beginning to show promise.

He made first-string as a senior and impressed Hal de Julio, a former University of San Francisco player, who recommended him to Phil Woolpert, the coach at San Francisco. His freshman coach, Ross Guidice, taught him the hook shot and other staples. Russell's roommate was K.C. Jones, who taught him to think not in terms of individual moves but about how combinations of players could function.

He grew to 6-9 in his sophomore year and was outstanding, but his team, hampered by injuries, was only fair with a 14-7 record. The next season San Francisco won its first two games and lost its third. From then on, Russell never played another losing game in college. In two seasons San Francisco won 55 straight games as Russell led his team to two NCAA titles.

Coach Red Auerbach of the Celtics traded two outstanding players—Ed Macauley and Cliff Hagan—for the draft rights to Russell, who played for the U.S. gold-medal team in the 1956 Olympic Games.

"There were people in Boston who told me that I was lucky to play for the Celtics, with all those great players," Russell recalled. "Wait a minute. The Celtics didn't go out to San Francisco and say, 'Here's a poor, black kid who needs money, let's draft him.' They got me because I was a great player.

"When I got to Boston, there was not a flag in the Garden, except for those of the Bruins. I'm proud of the fact that I helped put the Celtic flags up there."

He gave the Celtics a new weapon, a style of play that made defense a respectable part of the game. Intelligent and sharp-witted, Russell relied on psychology to a great extent in making his defensive skills more effective. If he could prevent a player from driving on him merely by intimidating him, then he had won a battle without moving a muscle.

Russell became the first black to coach a major-league sports franchise in 1966-67, when he became the Celtics' playing coach. In his second and third year at the helm, the Celtics won the NBA title. No team has won back-to-back crowns since then. He retired as a coach and a player following the 1968-69 season.

When Russell quit, he also divorced his wife of 13 years and headed to the West Coast. He was looking for new experiences and would work for Los Angeles radio station KABC before becoming coach and general manager of the SuperSonics in 1973 and later doing television commentary for ABC, CBS and WTBS.

Tom Burleson, who played for Russell at Seattle, thinks the legacy of the Celtics' success inspired Russell to coach the Kings.

"He'd have been a great player anywhere he went," Burleson said. "People give a lot of credit to Auerbach and the Celtics' organization for what Russell achieved. He probably wants to get back into it to prove he's a great coach without Boston. It's a challenge to him. He's doing it to clear up his reputation in people's minds and prove he can do it on his own."

Russell's first conversations about the Kings' job took place last February, long before then-Los Angeles Dodger general manager Al Campanis created a racial tempest when he questioned the abilities of blacks to take on executive positions in major-

Russell teamed up with Dick Stockton on CBS.

league sports. There were rumors, unfounded, that NBA Commissioner David Stern orchestrated Russell's hiring to placate the NAACP.

"I found that rumor very offensive," Russell said. "If one goes back and looks at my association with the NBA, there's not a remote possibility of anyone being more qualified than I am for this job. The idea that they needed to hire me to relieve civil rights pressure—that's racism."

Russell became deeply involved in the civil rights movement in the '60s and later would call Boston the country's most racist city.

In her article in *The New York Times Magazine* last summer, Karen Russell, a product of Bill's first marriage, recalled the time the family home in Massachusetts was burglarized. "Nigga" was spray-painted on the walls.

Bill once wrote an article on racism in the NBA for *The Saturday Evening Post*. He called the FBI after receiving threatening letters. Years afterward, he acquired the FBI files and found he had been referred to as "an arrogant Negro who won't sign autographs for white children."

(For the record, he will not sign for anyone, including his own children. He sees the act as "impersonal.")

Russell ventured to Mississippi at the height of racial tensions in 1964 to put on basketball camps. In *Second Wind,* he recalled dreading the trip:

"Fortunately, my teammates on the Celtics had cheered me up with the tender sympathy that was our trademark. 'You'll be just fine down there, Russ,' they'd drawl. 'Just make sure you stay inconspicuous. Incognito is the key.' That was a big help. In

Mississippi, I felt about as big as a target range . . ."

Russell opted not to be involved in his own Hall-of-Fame induction in 1975, partly for racial considerations (he was to be the first black player so honored), partly because he did not respect it as an institution.

In his autobiography, Russell described himself as "a triple threat . . . Not only am I tall enough to make a lot of people uncomfortable, but I am also black and infamous as an athlete. No wonder I have my quirks."

One of Russell's first moves on signing was to hire Willis Reed, another tall left-hander out of Louisiana. Reed had idolized the Celtics' center and drew inspiration from him.

"Nobody has been what he was and no one ever will," said the onetime star and later coach of the New York Knicks. "Akeem Olajuwon may come close, athletically and at the defensive end, but no has had Bill's impact. He was the master of the game."

Reed thinks that Russell's upbringing forged an intelligent man who can be alternately charming and intimidating. Reed grew up only about 50 miles from Russell's hometown and is eight years younger than Russell, but the similarity ends there. Reed is as friendly and open as Russell is standoffish.

"We grew up in two different worlds," Reed said. "I understood the difference between black and white, but I didn't encounter the stuff that Bill did growing up. Also, his mother died when he was young, and his father raised him. That probably made him as independent as he is."

"Russ is extremely private," Bob Cousy said. "He comes across as aloof. He's a militant, proud, black man who's extremely sensitive. He was deeply and profoundly affected by the civil rights movement and he acted predictably for a proud black man.

"Unless you can put yourself in his shoes, you might not understand him. Myself, I probably wouldn't have handled things as well as Russ has. Anyone extremely competitive, like Russ, has problems turning the other cheek. He's an extremely bright person who has chosen to react in his own way."

Sure, that way is often cold and intimidating. But it can be warm and humorous, too. Witness the cackling laugh that has been a trademark in his television work.

At Seattle, Russell compiled a 162-166 record and drew mixed reactions.

"I got the feeling he was indeed one of those individuals who could dominate a high-powered environment . . . He was in a position where he commanded enough respect to get some things done that had to be," said Blaine Johnson, who covered the

Classic confrontation: Russell and Wilt Chamberlain.

"On the down side, I had the idea he didn't put in enough time in the film room and into scouting, at least not as much as guys like John MacLeod and Jack Ramsay appear to. I thought he got bored with the routine stuff."

Tom Burleson, however, described Russell as "a real fine coach," though adding he had a laissez-faire approach.

"He left it up to the players to keep themselves in shape," Burleson recalled. "If you showed up to camp out of shape, if you were late to practice, he made you pay. But he thought we were men and wanted to treat us that way."

"The last year in Seattle was not a lot of fun, and I could see it coming in advance," Russell said. "I heard it said a lot that I was on the golf course every afternoon at 3 o'clock and that my assistant coaches did all the coaching. It just wasn't true, and it pissed me off."

Last year, Russell portrayed a judge on the take in an episode of "Miami Vice." At the end, he was seen holding a gun to his head and he supposedly shot himself off-camera (Russell would later joke he shot the gun like he did free throws, and missed.)

Russell is hard to get to know—at 6-foot-9 with a gray-flecked beard and a world-class glare, he can intimidate those he does not want to know.

"The most important thing to know about me is that you don't know anything about me," Russell said. "People complain that they don't understand me and that I don't go out of my way to make it easy on them. I don't know why I should. I just try to do the best I can."

THE IMITATION OF MICHAEL JORDAN

By BOB SAKAMOTO

It's the backyard in a small Midwestern town, and Dougie Vedra is re-enacting a scene that's played all over this land. This is life imitating art, and the stage can be a graffiti-marred, glass-jungle playground in Harlem as readily as the traditional driveway in middle America where youngsters shoot the hoops.

The 14-year-old Vedra, of Baileyville, Ill., is making his move to the basket. In one hand, he palms a miniature basketball, waving it about as if rehearsing some basketball ritual or art form. Then at precisely the right moment, before dunking into a downsized hoop, Vedra's mouth opens wide and his tongue comes dangling out.

Halfway 'round the world, 15-year-old Joyce Okamoto is strolling through downtown Kaiserslautern in West Germany when her mouth opens in disbelief. Walking right past her is a young man who has shaved his head and left the initials "MJ" standing out. This isn't the latest rage in punk-rock, new-wave exotica. This is a hair-raising tribute to America's most popular athlete.

Each time Michael Jordan hears another story of his impact on the world, he shakes his head and smiles. He doesn't completely understand the phenomenon he has created or why little kids and grownups alike want to be like Michael Jordan, wearing his gym shoes and sweat outfits or driving the cars he endorses or gobbling the hamburgers he consumes or downing the soft drinks he sips.

The tales of Jordan-mania are already becoming the stuff of

Bob Sakamoto's tongue is hanging out because he follows Michael Jordan as the Bulls' beat man for the Chicago Tribune.

Michael Jordan scored 3,041 points last season.

legends, and the 24-year-old Chicago Bulls' superstar has only been in the NBA for three years.

There was the horde of young, teenage girls that tried tearing his clothes after an exhibition game in his rookie season. There was the lady who so desperately wanted Jordan's autograph that she laid down in front of his car and refused to move. She said she wouldn't mind being run over as long as her hero was in the car. After selling out arenas in other cities, Jordan is escorted away by a cadre of security guards like some rock star or cult hero.

"The kids [at West Germany's Voselweh Air Force Base] dress like him, act like him, wear his wristbands, kneepads, shoes, and Air Jordan T-shirts," said Okamoto, whose father was a civilian employee of the U.S. Air Force before retiring in June and moving his family back to Florida. "The basketball players on our school team try to do his dunks. Kids will come to class all red-eyed in the morning after staying up til 4 A.M. to watch a Bulls' game. They look up his past, where he went to school. They cut out all the pictures and articles of him in newspapers and magazines and put them all over their lockers. Kids will beg and plead for a Michael Jordan poster."

Okamoto had never been much of a basketball fan and has yet to attend a pro game. But that didn't keep her from getting caught up in the Michael Jordan fever. She said it all began for her after Jordan scored a playoff-record 63 points last year in the Bulls' 135-131 double-overtime loss to the Boston Celtics.

Jordan's posters have even taken on a therapeutic value in Germany. Okamoto was fortunate enough to obtain one, but gave it away to 18-year-old Pat Wood, who shattered his jaw and cheekbone during a soccer match. Wood could hardly believe anyone would give up such a cherished possession.

"You hear all the bad things about kids coming out of college and getting into drugs after they make the pros," Okamoto said. "Michael Jordan is clean, and that's another big reason why we like him. He's not like a rock star, getting real big-headed, conceited and flaunting things. He sews his own clothes, cleans house and does things for himself. He's not living in a big mansion with a lot of servants. That's the impression you get from all the movie stars. He's like a normal person walking around. That's probably why he is so well-liked. He doesn't let success go to his head."

If ever Jordan had reason to gloat, the 1986-87 season was it. Although Magic Johnson was acclaimed the Most Valuable Player, Jordan was the force in the NBA. He became the first player in 24 years and the only one other than Wilt Chamberlain to score 3,000 points in a season when he racked up 3,041 in averaging 37.1 a game to lead the league. Almost singlehandedly, Jordan took the Bulls to a near .500 season with scoring exploits that boggle the mind. He had a stretch of nine straight games in which he scored 40 points or more. As a sign of things to come, Jordan scored 50 in an opening-night victory over the New York Knicks.

"What he's doing is incredible," said then-Knicks coach Hubie Brown. "We had Rory Sparrow in his face the last seven minutes, but he did things that were astounding. He had a couple shots off the glass that were unbelievable. You say: 'How the hell did he get that off?' But not only does he get it off, it backspins in like a feather. He was magic. Whatever arena he goes to, people are flocking to see him play."

He is a combination of Peter Pan and Luke Skywalker; the Pied Piper of the 80s; a genuine American hero. Watergate and Irangate and too many other scandals have reduced the supply of role models. When the news broke about Dwight Gooden's cocaine problem, Jordan sat quietly in his Washington, D.C., hotel room and reaffirmed his stance against drugs. He spoke with passion and emotion, at times his voice quivering.

"Every human being makes mistakes," Jordan said, "and his [Gooden's] mistakes came back to haunt him. My lifestyle is so positive that I'm not afraid of something from my past coming back to haunt me or upset the role-model image I've set. I live a clean, healthy life, and I'm happy about it. I've never done drugs, and I'll never have a reason to do drugs."

Jordan and Gooden were perceived as clean-cut figures worthy of emulation and adoration. Stories of Gooden succumbing to the pressures of fame and living up to the expectations of others encouraged Jordan to analyze how he has been able to handle all the things that caused Gooden's downfall.

"I'm not afraid of what I've become," Jordan said. "I don't think of it as pressure. I think of it as a compliment. Maybe it's because I didn't have the type of growing up that most superstars seem to have. I came on so suddenly. I was a late bloomer. I didn't have time to see myself in this situation. It's helped me act more naturally.

Jordan credited his upbringing for the attitude that "I don't think I'm better than the next person." He listened to the story of how Gooden was upset by the fan who walked up to him in a restaurant, replaced the fork he was holding with a pen and asked for an autograph.

"You have to accept that," Jordan said. "There are some things you have to give up when you become a superstar. Someone like Gooden or myself goes to a restaurant and gets seated faster than the average person. We get free food or someone pays for our meals. To get these things, you have to give up something.

"Taking time out to sign autographs or talking to people in an airport, this is what you have to give back. I don't want to ever isolate myself from the people. When they talk to me, I talk back to them just as if they were my friend. I can't speak for what Gooden's problems were. He was afraid of his public, but I'm not afraid. My personality won't let me. I've talked to Dwight. He's not as outgoing as I am. He seems to be more of a private person. I can look within myself to find something positive instead of looking around for things I shouldn't do to get my confidence back."

During a radio talk show in Chicago, one caller asked a sportswriter to publish quotes from Jordan on his anti-drug stance. "My two kids absolutely idolize Michael Jordan," the caller said. "One word from him and I know I'll never have to worry about them using drugs."

Jordan's all-American image, combining with his court charisma, helped make him the biggest box-office draw in the NBA last season. During one stretch, Jordan was primarily responsible for the Bulls playing before 11 sellout crowds in 12 games. His appearance against the Clippers in Los Angeles resulted in the Sports Arena's first capacity crowd in two years. Thanks to Jordan, the Bulls set a single-season attendance record last year, averaging close to 16,000 fans a game, while the rest of the league profited from his spectacular return. Jordan had missed 64 games in the 1985-86 season with a broken bone in his left foot.

"The moment word got out that he was injured, ticket sales for the Chicago game came to a halt," said Denver communications director Harve Kirkpatrick. "This last season, he sold out our building. When he was hurt, it cost us about $90,000 in ticket sales. There's no question he is the greatest drawing card in the game today."

Phoenix marketing director Harvey Shank said, "To the basketball fan, Michael Jordan is the Bruce Springsteen. He is like the great entertainers, the Frank Sinatras that come into Phoenix. It is an event when Michael Jordan comes to town."

Jordan's name is magic in the offseason as well. Helping promote the first annual Michael Jordan Celebrity Golf Tournament to benefit the Ronald McDonald House charity, more than 100 celebrities showed up last June in Lemont, a western suburb of Chicago. The outing raised more than $50,000 and included the Chicago Bears' Walter Payton, CBS-TV announcer Brent Musburger and ex-Bear great Gale Sayers.

Jordan was on the go all summer, including the filming of a movie *Heaven Is A Playground,* based on the book by Rick Telander. Jordan had one of the major roles in the movie, about a youngster making good in life through basketball.

He played in a number of pro-am and celebrity golf tournaments, worked at various basketball camps, including his own, and made an appearance at the Special Olympics International Summer Games at Notre Dame. He also made various promotional appearances and began work on a new commercial for Coca-Cola.

Jordan's contract calls for him to make about $830,000 this season, but there are indications he will renegotiate his current contract, which runs through the 1990-91 season. Under that pact, Jordan will not make $1 million a season until 1989-90. There are reports he and the Bulls' management will settle on something in the neighborhood of $2.3 million a year for eight years—in effect, a lifetime contract with the Bulls. Jordan has said he wants to play until he is 32 and then think about a career as a professional golfer.

Financially, the 6-6 guard is set for life. He makes close to $3 million a year in endorsements and off-court revenue. His sports management representative, Pro-Serv of Washington, D.C., filtered through an avalanche of endorsement opportunities in search of products that would reflect or enhance Jordan's image. Those turned out to be McDonald's, Coca-Cola, Nike, Chevrolet, Wilson Sporting Goods, Johnson Products and Guy LaRouche watches. Jordan also has limited real-estate partnerships in Miami, Kansas City, San Clemente, Cal., and Washington, D.C.

The fourth of five children, Jordan was born in Brooklyn, N.Y. Soon after his birth, James and Deloris Jordan moved their family to Wilmington, N.C., where Jordan spent his formative years. Much has been made of Jordan's domestic skills, developed under the wing of his mother. The story goes that he was so concerned he would never get married that he took a course in home economics in high school and learned how to take care of himself.

Somehow—between stitches and pots and pans—he found the time to develop as a basketball star at Wilmington's Laney High School. From there he went on to instant success at North Carolina, where as a freshman he hit on a 17-footer jumper with 15 seconds remaining to beat Georgetown for the 1982 NCAA title. He was an All-American as a sophomore and junior, and led the U.S. to gold in the 1984 Olympic Games.

Jordan left college after his junior year and was the No. 3 draft

Jordan had the most playing time in NBA in 1986-87.

pick in 1984 (Akeem Olajuwon and Sam Bowie were ahead of him). The awards came fast as Chicago's flying Bull was chosen Rookie of the Year and made the All-NBA team in 1984-85. And it has been more of the same with each succeeding season.

One of America's most eligible bachelors, Jordan is serious about a Chicago woman named Juanita Vanoy. But he says he doesn't want to get married until he is 27 or 28. He believes it doesn't make sense for a young man in his position doing all the traveling he does to settle down at a young age.

And the way Jordan takes off, it may be a while before he settles down.

"He's a rare occasion," Los Angeles Laker star James Worthy said. "He's probably the most flamboyant talent in the NBA. He's gonna be a superstar for a long time."

Perhaps the single most intriguing characteristic of Air Jordan is his ability to defy gravity. He is giving a whole new meaning to the term "Hang Time." He is taking the game of basketball to new heights and awakening a fantasy in all of us—the wish to fly.

"Fly? I don't know. But when I do, I'll let you know," Jordan said. "I'm getting close. I remember one game in Milwaukee last year. I've got it on tape, where it looks just like I'm taking off. I stole the ball and I'm rising up. Then, I just stop in midair and start my descent. I shot the ball coming down."

Jordan won the Slam-Dunk Contest last February with a couple of airborne maneuvers. In one, he sailed in from the free-throw line and double-pumped his way to the hoop. In another, his body appeared to be perpendicular to the ground, his lips about to kiss the rim.

His army of young imitators steadily increases, with probably more than a few casualties as a result—tongues that get bitten and crash-landings.

THE FUNNIEST MAN IN PRO BASKETBALL

By PAUL DAUGHERTY

If life were a honeymoon, Frank Layden would be Ed Norton. The world's best-loved shirttail, forever hanging out.

Layden is every laugh you never had, every joke you ever told and then forgot. He never met a moment he didn't like.

The 300-pound, Brooklyn-born coach and general manager of the Utah Jazz roams the blue-suited NBA in gray sweats. He's beginning his 31st year in basketball now, his 11th in the league, seventh as coach of the Jazz. The league still doesn't know quite what to make of him.

And why should it? As a member of the NBA's Competition and Rules Committee, Layden once suggested that referees learn to throw the ball up straight for the center jump.

Once in 1984, as the Jazz were playing the Lakers in Los Angeles, he walked off the bench and out the door of The Forum. While his team lost handily, Layden was eating a bacon, lettuce and tomato sandwich in a hotel coffee shop.

Did you hear the one about Frank Layden? He's only funny when he's awake. Billy Crystal in cellulite.

Oddly, the folks at Miller Brewing turned him down. Layden had looked into making a Miller Lite commercial, but he was judged too overweight.

"I was standing on the corner, with a yellow hat and a blue suit on. Three people pulled up to me and dropped off film." Layden was speaking at a chamber of commerce luncheon in Cedar City, Utah, where the Jazz were playing a preseason game. Everyone was laughing. "I'm on a diet because the last time I

Paul Daugherty is a sports feature writer on Newsday.

© *1986,* Newsday, Inc. *Reprinted by permission.*

"There's only room on this team for one pot-belly."

stepped on a scale, it gave me a fortune card. It said, 'Come back in 15 minutes. Alone.'"

One night several years ago, Layden gave a valet on Long Island two bucks to park his car, and the guy stole the car. And that's a *true* story. But there is more. Inside this body, there has to be.

If Layden is unique in his game, it isn't because he can do 30 minutes of stand-up humor without notes (he can), or because he's the only coach in the NBA who could double as the Michelin Tire Man.

Layden's gift comes from seeing the considerable gap between what's real and what's sports. He and perspective met some time ago. It has been a pleasant and lasting friendship. Now, what is left is to enjoy.

"Frank knows it's not Iwo Jima," Jazz center Mark Eaton said. "And that's the way he coaches."

Layden is a man of many faces, not just funny ones. He is an original in a league of cutouts.

And Layden, 55, is steadfast in a profession of gypsies. Only five active NBA coaches have been in one spot longer than Layden, who came to Utah in 1979. Layden signed a 10-year contract with the Jazz in 1983. Since then, he has been wooed by the New Jersey Nets, who play in a richer, more visible market than the Jazz. He turned them down.

He is a fat man charged with the conditioning of athletes, a quipster among grinders, a raucous Irish Catholic in a sedate town of Mormons. An oblong peg in a round hole.

Layden is a professed lover of baseball and the theater who labels his coaching position in the pros "an accident." If he had life to do over, he'd study harder and be a lawyer.

Maybe above all, Layden is a mortalist in a business that doesn't have much use for that sort of thing. Somehow, he makes it work.

"He believes he is in debt to the world, because life has been good to him," said ex-Sacramento Kings' coach Phil Johnson, a former Layden assistant. "He's willing to pay that debt any way he can."

Just when you're sure he is nothing but a waddling, shambling laugh track, Frank Layden will make you think.

He might talk about John Drew, who played for Layden in Utah between 1982 and 1984. Or Terry Furlow, who played most of a year in Utah, before he died in a drug-related, one-car wreck in May 1980. Layden was the first to try to quiet Drew's sad song of drug abuse, and the first to suggest to the league office that the NBA had a drug problem.

"Frank did everything he could for John," Johnson said. "I think he's still very interested in John's life."

In 1984, Layden offered Drew a job in Utah's front office, he said, "to learn some basic literacy skills. I wanted him capable of living in society without basketball."

Drew declined the offer. Subsequently, he was banned from the league for drug use, and now is in jail.

Layden also can coach, a fact that sometimes escapes the general public. He spent 12 years as a high school and small college (Adelphi-Suffolk, now Dowling College) coach on Long Island,

He's sought as a speaker for all occasions.

the next eight as head man at Niagara, the past 11 in the NBA with Atlanta and Utah.

As coach and GM at Utah, Layden gets more bang for a team's bucks than anyone in the NBA. In 1985-86, the Jazz payroll ranked last in the NBA, at $2.9 million. In comparison, the Lakers paid Magic Johnson alone $2.5 million. Nevertheless Utah, at 42-40, finished with the 10th-best record in the league.

In 1982-83, the Jazz were 30-52; a year later, they were 45-37 and Midwest Division champions, and Layden was NBA Coach and Executive of the Year.

Last season the 44-38 Jazz, runnerup to Dallas in the Midwest Conference, had the ninth-best record overall.

Through force of personality and solid basketball and business sense, he has made the basketball business work. In Utah, of all places. "Players here know that I *am* the Jazz. There is no player in our organization bigger than I am," Layden said.

Pause.

"Literally and figuratively, of course."

Layden is a funny guy, all right. But he's no comedian. He uses laughs the way a judge uses a gavel. They give him a voice that otherwise he might not have had.

"I never really looked at myself as a humorous person," Layden said. "But no one believes that. I walk into a room, people expect me to slip on a banana."

But Layden created this monster, one-liner by one-liner. Now he has to feed it. It's not real hard.

Given the choice, Layden will step lightly through the days. "Life's short," he said. "Why not leave 'em dancin'?"

*   *   *

The long, loud Greyhound with the tinted windows and bellowing air-conditioner rumbled through the Utah desert, carrying the Jazz to Cedar City, some 280 miles south of Salt Lake.

Layden sat alone, his considerable self sprawled across the front two seats. A visit in August to the Pritikin Institute in Santa Monica, Calif., at the urging of the Jazz brass, had started Layden down another dietary road.

He has tried every diet known to calories, with no lasting effect. This one, he vows, will work.

He said he lost 35 pounds the first six weeks. He eats a lot of fruit now. The Fatman Slimmeth. But his roundness still fills most of both seats.

"Fat people are not happy," he said. Layden put down the Stephen King book he was reading, adjusted the glasses on his nose, collected all of himself in basically one spot. "I don't know one happy fat person. They don't like themselves."

Layden likes himself, though. And, because of the way he is, everyone else does, too. Laugh and the world laughs with you. If Layden has a lot to laugh about, he has earned it.

His mother died when Frank was an infant. He was raised, along with two sisters, in a third-floor walkup in Brooklyn, N.Y., by his father.

Mike Layden was a longshoreman, an ex-boxer, the sort of guy who talked with his sleeves rolled up. He also saw the potential in his only son. "We all have to get behind Frank, because he's got a shot at becoming somebody someday" Layden remembered his father saying.

Sports dominated Layden's youth. The bus to Ebbets Field stopped right in front of his house. Layden was a big Dodger fan, who says now that "sports lost a lot of its innocence when the Dodgers left Brooklyn."

He played basketball and baseball at Fort Hamilton High. Not, incidentally, at Boys High, as has been reported. Layden has made so many jokes about Boys ("great athletic program, wonderful teachers, strange proms") that last year the school's West

A LAYDEN SAMPLER

About a player: "He knows plenty. He just can't think of it."

"We were going to erect a statue to a player in Liberty Park near downtown, but why scare the pigeons?"

About a player: "His life has been a series of trials . . . but no convictions."

On a player's body: "If he was a building, he'd be condemned."

On player adjustment to the NBA: "I figure it takes three years just to find out when the planes leave."

Describing a player: "I didn't know if he was a player. He looked like a player. I figured he'd look good in the team picture. After all, we've got a coach who doesn't look like a coach."

After a player got just one rebound in a game: "Congratulations, son, you just got one more rebound than a dead man."

"Talk about John Stockton having quick hands. In my neighborhood they didn't consider you to have quick hands unless you could take the hubcaps off moving cars."

To a player packing extra weight: "There's only room on this team for one pot-belly."

"The Jazz are America's Team . . . the Americans just don't know it yet."

"A good point guard and a good scorer should go hand in hand . . . but not in the locker room or shower."

After a 4½-hour bargaining session on a player contract: "Even the Good Lord kept his sermons to 40 minutes."

Informed that a player was being flown to a specialist for a second opinion on an injury, "I'll give a second opinion and save us the airfare."

Discussing a free agent's college career: "He didn't have a very good career. But it was the best seven years of his life."

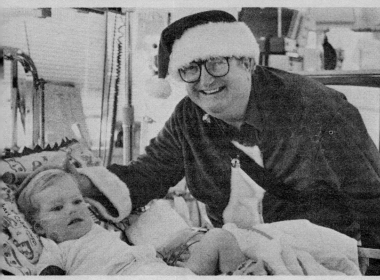

Layden is Santa Claus at Children's Medical Center.

Coast alumni association wanted to make him their man of the year. He had to come clean with them.

During the summers, Layden played first base for a neighborhood team that traveled to Long Island and the other boroughs.

At one time or another, Layden hit against Sandy Koufax and Whitey Ford and matched bats with Joe and Frank Torre, and Bob and Ken Aspromonte.

Team members often would be paid to play. "It wasn't much," Layden recalled. "We'd usually just turn around and bet the money on the game."

By Layden's senior year at Fort Hamilton, gambling had infiltrated the area colleges. Combined with a teachers' strike in the high schools, it shut down athletics in and around the city. Many schools, including Long Island University, where Layden had planned to enroll, simply dropped sports.

Layden kept playing, becoming a player/coach on his Catholic Youth Organization team in Bay Ridge—and on several others.

To maintain his eligibility, Layden played under a whole roster of assumed names. On one team, he was Lash LaRue, on another Happy Daily.

"There were so many teams, you could get away with it," he

said. "I would go to games and play, and later I'd hear other coaches say stuff like, 'That LaRue, you know, he sure plays a lot like Layden.'"

He got a basketball scholarship to Niagara, where he roomed with Hubie Brown. (Layden later would work as an assistant to Brown with the Atlanta Hawks. A falling out with Brown led to Layden's move to the Jazz as general manager in 1979. He replaced Tom Nissalke as coach during the 1981-82 season.)

After high school, and again after he left Niagara, Layden had the chance to play baseball. The New York Giants offered him a Class D contract as an 18-year-old; four years later, scouts from Detroit and Cleveland came calling. He turned them all down.

"I was always practical enough never to go off half-cocked," he said. "I wanted to get on with my life. Sports just aren't that important."

That's not an above-it-all pronouncement from Layden. He isn't above anything, except perhaps the weight limit for his height.

"He's not in love with what he does for a living," said Jack Donohue, one of the coach's best friends for more than 30 years. "He's a well-rounded human being who happens to coach basketball."

Layden's first job was on Long Island, coaching and teaching high-school history. To supplement his income, Layden took odd jobs in the summer. One year he went door-to-door, peddling *Newsday* subscriptions; the next, he worked a hot dog stand for the Long Island Parks Department.

Layden was ready to become Lou Carnesecca's assistant at St. John's when Niagara called. He coached a decade at his alma mater, winning 119 games and finishing second in the NIT in 1972. Calvin Murphy played for Layden.

Brown called next, and Layden packed for Atlanta. Even then, he wasn't convinced that coaching basketball was what he wanted to do.

"Frank may have been forced into the NBA," Donohue said. "He was 40 then, not really the time to jump into the pros as an assistant. When he left Niagara, the NBA was just a way to make a living until he found something he really wanted to do."

Layden doesn't regret the move, of course. Layden doesn't have time for regrets.

His favorite people are Casey Stengel, John Madden and Al McGuire. Leave-em-laughing guys. "Guys," he said, "who sport a comic figure." They have room for humor in their lives, Layden thinks, "because they realized that what they did wasn't work."

Jazzcaster Hot Rod Hundley shares laugh with Layden.

Layden met his wife, Barbara, in a Rockaway Beach bar owned by McGuire's parents. He and the ex-Marquette coach remain close.

"Frank has a lot of Al McGuire in him," said Donohue, who now coaches the Canadian Olympic Team. Donohue grew up in the Bronx and met Layden when both were coaching in high school. "It's easy when you talk to Frank not to realize how important basketball is to him. McGuire used to tell people that if he ran into three of his players in a bar, that was a practice. It wasn't true, of course, but that was Al. Frank's a little bit like that."

Said Mark Eaton: "Frank's the kind of guy who will say one minute that he doesn't need you, that the Jazz is his show. The next, he'll be after you to call your mother on Mother's Day.

"He's a good coach, mainly because he understands players. He knows there are going to be ups and downs in an 82-game season. In the NBA, you need to keep things a little off balance. If you can instill the attitude that it's not life and death every night, it makes it easier on the players."

Layden's perspective and good-humor-man approach to his game have been tested only once. He and former Jazz all-star forward Adrian Dantley commenced a running feud in the fall of 1985, while Dantley held out to have his contract renegotiated.

Things got serious late that season, when Layden suspended Dantley for one game and fined him 30 dimes, representing the 30 pieces of silver for which Judas betrayed Christ.

Layden, the loyalist, figured Dantley betrayed the trust the Jazz had placed in him, by holding out. "I just cannot tolerate a player who chooses to violate his contract," Layden said.

Mr. Jazz won out in the end. "My standards were tested," he said. "What happened was we got rid of Adrian [to the Detroit Pistons for Kelly Tripucka and Kent Benson]. Players are temporary; I'm staying."

* * *

Nearing Cedar City, the Greyhound slowed, ground its gears and eased its pursuit of the sun. It was twilight, a good time for introspection. Layden obliged.

"You know," he said, "I don't like people to think, 'There goes Frank Layden, he's very funny.' I like to leave them thinking, not laughing. Thinking that, you know, I'm not so shallow. I have a lot more to offer than jokes.

"I'm lucky I'm in coaching. I don't think I'd be in it now if I had a choice, but it was what was dealt to me. It beats having a real job."

Layden shifted in his seats and watched the day end.

The next morning, he climbed into the bus that was taking the Jazz to a morning workout.

"They gave me a suite with a waterbed at the hotel," Layden announced. "It was really nice, but I didn't get much sleep. All I did was get seasick and fantasize about what must have went on there last week."

Given a choice, he'll leave 'em dancin'. He's good at that. After all, life really should be a honeymoon, shouldn't it?

INSIDE THE NBA

By FRAN BLINEBURY and KEVIN KERNAN

PREDICTED ORDER OF FINISH

ATLANTIC	CENTRAL	MIDWEST	PACIFIC
Boston	Detroit	Dallas	LA Lakers
Philadelphia	Atlanta	Houston	Seattle
New Jersey	Chicago	Utah	Portland
Washington	Indiana	Sacramento	Golden State
New York	Milwaukee	Denver	LA Clippers
	Cleveland	San Antonio	Phoenix

EASTERN CONFERENCE: Boston
WESTERN CONFERENCE: LA Lakers
CHAMPION: Boston

OK, let's get this straight. The '60s were the "We Decade," the '70s were the "Me Decade," and the '80s are "Their Decade." Who?

Why, Magic Johnson and Larry Bird, of course. Has there been anybody else playing ball in the NBA in the 1980s?

Stop and think about it. Between them, they have won a Rookie-of-the-Year Award (Bird), four regular-season MVP Awards (Bird 3, Johnson 1), six playoff MVP Awards (Bird 3, Johnson 3) and seven NBA championships (Johnson 4, Bird 3) since entering the league at the start of the 1979-80 season.

Have there ever been two players whose careers have been so intertwined? They even played for the NCAA title in the final game of their respective college careers.

Fran Blinebury is a sports columnist for the Houston Chronicle *and Kevin Kernan covers pro basketball for the* New York Post. *Kernan wrote the Eastern Conference, Blinebury the Western Conference and the introduction.*

Bird and Johnson. Or Johnson and Bird. No matter how you say it, they are the best and the brightest that the NBA has had to offer in the '80s. And since the decade has not yet run its course, there is no reason to think that things will be any different during the 1987-88 season.

Bird is Johnson East and Johnson is Bird West and together they will once more lift their respective teams up on their shoulders and set the pace for the 21 other clubs to follow.

Oh, for sure there are other names and teams to watch throughout the winter. There are the up-and-coming Detroit Pistons, who came perhaps within a head-butt between Adrian Dantley and Vinnie Johnson of upsetting the Celtics last spring, and the high-flying Atlanta Hawks, who abruptly had their wings clipped in the playoffs—the most noted challengers in the Eastern Conference. The Philadelphia 76ers will be playing without the great Julius Erving and the Milwaukee Bucks will take the floor without the guidance of Don Nelson, who has been replaced by Del Harris.

Over in the Western Conference, Houston will be looking to re-establish itself as a young power after a slip last season. Dallas, under the direction of new boss John MacLeod, is coming off a 55-win campaign. Seattle, under the hand of Bernie Bickerstaff, has a wealth of young talent and hope. And even the perennial doormat LA Clippers are optimistic with the addition of three first-round draft choices in Reggie Williams, Joe Wolf and Ken Norman. Golden State will continue growing and San Antonio will tread water and wait for Navy man David Robinson in two years.

But when all is said and done, the scene next June will look very familiar. The Lakers and the Celtics, Magic and Bird. They'll be back at center stage, playing for all the marbles. And this time it will be Boston coming out on top.

Why?

Two reasons.

First, in the NBA nobody repeats. Second, it's Bird's turn.

ATLANTA HAWKS

TEAM DIRECTORY: Pres./GM: Stan Kasten; Dir. Pub. Rel: Bill Needle; Coach: Mike Fratello; Asst. Coaches: Brendan Suhr, Brian Hill, Don Chaney. Arena: The Omni (16,074). Colors: Red and white.

SCOUTING REPORT

SHOOTING: When you are a gunslinger it's hard to holster your weapon. Dominique Wilkins is trying his best not to be a one-man show, but he still shoots too much. His percentage actually dropped for the second straight year, down to .463. Dominique took 110 shots less than the previous season and his assists jumped from 206 to 261.

In all, Wilkins heaved 1787 shots. Only one other Hawk took as many as 1000—Kevin Willis, 1003. Randy Wittman was next with 792. Wittman, the Hawks' best outside shooter, went from .530 to .503 from the field. Overall, the Hawks' shooting dropped from .490 to .481.

They did, however, pick up a new weapon in three-point ace Mike McGee, who made 53 more three-pointers than the entire team did two years ago. Still, Mike Fratello has to spread out the offense a little more for the Hawks to make the next step beyond in the playoffs.

PLAYMAKING: Doc Rivers continues to grow into one of the game's best point guards, finishing fourth in the league in assists at 10 a game. He completely fell apart in the playoffs against Detroit, however, and that spelled doom for the Hawks.

The Hawk frontline is one of the worst passing frontlines in existence. Tree Rollins gets one assist every 80.2 minutes, Jon Koncak one assist every 54.3 minutes, Cliff Levingston one assist every 46.2 minutes and Kevin Willis one assist every 32 minutes.

DEFENSE: The Hawks led the league in defense, holding opponents to an average of 102.8 points a game and also a league-low .451 shooting percentage. They rolled up 110 a night so that's a 7.2 plus; only the Lakers had a bigger bulge. Fratello obviously has learned well from the master, Hubie Brown, on how to create chaos with traps, switches and illegal zones. Tree Rollins anchors the "D" and players like Willis, Koncak and Levingston make it nearly impossible to go in deep against the Hawks and get your

Dominique Wilkins shows stuff of a 29 ppg Hawk.

HAWK ROSTER

No.	Veteran	Pos.	Ht.	Wt.	Age	Yrs. Pro	College
12	John Battle	G	6-2	175	25	2	Rutgers
33	Antoine Carr	F	6-9	235	26	3	Wichita State
44	* Scott Hastings	C	6-10	235	27	5	Arkansas
55	Jon Koncak	C	7-0	250	24	2	SMU
53	Cliff Levingston	F	6-8	210	26	5	Wichita State
40	Mike McGee	G	6-5	190	28	6	Michigan
25	Glenn Rivers	G	6-4	185	26	4	Marquette
30	Tree Rollins	C	7-1	240	32	10	Clemson
4	Spud Webb	G	5-7	130	24	2	North Carolina St.
21	Dominique Wilkins	F	6-8	200	27	5	Georgia
42	Kevin Willis	F	7-0	235	25	3	Michigan State
10	Randy Wittman	G	6-6	210	28	4	Indiana

*Free agent unsigned at press time

Rd.	Top Rookies	Sel. No.	Pos.	Ht.	Wt.	College
1	Dallas Comegys	21	F	6-9	205	DePaul
2	Terrance Bailey	42	G	6-2	185	Wagner
2	Terry Coner	44	G	6-3	170	Alabama
3	Song Tau	67	F	6-10	220	China
4	Theofanis Christodouluo	90	F	6-10	220	Greece

own rebound. Atlanta also blocked 77 more shots than the year before.

REBOUNDING: With all the tall trees up front, Atlanta's best offense is probably the missed shot. They retrieved 37 percent of their misses, a league high. The Hawks finished second in the league in rebounding and figure to dominate the boards for a long while. The drafting of DePaul's Dallas Comegys should also help. Balance is the watchword, with Willis grabbing 849 rebounds, Levingston 532, Koncak 498, Wilkins 494 and Rollins 488.

OUTLOOK: This is the year the Hawks have to mature as a team and that means winning in the playoffs. Although they set a franchise record for victories (57), they disintegrated for the second straight year in postseason play. It should be interesting to see how the departure of Willis Reed affects the team up front. Perhaps it's time for Antoine Carr to play a much bigger role. This team is too big to keep down. The Hawks, Celtics and Pistons should create a monster dogfight in the East.

HAWK PROFILES

DOMINIQUE WILKINS 27 6-8 200   Forward

"Human Highlight Film" was edited into more of a team player last season...Was NBA scoring king two years ago at 30.3, finished last season at 29.0, second to Michael Jordan's 37.1...Scored 50-plus points three times, including a career-high 57 on Dec. 10 vs. the Bulls...Has five of the top six scoring games in Atlanta history...Lou Hudson rolled the dice for 57 on Nov. 10, 1969...Assists climbed from 206 to 261 as he made big effort to improve his passing...Just like season before, had difficult time in playoff series in which Hawks were ousted, but was bothered by sore leg...Nicknamed 'Nique, he's not afraid to work his apostrophe off...Still plays out of control at times...Born Jan. 12, 1960, in Sorbonne, France, where father was stationed in the Air Force...Full name is Jacques Dominique Wilkins...Utah chose Georgia grad third overall in 1982, but dealt rights to Hawks for John Drew, Freeman Williams and cash...May be best deal Ted Turner ever made...Signed five-year pact that gives him $1.3 million a year...Brother, Gerald, plays for the Knicks...First "sport" he ever mastered was marbles.

Year	Team	G	FG	FG Pct.	FT	FT Pct.	Reb.	Ast.	TP	Avg.
1982-83	Atlanta..............	82	601	.493	230	.682	478	129	1434	17.5
1983-84	Atlanta..............	81	684	.479	382	.770	582	126	1750	21.6
1984-85	Atlanta..............	81	853	.451	486	.806	557	200	2217	27.4
1985-86	Atlanta..............	78	888	.468	577	.818	618	206	2366	30.3
1986-87	Atlanta..............	79	828	.463	607	.818	494	261	2294	29.0
	Totals..............	401	3854	.469	2282	.792	2729	922	10061	25.1

KEVIN WILLIS 25 7-0 235   Forward

Member of the Dow Jones' team...Too often his performance is up and down, but is beginning to pay huge dividends...Became much more consistent last season...Concentration has improved thanks to coaching of ex-assistant Willis Reed...Can be absolutely frightening when all rockets are ignited...Scored and rebounded in double figures 45 games...Hawks won 34 of those...Enthusiastic, he's liable to get in shoving match before opening tip...Will earn $400,000 this season...Led team in rebounds (10.4) and was second in scoring (16.1)...Was 11th pick overall in 1984 draft, out of

Michigan State...Taken after Leon Wood and Lancaster Gordon...Late bloomer did not start playing ball until junior year in high school...Hawks believe he is answer to Kevin McHale...Bad passer...Had just 62 assists...Born Sept. 6, 1962, in Los Angeles...Doug Moe calls him "the most underrated player in our league."...Likes to design his own clothes ...In position to design a great career.

Year	Team	G	FG	FG Pct.	FT	FT Pct.	Reb.	Ast.	TP	Avg.
1984-85	Atlanta	82	322	.467	119	.657	522	36	765	9.3
1985-86	Atlanta	82	419	.517	172	.654	704	45	1010	12.3
1986-87	Atlanta	81	538	.536	227	.709	849	62	1304	16.1
	Totals	245	1279	.511	518	.678	2075	143	3079	12.6

RANDY WITTMAN 28 6-6 210   Guard

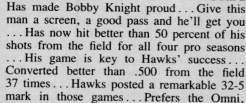

Has made Bobby Knight proud...Give this man a screen, a good pass and he'll get you ...Has now hit better than 50 percent of his shots from the field for all four pro seasons ...His game is key to Hawks' success... Converted better than .500 from the field 37 times...Hawks posted a remarkable 32-5 mark in those games...Prefers the Omni, where he shoots .544 from the field, over the road, .466...Born Oct. 28, 1959, in Indianapolis, Ind....Stayed home for college and helped bring national championship to Indiana in 1981... Two-time academic All-American...Drafted 22nd overall by the Bullets in 1983, then sent to Hawks for second-round pick and forward Tom McMillen shortly thereafter...Will earn $325,000 this season...Important piece to a winning team.

Year	Team	G	FG	FG Pct.	FT	FT Pct.	Reb.	Ast.	TP	Avg.
1983-84	Atlanta	78	160	.503	28	.609	71	71	350	4.5
1984-85	Atlanta	41	187	.531	30	.732	73	125	406	9.9
1985-86	Atlanta	81	467	.530	104	.770	170	306	1043	12.9
1986-87	Atlanta	71	398	.503	100	.787	124	211	900	12.7
	Totals	271	1212	.517	262	.751	438	713	2699	10.0

GLENN RIVERS 26 6-4 185   Guard

A rising star...Made great strides in his game last season and then was burned at the stake by Isiah Thomas in the playoffs...Will he be able to recover from that dreadful performance?...Shot 40 percent from the field (16-40) and 50 percent from the line (10-20) against Pistons...Admitted he had lost his confidence...During the season he

was remarkable . . . Came off a broken wrist to play all 82 games
. . . Finished in top 10 in assists (fourth) and steals (ninth) . . .
Dedicated himself to improving free-throw percentage, including
practicing daily on his honeymoon . . . Zoomed from .602 to
team-leading .828 . . . Got married in style, wearing pink hightops to match his wife's dress . . . "Doc" was born Oct. 13, 1961,
in Maywood, Ill. . . . Was thought to have made a mistake when
he left Marquette a year early after poor season and was not taken
until 31st pick of the draft by Hawks in 1983 . . . Made $450,000
last season.

Year	Team	G	FG	FG Pct.	FT	FT Pct.	Reb.	Ast.	TP	Avg.
1983-84	Atlanta............	81	250	.462	255	.785	220	314	757	9.3
1984-85	Atlanta............	69	334	.476	291	.770	214	410	974	14.1
1985-86	Atlanta............	53	220	.474	172	.608	162	443	612	11.5
1986-87	Atlanta............	82	342	.451	365	.828	299	823	1053	12.8
	Totals.............	285	1146	.465	1083	.759	895	1990	3396	11.9

MIKE McGEE 28 6-5 190   Guard

Have three-pointer, will travel . . . Got away
from Jack Nicholson and Lakers on June 17,
1986, along with rights to Ken Barlow for
Billy Thompson and Ron Kellogg . . . Smashed
Hawk three-point records, making 86-229
from down deep . . . Previous season Hawks
had just 33 three-point field goals from entire
team . . . Showed he could do more than shoot
from long range, playing defense and passing . . . Shot just
58 percent from free-throw line . . . Went down the tubes in
playoffs, shooting just 26 percent from the field and had five
shots blocked by Vinnie Johnson . . . Was massive scorer at
Michigan . . . In five years with the Lakers he could never get the
time or consistency needed to become NBA scoring wizard . . .
Something seems to be missing in his overall makeup that would
bring all his talents out . . . Lakers made him No. 19 pick overall
in 1981 and had big plans for him . . . Hawks may trade him because of all the talent in the backcourt.

Year	Team	G	FG	FG Pct.	FT	FT Pct.	Reb.	Ast.	TP	Avg.
1981-82	Los Angeles.........	39	80	.465	31	.585	49	16	191	4.9
1982-83	Los Angeles.........	39	69	.423	17	.739	53	26	156	4.0
1983-84	Los Angeles.........	77	347	.594	61	.540	193	81	757	9.8
1984-85	L.A. Lakers.........	76	329	.538	94	.588	165	71	774	10.2
1985-86	L.A. Lakers.........	71	252	.463	42	.656	140	83	587	8.3
1986-87	Atlanta.............	76	311	.459	80	.584	159	149	788	10.4
	Totals.............	378	1388	.504	325	.591	759	426	3253	8.6

ANTOINE CARR 26 6-9 235   Forward

Get ready for the big bang . . . Is due to explode any time . . . His playoff performance was a hint of things to come . . . Hit 39-56 from the field . . . Can shoot, pass and dribble . . . One of the team's few big men who can be credited with an assist . . . Freak accident in preseason in which he scalded himself stepping into a tub set him back . . . Bugged by injuries throughout career . . . Broke a thumb three years ago . . . Suffered stress fracture in his leg two years back . . . Girlfriend convinced him to sprinkle holy water on the leg to ensure full recovery . . . This Carr carrying extra passenger . . . Must lose weight to live up to advance billing as eighth player chosen overall by Pistons in 1983, out of Wichita State . . . Came to Atlanta along with Cliff Levingston on June 18, 1984, for Dan Roundfield . . . Played first pro season in Italy after contract squabble . . . Born July 23, 1961, in Oklahoma City.

Year	Team	G	FG	FG Pct.	FT	FT Pct.	Reb.	Ast.	TP	Avg.
1984-85	Atlanta............	62	198	.528	101	.789	232	80	499	8.0
1985-86	Atlanta............	17	49	.527	18	.667	52	14	116	6.8
1986-87	Atlanta............	65	134	.506	73	.709	156	34	342	5.3
	Totals............	144	381	.520	192	.744	440	128	957	6.6

JOHN BATTLE 24 6-2 175   Guard

One man's ceiling is another man's floor . . . Spud Webb's injury problems opened the door for Battle when he averaged eight points in 16 minutes during Spudster's absence . . . Born Nov. 9, 1962, in Washington, D.C. . . . Has been fighting for a spot since being drafted 84th overall by Hawks in 1986, out of Rutgers . . . Once fled practice in tears, but has grown to accept the challenge . . . This power point guard has had some sensational games . . . Hit nine of 10 from the field vs. Rockets and scored career-high 27 points on Feb. 2 . . . "I used to wonder about my future," he says, "but now I know I belong in this league and it's given me peace of mind." . . . A self-taught piano player, he must find a way to teach Mike Fratello to give him more time.

Year	Team	G	FG	FG Pct.	FT	FT Pct.	Reb.	Ast.	TP	Avg.
1985-86	Atlanta............	64	101	.455	75	.728	62	74	277	4.3
1986-87	Atlanta............	64	144	.457	93	.738	60	124	381	6.0
	Totals............	128	245	.456	168	.734	122	198	658	5.1

CLIFF LEVINGSTON 26 6-8 210   Forward

Tale of two Shockers...Increased time for Antoine Carr means less time for Levingston ...Two were teammates at Wichita State... Somehow, somewhere, time has to be made available for this jumping demon...Made $375,000 last season...Averaged 22 minutes during the season, third straight season his playing time has dropped, which can't make him too happy...Bottom really fell out in playoffs when he got into the combat zone just 13 minutes a night...Free-throw shooting finally became respectable...Was ninth player chosen in 1982 draft, going to Detroit...Prior to 1984-85 season was dealt to Hawks along with Carr for Dan Roundfield...Born Jan. 4, 1961, in San Diego...Must have liked the aquarium because he has an extensive collection of tropical fish.

Year	Team	G	FG	FG Pct.	FT	FT Pct.	Reb.	Ast.	TP	Avg.
1982-83	Detroit	62	131	.485	84	.571	232	52	346	5.6
1983-84	Detroit	80	229	.525	125	.672	545	109	583	7.3
1984-85	Atlanta	74	291	.527	145	.653	566	104	727	9.8
1985-86	Atlanta	81	294	.534	164	.678	534	72	752	9.3
1986-87	Atlanta	82	251	.506	155	.731	533	40	657	8.0
	Totals	379	1196	.519	673	.667	2410	377	3065	8.1

JON KONCAK 24 7-0 250   Center

The honeymoon is over...Made $650,000 despite minimum-wage stats, 5.6 points and six rebounds a night...Willis Reed spent long hours working to improve Koncak's game, especially developing a hook shot...This should be the year Koncak starts fully absorbing what he's been taught and start producing bigger numbers...Positioning is a problem for this massive body...Had just 20 points in eight playoff games...Team went 15-3 in games he started...Born May 17, 1963, in Cedar Rapids, Iowa...Was 1984 Olympian, then was chosen No. 5 by Hawks in 1985, out of SMU...Mustangs' all-time leading rebounder and shot-blocker and its second-best scorer.

Year	Team	G	FG	FG Pct.	FT	FT Pct.	Reb.	Ast.	TP	Avg.
1985-86	Atlanta	82	263	.507	156	.607	467	55	682	8.3
1986-87	Atlanta	82	169	.480	125	.654	493	31	463	5.6
	Totals	164	432	496	281	.627	960	86	1145	7.0

SPUD WEBB 24 5-7 130   Guard

This Spud's for all the short guys out there with tall dreams...Just the fact he was in NBA second straight season is a credit to his drive and talent...Jumping and hanging ability allow him to play much bigger...Won the hearts of America when he became The Little Guard That Could, winning the NBA's Slam Dunk contest two years ago...Had a frustrating time last season because of injuries...Missed a total of 56 games, 44 because of ligament damage in right knee that necessitated surgery...Originally hurt his knee on Dec. 5 against Pacers and did not return to lineup until March 13 in Dallas... That's his hometown and site of his Slam Dunk triumph...Born July 13, 1963...Will make $250,000 on the court and much more off it in endorsements...An ad-man's dream...His autobiography is called *Flying Inside*...Nicknamed Sputnikhead as a baby...Drafted 87th overall by Pistons in 1985, out of North Carolina State, he was cut before camp and signed by Hawks... An inspiration to all.

Year	Team	G	FG	FG Pct.	FT	FT Pct.	Reb.	Ast.	TP	Avg.
1985-86	Atlanta............	79	199	.483	216	.785	123	337	616	7.8
1986-87	Atlanta............	33	71	.438	80	.762	60	167	223	6.8
	Totals............	112	270	.470	296	.779	183	504	839	7.5

SCOTT HASTINGS 27 6-10 235   Center

Pure roster fodder...Biggest contribution is making an inbounds pass every few weeks... Has become somewhat of a thug to keep himself in the league...Too bad for reporters he doesn't play more...Always entertaining in the locker room...Majored in public relations at Arkansas and that has paid off...Born June 3, 1960 in Independence, Kan.... Knicks chose him 29th overall in 1982...Went to Hawks along with $600,000 for guard Rory Sparrow in February 1983... Does passable imitations of Bruce Springsteen, Bill Murray, John Wayne, and, at rare times, an NBA player.

Year	Team	G	FG	FG Pct.	FT	FT Pct.	Reb.	Ast.	TP	Avg.
1982-83	N.Y.-Atl...........	31	13	.342	11	.550	41	3	37	1.2
1983-84	Atlanta............	68	111	.468	82	.788	270	46	305	4.5
1984-85	Atlanta............	64	89	.473	63	.778	159	46	241	3.8
1985-86	Atlanta............	62	65	.409	60	.857	124	26	193	3.1
1986-87	Atlanta............	40	23	.338	23	.793	70	13	71	1.8
	Totals............	265	301	.436	239	.786	664	134	847	3.2

WAYNE (TREE) ROLLINS 32 7-1 240   Center

Always, his roots have been defense... Hawks' all-time leading shot-blocker dropped out of the league's top 10 for the first time in his career in that category, but still averaged nearly two a game... You know exactly what you're getting with him—defense, shot-blocking, oak-tree picks and zero offense... Average of 5.4 was lowest in 10-year career... Richly rewarded for his work with a million-dollar-a-year salary... Fouled out of the fewest games of his career, which means he's learning to control aggression... Or perhaps, he's not as aggressive as he once was... Total of 22 assists for the season is hard to believe... You'd think he'd get one every now and then by accident... Team's elder statesman... Born June 16, 1955, in Cordele, Ga.... Hawks chose him 14th overall in 1977, out of Clemson, and he's been in the pivot ever since.

Year	Team	G	FG	FG Pct.	FT	FT Pct.	Reb.	Ast.	TP	Avg.
1977-78	Atlanta.	80	253	.487	104	.703	552	79	610	7.6
1978-79	Atlanta.	81	297	.535	89	.631	588	49	683	8.4
1979-80	Atlanta.	82	287	.558	157	.714	774	76	731	8.9
1980-81	Atlanta.	40	116	.552	46	.807	286	35	278	7.0
1981-82	Atlanta.	79	202	.584	79	.612	611	59	483	6.1
1982-83	Atlanta.	80	261	.510	98	.726	743	75	620	7.8
1983-84	Atlanta.	77	274	.518	118	.621	593	62	666	8.6
1984-85	Atlanta.	70	186	.549	67	.720	442	52	439	6.3
1985-86	Atlanta.	74	173	.499	69	.767	458	41	415	5.6
1866-87	Atlanta.	75	171	.546	63	.724	488	22	405	5.5
	Totals.	738	2220	.530	890	.690	5535	550	5330	7.2

TOP ROOKIE

DALLAS COMEGYS 23 6-9 205   Forward

Hawks were pleasantly surprised he was still around when they chose him with the 21st pick... DePaul's all-time leading shot-blocker with 297 and No. 4 scorer with 1,613 points... Was one of the main reasons Blue Demons were ranked in top 10 nearly his entire senior season... Quick jumper with good hands... Will need to build strength but will make Hawks' deep frontline that much deeper... Born Aug. 17, 1964, in Philadelphia.

COACH MIKE FRATELLO: Had stirring encore to Coach-of-the-Year season, despite playoff collapse . . . In his fourth year as a head coach, Fratello had completely reshaped Hawks . . . Just three players remain from team he inherited from Kevin Loughery—Dominique Wilkins, Tree Rollins and Scott Hastings . . . Was wound a bit too tight when he came to the team—remember, he was weened on the NBA by highstrung Hubie Brown—but has reached a level of respect from players, peers and public . . . Son of a former Golden Gloves champion and pro middleweight, he knows how to take a punch and come back with a flurry of his own . . . Has completely escaped from Hubie's shadow and the absurd belief some held he was too short at 5-7 to coach in the NBA . . . Hard work, perseverance, dedication and communication paid off this season in Central Division crown, team's first in seven seasons . . . The 57 wins were a franchise record and marked the first time the Hawks have won 50-plus games in back-to-back seasons . . . Born Feb. 24, 1947, in Hackensack, N.J. . . . Attended Montclair State (N.J.) College . . . Three-year record is 181-147.

GREATEST COACH

This is a case where the student earns better grades than the teacher. Mike Fratello is chosen over Hubie Brown not only on basis of performance, but potential.

Fratello, of course, broke into the NBA under Brown as assistant coach of the Hawks from 1978-82 and then followed Brown to New York. From Hubie he learned organization, preparation and fine-tuned his knowledge of the game. But he did not pick up Brown's fatal flaw—his tendency to over-berate players—and that is the difference.

After a 49-42 rookie year in 1983-84 he slumped to 34-48 and there was talk he might be fired. The Hawks, however, stayed with their Little Big Man and it paid off in a large way. Fratello racked up 50 wins the following year, when he was Coach of the Year, and last season was marked by Atlanta's winning the Central Division crown.

Where does he go from here? Well, he could cite the coach of the Tri-Cities Blackhawks in 1949-50. They managed a 28-29 record, only a little better than Fratello's mark in 1984-85. The Tri-Cities' coach? Red Auerbach.

ALL-TIME HAWK LEADERS

SEASON

Points: Bob Pettit, 2,429, 1961-62
Assists: Glenn Rivers, 823, 1986-87
Rebounds: Bob Pettit, 1,540, 1960-61

GAME

Points: Dominique Wilkins, 57 vs. New Jersey, 4/10/86
           Lou Hudson, 57 vs. Chicago, 11/10/69
           Bob Pettit, 57 vs. Detroit, 2/18/61
Assists: Glenn Rivers, 21 vs. Philadelphia, 3/4/86
Rebounds: Bob Pettit, 35 vs. Cincinnati, 3/2/58
             Bob Pettit, 35 vs. New York, 1/6/56

CAREER

Points: Bob Pettit, 20,880, 1954-65
Assists: Lenny Wilkins, 3,048, 1960-68
Rebounds: Bob Pettit, 12,851, 1954-65

BOSTON CELTICS

TEAM DIRECTORY: Chairman: Don F. Gaston; Pres.: Arnold (Red) Auerbach; VP/GM: Jan Volk: Dir. Pub. Rel.: Jeff Twiss; Coach: K.C. Jones; Asst. Coaches: Jim Rodgers, Chris Ford. Arena: Boston Garden (14,890) and Hartford Civic Center (15,134). Colors: Green and white.

SCOUTING REPORT

SHOOTING: There is no better shooting team in the league than the Celts, whose regular-season mark (.517) just nipped the Lakers (.516). For four straight years now the Celtics have shot better than 50 percent from the field and last year's mark was a team record. Usually, the bigger the game, the better they shoot. Also, the .808 mark from the line was a team record and Boston became the only team in the league to shoot better than 80 percent from the charity stripe.

Kevin McHale (.604) led the league in shooting percentage, while Robert Parish (.556) also was in the Top Ten. Larry Bird was the third starter over 50 percent with a .525 mark. Bird, however, wore down in the playoffs, shooting just 44 percent against the Lakers and vowed to work on weights for the first time in his career this season to improve his strength.

PLAYMAKING: One reason the Celtics shoot so well is because they pass so well. Their around-the-horn offense is the best in the league. Kind of ironic that they don't have a true playmaker with Dennis Johnson, Danny Ainge and Bird all getting a piece of the passing action. DJ led the team in assists with 594, but Bird was right behind with 566 while Ainge added 400. They play the game the way it should be played.

DEFENSE: The Celtic defense, of course, makes their offense go. Two years ago they led the league, holding opponents to .461 shooting accuracy. Last year the number was .463, fifth best in the NBA. They are masters at playing the zone defense, allowing Bird to be a free safety.

McHale was named by the coaches as the top defensive player in the league and Johnson, the best "in-your-face" guard in the league, was named to the All-Defensive team as well.

One final note: Bird's steal of Isiah Thomas' inbounds pass in Game 5 of the Detroit series was the most dramatic example of playing hard defense to the final second.

Crownless: (from left) Vincent, Bird, Henry, Ainge.

REBOUNDING: Parish led the team in rebounding with 851. That was good enough for 10th in the league at 10.6. McHale (763) is just as relentless on the boards, especially on the offensive end, while Bird added 682 rebounds. Two years ago Celtics led the league in rebounding, but that was before Bill Walton was hurt. Last year they finished 18th. Walton had but 31 rebounds last season after rolling up 544 the season before. The Celts are hoping 7-0 rookie Brad Lohaus can help pick up the rebound slack off the bench.

OUTLOOK: Just think of what might have been if Len Bias hadn't died. The Celtics must regroup this season after courageous defeat at the hand of the Lakers. A rebuilt McHale should pay huge dividends in the playoffs. Walton's career is probably over, so the Celts have to get new life from rookies. Reggie Lewis will give them scoring spark off the bench and another big man has to come through.

Through it all there is Bird and that, more than any other factor, is the reason to believe the Celtics will battle the Lakers one more time in the finals. Don't count K.C. Jones' aging team out just yet. This could be their fine wine year.

CELTIC ROSTER

No.	Veteran	Pos.	Ht.	Wt.	Age	Yrs. Pro	College
44	Danny Ainge	G	6-5	190	28	6	Brigham Young
33	Larry Bird	F	6-9	220	30	8	Indiana State
34	Rick Carlisle	G	6-5	210	28	3	Virginia
20	Darren Daye	G-F	6-8	220	26	4	UCLA
43	Conner Henry	G	6-7	195	24	1	Cal-Santa Barbara
3	Dennis Johnson	G	6-4	200	33	11	Pepperdine
50	Greg Kite	C	6-11	255	26	4	Brigham Young
32	Kevin McHale	F	6-10	240	29	7	Minnesota
00	Robert Parish	C	7-1	240	34	11	Centenary
31	Fred Roberts	F	6-10	220	27	3	Brigham Young
12	Jerry Sichting	G	6-1	175	30	7	Purdue
11	Sam Vincent	G	6-2	185	24	2	Michigan State
5	Bill Walton	C	6-11	235	34	13	UCLA
8	Scott Wedman	F	6-7	225	35	13	Colorado

Rd.	Top Rookies	Sel. No.	Pos.	Ht.	Wt.	College
1	Reggie Lewis	22	G-F	6-7	195	Northeastern
2	Brad Lohaus	45	F	7-0	230	Iowa
3	Tom Sheehey	70	F	6-7	225	Virginia
4	Darryl Kennedy	91	F	6-5	220	Oklahoma
5	David Butler	114	F	6-9	225	California

CELTIC PROFILES

LARRY BIRD 30 6-9 220   Forward

"Bird stole the ball! Bird stole the ball!"... That one play is all you need to know about his career...Game 5 against Detroit, Bird steals Isiah Thomas' inbounds pass with four seconds left and sets up a darting Dennis Johnson for the game-winning layup... Afterwards teammate Jerry Sichting put it best: "The legend of Larry Bird goes on."... Three-time MVP, however, took a back seat to Magic Johnson in the finals...After carrying Celtics to seven-game victories over Bucks and Pistons, Bird simply wore down against Lakers... Shot just 44 percent in that series...Led NBA in free-throw shooting again...Became first Celtic to register 2,000 points three consecutive seasons...Finished fourth in league in scoring ...Born Dec. 7, 1956, in French Lick, Ind....Keeps one of his MVP trophies on refrigerator in the basement of French Lick home...A future eligible pick by Celtics, who chose him sixth overall in 1978 draft, out of Indiana State...Makes $1.8 million...Many consider him the best to ever play the game... "The truth is, Bill Russell was a better basketball player than I am, and I'm not afraid to admit it," Bird says. "When you look at Russell winning 11 championships in 13 seasons, that's amazing. That's something that will never be done again."

Year	Team	G	FG	FG Pct.	FT	FT Pct.	Reb.	Ast.	TP	Avg.
1979-80	Boston	82	693	.474	301	.836	852	370	1745	21.3
1980-81	Boston	82	719	.478	283	.863	895	451	1741	21.2
1981-82	Boston	77	711	.503	328	.863	837	447	1761	22.9
1982-83	Boston	79	747	.504	351	.840	870	458	1867	23.6
1983-84	Boston	79	758	.492	374	.888	796	520	1908	24.2
1984-85	Boston	80	918	.522	403	.882	842	531	2295	28.7
1985-86	Boston	82	796	.496	441	.896	805	557	2115	25.8
1986-87	Boston	74	786	.525	414	.910	682	566	2076	28.1
	Totals	635	6128	.500	2895	.874	6579	3900	15508	24.4

KEVIN McHALE 29 6-10 240   Forward

Gutted out one of the most courageous seasons possible...Broke his right foot on March 11 against Phoenix, missed five games and then played rest of regular season and throughout playoffs...Averaged 21 points in playoffs ...Had surgery after season and may miss a major portion of this year...Led league in field-goal percentage and also was among leaders in scoring and blocked shots...Top vote-getter on All-Defensive team in poll by coaches...Most down-to-earth player in the league...Loves to fish, golf, shoot the breeze and have a few brews...Kind of guy you'd expect to find in a VFW hall, not on CBS on Sundays in the spring...Second on club to Larry Bird in scoring...No. 3 pick overall by Celts in 1980 draft, out of Minnesota...Born Dec. 19, 1957, in Hibbing, Minn., also home of Bob Dylan...Averages $1.6 million a year...A winner.

Year	Team	G	FG	FG Pct.	FT	FT Pct.	Reb.	Ast.	TP	Avg.
1980-81	Boston	82	355	.533	108	.679	359	55	818	10.0
1981-82	Boston	82	465	.531	187	.754	556	91	1117	13.6
1982-83	Boston	82	483	.541	193	.717	553	104	1159	14.1
1983-84	Boston	82	587	.556	336	.765	610	104	1511	18.4
1984-85	Boston	79	605	.570	355	.760	712	141	1565	19.8
1985-86	Boston	68	561	.574	326	.776	551	181	1448	21.3
1986-87	Boston	77	790	.604	428	.836	763	198	2008	26.1
	Totals	552	3846	.563	1933	.769	4104	874	9626	17.4

ROBERT PARISH 34 7-1 240   Center

Chief Thunderfist... His savage attack on Bill Laimbeer helped key dramatic Game 5 victory in Eastern Conference finals... Another one of the walking wounded... Played throughout playoffs on severely sprained ankle, averaging 18 points, 9.4 rebounds and 1.5 times a night was helped off the court... People tend to get the wrong impression because he is sullen on the floor and in the locker room, but Parish is a charming person ...High, arching jumper is maddeningly accurate... Makes $1.5 million a season... Born Aug. 30, 1953, in Shreveport, La.... Warriors picked him eighth overall in 1976... Came to Celtics as part of one of the most one-sided trades ever made... Wound up in Boston along with draft pick that became Kevin McHale, for two first-round picks, one of which became Joe Barry Carroll... After getting blasted by Kareem Abdul-Jabbar in finals, he went home to Boston to discover thieves had robbed his home, taking his wedding ring, seven All-Star rings and three championship rings... That's a tough series.

Year	Team	G	FG	FG Pct.	FT	FT Pct.	Reb.	Ast.	TP	Avg.
1976-77	Golden State	77	288	.503	121	.708	543	74	697	9.1
1977-78	Golden State	82	430	.472	165	.625	680	95	1025	12.5
1978-79	Golden State	76	554	.499	196	.698	916	115	1304	17.2
1979-80	Golden State	72	510	.507	203	.715	783	122	1223	17.0
1980-81	Boston	82	635	.545	282	.710	777	144	1552	18.9
1981-82	Boston	80	669	.542	252	.710	866	140	1590	19.9
1982-83	Boston	78	619	.550	271	.698	827	141	1509	19.3
1983-84	Boston	80	623	.546	274	.745	857	139	1520	19.0
1984-85	Boston	79	551	.542	292	.743	840	125	1394	17.6
1985-86	Boston	81	530	.549	245	.731	770	145	1305	16.1
1986-87	Boston	80	588	.566	227	.735	851	173	1403	17.5
	Totals	867	5997	.530	2528	.713	8710	1413	14522	16.7

DANNY AINGE 28 6-5 190   Guard

The gnat... Always buzzing around the ball on defense... His three-pointer was killer blow in Game 7 vs. Pistons... Larry Bird likes to get on his case and sometimes Ainge appears to try too hard... His 1-9 outing in final game of Laker series proved extremely costly... Has improved year in and year out showing the world he made the right decision leaving the Toronto Blue Jays for Celtics... Negotiated his own contract, which pays him about $600,000 a season... Feisty player who is hated by opposing fans because his boyish face can take on the expression: "I want my Maypo!"... In reality Brigham Young product is nothing like that... A wonderful person... People always get the wrong impression... They think he bit Tree Rollins' finger in infamous incident when it was the other way around... Born March 17, 1959, in Salt Lake City, Utah... Tough, played despite knee and ankle problems in playoffs and started season with a fractured transverse bone in his back... Drafted 31st by Celtics in 1981, even though he was playing for the Blue Jays at the time... The only young buck on an aging team.

Year	Team	G	FG	FG Pct.	FT	FT Pct.	Reb.	Ast.	TP	Avg.
1981-82	Boston	53	79	.357	56	.862	56	87	219	4.1
1982-83	Boston	80	357	.496	72	.742	214	251	791	9.9
1983-84	Boston	71	166	.460	46	.821	116	162	384	5.4
1984-85	Boston	75	419	.529	118	.868	268	399	971	12.9
1985-86	Boston	80	353	.504	123	.904	235	405	855	10.7
1986-87	Boston	71	410	.486	148	.897	242	400	1053	14.8
	Totals	430	1784	.490	563	.860	1131	1704	4273	9.9

JERRY SICHTING 30 6-1 175   Guard

A playoff disappointment... After shooting 51 percent during the regular season, he managed just 43 percent in postseason... Had some good moments against Isiah Thomas in Piston series, but made just 4-15 shots vs. Lakers... Benchless Celtics needed his outside shooting to survive... Escaped from a career on the garbage heap in Indiana to win a championship ring two years ago... Celts signed free agent for $825,000 over four years... Extremely witty individual... After taking Ralph Sampson's one-two punch to the face in 1986 finals, he said, "I don't know if that was a punch or a mosquito. My son hits harder than that and he's only three years old."... Born Nov. 29, 1956, in Martinsville, Ind.... Drafted 82nd overall by Warriors in 1979, out of Purdue.

Year	Team	G	FG	FG Pct.	FT	FT Pct.	Reb.	Ast.	TP	Avg.
1980-81	Indiana	47	34	.358	25	.781	43	70	93	2.0
1981-82	Indiana	51	91	.469	29	.763	55	117	212	4.2
1982-83	Indiana	78	316	.478	92	.860	155	433	727	9.3
1983-84	Indiana	80	397	.532	117	.867	171	457	917	11.5
1984-85	Indiana	70	325	.521	112	.875	114	264	771	11.0
1985-86	Boston	82	235	.570	61	.924	104	188	537	6.5
1986-87	Boston	78	202	.508	37	.881	91	187	448	5.7
	Totals	486	1600	.511	473	.863	733	1716	3705	7.6

DENNIS JOHNSON 33 6-4 200   Guard

Rock steady...One of the all-time "big-game" players...When Bird stole the ball, his cut to basket and difficult reverse layup in Game 5 vs. Pistons was exclamation point to fantastic play...How many players would have had the sense to do that?...Where would the Celtics be without him?...How could the Suns and Sonics make such terrible deals, dumping DJ?...Hard to believe Lenny Wilkins once called him "a cancer."...Only Celtic to shine in Laker finale, rolling up 33 points...Ultimate team player...Born Sept. 18, 1954, in San Pedro, Cal....Drafted 29th overall by Sonics in 1976, out of Pepperdine...Earns about $800,000 a season... Was MVP in 1978-79 playoffs...Big and durable, for nine straight years he has been named first- or second-team All-Defense...If your life depended on one game, this guy would be on the team.

Year	Team	G	FG	FG Pct.	FT	FT Pct.	Reb.	Ast.	TP	Avg.
1976-77	Seattle	81	285	.504	179	.624	302	123	749	9.2
1977-78	Seattle	81	367	.417	297	.732	294	230	1031	12.7
1978-79	Seattle	80	482	.432	306	.781	374	280	1270	15.9
1979-80	Seattle	81	574	.422	380	.780	414	332	1540	19.0
1980-81	Phoenix	79	532	.436	411	.820	363	291	1486	18.8
1981-82	Phoenix	80	577	.470	399	.806	410	369	1561	19.5
1982-83	Phoenix	77	398	.462	292	.791	335	388	1093	14.2
1983-84	Boston	80	384	.437	281	.852	280	338	1053	13.2
1984-85	Boston	80	493	.462	261	.853	317	543	1254	15.7
1985-86	Boston	78	482	.455	243	.818	268	456	1213	15.6
1986-87	Boston	79	423	.444	209	.833	261	594	1062	13.4
	Totals	876	4997	.447	3258	.791	3618	3944	13312	15.2

BILL WALTON 34 6-11 235   Center

Oh, no Mr. Bill...After tasting champagne two years ago, Big Red had one of the most frustrating years of injury-riddled career, playing just 10 regular-season games and 12 in the playoffs...Even though he's well over 7-feet, he refuses to be listed over 6-11...Was stumbling shadow of himself during those 102 playoff minutes...Career could be over... Foot problems intensified last season and he had offseason surgery...Has missed nearly five seasons due to foot woes... First pick overall in 1974 draft by Trail Blazers...Starred at UCLA, leading Bruins to two NCAA titles...Considered by many to be the greatest college player of all time . . . Led Blazers to their only NBA championship in 1977 and was named MVP of playoffs . . . Was picked off the Clipper junk pile by Red Auerbach in September 1985 for Cedric Maxwell and a No. 1 pick . . . In last year of contract that pays him $450,000.

Year	Team	G	FG	FG Pct.	FT	FT Pct.	Reb.	Ast.	TP	Avg.
1974-75	Portland............	35	177	.513	94	.686	441	167	448	12.8
1975-76	Portland............	51	345	.471	133	.583	681	220	823	16.1
1976-77	Portland............	65	491	.528	228	.697	934	245	1210	18.6
1977-78	Portland............	58	460	.522	177	.720	766	291	1097	18.9
1978-79	Portland............					Injured				
1979-80	San Diego..........	14	81	.503	32	.593	126	34	194	13.9
1980-81	San Diego..........					Injured				
1981-82	San Diego..........					Injured				
1982-83	San Diego..........	33	200	.528	65	.536	323	120	465	14.1
1983-84	San Diego..........	55	288	.556	92	.597	477	183	668	12.1
1984-85	L.A. Clippers........	67	269	.521	138	.680	600	156	676	10.1
1985-86	Boston.............	80	231	.562	144	.713	544	165	606	7.6
1986-87	Boston.............	10	10	.385	8	.533	31	9	28	2.8
	Totals.............	468	2552	.521	1111	.660	4923	1590	6215	13.3

GREG KITE 26 6-11 255   Center

Plays crustacean basketball . . . Gets into his lobster mode and claws and bangs opponents . . . Received most acclaim ever given to the scoreless after his performance in Celts' Game 3 victory against Lakers . . . That nine-rebound game justified his NBA existence in some small way . . . Ironically, K.C. Jones completely forgot about him in finale when Celtics needed a big body to combat Kareem Abdul-Jabbar and Mychal Thompson . . . Is much more intelligent than he looks . . . In fact, he is a reporter's best friend in the locker room . . . With injury to Bill Walton, he played nearly twice as many minutes than any previous season . . . Sets bone-jarring picks . . . Same can be said for his shot . . . Born Aug. 5, 1961, in Houston . . . Drafted 21st overall in 1983, out of Brigham Young . . . Known as a thug, his takedown of James Worthy made Laker come up swinging . . . Does whatever it takes to survive, legal or not.

Year	Team	G	FG	FG Pct.	FT	FT Pct.	Reb.	Ast.	TP	Avg.
1983-84	Boston.............	35	30	.455	5	.313	62	7	65	1.9
1984-85	Boston.............	55	33	.375	22	.688	89	17	88	1.6
1985-86	Boston.............	64	34	.374	15	.385	128	17	83	1.3
1986-87	Boston.............	74	47	.427	29	.382	169	27	123	1.7
	Totals.............	228	144	.406	71	.436	448	68	359	1.6

SCOTT WEDMAN 35 6-7 225   Forward

Another member of the Blue Cross/Blue Shield Celtics... Was placed on the injured list on Oct. 30 with a sore left heel and was not activated until Nov. 25... He played in just six games, 78 total minutes, the entire season... His outside shot was desperately missed... Was a key ingredient to Celts' championship two years ago... Born July 29, 1952, in Harper, Kan.... Kings chose him sixth overall in 1974, out of Colorado... Came to Celts from Cavaliers in January 1983 for Darren Tillis, cash and a 1983 first-rounder... Streak shooter's career is in doubt... A health nut, he often travels on the road with his own water... May have to dip his heel in the Fountain of Youth if he ever hopes to play again.

Year	Team	G	FG	FG Pct.	FT	FT Pct.	Reb.	Ast.	TP	Avg.
1974-75	K.C.-Omaha	80	375	.465	139	.818	490	129	889	11.1
1975-76	Kansas City	82	538	.456	191	.780	606	199	1267	15.5
1976-77	Kansas City	81	521	.460	206	.855	506	227	1248	15.4
1977-78	Kansas City	81	607	.509	221	.870	463	201	1435	17.7
1978-79	Kansas City	73	561	.534	216	.797	386	144	1338	18.3
1979-80	Kansas City	68	569	.512	145	.801	386	145	1290	19.0
1980-81	Kansas City	81	685	.477	140	.686	433	226	1535	19.0
1981-82	Cleveland	54	260	.441	66	.733	304	133	591	10.9
1982-83	Clev.-Bos.	75	374	.475	85	.794	282	117	843	11.2
1983-84	Boston	68	148	.444	29	.829	139	67	327	4.8
1984-85	Boston	78	220	.478	42	.764	159	94	499	6.4
1985-86	Boston	79	286	.473	45	.662	192	83	634	8.0
1986-87	Boston	6	9	.333	1	.500	9	6	20	3.3
	Totals	906	5153	.481	1526	.794	4355	1771	11916	13.2

FRED ROBERTS 27 6-10 220   Forward

Punk haircut inspired one of the great nicknames... Teammates call him "Norman," as in Norman Bates of "Psycho" fame... Grabbed from Jazz prior to the start of the season for a third-round draft pick and cash ... Can run the floor but has hands of stone ... Many times he was set up by teammates, only to bounce the ball out of bounds... Larry Bird's caddie, he is a classic garbageman... Does not possess any great skills, just a willingness to work... Saw very little time in finals, which may have been a mistake by K.C. Jones... His biggest claim to fame is that he was traded for a coach... When Stan Albeck bolted as the boss of the Spurs to sign with New Jersey, San Antonio demanded this guy as compensation... Born Aug. 14, 1960, in Provo, Utah... Starred at Brigham Young, where he earned a reputation as a banger... Returned to Utah in trade for a second-round draft pick in December 1984... No. 27 pick overall in 1982 by Milwaukee... Played in Italy for a year.

Year	Team	G	FG	FG Pct.	FT	FT Pct.	Reb.	Ast.	TP	Avg.
1983-84	San Antonio	79	214	.536	144	.837	304	98	573	7.3
1984-85	S.A.-Utah	74	208	.498	150	.824	186	87	567	7.7
1985-86	Utah	58	74	.443	67	.770	80	27	216	3.7
1986-87	Boston	73	139	.515	124	.810	190	62	402	5.5
	Totals	284	635	.506	485	.816	760	274	1758	6.2

SAM VINCENT 24 6-2 185   Guard

Now you see him, now you don't... After playing important role vs. Pistons, he was totally forgotten in Laker series... If Celts have future plans for this guy, they have a funny way of showing it... A fine free-throw shooter, he made some big ones from the line against Detroit (19-23)... Was drafted 20th overall in 1985, out of Michigan State... Averaged just eight minutes a game his first two years and has sat out 61 games altogether, only 16 of those due to injury... Will make $380,000 this year, so at least he earns while he learns... Made 51 of 55 free throws in regular season... Born May 18, 1963, in Lansing, Mich.... Younger brother of Washington's Jay Vincent... Part of the Isiah Thomas, Magic Johnson Michigan connection... Isiah openly laughed in his face during Game 1, which incited Celtics... It's time Celts find out for sure if this guy can play.

Year	Team	G	FG	FG Pct.	FT	FT Pct.	Reb.	Ast.	TP	Avg.
1985-86	Boston	57	59	.364	65	.929	48	69	184	3.2
1986-87	Boston	46	60	.441	51	.927	27	59	171	3.7
	Totals	103	119	.399	116	.928	75	128	355	3.4

DARREN DAYE 26 6-8 220   Guard-Forward

Wouldn't know him from Doris Day until this season... Waived in December by the Bulls and then wound up playing in the finals... Such is life in the NBA when you are a decent one-on-one player and the Celtic bench is pitiful... Earned a job for this season with his playoff performance (42-72, 58 percent from the field)... Bullets drafted him 57th overall, out of UCLA... Born Nov. 30, 1960, in Des Moines, Iowa... Ignored by Kevin Loughery in Washington... Played in 61 games for Celts, shooting 50 percent from the field... A horrid free-throw shooter and not a good rebounder . . . It should be interesting to see what kind of role he will play for the Celtics this season . . . Will he go back to being a faceless pro or become important role player?

Year	Team	G	FG	FG Pct.	FT	FT Pct.	Reb.	Ast.	TP	Avg.
1983-84	Washington.........	75	180	.441	95	.714	188	176	455	6.1
1984-85	Washington.........	80	258	.512	178	.715	272	240	695	8.7
1985-86	Washington.........	64	198	.496	159	.671	183	109	556	8.7
1986-87	Chi.-Bos.............	62	101	.500	34	.523	125	76	236	3.8
	Totals.............	281	737	.487	466	.681	768	601	1942	6.9

CONNER HENRY 24 6-7 195   Guard

Great name . . . Sounds like the protagonist in a Leon Uris novel . . . Rookie was so obscure he wasn't even listed in the official NBA register last season even though guys like Panagiotas Fasoulas were . . . Drafted in the fourth round by Rockets (89th overall), out of Cal-Santa Barbara, where he averaged 17 points . . . Played 18 games with Houston before being waived on Dec. 22 . . . In his first game with Boston on Jan. 7 vs. Milwaukee, he scored 11 points . . . That earned him second 10-day contract and season-long stay . . . Has excellent outside shot, which gives him chance to stick . . . Born July 21, 1961, in Claremont, Cal. . . . Hero is Pete Maravich.

Year	Team	G	FG	FG Pct.	FT	FT Pct.	Reb.	Ast.	TP	Avg.
1986-87	Hou.-Bos............	54	46	.338	17	.630	34	35	122	2.3

RICK CARLISLE 28 6-5 210   Guard

Just another pretty face who looks like perfect Minnesota Timberwolve material . . . Dropped off the face of the Celtic earth at the end of March and was placed on the injured list and never again played . . . Conner Henry and Darren Daye's acquisitions made him Mr. Forgettable . . . Born Oct. 27, 1959, in Ogdensburg, N.Y. . . . Celtics chose him 69th overall in 1984, out of Virginia, where teammate was Ralph Sampson . . . Averaged just seven minutes when he did get on the parquet . . . Made just 30 of 92 shots . . . Going, going, gone.

Year	Team	G	FG	FG Pct.	FT	FT Pct.	Reb.	Ast.	TP	Avg.
1984-85	Boston.............	38	26	.388	15	.882	21	25	67	1.8
1985-86	Boston.............	77	92	.487	15	.652	77	104	199	2.6
1986-87	Boston.............	42	30	.326	15	.750	30	35	80	1.9
	Totals.............	157	148	.425	45	.750	128	164	346	2.2

TOP ROOKIE

REGGIE LEWIS 22 6-7 195   **Guard-Forward**

One of the three Dunbar High School (Baltimore) teammates chosen in first round... Georgetown's Reggie Williams and Wake Forest's Tyrone Bogues were the others... Northeastern's all-time leading scorer (2,709 points) will have to make the switch to shooting guard... Also ranks as Huskies' all-time leader in blocked shots with 155... Born Nov. 21, 1965, in Baltimore... Will play a sixth-man role and give Celtics much needed instant offense off the bench.

COACH K. C. JONES: Like old man river, he keeps on rollin' along, chalking up the wins... Most successful coach ever over a four-year period with 251-77 record (.765) since coming to the Celtics... His career mark is 406-168 (.707) ... Took a bad rap when Washington Bullets were bounced in four straight by Warriors in 1974-75 and was fired after the following season... Member of the 1956 Olympic team ... San Francisco product played on eight NBA title teams during nine-year career with Celtics... Absolutely devoted to Red Auerbach... Just like Red, he said referee Earl Strom should have been wearing a Laker uniform after Game 4 loss in finals ... Had career .387 shooting percentage... Was Celts' second-round pick in 1956... Rams took him on 30th round of NFL draft in 1955... Ever affable, he loves to play self-deprecating role, laughing all the way to the bank and probably the Hall of Fame... Has 10 championship rings in 13 years... Only coach in history to post 60-plus victory seasons with two teams... Low-key demeanor is vital to Celts' success... His mother, Eula, passed away during playoffs, hurting him deeply... A wonderful singer, he loves to entertain in piano-bar settings... Born May 25, 1932, in Tyler, Tex.... Initials?... His father was fond of legendary railroader Casey Jones... A lovely, lovely man.

GREATEST COACH

You weren't expecting Alvin (Doggy) Julian, were you? Doggy, who coached the Celtics for two seasons (1948-49,

1949-50), running up a 47-71 mark, gave way to a brassy 34-year-old named Arnold (Red) Auerbach in 1950-51 and thus began a legend.

After six decent years, Auerbach the coach came into his glory because Auerbach the GM dealt for Bill Russell. The Celtics then went on to win 11 championships in 13 years.

Auerbach revolutionized the game with tactics such as the sixth man. When he retired from coaching in 1966 he had led his team to championships in nine of his last 10 seasons. He is the NBA's winningest coach with a 938-479 record and has moved on to GM and club president three times, rebuilding the franchise into a championship team with mind-bending acquisitions like Larry Bird and Kevin McHale.

The secret of his success?

"Pride, that's all," he says, taking a long puff from his trademark cigar. "Pride of excellence and of accomplishment. I always like to tell our guys during the playoffs, 'Wouldn't it be nice to go around all summer and say you're a member of the greatest basketball team in the world?'"

ALL-TIME CELTIC LEADERS

SEASON

Points: John Havlicek, 2,388, 1970-71
Assists: Bob Cousy, 715, 1959-60
Rebounds: Bill Russell, 1,930, 1963-64

GAME

Points: Larry Bird, 60 vs. Atlanta, 3/12/85
Assists: Bob Cousy, 28 vs. Minneapolis, 2/27/59
Rebounds: Bill Russell, 51 vs. Syracuse, 2/5/60

CAREER

Points: John Havlicek, 26,395, 1962-78
Assists: Bob Cousy, 6,945, 1950-63
Rebounds: Bill Russell, 21,620, 1956-69

CHICAGO BULLS

TEAM DIRECTORY: Chairman: Jerry Reinsdorf; VP-Operations: Jerry Krause; Dir. Pub. Rel.: Tim Hallam; Coach: Doug Collins; Asst. Coaches: Gene Littles, John Bach, Tex Winter, Billy McKinney. Arena: Chicago Stadium (17,374). Colors: Red, white and black.

Michael Jordan frustrated foes with 37.1 ppg.

SCOUTING REPORT

SHOOTING: If Al Capone's gang shot like this, The Untouchables would have cleaned up Chicago in no time. For the second straight season the Bulls were the third-worst shooting team in the East. Of the players who started at least half the games, only Gene Banks shot better than 50 percent, but he is likely to be out for the season as a result of a ruptured Achilles tendon. If Michael Jordan (.482) weren't firing it up at every opportunity, this team might never score 100 points.

You can understand why coach Doug Collins and GM Jerry Krause sought and wound up with Central Arkansas forward Scottie Pippen. Pippen blistered along at a .594 last season and can drain it from long range. Seven-footer Artis Gilmore, a career 58-percent shooter, can put it in the hole from up close and should prove to be an excellent acquisition from San Antonio.

PLAYMAKING: It's Jordan's ball and game. He controls the pace. He is the show. John Paxson had the best year of his career (5.6 assists) and will be counted on to keep it up. Pippen figures to move the ball around up front. He may even move into the backcourt. Oakley is a fine passer and now should have someone else to throw it to besides Magical Michael.

DEFENSE: Collins cracked the whip and the Bulls responded. Two years ago under Stan Albeck, the Bulls allowed 113 points a night. That number was cut to 104 last season, a huge improvement. Ex-Mavs coach Dick Motta put Jordan on his all-defensive team. Jordan led the Bulls in blocked shots with 125.

His closest teammate was Dave Corzine with 87. In that department the Bulls missed Jawann Oldham. In exchange for Oldham, however, they picked up the eighth pick, which they used to swap for Pippen. Tenth pick, Clemson bruiser forward Horace Grant, will be rock solid up front.

Elston Turner, whose defense is the best part of his game, will have to battle for a job with Sedale Threatt and rookie Tony White as backup guard.

REBOUNDING: Oakley finished second in the league to Charles Barkley. The Bulls led the league in defending their own

BULL ROSTER

No.	Veteran	Pos.	Ht.	Wt.	Age	Yrs. Pro	College
20	Gene Banks	F	6-7	223	28	6	Duke
17	Mike Brown	F-C	6-9	250	24	1	George Washington
40	* Dave Corzine	C	6-11	265	31	9	DePaul
53	Artis Gilmore	C	7-2	265	38	16	Jacksonville
23	Michael Jordan	G	6-6	198	24	3	North Carolina
10	Pete Myers	F	6-7	190	24	1	Ark.-Little Rock
34	Charles Oakley	F	6-9	245	23	2	Virginia Union
5	John Paxson	G	6-2	185	27	4	Notre Dame
50	Ben Poquette	F	6-9	235	32	10	Central Michigan
6	Brad Sellers	F	7-0	212	24	1	Ohio State
3	Sedale Threatt	G	6-2	180	26	4	West Virginia Tech
21	Elston Turner	G	6-5	220	28	6	Mississippi
31	* Granville Waiters	C	6-11	225	26	4	Ohio State

*Free agent unsigned at press time

Rd.	Top Rookies	Sel. No.	Pos.	Ht.	Wt.	College
1	**Scott Pippen	5	F	6-7	210	Central Arkansas
1	Horace Grant	10	F-C	6-10	220	Clemson
2	Ricky Winslow	28	F	6-8	225	Houston
2	Tony White	33	G	6-2	170	Tennessee
3	John Fox	56	F	6-9	220	Millersville (Pa.)

**Drafted by Seattle and traded to Chicago

board by grabbing 70 percent of the available defensive rebounds. Grant and Pippen should help immensely in this area and Gilmore will take up a lot of space in the middle. The Bulls have become big overnight.

Rebounding is all hard work and under Albeck this team did not try, finishing eighth in the East two years ago. Last year they moved up to fourth best overall. Collins has them breaking a sweat.

OUTLOOK: Collins is one of the game's brightest and best. No longer is it a case of Michael and the Jordanaires. The Bulls have some excellent young talent to go along with the game's most exciting player. Michael even may be able to put his tongue back in his mouth occasionally this season and take a breather.

A young center is needed, however, before the Bulls can be taken seriously. Artis is just too old to depend upon and Dave Corzine never was the Hall-of-Fame type. Still, the Bulls should break the .500 barrier for the first time in seven years as they prove they're a team on the move.

BULL PROFILES

MICHAEL JORDAN 24 6-6 198   Guard

The Ultimate Weapon...Doug Collins explains: "It's nice to have a nuclear weapon on your side"...Missed out on MVP to Magic Johnson, but Bulls wouldn't have won 10 games without him...League scoring champ at 37.1, the top scoring guard ever in the NBA...Poured in 35.7 a game during three-game playoff vs. Celts...His 3,041 points were third-highest output in NBA history...He and a guy named Wilt are the only two players to break 3,000-point barrier... Says if he ever scores 100 in a game he will retire...Will make $810,000 this season and is vastly underpaid...Reportedly triples his income on off-the-court endorsements...Led NBA in scoring on Opening Day, 50 vs. New York, and never let up... Had two 61-point outings...Was plus 50 eight times...Became only player in history to record more than 200 steals and block 100-plus shots...Enthusiasm carries over to defense and is one of the best on that end of the floor...Obviously made up for missing 64 games season before with foot fracture...Born Feb. 17, 1963, in Wilmington, N.C....NBA Rookie of the Year in 1984-85 after being drafted No. 3 out of North Carolina...Only question is: Can he hold up physically?...Larry Bird said it best: "He's God disguised as Michael Jordan."

Year	Team	G	FG	FG Pct.	FT	FT Pct.	Reb.	Ast.	TP	Avg.
1984-85	Chicago	82	837	.515	630	.845	534	481	2313	28.2
1985-86	Chicago	18	150	.457	105	.840	64	53	408	22.7
1986-87	Chicago	82	1098	.482	833	.857	430	377	3041	37.1
	Totals	182	2085	.493	1568	.851	1028	911	5762	31.7

CHARLES OAKLEY 23 6-9 245   Forward

Windex on the glass...Collins calls him best defensive rebounder in NBA...Ultra-impressive in playoffs with 20 points and 15 rebounds a night...Born Dec. 19, 1963, in Cleveland...NCAA II Player of the Year in senior season at Virginia Union, when he led team to 31-1 record...Chosen No. 9 overall by Cavs in 1985, he was dealt with Calvin Duncan for Keith Lee and Ennis Whatley...Not a bad deal, hey...When he and Charles Barkley square off, it's like Godzilla vs. King Kong...Oakley grabbed most rebounds in league (1,074)...His 13.1 average was second to Barkley... Excellent passer, his 3.6 assists per game were most by any power forward...Gets carried away, though...Oakley's 299 turnovers were fourth most in league...Despite fine outside touch, free throws aren't free, shooting just .686 from the line ...True workhorse, a pleasure to watch sweat.

Year	Team	G	FG	FG Pct.	FT	FT Pct.	Reb.	Ast.	TP	Avg.
1985-86	Chicago	77	281	.519	178	.662	664	133	740	9.6
1986-87	Chicago	82	468	.445	245	.686	1074	296	1192	14.5
	Totals	159	749	.470	423	.676	1738	429	1932	12.2

JOHN PAXSON 27 6-2 185   Guard

Middle name is MacBeth...Up until now career has been *Much Ado About Nothing*... Point guard proved last season he's not the only Paxson who can drill it...Brother, Jim, is Portland Trail Blazer star...More than doubled scoring average to 11.1 and nearly doubled assists to 5.7...Set personal highs in all major categories, except field-goal percentage, the most important of which was minutes played (33 a game)...Spurs picked him 12th overall in 1983, out of Notre Dame...Snatched by Chicago as free agent on Oct. 30, 1985 ...Born Sept. 29, 1960, in Kettering, Ohio...It's all in the genes...Father, Jim Sr., played in NBA for Cincinnati and Minneapolis...Quiet, unselfish type, somewhere between Bob Newhart and the football Giants' Mark Bavaro.

Year	Team	G	FG	FG Pct.	FT	FT Pct.	Reb.	Ast.	TP	Avg.
1983-84	San Antonio	49	61	.445	16	.615	33	149	142	2.9
1984-85	San Antonio	78	196	.509	84	.840	68	215	486	6.2
1985-86	Chicago	75	153	.466	74	.804	94	274	395	5.3
1986-87	Chicago	82	386	.487	106	.809	139	467	930	11.3
	Totals	284	796	.484	280	.802	334	1105	1953	6.9

ARTIS GILMORE 38 7-2 265   Center

The A-Train is just an old freight train whose caboose is dragging now as he chugs into Chicago from San Antonio for the Bulls' 1988 second-round draft pick...He's lucky he can run down the floor before the 24-second clock expires...Still tough to stop inside, but his stamina is gone and he's not a consistent offensive threat anymore...Doesn't have the quickness to keep up with the young horses in the NBA...Had lowest scoring average of his career...Second-best percentage shooter in the NBA last season . . . Born Sept. 21, 1949, in Chipley, Fla. . . . Has an honorary doctoral degree from Jacksonville, where he led Dolphins to the NCAA title game and was named All-American . . . Shows up all the time. Has missed just 66 of 1,359 games in career . . . Won ABA championship with the Kentucky Colonels . . . Started NBA career in Chicago . . . All-time NBA field-goal percentage leader . . . An avid scuba diver who must scare the daylights out of the fish.

Year	Team	G	FG	FG Pct.	FT	FT Pct.	Reb.	Ast.	TP	Avg.
1971-72	Kentucky (ABA)	84	806	.598	391	.646	1491	230	2003	23.8
1972-73	Kentucky (ABA)	84	687	.559	368	.643	1476	295	1743	20.9
1973-74	Kentucky (ABA)	84	621	.494	326	.667	1538	329	1568	18.7
1974-75	Kentucky (ABA)	84	784	.580	412	.696	1361	208	1081	23.1
1975-76	Kentucky (ABA)	84	773	.552	521	.682	1303	211	2067	24.6
1976-77	Chicago	82	570	.522	387	.660	1070	199	1527	18.6
1977-78	Chicago	82	704	.559	471	.704	1071	263	1879	22.9
1978-79	Chicago	82	753	.575	434	.739	1043	274	1940	23.7
1979-80	Chicago	48	305	.595	245	.712	432	133	855	17.8
1980-81	Chicago	82	547	.670	375	.705	828	172	1469	17.9
1981-82	Chicago	82	546	.652	424	.768	835	136	1517	18.5
1982-83	San Antonio	82	556	.626	367	.740	984	126	1479	18.0
1983-84	San Antonio	64	351	.631	280	.718	662	70	982	15.3
1984-85	San Antonio	81	532	.623	484	.749	846	131	1548	19.1
1985-86	San Antonio	71	423	.618	338	.701	600	102	1184	16.7
1986-87	San Antonio	82	346	.597	242	.680	579	150	934	11.4
	Totals	1258	9304	.582	6065	.700	16119	3029	24676	19.6

SEDALE THREATT 26 6-2 180   Guard

Can be trick or threatt . . . Fell out of favor in Philly after fine playoff performance two years ago and was dealt to Bulls for guard Steve Colter and future second-round pick on Dec. 31, 1986 . . . Wasn't a happy New Year . . . Just four games into new career, Threatt broke the ring finger on his right hand and missed 14 games . . . Speed is his ally . . . Explosive scorer, averaged 8.5 in 21 minutes a night . . . Loves to make the blindside steal . . . Born Sept. 10, 1961, in Atlanta . . . Made NBA as sixth-round pick (139th overall) out of West Virginia Tech . . . School's all-time leading scorer with 2,488 points . . . People have a tough time with his name . . . Don Nelson once referred to him as Street.

Year	Team	G	FG	FG Pct.	FT	FT Pct.	Reb.	Ast.	TP	Avg.
1983-84	Philadelphia	45	62	.419	23	.821	40	41	148	3.3
1984-85	Philadelphia	82	188	.452	66	.733	99	175	446	5.4
1985-86	Philadelphia	70	310	.453	75	.833	121	193	696	9.9
1986-87	Phi.-Chi.	68	239	.448	95	.798	108	259	580	8.5
	Totals	265	799	.448	259	.792	368	668	1870	7.1

GENE BANKS 28 6-7 223   Forward

His star has never risen to heights expected . . . And now indications are that he'll miss the entire season due to a ruptured Achilles tendon suffered in summer play . . . Does a little bit of everything, including looking out for team harmony . . . Season literally started off on the wrong foot when he broke a bone in his right foot in exhibition season . . . Missed first 17 games, snapping consecutive-games-played streak at 195 . . . Traded by San Antonio for Steve Johnson and a 1985 second-round pick on June 16, 1985 . . . Born May 15, 1959, in Philadelphia . . . Deep-thinking sort with political ambitions . . . A Christian who has studied Hebrew . . . Drafted No. 28 overall in 1981 out of Duke . . . Led ACC in scoring senior year at Duke . . . Schoolboy legend.

Year	Team	G	FG	FG Pct.	FT	FT Pct.	Reb.	Ast.	TP	Avg.
1981-82	San Antonio	80	311	.477	145	.684	411	147	767	9.6
1982-83	San Antonio	81	505	.550	196	.705	612	279	1206	14.9
1983-84	San Antonio	80	424	.568	200	.741	582	254	1049	13.1
1984-85	San Antonio	82	289	.586	199	.774	445	234	778	9.5
1985-86	Chicago	82	356	.517	183	.718	360	251	895	10.9
1986-87	Chicago	63	249	.539	112	.767	308	170	610	9.7
	Totals	468	2134	.539	1035	.730	2718	1335	5305	11.3

BRAD SELLERS 24 7-0 212   Forward

Keep those bananas and milk shakes coming . . . Rookie season proved one thing: Sellers has to put on weight to be effective . . . Was suspended by Doug Collins for missing a team flight on Christmas . . . Bah . . . Humbug . . . Doesn't seem to be a problem-type, though . . . Made crucial mistake in Celtic series watching play develop from out of bounds . . . Michael Jordan's pass surprised him . . . Oops . . . Born Dec. 17, 1962, in Cleveland . . . Ohio State Buckeye was MVP of 1986 NIT . . . Bulls took much heat for passing on Johnny Dawkins and selecting Sellers ninth overall in 1986 draft . . . Collins says Sellers has potential to get 17 points and nine rebounds a night and expects him to be a great wing on the break . . . Soft shooting touch, but he's got to get more physical.

Year	Team	G	FG	FG Pct.	FT	FT Pct.	Reb.	Ast.	TP	Avg.
1986-87	Chicago	80	276	.455	126	.728	373	102	680	8.5

DAVE CORZINE 31 6-11 265   Center

The race doesn't always go to the swiftest... Entering 10th season and figures to hang around a while longer... "A lot of guys who came in the league with me aren't around anymore," he says. "They've dropped out one by one. Some guys are sprinters, I'm a marathoner."... Played in all 82 games, the sixth time he's done it... Nets made him wealthy by giving him offer sheet that got him $710,000 last season... Was No. 18 pick overall by Bullets in 1978, out of DePaul... Came to Bulls with Mark Olberding and cash via San Antonio underground railroad for Artis Gilmore on July 22, 1982... That's a lot of beef... Born April 25, 1956, in Arlington Heights, Ill.... Deft outside touch, fine pivot passer... The original Bill Laimbeer.

Year	Team	G	FG	FG Pct.	FT	FT Pct.	Reb.	Ast.	TP	Avg.
1978-79	Washington	59	63	.534	49	.778	147	49	175	3.0
1979-80	Washington	78	90	.417	45	.662	270	63	225	2.9
1980-81	San Antonio	82	366	.490	125	.714	636	117	857	10.5
1981-82	San Antonio	82	336	.519	159	.746	629	130	832	10.1
1982-83	Chicago	82	457	.497	232	.720	717	154	1146	14.0
1983-84	Chicago	82	385	.467	231	.840	575	202	1004	12.2
1984-85	Chicago	82	276	.486	149	.745	422	140	701	8.5
1985-86	Chicago	67	255	.491	127	.743	433	150	640	9.6
1986-87	Chicago	82	294	.475	95	.736	540	209	683	8.3
	Totals	696	2522	.487	1212	.750	4369	1214	6263	9.0

MIKE BROWN 24 6-9 250   Forward-Center

He'd be seven-footer if he had a neck... Played in Italy two years ago... Not only came back with league's Rookie-of-the-Year award, but returned with even more important trophy, an Italian wife... Sweetheart of a guy ... Big things were predicted for him after junior season at George Washington... But Washington Monument suffered toe injury midway through senior season that changed the picture... Drafted in third round (69th overall) in 1985... Born July 19, 1963, in Newark, N.J.... Saw limited action, but shot .527 from the field and had season-high 12 rebounds and 16 points in 24 minutes against Washington's Moses Malone on Feb. 3... A project worth watching.

Year	Team	G	FG	FG Pct.	FT	FT Pct.	Reb.	Ast.	TP	Avg.
1986-87	Chicago	62	106	.527	46	.639	214	24	258	4.2

PETE MYERS 24 6-7 190   Forward

You think you have a tough job?... Myers is Michael Jordan's punching bag... For two hours a day he gets stomped on in practice... "It's like being Marvin Hagler's sparring partner," Doug Collins says... For a season of abuse, Myers got to play for real a grand total of 155 minutes... Born Sept. 15, 1963, in Mobile, Ala.... A sixth-round choice (120th overall) out of Arkansas-Little Rock... Of the 162 players chosen in the draft, only Tim Kempton of the Los Angeles Clippers was taken after Myers and managed to earn a spot on opening-day rosters... Though he played just two years at Arkansas-Little Rock, he ranks fourth on school's all-time scoring list... Transferred from Faulkner State.

Year	Team	G	FG	FG Pct.	FT	FT Pct.	Reb.	Ast.	TP	Avg.
1986-87	Chicago	29	19	.365	28	.651	17	21	66	2.3

BEN POQUETTE 32 6-9 235   Forward

NBA handyman, it's no surprise Gentle Ben would love to fix up old homes and sell them ... Classic journeyman is nearing the end of the line after 10 seasons and four teams... Acquired from Cavs on Feb. 15 last season in exchange for second-round pick... Central Michigan star was chosen No. 36th in draft by Pistons in 1977... Born May 7, 1955, in Ann Arbor, Mich.... Has great corner jumper... Did not see any time in the playoffs and played in just 23 of the Bulls' last 53 games... Good shot-blocker... Expansion may help keep him around... Best season as a pro was 1983 in Utah, when he averaged 11 points... That was only year he managed to hit double figures.

Year	Team	G	FG	FG Pct.	FT	FT Pct.	Reb.	Ast.	TP	Avg.
1977-78	Detroit	52	95	.422	42	.700	145	20	232	4.5
1978-79	Detroit	76	198	.427	111	.782	336	57	507	6.7
1979-80	Utah	82	296	.523	139	.832	560	131	731	8.9
1980-81	Utah	82	324	.528	126	.778	629	161	777	9.5
1981-82	Utah	82	220	.514	97	.808	411	94	540	6.6
1982-83	Utah	75	329	.472	166	.751	521	168	825	11.0
1983-84	Cleveland	51	75	.439	34	.791	182	49	185	3.6
1984-85	Cleveland	79	210	.460	109	.796	473	79	532	6.7
1985-86	Cleveland	81	166	.477	72	.720	373	78	406	5.0
1986-87	Cle.-Chi.	58	62	.508	40	.800	101	35	164	2.8
	Totals	718	1975	.483	936	.779	3731	872	4899	6.8

GRANVILLE WAITERS 26 6-11 225   Center

Looks and plays like he should be waiting on tables . . . Has more hair than career points . . . How desperate were the Bulls in the middle this season? . . . Waiters actually started the first 17 games . . . Came to Chicago from Houston prior to season in blockbuster deal that sent either a third- or fourth-round pick to Rockets . . . Born Jan. 8, 1961, in Columbus, Ohio . . . Drafted No. 39 overall by Portland in 1983, he was traded to Indiana before the 1983-84 season began . . . Houston gave up fifth-round pick to get him two years ago . . . But Rocket fizzled . . . Busted out last year for season-high six points vs. Celtics in final regular-season game.

Year	Team	G	FG	FG Pct.	FT	FT Pct.	Reb.	Ast.	TP	Avg.
1983-84	Indiana............	78	123	.517	31	.608	227	60	277	3.6
1984-85	Indiana............	62	85	.447	29	.580	170	30	199	3.2
1985-86	Houston............	43	13	.333	1	.167	28	8	27	0.6
1986-87	Chicago............	44	40	.430	5	.556	87	22	85	1.9
	Totals.............	227	261	.466	66	.569	512	120	588	2.6

ELSTON TURNER 28 6-5 220   Guard

Time may be running out for "E.T." . . . He's lost confidence as a shooter and he didn't get much playing time, but his defensive forte brought him guarding assignments on Larry Bird and Dominique Wilkins . . . Came to the Bulls last season from Denver for a 1988 draft pick . . . Born July 10, 1959, in Knoxville, Tenn. . . . Went to Ol' Miss and helped the Rebs go to the NIT . . . Was the 43rd pick of the 1981 draft, spending three years with the Mavs before signing offer sheet by Denver and being acquired for Howard Carter prior to 1984-85.

Year	Team	G	FG	FG Pct.	FT	FT Pct.	Reb.	Ast.	TP	Avg.
1981-82	Dallas.............	80	282	.441	97	.703	301	189	661	8.3
1982-83	Dallas.............	59	96	.403	20	.667	152	88	214	3.6
1983-84	Dallas.............	47	54	.360	28	.824	93	59	137	2.9
1984-85	Denver.............	81	181	.466	51	.785	216	158	414	5.1
1985-86	Denver.............	73	165	.435	39	.736	201	165	369	5.1
1986-87	Chicago............	70	112	.444	23	.742	115	102	248	3.5
	Totals.............	410	890	.435	258	.735	1078	761	2043	5.0

TOP ROOKIES

SCOTTIE PIPPEN 22 6-7 210   Forward

Most intriguing player in the draft . . . Detroit's Jack McCloskey said University of Central Arkansas star will become "a superstar"... Came to Bulls from Seattle in draft-day swap for Olden Polynice and draft picks... Was ignored by major-college recruiters because he was only 6-1 after graduating from high school... Born Sept. 25, 1965, in Hamburg, Ark.... Will wind up in backcourt alongside Michael Jordan and will play some point forward.

HORACE GRANT 22 6-10 220   **Forward**
Slipped all the way to No. 10 and Bulls couldn't have been happier... Gives them beef up front... Clemson star was consensus ACC Player of the Year after averaging 21 points and 9.6 rebounds... Never missed a game at Clemson... Born July 4, 1965, in Sparta, Ga.... Younger brother Harvey stars for Oklahoma... May be the best forward in the draft... Great hands... Excellent leader... Third-highest field-goal percentage (.656) in NCAA.

COACH DOUG COLLINS: Big deal, hand the ball to Michael Jordan and get out of the way... Is that all there is to coaching the Bulls?... No way... The 36-year-old Collins showed signs that the Bulls may have their best coach since Dick Motta left town in 1976... Although there were early discipline problems with Charles Oakley and Earl Cureton, who was dealt away, Collins' fairness doctrine paid off as the Bulls went further than anyone expected... Collins has always been able to make it through rough times... As a player it was a sad case of what might have been, but it still wasn't that bad... He had seven surgeries in eight years with the Sixers, yet managed to average 17.9 points per game... When healthy he was a sensational second guard possessed by a hell-bent slashing style of play... The No. 1 pick in the draft following the wretched 9-73 Sixer season of 1972-73, Collins was named to the all-star team four times... Born July 28, 1951, in Christopher, Ill.... Starred at Illinois State... Starter on the 1972 Olympic team that was jobbed out of a gold medal by the Russians... His two free throws put the U.S. ahead, before theft... A great talker, Collins came to the Bulls through the Pat Riley school of coaching... Direct from the microphone to the sideline... Bulls believe in him and he in them.

GREATEST COACH

Michael Jordan has proven to be the best at everything else, so the temptation is to name him the Bulls' greatest coach because there have been so many flops.

But this is one honor Air Jordan can't claim. Dick Motta spent eight years along the Bulls' bench and established himself as one of the finest coaches in the game.

Motta currently ranks third in all-time wins in the NBA with 811 victories, 356 in Chicago. In 1970-71, the first of four straight 50-plus-win seasons, Motta was named Coach of the Year.

That team finished second in the Midwest at 51-31 and was known for its rugged style of play with Bob Love, Chet Walker, Jerry Sloan and Tom Boerwinkle. Unfortunately for Motta during that era, a big fella named Kareem Abdul-Jabbar was also in the Midwest and Motta's teams never really got out from his shadow.

Since Motta left Chicago after 1975-76, there have been nine coaches. In five of Motta's eight seasons he posted a better than .500 mark. In the 11 years he has been gone, the Bulls have been over .500 but two times. Enough said.

ALL-TIME BULL LEADERS

SEASON

Points: Michael Jordan, 3,041, 1986-87
Assists: Guy Rodgers, 908, 1966-67
Rebounds: Tom Boerwinkle, 1,133, 1970-71

GAME

Points: Michael Jordan, 61 vs. Detroit, 3/4/87
        Michael Jordan, 61 vs. Atlanta, 4/16/87
Assists: Ennis Whatley, 22 vs. New York, 1/14/84
        Ennis Whatley, 22 vs. Atlanta, 3/3/84
Rebounds: Tom Boerwinkle, 37 vs. Phoenix, 1/8/70

CAREER

Points: Bob Love, 12,623, 1968-76
Assists: Norm Van Lier, 3,676, 1971-78
Rebounds: Tom Boerwinkle, 5,745, 1968-78

CLEVELAND CAVALIERS

TEAM DIRECTORY: Chairmen: George Gund III, Gordon Gund; GM: Wayne Embry; Dr. Pub. Rel.: Bob Price; Coach: Lenny Wilkens; Asst. Coaches: Brian Winters, Dick Helm. Arena: The Coliseum (20,900). Colors: Orange, blue and white.

Shoot-'em-up Ron Harper leads Cav youth movement.

SCOUTING REPORT

SHOOTING: A little self control is needed here, guys. There's no doubt Ron Harper has Ervinesque talents, but sometimes he thinks he's back at a Miami of Ohio pickup game, firing 'em up from everywhere. Only Michael Jordan, Dominique Wilkins and Alex English let fly more than Harper's 1,614 shots. Harper took 117 more shots than Larry Bird and nearly 700 more than any teammate. He's not that good, yet. Especially when he's going along at a .455 clip.

All that helped make Cleveland the fourth-worst shooting team in the league (.470). Now the really scary part—the Cavs shot .697 from the free-throw line, the worst mark by far in the league. Phil Hubbard shot .531 from the field and .596 from the line to give you an idea how messy a night in Richfield can really get.

PLAYMAKING: Pipsqueak point guards are getting to be a Cav tradition. John Bagley and Mark Price have to be proofed at the local bars. On draft day Cavs added another in California's Kevin Johnson. He's ultra-athletic but out of control at times. Only the Bullets had fewer assists than the Cavs (1,912).

Bagley, who had been fourth in the league in assists the previous season (9.4), dropped to 5.2 last season. Finally, Cleveland and New Jersey turned the ball over more than anyone else (19.7 a game). That's got to change.

DEFENSE: Lenny Wilkens' Cavs ranked 17th in steals last season and would have been in a lot worse shape if Harper wasn't there to ballhawk. His 2.55 a game was fourth best in the league. He finished with 209. His closest teammate was Bagley with 91. John Williams' shot-blocking (2.1 a game) and defensive presence helps make up for Brad Daugherty's softness in the middle. Although the Cavs didn't light it up from the field, neither did their opponents, who shot 48 percent. Ugly Ball can be catching.

REBOUNDING: John Williams is a man's man. Mel Turpin is a tub of goo. Need we say more. Okay, one more thing. Turpin was outrebounded by Bagley. Brad Daugherty (8.0) did better than anyone expected. Keith Lee, who wouldn't have been missed, wound up back in Cleveland after Portland called off the June deal which would have made Jim Paxson a Cavalier.

OUTLOOK: They say that youth is wasted on the young. Not in the Cavs' case. The three young studs—Harper, Williams and

CAVALIER ROSTER

No.	Veteran	Pos.	Ht.	Wt.	Age	Yrs. Pro	College
5	John Bagley	G	6-0	195	27	5	Boston College
23	* Tyrone Corbin	F	6-6	222	24	2	DePaul
43	Brad Daugherty	C	7-0	245	22	1	North Carolina
3	* Craig Ehlo	G	6-7	185	26	4	Washington State
4	Ron Harper	G	6-6	205	23	1	Miami, Ohio
35	* Phil Hubbard	F	6-8	205	30	8	Michigan
24	Keith Lee	F	6-10	230	24	2	Memphis State
22	Johnny Newman	G	6-7	190	23	1	Richmond
25	Mark Price	G	6-1	174	23	1	Georgia Tech
54	Mel Turpin	C	6-11	280	26	3	Kentucky
41	* Mark West	C	6-10	225	26	4	Old Dominion
18	John Williams	F	6-11	230	26	1	Tulane

*Free agent unsigned at press time

Rd.	Top Rookies	Sel. No.	Pos.	Ht.	Wt.	College
1	Kevin Johnson	7	G	6-1	180	California
2	Kannard Johnson	41	F	6-9	220	Western Kentucky
3	Donald Royal	52	F	6-7	220	Notre Dame
4	Chris Dudley	75	C	6-10	235	Yale
4	Carven Holcombe	80	G	6-5	200	Texas Christian

Daugherty—have to keep improving. So much depends on Harper. He can take this team a long way . . . as long as he allows other people to get involved, too. The problem is he has to draw a very fine line because there just aren't enough pieces to complete the puzzle. He has to play a dominating role, yet develop a team atmosphere. That's a lot to ask.

CAVALIER PROFILES

RON HARPER 23 6-6 205   Guard

Has hands the size of Lake Erie . . . A high-wire act, he takes the game to its outer limits . . . Named to All-Rookie team . . . Topped all rookies in scoring at 22.9 to rank 16th in league . . . Was fourth in steals with an average of 2.55 . . . Cavs paid $750,000 for supplemental pick used to grab Harper . . . Steal of 1986 draft . . . Taken first round (eighth overall) out of Miami of Ohio . . . Reminds many of Clyde Frazier with cool demeanor . . . Knicks were begged by New York media to take Harper instead of Kenny Walker, but declined, saying

Harper wasn't intelligent enough... "That just goes to show you," says Cavs' GM Wayne Embry. "Sometimes you can out-smart yourself."... Has overcome speech impediment and works with children with similar problems... Explosive dunker... All-time leading scorer (2,377 points) in Mid-American Conference ... Born Jan. 20, 1964, in Dayton, Ohio... Tends to throw up wild shots but will learn... Scored season-high 40 vs. Boston on Feb. 4... Already owns Cavs' single-season record for steals (209) and free throws (564)... Will own many more records before he's through.

Year	Team	G	FG	FG Pct.	FT	FT Pct.	Reb.	Ast.	TP	Avg.
1986-87	Cleveland..........	82	734	.455	386	.684	392	394	1874	22.9

BRAD DAUGHERTY 22 7-0 245   Center

Not as hard as nails, but not as soft as people said... Led Cavs in rebounding with 8.1 average... Second behind Harper in scoring (15.7)... Led Cav starters in field-goal percentage (.538) and was 15th in NBA... All-Rookie selection... Often compared to Bill Cartwright, but much better... Led all NBA centers in assists (3.8)... If he's supposed to be soft, how come he spends offseason rattlesnake hunting?... Also loves to fish... North Carolina star was No. 1 choice in 1986 draft... Sixers got Roy Hinson and $750,000 in exchange for pick... Born Oct. 19, 1965, in Black Mountain, N.C.... Trying to add hook shot to arsenal... Grandson of a full-blooded Cherokee Indian... Grew from 6-3 to 6-10 between eighth and ninth grades... Needs to work on free-throw shooting... A solid base for future.

Year	Team	G	FG	FG Pct.	FT	FT Pct.	Reb.	Ast.	TP	Avg.
1986-87	Cleveland..........	80	487	.538	279	.696	647	304	1253	15.7

JOHN WILLIAMS 26 6-11 230   Forward

Congratulations... Has overcome stigma of Tulane point-shaving scandal... Acquitted of sports bribery charges... Pardon the expression, but GM Harry Weltman gambled and won when he chose Williams in the second round (45th pick) of the 1985 draft... A quiet, genuine person who is so naive he once asked his attorney what language is spoken in Italy... Hard to believe his nickname is "Hot Rod," acquired when he was a baby and scooted across the floor making engine sounds... Made All-Rookie team... Cavs' third leading scorer at 14.6, second-leading rebounder at 7.9 and top shot-blocker with 167 (11th best in league)... Has ferocious ability to get rebound in traffic... Born Aug. 9, 1961, in Sorrento, La.... Second-leading scorer in Tulane history with 16 ppg... Played two years in USBL while awaiting Tulane verdict... In second year of three-year $750,000 contract... Much bigger money and future ahead.

Year	Team	G	FG	FG Pct.	FT	FT Pct.	Reb.	Ast.	TP	Avg.
1986-87	Cleveland..........	80	435	.485	298	.745	629	154	1168	14.6

MEL TURPIN 26 6-11 280 Center

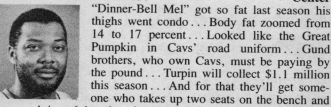

"Dinner-Bell Mel" got so fat last season his thighs went condo... Body fat zoomed from 14 to 17 percent... Looked like the Great Pumpkin in Cavs' road uniform... Gund brothers, who own Cavs, must be paying by the pound... Turpin will collect $1.1 million this season... And for that they'll get someone who takes up two seats on the bench and averaged just 6.1 points last season... Logged 13 minutes a night... Ate more pizzas than scored points last season (393) ... Only person Turpin seems to play hard against is Patrick Ewing... Born Dec. 28, 1960, in Lexington, Ky.... He has the talent; if only he could shed the appetite... Bullets picked him No. 6 overall in 1984 out of Kentucky... Was involved in draft day, three-way trade that cost Cavs Cliff Robinson and a No. 1 pick... Weight clause in contract but obviously it makes no difference.

Year	Team	G	FG	FG Pct.	FT	FT Pct.	Reb.	Ast.	TP	Avg.
1984-85	Cleveland..........	79	363	.511	109	.784	452	36	835	10.6
1985-86	Cleveland..........	80	456	.544	185	.811	556	55	1097	13.7
1986-87	Cleveland..........	64	169	.462	55	.714	190	33	393	6.1
	Totals.............	223	988	.516	349	.786	1198	124	2325	10.4

PHIL HUBBARD 30 6-8 205 Forward

Emergency room's best friend... Injuries have kept him from being one of better forwards in the league, but still not so bad... Terribly underrated... Eight-year veteran gives young Cavs much needed experience ... How valuable?... Over last three seasons with Hubbard in the starting lineup Cavs are 69-75 (.479), 27-75 (.265) without him starting... Coming off his best shooting season (.531)... Came back to play 68 games after missing 59 the season before with a torn ligament in right wrist...Knee injury while at Michigan robbed him of much of his mobility...Pistons chose him No. 15 overall in 1979 after he left college a year early...Born Dec. 13, 1956, in Canton, Ohio...Acquired from Pistons with Paul Mokeski and two draft picks for Kenny Carr and Bill Laimbeer in February 1982...Has degree in special ed...Married to Dr. Jackie Williams, a Cleveland dentist.

Year	Team	G	FG	FG Pct.	FT	FT Pct.	Reb.	Ast.	TP	Avg.
1979-80	Detroit............	64	210	.466	165	.750	320	70	585	9.1
1980-81	Detroit............	80	433	.492	294	.690	586	150	1161	14.5
1981-82	Det.-Clev..........	83	326	.490	191	.682	473	91	843	10.2
1982-83	Cleveland..........	82	288	.482	204	.689	471	89	780	9.5
1983-84	Cleveland..........	80	321	.511	221	.739	380	86	863	10.8
1984-85	Cleveland..........	76	415	.505	371	.751	479	114	1201	15.8
1985-86	Cleveland..........	23	93	.470	76	.679	120	29	262	11.4
1986-87	Cleveland..........	68	321	.531	162	.596	388	136	804	11.8
	Totals............	556	2407	.497	1684	.702	3217	765	6499	11.7

MARK PRICE 23 6-1 174   Guard

Another munchkin point guard...Led Cavs in three-point field-goal shooting (.329) and shot .833 from the line...Season was disrupted midway when Price had appendectomy...Sidelined Jan. 13 to Feb. 10 and was really never the same after surgery...Born Feb. 16, 1964, in Enid, Okla....Not only has choirboy looks but actually sings in Christian group...Dad, Denny, is a former head coach at Sam Houston State and assistant coach for Phoenix Suns...Second all-time leading scorer in Georgia Tech history, he had to learn a new role, star to sub...Selected in the second round (25th overall) in the 1986 draft by Mavericks...Dealt for 1989 second-rounder and cash.

Year	Team	G	FG	FG Pct.	FT	FT Pct.	Reb.	Ast.	TP	Avg.
1986-87	Cleveland..........	67	173	.408	95	.833	117	202	464	6.9

JOHN BAGLEY 27 6-0 195   Guard

Looks like Turpin's little brother...Binge scorer and eater...His extra weight goes right to his legs...Needs to become more consistent...Averaged 5.3 assists to lead Cavs, down nearly four a game from previous season...Part of the reason is because he's not handling the ball nearly as much with Harper in the lineup...Minutes down a bit, too, about four less a game ... Scoring (10.7) down, but has hit double figures two straight years ... No longer is Bags or team ridiculed for being No. 12 pick overall in 1982 ... Born April 30, 1960, in Bridgeport, Conn. ... Made $300,000 last season ... Most onlookers believe he made a big mistake jumping Boston College a year early ... Lack of height a disadvantage, but has accomplished more than a lot of people thought he could.

Year	Team	G	FG	FG Pct.	FT	FT Pct.	Reb.	Ast.	TP	Avg.
1982-83	Cleveland	68	161	.432	64	.762	96	167	386	5.7
1983-84	Cleveland	76	257	.423	157	.793	156	333	673	8.9
1984-85	Cleveland	81	338	488	125	.749	291	697	804	9.9
1985-86	Cleveland	78	366	.423	170	.791	275	735	911	11.7
1986-87	Cleveland	72	312	.426	113	.831	252	379	768	10.7
	Totals	375	1434	.439	629	.786	1070	2311	3542	9.4

TYRONE CORBIN 24 6-6 222   Forward

A scrapper ... Strong, but pushes people around too much ... Has not learned to play defense with his legs ... DePaul's all-time leading rebounder ... Quite an accomplishment since he's only 6-6 ... Joined the Cavs on Jan. 24 after being waived by Spurs ... Started 15 games for Spurs but disappeared once Mike Mitchell returned and Walter Berry was acquired ... Scored career-high 24 points vs. Bucks on April 11 ... Born Dec. 12, 1962, in Columbia, S.C. ... Drafted 35th overall by San Antonio in 1985 ... Studies computers, real estate and financial planning, just in case ... Obviously, shooting has to improve ... Finished .386 from the field for Cavs over 32 games ... One of those guys on the bubble.

Year	Team	G	FG	FG Pct.	FT	FT Pct.	Reb.	Ast.	TP	Avg.
1985-86	San Antonio	16	27	.422	10	.714	25	11	64	4.0
1986-87	S.A.-Clev.	63	156	.409	91	.734	215	97	404	6.4
	Totals	79	183	.411	101	.732	240	108	468	5.9

MARK WEST 26 6-10 225   Center

Called "The Hammer" by teammates because of brick-like free throws ... Has hammered his way into the league ... Shot .514 from the line and .543 from the field ... That's because he rarely takes shots from beyond five feet ... Mavericks picked him No. 30 in 1983 out of Old Dominion ... Signed as a free agent on Nov. 25, 1984 ... Has always been a good shot-blocker because of long arms ... Born Nov. 1960, in Ft.

Campbell, Ky. . . . Loves to sail in the offseason . . . Grew up in Petersburg, Va., Moses Malone's original stomping grounds . . . Scoring average "zoomed" from 4.2 to 6.5 . . . Had career-high 27 points vs. Malone's Bullets on Nov. 1 . . . Averaged 9.5 ppg over last six games on .676 (23-34) shooting . . . Lenny Wilkens has spent a lot of time working on low-post moves and it's helped turn a marginal player into an important one.

Year	Team	G	FG	FG Pct.	FT	FT Pct.	Reb.	Ast.	TP	Avg.
1983-84	Dallas.	34	15	.357	7	.318	46	13	37	1.1
1984-85	Mil.-Clev.	66	106	.546	43	.494	251	15	255	3.9
1985-86	Cleveland.	67	113	.541	54	.524	322	20	280	4.2
1986-87	Cleveland.	78	209	.543	89	.514	339	41	507	6.5
	Totals.	245	443	.534	193	.501	958	89	1079	4.4

JOHNNY NEWMAN 23 6-7 190   Guard

Give him time . . . Had to make the transition last season from big-time scoring forward in college to little-used big guard . . . Lost in the shuffle, but is a talented player . . . Picked 29th overall out of Richmond in 1986 draft . . . Richmond's all-time leading scorer with 2,383 points . . . Born Nov. 28, 1963, in Danville, Va. . . . Tremendous free-throw shooter led Cavs with .868 percentage . . . Has fine outside shot even though he was 1-22 from three-point range and finished .411 from the field . . . Great attitude, great kid . . . When he competed in European tour during college, he wrote thank-you letters to everyone involved . . . That's rare.

Year	Team	G	FG	FG Pct.	FT	FT Pct.	Reb.	Ast.	TP	Avg.
1986-87	Cleveland.	59	113	.411	66	.868	70	27	293	5.0

CRAIG EHLO 26 6-7 185   Guard

Was Bill Fitch's pet project in Houston, which explains why he's lasted so long in the league . . . Joined Cavs on Jan. 13 after being waived by Rockets, but quickly made an impression filling in for the sidelined Mark Price and John Bagley . . . Had pro-high 18- and 26-point efforts first two weeks as a Cav . . . Born Aug. 11, 1961, in Lubbock, Tex. . . . Had to go all the way to Washington State to play his college ball . . . Mother played basketball for Wayland Baptist College . . . Rockets made him 48th pick overall in 1983 . . . Blond and blue-eyed, he looks more like a member of the Beach Boys than the NBA...Snuck up on opponents to make 30 blocks last season...Played point guard, off guard and small forward for Cavs...Has a chance to stick because of his versatility.

Year	Team	G	FG	FG Pct.	FT	FT Pct.	Reb.	Ast.	TP	Avg.
1983-84	Houston	7	11	.407	1	1.000	9	6	23	3.3
1984-85	Houston	45	34	.493	19	.633	25	26	87	1.9
1985-86	Houston	36	36	.429	23	.793	46	29	98	2.7
1986-87	Cleveland	44	99	.414	70	.707	161	92	273	6.2
	Totals	132	180	.430	113	.711	241	153	481	3.6

KEITH LEE 24 6-10 230   Forward

Played only 870 minutes with the Cavs last season and was traded to Portland for Jim Paxson in June, but the Blazers rescinded the deal because Lee's knees didn't pass a medical...A lot of scouts say he's overrated ...Cavs gave up Charles Oakley for him on draft day, 1985...An outright swindle for Bulls...Set six records at Memphis State, including rebounds (1,329) and points (2,398)...For two straight seasons has averaged a foul every 5.9 minutes...Scored more than 20 points just one time last season...For that Cavs shelled out $301,666...Bad knees have contributed to his weak performance...Biggest problem, though, is that he's not a hard worker...Born Dec. 28, 1962, in West Memphis, Ark....Won 60 straight games in high school and was a teammate with Michael Cage...Has to realize those days are over.

Year	Team	G	FG	FG Pct.	FT	FT Pct.	Reb.	Ast.	TP	Avg.
1987-86	Cleveland	58	177	.466	75	.781	351	67	431	7.4
1986-87	Cleveland	67	170	.455	72	.713	251	69	412	6.1
	Totals	125	347	.460	147	.746	602	136	843	6.7

TOP ROOKIE

KEVIN JOHNSON 21 6-1 180   Guard

Cavs desperately wanted North Carolina's Kenny Smith, but Kings stole him with sixth pick, leaving California speed merchant at No. 7...Born March 4, 1966, in Sacramento, Cal.... He's really a shooting guard in point guard's body...Has to learn to make right moves on the break...Tremendous athlete ...Played shortstop in Oakland A's minor-league system...A greyhound.

Cavaliers went for Cal's Kevin Johnson as No. 7.

COACH LENNY WILKENS: The perfect coach for a young team . . . Wilkens is a teacher with a gentle, guiding attitude . . . Named as George Karl's replacement, after four months as Seattle SuperSonics' VP-GM after 11 seasons as head coach . . . A change of scenery was desperately needed by both parties because Wilkens appeared to become aloof from his players . . . Was a nine-time all-star as a player in 15 NBA seasons after outstanding career at Providence College . . . Played eight seasons with the St. Louis Hawks and two each with the Portland Trail Blazers and the Cavaliers . . . Named to 1973 all-star team as a Cav . . . Guard ranks among the career all-time leaders in assists (second with 7,211), games played, minutes played, free throws made and free throws attempted . . . Born Oct. 28, 1937, in Brooklyn, N.Y. . . . Needs four victories to jump ahead of Cotton Fitzsimmons to become sixth winningest coach in NBA history.

GREATEST COACH

In the sorry 17-year history of this franchise not one coach has managed to post a .500 record. Only three of the team's 10 coaches have a winning percentage over .400.

Just by the fact that he rode herd for nine seasons in Cleveland, Wild Bill Fitch should be recognized as the Cavs' top coach.

He certainly was the funniest. A master manipulator, Fitch kept everyone laughing, just to keep himself from crying. He also deflected criticism with his never-ending stream of jokes.

The expansion Cavs grabbed Fitch from the University of Minnesota in 1970. "Just remember," the new coach quipped, "the name is Fitch, not Houdini." That point was driven home when the Cavs dropped their first 15 games. Cleveland finished 15-67 that season. Overall, Fitch posted a 304-434 mark.

The franchise high-water mark occurred in Fitch's sixth season, when the Cavs made the playoffs for the first time. Before one of the largest and loudest home crowds in NBA history, they knocked out Washington, only to lose to eventual champion Boston.

Five years later, the hard-driving Fitch would win a championship with the Celtics.

ALL-TIME CAVALIER LEADERS

SEASON

Points: Mike Mitchell, 2,012, 1980-81
Assists: John Bagley, 735, 1985-86
Rebounds: Jim Brewer, 891, 1975-76

GAME

Points: Walt Wesley, 50 vs. Cincinnati, 2/19/71
Assists: Geoff Huston, 27 vs. Golden State, 1/27/82
Rebounds: Rick Roberson, 25 vs. Houston, 3/4/72

CAREER

Points: Austin Carr, 10,265, 1971-80
Assists: John Bagley, 2,311, 1982-87
Rebounds: Jim Chones, 3,790, 1974-79

DETROIT PISTONS

TEAM DIRECTORY: Pres.: Bill Davidson; GM: Jack McCloskey; Dir. Pub. Rel.: Matt Dobek; Coach: Chuck Daly; Asst. Coaches: Ron Rothstein, Dick Versace. Arena: Pontiac Silverdome (22,366). Colors: Red, white and blue.

SCOUTING REPORT

SHOOTING: If only the Detroit car makers could do as well. The Pistons set a club record for field-goal percentage, knocking down .490 of their shots. It was the third straight year the Pistons have improved in that area. Two seasons ago they shot .484. The acquisition of Adrian Dantley (.534) was the big reason for the rise. The Pistons' leading scorer (21.5) gives them strong inside scoring to mesh with Bill Laimbeer's outside game.

Isiah Thomas, however, slipped badly, dropping from .488 to .463. Thomas was coming off thumb surgery, which accounted for part of the problem. The other reason is in his head. He has a tendency to shoot too often, trying to get the job done all by his 6-1 self. There is too much talent across the board for the Pistons to be a one-man team.

PLAYMAKING: It's ironic that all the great passes Thomas made over the years were overshadowed by his lazy inbounds pass that was stolen by Larry Bird in the closing seconds of Game 5. That eventually cost the Pistons the series. Even though he was third in the league in assists (10.0), Thomas has to get his teammates even more involved before he can dare to think about stepping into Magic Johnson's class. Fellow guard Joe Dumars is a good one and should be given the ball more.

DEFENSE: The Pistons ranked eighth in the league in scoring at 111.2 and 10th in defense, allowing 107.8 a night. The year before, the Pistons were allowing 113 points a game. That's quite an improvement for Chuck Daly's give-and-take philosophy of basketball. The key, of course, is to take more than you give and that's why the Pistons (52-30) were able to equal a franchise record for victories last season.

Thomas is the Pistons' most active defender (153 steals). Kelly Tripucka was not around for opponents to abuse at small forward, which helped. Rookie forwards Dennis Rodman and John Salley, a team-high 125 blocks, were a wild combination off the bench and provide a bright future. Despite all the improve-

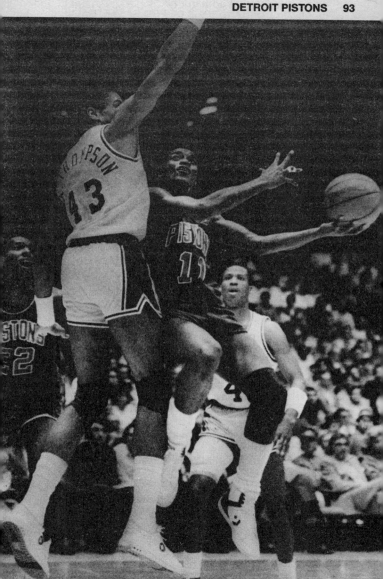

Isiah Thomas must learn a team needs all its Pistons.

PISTON ROSTER

No.	Veteran	Pos.	Ht.	Wt.	Age	Yrs. Pro	College
25	William Bedford	C	7-0	225	23	1	Memphis State
00	* Tony Campbell	F	6-7	215	25	3	Ohio State
45	Adrian Dantley	F	6-5	210	31	11	Notre Dame
4	Joe Dumars	G	6-3	190	24	2	McNeese State
12	* Sidney Green	F	6-9	220	26	4	Nevada-Las Vegas
15	* Vinnie Johnson	G	6-2	200	31	8	Baylor
40	Bill Laimbeer	C	6-11	260	30	7	Notre Dame
44	* Rick Mahorn	C-F	6-10	255	30	7	Hampton Institute
42	Chuck Nevitt	C	7-5	230	28	4	North Carolina St.
41	* Kurt Nimphius	C	6-10	218	29	6	Arizona State
10	Dennis Rodman	F	6-8	210	26	1	SE Oklahoma St.
22	John Salley	C-F	6-11	231	23	1	Georgia Tech
11	Isiah Thomas	G	6-1	185	26	6	Indiana

*Free agent unsigned at press time

Rd.	Top Rookies	Sel. No.	Pos.	Ht.	Wt.	College
2	Freddie Banks	24	G	6-2	155	Nevada-Las Vegas
3	Eric White	65	F	6-8	210	Pepperdine
4	David Popson	88	F	6-10	220	North Carolina
6	Gerry Wright	134	F	6-8	210	Iowa
7	Mark Gottfried	157	G	6-2	185	Alabama

ments, the Pistons do not play down-in-the-dirt defense and probably never will.

REBOUNDING: A vastly improved area. So much so they led the league. Bill Laimbeer went from first to fifth in the league, but still hauled in 11.6 a night. Salley and Rodman did their share and Rick Mahorn came alive in the late stages of the regular season and playoffs, making Sidney Green a memory. The acquisition of 7-0 William Bedford from Phoenix for a 1988 draft pick should also help the board work.

OUTLOOK: The Pistons came one mistake away from going to the finals last season. In many people's minds they were the better team—physically. They now have to cross that barrier and become a great team mentally as well. On the surface, Bedford's arrival should help matters, but he has to overcome personal problems for his acquisition to pay off and not disrupt the delicate chemistry of a successful team. A little more maturity, a little less Isiah shooting the ball, and this club is the best in the East.

PISTON PROFILES

ISIAH THOMAS 26 6-1 185   **Guard**

Of all the great plays he has made in his career, he will be tortured by the lazy pass that was stolen by Larry Bird in Game 5 of the Eastern Conference finals...Known as "Pocket Magic," he is one of the most dynamic small men ever to play the game...Confidence is his greatest asset...Sometimes that gets him in trouble because he tries to do too much...Game 1 (6-24 from the floor) against the Celtics was such a game...Destroyed Doc Rivers and the Hawks in the Eastern Conference semifinals...Rolled up 25 points during third quarter of Game 3 vs. Hawks...Had all-star year after offseason thumb surgery, but had bad series vs. Celtics...Came into NBA a year early because of differences with Bobby Knight and was drafted No. 2 overall by Pistons in 1982, after leading Indiana to NCAA title...Winner of 1987 Walter Kennedy Citizenship Award for community service...Born April 30, 1961, in Chicago...Youngest of nine children...Sensitive type...After Celtic loss, made stupid comments about Larry Bird being overrated because he is white...Has written some touching poetry ...Twice named All-Star Game MVP...Completed fourth year of 12-year contract that paid him $759,000 last season... Wouldn't it be great to see him running the floor with best friend Magic Johnson?

Year	Team	G	FG	FG Pct.	FT	FT Pct.	Reb.	Ast.	TP	Avg.
1981-82	Detroit............	72	453	.424	302	.704	209	565	1225	17.0
1982-83	Detroit............	81	725	.472	368	.710	328	634	1854	22.9
1983-84	Detroit............	82	669	.462	388	.733	327	914	1748	21.3
1984-85	Detroit............	81	646	.458	399	.809	361	1123	1720	21.2
1985-86	Detroit............	77	609	.488	365	.790	277	830	1609	20.9
1986-87	Detroit............	81	626	.463	400	.768	319	813	1671	20.6
	Totals.............	474	3728	462	2222	.753	1821	4879	9827	20.7

ADRIAN DANTLEY 31 6-5 210   **Forward**

Got the last laugh on Jazz funnyman Frank Layden, whose intense dislike for him led to trade ...Whirling dervish came east along with two second-round draft picks in exchange for Kelly Tripucka and Kent Benson, prior to the start of the season...Tripucka flopped in Utah while A.D. posted up Pontiac...Two-time NBA scoring champ showed the world he could be a team player as average dropped from 29.8 to 21.5... Still good enough to lead Pistons, but it was his lowest mark in eight years... "There's not another forward in the league who's done what I've done," he says of his ppg sacrifice... Was the Pistons' only real low-post threat... Season could have had a much different ending if A.D. hadn't collided heads with Vinnie Johnson in third quarter of Game 7 vs. Celtics and suffered game-ending concussion... Ironically, he's never been known for diving after loose balls... Roamed from Buffalo to Indiana to Los Angeles and to Utah before finding a home with Pistons... Born Feb. 28, 1956, in Washington, D.C... DeMatha H.S. product went to Notre Dame... No. 6 pick overall in 1976 by Buffalo and went on to win Rookie-of-the-Year honors... Will earn $975,000 this season... Has scored 19,678 points, 13th best in league history... Never met a foul line he didn't own... Listed 6-5, but more like 6-3.

Year	Team	G	FG	FG Pct.	FT	FT Pct.	Reb.	Ast.	TP	Avg.
1976-77	Buffalo	77	544	.520	476	.818	587	144	1564	20.3
1977-78	Ind.-L.A.	79	578	.512	541	.796	620	253	1697	21.5
1978-79	Los Angeles	60	374	.510	292	.854	342	138	1040	17.3
1979-80	Utah	68	730	.576	443	.842	516	191	1903	28.0
1980-81	Utah	80	909	.559	632	.806	509	322	2452	30.7
1981-82	Utah	81	904	.570	648	.792	514	324	2457	30.3
1982-83	Utah	22	233	.527	210	.847	140	105	676	30.7
1983-84	Utah	79	802	.558	813	.859	448	310	2418	30.6
1984-85	Utah	55	512	.531	438	.804	323	186	1462	26.6
1985-86	Utah	76	818	.563	630	.791	395	264	2267	29.8
1986-87	Detroit	81	601	.534	539	.812	332	162	1742	21.5
	Totals	758	7005	.549	5662	.817	4726	2399	19678	26.0

BILL LAIMBEER 30 6-11 260   Center

May be the most hated player in the league because of his crybaby face and sly tricks... NBA's No. 1 flopper... His mom and wife say he's really a nice guy, though... Threw down Dominique Wilkins in playoffs and did same to Larry Bird... In Bird's case he said he was just trying to break his fall... Too bad he used Larry's face for a railing... Celts got even when Robert Parish blindsided him with three thunderous punches in Game 5... Showed he could make cheap shots as well as take them with accurate shooting of wide-open jumpers throughout Celt series, but has absolutely no inside moves ... Was on the receiving end of Isiah Thomas' ill-fated pass in Game 5 and made cardinal sin of not moving to the ball... Has played in 564 consecutive games, currently the league's longest

mark... After leading the NBA in rebounding previous season
slipped from 13.1 to 11.6 rpg... Grabbed 955 rebounds for the
season, despite never leaving the floor, snapping his streak of
three straight seasons with 1,000 or more rebounds... Born
May 19, 1957, in Boston... Drafted No. 65 overall by Cavs
in 1979, out of Notre Dame... Played one season in Italy
... Acquired from Cleveland with Kenny Carr for Phil Hubbard,
Paul Mokeski and two second-round picks in 1982... Will earn
$650,000 this season.

Year	Team	G	FG	FG Pct.	FT	FT Pct.	Reb.	Ast.	TP	Avg.
1980-81	Cleveland	81	337	.503	117	.765	693	216	791	9.8
1981-82	Clev.-Det.	80	265	.494	184	.793	617	100	718	9.0
1982-83	Detroit	82	436	.497	245	.790	993	263	1119	13.6
1983-84	Detroit	82	553	.530	316	.866	1003	149	1422	17.3
1984-85	Detroit	82	595	.506	244	.797	1013	154	1438	17.5
1985-86	Detroit	82	545	.492	266	.834	1075	146	1360	16.6
1986-87	Detroit	82	506	.501	245	.894	955	151	1263	15.4
	Totals	571	3237	.504	1617	.825	6349	1179	8111	14.2

VINNIE JOHNSON, 31 6-2 200 Guard

The Microwave... Heats up faster than anybody in the NBA... The original streak
shooter... Can be counted on to win a couple
games a season all by himself... Did just that
in Game 6 against Celtics... Pistons' third-
leading scorer in sixth-man capacity... His
15.7 average was second-highest output of
eight-year career... Perhaps the NBA's
strongest guard, he simply overpowers rivals down low, but because of his lack of height, he can be posted up... Rock-like
physique... Ask Adrian Dantley how hard his head is... Made
$491,667 last season... Born Sept. 1, 1956, in Brooklyn, N.Y.
... Drafted No. 7 overall by Seattle in 1979 out of Baylor...
Acquired from the Sonics for Greg Kelser in November 1981 in
proverbial NBA steal of a trade... Knicks would love to have
him.

Year	Team	G	FG	FG Pct.	FT	FT Pct.	Reb.	Ast.	TP	Avg.
1979-80	Seattle	38	45	.391	31	.795	55	54	121	3.2
1980-81	Seattle	81	419	.534	214	.793	366	341	1053	13.0
1981-82	Sea.-Det.	74	217	.489	107	.754	159	171	544	7.4
1982-83	Detroit	82	520	.513	245	.778	353	301	1296	15.8
1983-84	Detroit	82	426	.473	207	.753	237	271	1063	13.0
1984-85	Detroit	82	428	.454	190	.769	252	325	1051	12.8
1985-86	Detroit	79	465	.467	165	.771	226	269	1097	13.9
1986-87	Detroit	78	533	.462	158	.786	257	300	1228	15.7
	Totals	596	3053	.481	1317	.773	1905	2032	7453	12.5

JOE DUMARS 24 6-3 190   Guard

The Quiet Man...Super scorer from McNeese State is lost in the backcourt shadows of Isiah Thomas and Vinnie Johnson ...In Game 7 vs. the Celtics he erupted for 35 points and nearly pushed the Pistons over the parquet hump...Became the starting off-guard in training camp and started 72 of 79 games...Defense may be strongest suit ...Named to NBA's All-Defense team and Chuck Daly said he was the first defense-oriented player he ever had in Detroit... Averaged over 25 a game in college...Drafted No. 18 overall by Pistons in 1985...Born May 24, 1963, in Natchitoches, La.... Brother, David, played in USFL...A steal for the Pistons... Made $120,000 last season and jumps to $225,000 this year...Can play the point as well...Has bright future, but needs more playing time.

Year	Team	G	FG	FG Pct.	FT	FT Pct.	Reb.	Ast.	TP	Avg.
1985-86	Detroit.............	82	287	.481	190	.798	119	390	769	9.4
1986-87	Detroit.............	79	369	.493	184	.748	167	352	931	11.8
	Totals.............	161	656	.487	374	.773	286	742	1700	10.6

SIDNEY GREEN 26 6-9 220   Forward

The forgotten man...Started 69 games for the Pistons during the regular season, then was lost in the sauce because of the play of Rick Mahorn and rookie John Salley...There has been talk he's difficult to get along with... Ironically, Salley, like Green a Brooklyn, N.Y., native, idolized him growing up... Came to Pistons from Bulls for Earl Cureton and a second-round draft choice prior to start of season...Had to battle his way off the bench for playing time with Chicago after being drafted No. 5 overall in 1983 out of UNLV...Finished as the Bulls' No. 2 rebounder, but they were eager to dump him... Led Pistons in rebounding 18 times, including a career-high 23 vs. Bucks on Dec. 30...Born Jan. 4, 1961, in Brooklyn, N.Y. ...Earned $400,000 in final year of contract...Too good to sit.

Year	Team	G	FG	FG Pct.	FT	FT Pct.	Reb.	Ast.	TP	Avg.
1983-84	Chicago............	49	100	.439	55	.714	174	25	255	5.2
1984-85	Chicago............	48	108	.432	79	.806	246	29	295	6.1
1985-86	Chicago............	80	407	.465	262	.782	658	139	1076	13.5
1986-87	Detroit.............	80	256	.472	119	.672	653	62	631	7.9
	Totals.............	257	871	.460	515	.747	1731	255	2257	8.8

DENNIS RODMAN 26 6-8 210   Forward

Has one of the league's most intriguing nicknames: The Worm...Along with Isiah Thomas, he infuriated Celtics with statement following Game 7 when he said Larry Bird is overrated because he's white...Turned out to be one of the finds of the draft as he was selected 27th overall in 1986 out of Southeastern Oklahoma State...He fills the lane like a hockey player...Offered up some memorable dunks in playoffs but no outside shots...Named the Small College Player of the Year when he averaged 24 points and 17 rebounds...Talent runs in the family...Sisters, Debra and Kim, were high-school All-Americans and Kim went on to Louisiana Tech, won a national championship and was named All-American three times...Born May 13, 1961, in Dallas...Has habit of pumping his arm in the air after baskets, which angers opponents...A fun guy to watch ...Perpetual motion...He really does run circles around opponents in trips up and down the floor.

Year	Team	G	FG	FG Pct.	FT	FT Pct.	Reb.	Ast.	TP	Avg.
1986-87	Detroit.............	77	213	.545	74	.587	332	56	500	6.5

JOHN SALLEY 23 6-11 231   Center-Forward

Long, tall Salley...Was tabbed 11th overall in 1986 draft out of Georgia Tech... Discovered by Bobby Cremmins on the streets of Brooklyn and went on to become Tech's all-time leading shot-blocker and fourth-best scorer..."The Spider" blocked 125 shots for the Pistons, most since Terry Tyler in 1982-83 ...Tons of athletic talent, he must learn how to shoot...Better yet, how to dunk...Blew two dunks in Game 1 vs. Celtics and another in Game 7...Still, has come a long way when you consider last time he was in Boston Garden for a playoff game he happened to be seated next to exotic dancer Busty Heart...Pitiful free-throw shooter...Hard work, combined with natural talents, should create package of dynamite over the next few years...Born May 16, 1964, in Brooklyn, N.Y.

Year	Team	G	FG	FG Pct.	FT	FT Pct.	Reb.	Ast.	TP	Avg.
1986-87	Detroit.............	82	163	.562	105	.614	296	54	431	5.3

RICK MAHORN 30 6-10 255   Center-Forward

Burp... Was on the way to eating his way out of the league, then it dawned on him he would be a free agent... Earned a cool half-million last season... After being a one-arm gang, he came on like gangbusters... Started the final six games of the season and did a job on the Hawks in the playoffs to finally become the power forward the Pistons have been searching for... They gave up power forward failure No. 1 Dan Round-field to Washington for him in June 1985... Sets the meanest picks in the world... While you wouldn't want to meet him on a dark basketball court, he's an absolute prince away from the game... Johnny Most's most hated player, if that's possible... Born to maim on Sept. 21, 1958, in Hartford, Conn.... Bullets made him the 35th pick overall, out of Hampton Institute in 1980... Was a better football prospect than a basketball prospect in high school.

Year	Team	G	FG	FG Pct.	FT	FT Pct.	Reb.	Ast.	TP	Avg.
1980-81	Washington.........	52	111	.507	27	.675	215	25	249	4.8
1981-82	Washington.........	80	414	.507	148	.632	704	150	976	12.2
1982-83	Washington.........	82	376	.490	146	.575	779	115	898	11.0
1983-84	Washington.........	82	307	.507	125	.651	738	131	739	9.0
1984-85	Washington.........	77	206	.499	71	.683	608	121	483	6.3
1985-86	Detroit.............	80	157	.455	81	.681	412	64	395	4.9
1986-87	Detroit.............	63	144	.447	96	.821	375	38	384	6.1
	Totals.............	516	1715	.492	694	.655	3831	644	4124	8.0

WILLIAM BEDFORD 23 7-0 225   Center

A big disappointment as a Suns' rookie, he comes to Detroit for a draft pick... Was supposed to be the cornerstone of a Phoenix rebuilding program... Missed the first 14 games with a knee injury... Never showed the aggessiveness that the Suns wanted... Was a great shot-blocker and regarded as the best "pure center" available from the college ranks in 1986... But also suspected of existing on a diet of Ken-L-Ration... Born Dec. 14, 1963, in Memphis, Tenn.... Left college after junior year at Memphis State to turn pro... Suns were surprised he was still available at No. 6 spot... Now they know why.

Year	Team	G	FG	FG Pct.	FT	FT Pct.	Reb.	Ast.	TP	Avg.
1986-87	Phoenix............	50	142	.397	50	.581	246	57	334	6.7

KURT NIMPHIUS 29 6-10 218 Center

With his long, wavy hair, looks a little bit like Kelly Tripucka... Maybe that's why the Pistons gave up a 1987 first-round pick and a second-rounder to Clippers for him during the season... Has reputation of being an odd-ball ...When he was traded to the Clippers in exchange for James Donaldson, he said he was leaving his pet iguana behind: "I hope it grows up and eats all of Dallas."... Now says he's getting tired of that rep...Didn't get off the bench much in playoffs...Fairly agile swingman when he plays...Signed as free agent by Dallas in 1981 and spent four seasons with the club...Born March 13, 1958, in Milwaukee...Played at Arizona State, where the entire starting five in his senior year—Fat Lever, Sam Williams, Alton Lister, Byron Scott and him—made it to the NBA...Spent the 1985 All-Star Game break in a haunted mansion in Louisiana and reported no ghosts...Taken 47th overall in the 1980 draft by Denver...Earned $225,000 last season before becoming free agent.

Year	Team	G	FG	FG Pct.	FT	FT Pct.	Reb.	Ast.	TP	Avg.
1981-82	Dallas............	63	137	.461	63	.583	295	61	337	5.3
1982-83	Dallas............	81	174	.490	77	.550	404	115	426	5.3
1983-84	Dallas............	82	272	.520	101	.623	513	176	646	7.9
1984-85	Dallas............	82	196	.452	108	.771	408	183	500	6.1
1985-86	Dal.-LAC.........	80	351	.506	194	.740	453	62	896	11.2
1986-87	LAC-Det..........	66	155	.470	81	.675	187	25	391	5.9
	Totals............	454	1285	.488	624	.670	2260	622	3196	7.0

TONY CAMPBELL 25 6-7 215 Forward

Going, going, gone...Had by far his worst season of ineffective career...Played in just 40 games after seeing action in all 82 season before...Shot career lows from the field (.393) and the line (.615)...Has a good shooting touch but never got the time to work it out...Lack of size has always been his big problem...Use to sit behind Kelly Tripucka, now young studs John Salley and Dennis Rodman have rendered free agent obsolete...Born May 7, 1962, in Teaneck, N.J.... Big-time scorer at Ohio State...Buckeye was selected Big 10 Player of the Year by one wire service his senior season...Taken

20th overall by the Pistons in 1984 draft . . . Expansion may save him.

Year	Team	G	FG	FG Pct.	FT	FT Pct.	Reb.	Ast.	TP	Avg.
1984-85	Detroit............	56	130	.496	56	.800	89	24	316	5.6
1985-86	Detroit............	82	294	.484	58	.795	236	45	648	7.9
1986-87	Detroit............	40	57	.393	24	.615	58	19	138	3.5
	Totals............	178	481	.474	138	.758	383	88	1102	6.2

CHUCK NEVITT 28 7-5 230   Center

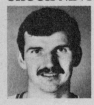

A walking cartoon character . . . Now with his third team in four years . . . Keeps things loose in the clubhouse . . . Always ready with a friendly smile . . . When reporters asked John Salley in Game 1 of Celtics series, how he could blow two dunks, Nevitt overheard and said, "What's the big deal? I've missed lots of dunks. It's not an easy shot with guys hanging all over you." . . . Had his career game vs. the Knicks on Jan. 7 when he scored a career-high 12 points, adding career bests in rebounds (10) and blocked shots (5) . . . Signed as a free agent in middle of 1985-86 season . . . North Carolina State product was 63rd pick overall by Houston in 1982 . . . Born June 13, 1959, in Cortex, Colo. . . . Gotta love his nickname: Chuck E. Cheese.

Year	Team	G	FG	FG Pct.	FT	FT Pct.	Reb.	Ast.	TP	Avg.
1982-83	Houston............	6	11	.733	1	.250	17	0	23	3.8
1984-85	L.A. Lakers.........	11	5	.294	2	.250	20	3	12	1.1
1985-86	LAL-Det.............	29	15	.349	19	.731	32	7	49	1.7
1986-87	Detroit............	41	31	.492	14	.583	83	4	76	1.9
	Total.............	87	62	.449	36	.581	152	14	160	1.8

TOP ROOKIE

FREDDIE BANKS 22 6-2 155   Guard

UNLV wizard was first pick of second round . . . Pistons gave away their No. 1 in Kurt Nimphius deal . . . A three-point maverick, having made 152-358 (.425) his senior season . . . Born March 6, 1965, in Las Vegas, Nev. . . . Averaged 19.5 points to help lead Runnin' Rebels to Final Four . . . Another shooting guard who will have to make the switch to point . . . Ended college career on a high note, scoring career-high 38 vs. Indiana.

COACH CHUCK DALY: Nice guys don't always finish last

... Became the winningest coach in the history of the franchise this past season and has now directed the Pistons to four straight winning campaigns and four straight postseason appearances ... His four-year record with Detroit is 211-150 ... Prior to his stint, no Piston coach had ever compiled back-to-back winning seasons ... Despite all that success, he longs to get out of coaching and into the front office ... Thought he had found his Holy Grail when Knicks came within an eyelash of signing Piston boss Jack McCloskey as their GM, which would have opened up the post in Detroit ... Two years ago, he wanted to return to Philadelphia as head coach but McCloskey wouldn't let him ... In final year of contract that pays him about $225,000 ... Extremely personable, also does color commentary for several TV outlets ... Great dresser ... Born July 20, 1930, in St. Mary's, Pa. ... Was given much credit for helping Billy Cunningham make transition from player to coach while assistant with 76ers ... Graduated from Bloomsburg State (Pa.) College, where he averaged career 13.1 ppg over two seasons ... Had eight-year collegiate coaching mark of 151-62 ... Didn't get his first head-coaching job in pros until he was 51 ... Good things come to those who wait.

GREATEST COACH

Not only is Chuck Daly the best coach the Pistons ever had, he is the best dresser.

This was an easy choice because Daly is only the second coach in the 20-year history of the franchise to post a better than .500 record. In a city known for some classy cars, the Pistons have had their share of Edsels on the sidelines.

The names don't exactly strike fear into the hearts of opponents: Charles Eckman, Red Rocha, Paul Seymour, Earl Lloyd, Dick Vitale, and poor Richie Adubato, who still hasn't overcome the stigma of a 12-58 record after inheriting Vitale's vanquished squad in 1980.

In a franchise of losers, Daly has rung up four straight seasons of winning teams. Only Ray Scott had been able to put together back-to-back winning seasons before and he won Coach of the Year honors in 1973-74.

No other Piston coach, of course, has been lucky enough to have an Isiah Thomas. Certainly, a huge part of Daly's success is his common sense to let Isiah run the show.

After all, once you get a great set of wheels, you don't let anybody else drive.

ALL-TIME PISTON LEADERS

SEASON

Points: Dave Bing, 2,213, 1970-71
Assists: Isiah Thomas, 1,123, 1984-85
Rebounds: Bob Lanier, 1,205, 1972-73

GAME

Points: Kelly Tripucka, 56 vs. Chicago, 1/29/83
Assists: Kevin Porter, 25 vs. Phoenix, 4/1/79
　　　　　Kevin Porter, 25 vs. Boston, 3/9/79
　　　　　Isiah Thomas, 25 vs. Dallas, 2/13/85
Rebounds: Bob Lanier, 33 vs. Seattle, 12/22/72

CAREER

Points: Bob Lanier, 15,488, 1970-80
Assists: Isiah Thomas, 4,879, 1981-87
Rebounds: Bob Lanier, 8,033, 1970-80

INDIANA PACERS

TEAM DIRECTORY: Owners: Herb Simon, Melvin Simon; GM: Donnie Walsh; Dir. Player Personnel: George Irvine; Media Rel. Dir.: Dale Ratermann; Coach: Jack Ramsay; Asst. Coaches: Dick Harter, Dave Twardzik, Mel Daniels. Arena: Market Square Arena (16,912). Colors: Blue and gold.

SCOUTING REPORT

SHOOTING: Field-goal accuracy has to be improved before these Hoosiers are to make it big. Pacers shot .472 from the field, fifth worst in the league. No need to ask why they drafted UCLA sharpshooter Reggie Miller (a .547 career mark) with the 11th pick. The Pacers need to get inside scoring from the center spot, an impossible dream with Steve Stipanovich in the middle. Stipo does get the most of his ability, however, and shot .503, a jump from .470. Imagine if he ventured into the paint.

Wayman Tisdale backed his way to the hoop to shoot a team-leading .513 and underrated guard Vern Fleming had an impressive .509. John Long, a lifetime .471 shooter, dropped to .419. Chuck Person, the NBA's Future Monster Small Forward, moved along at a .468 clip. And the Pacers set a francise record by making 78.2 percent of their free throws.

PLAYMAKING: Person is one of those "point forward" types who can pass the ball, making his teammates all the better. Jack Ramsay's disciplined offense did wonders for the Pacers, who consistently hit the open man usher the season before. Fleming, who led the Pacers in assists with 473, cut down his turnovers from 208 to 167. Draft-day trade that brought tough-guy Scott Skiles from Milwaukee will give much needed spark off the bench, providing Skiles is over his back woes.

DEFENSE: This is where the teachings of Dr. Jack had the most influence on his students. The Pacers cut their point differential from 3.3 to 0.6. Two years ago only one Pacer, Fleming, had more than 75 steals. Last season four Pacers had 90 or more steals, with Fleming's 109 leading the pack. The Pacers also improved their crunch-time defense, and that is as big a reason as any for their improvement. Isn't it something how Fleming's name pops up in every category?

In Person: The NBA's Rookie of the Year.

PACER ROSTER

No.	Veteran	Pos.	Ht.	Wt.	Age	Yrs. Pro	College
15	Ron Anderson	F	6-7	215	29	3	Fresno State
54	Greg Dreiling	C	7-1	250	23	1	Kansas
10	Vern Fleming	G	6-5	195	25	3	Georgia
55	Stuart Gray	C	7-0	245	24	3	UCLA
25	John Long	G	6-5	195	31	9	Detroit
44	* Kyle Macy	G	6-3	195	30	7	Kentucky
45	Chuck Person	F	6-8	225	23	1	Auburn
4	Clint Richardson	G	6-3	195	31	8	Seattle
31	* Walker Russell	G	6-5	195	27	5	Western Michigan
00	Scott Skiles	G	6-2	190	23	1	Michigan State
40	Steve Stipanovich	C	7-0	250	26	4	Missouri
23	Wayman Tisdale	F	6-9	240	23	2	Oklahoma
32	Herb Williams	F	6-10	240	28	6	Ohio State

*Free agent unsigned at press time

Rd.	Top Rookies	Sel. No.	Pos.	Ht.	Wt.	College
1	Reggie Miller	11	G-F	6-7	190	UCLA
2	Brian Rowsom	34	F	6-9	225	NC-Wilmington
3	Sean Couch	60	G	6-11½	185	Columbia
5	Mike Milling	103	G	6-6	210	NC-Charlotte
6	Gary Graham	126	G	6-4	185	Nevada-Las Vegas

REBOUNDING: Where would they be without Person? Not only did he lead the team in scoring, but rebounding, too, with 8.2 a game. The Pacers grabbed .496 percent of available rebounds, 14th best in the league. They went from second in total rebounds to 14th. The absence of Clark Kellogg for the second straight season hurt, and last summer he announced his retirement after testing his knees in pickup games. Some toughness is in order because the Pacers are stocked with bulky frontcourt players.

OUTLOOK: The 41-41 mark was a 15-game improvement from the previous year. That's the most dramatic rise of any club in the league last year. Certainly, stealing Rookie of the Year Chuck Person with the fourth pick was the key move. The addition of Reggie Miller (No. 11 in the draft) will help this season. And the front-office smarts of GM Donnie Walsh and the presence of Jack Ramsay assure that the Pacers will not be a joke for quite some time. Until a power center arrives, however, this team will only be good, never great.

PACER PROFILES

CHUCK PERSON 23 6-8 225   Forward

The Rifleman was on target all season as he tore up the NBA and captured Rookie-of-the-Year honors...Full name is Chuck Connors Person, named after TV's Rifleman...Led Pacers in scoring (18.8), rebounding (8.3) and minutes (36)...Averaged 3.6 assists...Lit up scoreboard for 27 points a night in four-game playoff series against Hawks...Total player...Can shoot from the moon...Set an NBA record when he drained all six three-pointers at Phoenix on Feb. 11...Surprise pick at No. 4...Indiana fans booed GM Donnie Walsh for taking another forward instead of center William Bedford...
"It shows how dumb people are," proclaimed Denver coach Doug Moe. "The other guy [Bedford] is a total stiff."...Knicks, picking right behind Pacers, already had a "Person" jersey made up and were shattered as they had to settle for SEC rival Kenny Walker...Born June 27, 1964, in Brantley, Ala....Was high-school teammate of Buck Johnson and was overlooked at Auburn because of Charles Barkley...Overcame twin hernia and a near-fatal appendicitis attack in college...This Person has a huge, huge future.

Year	Team	G	FG	FG Pct.	FT	FT Pct.	Reb.	Ast.	TP	Avg.
1986-87	Indiana............	82	635	.468	222	.747	677	295	1541	18.8

JOHN LONG 31 6-5 195   Guard

Came the long way around to make his point...Never happy as a Piston, he was dealt to Seattle the day before training camp and then landed in Indiana the very next day for Terence Stansbury and Russ Schoene...Got sweet revenge when he burned Pistons on opening-night victory with three-pointer at the buzzer...Scored 40-plus points twice last season, including a career-high 44 vs. Philly on Nov. 4...Born Aug. 28, 1956, in Romulus, Mich....Pistons made him 29th player chosen in 1978, out of Detroit, where he played for Dick Vitale, later his Piston coach...One of the game's better free-throw shooters, he set Pacer NBA record by converting 89 percent...Accurate set shot can torture opponents...Big knock is his image as poor pressure player . . . Didn't help himself when he made just 31 percent of his shots (16-52) in playoffs.

Year	Team	G	FG	FG Pct.	FT	FT Pct.	Reb.	Ast.	TP	Avg.
1978-79	Detroit............	82	581	.469	157	.826	266	121	1319	16.1
1979-80	Detroit............	69	588	.505	160	.825	337	206	1337	19.4
1980-81	Detroit............	59	441	.461	160	.870	197	106	1044	17.7
1981-82	Detroit............	69	637	.492	238	.865	257	148	1514	21.9
1982-83	Detroit............	70	312	.451	111	.760	180	105	737	10.5
1983-84	Detroit............	82	545	.472	243	.884	289	205	1334	16.3
1984-85	Detroit............	66	431	.487	106	.862	190	130	973	14.7
1985-86	Detroit............	62	264	.482	89	.856	98	82	620	10.0
1986-87	Indiana............	80	490	.419	219	.890	217	258	1218	15.2
	Totals............	639	4289	.471	1483	.854	2031	1361	10096	15.8

HERB WILLIAMS 28 6-10 240   Forward

Rock steady . . . Past six years Williams has been one consistent Pacer . . . Some people would like him to do more, but what you see is what you get, night in, night out . . . Fifteen points, seven rebounds, a couple blocked shots . . . Co-captain now holds club records for games, minutes, field goals, rebounds and blocked shots . . . After earning embarrassingly small salary of $275,000 two years ago, he will earn $1 million this season . . . Has wondrous body . . . Born Feb. 19, 1959, in Columbus, Ohio . . . Was Clark Kellogg's teammate at Ohio State . . . Pacers drafted him 14th overall in 1981 . . . Had best year ever from free-throw line with .740

Year	Team	G	FG	FG Pct.	FT	FT Pct.	Reb.	Ast.	TP	Avg.
1981-82	Indiana............	82	407	.477	126	.670	605	139	942	11.5
1982-83	Indiana............	78	580	.499	155	.705	583	262	1315	16.9
1983-84	Indiana............	69	411	.478	207	.702	554	215	1029	14.9
1984-85	Indiana............	75	575	.475	224	.657	634	252	1375	18.3
1985-86	Indiana............	78	627	.492	294	.730	710	174	1549	19.9
1986-87	Indiana............	74	451	.480	199	.740	543	174	1101	14.9
	Totals............	456	3051	.484	1205	.702	3629	1216	7311	16.0

WAYMAN TISDALE 23 6-9 240   Forward

Now people are only laughing at his haircut . . . After being taken second in 1985 draft and becoming a major disappointment the first half of his rookie season, former Oklahoma star has found a role for himself as a sixth man . . . Lefty low-post game produced a career-high 35 points vs. Sacramento on Feb. 22, the highest point total for any sub last season in a 48-minute game . . . Always fighting his weight and complains:

"I'm forever on a diet but I've got to eat to stay alive."... Made difficult switch from college center to small forward... A three-time All-American, Tisdale was the Big Eight's all-time leading scorer (2,661 points) and a member of the 1984 U.S. Olympic team... Durable, has missed just one game in each of his first two seasons... Born June 9, 1964, in Tulsa, Okla.... Son of a reverend has formed "Tisdale's Team," an anti-drug group from local high schools... Contract zooms to $987,000 this year.

Year	Team	G	FG	FG Pct.	FT	FT Pct.	Reb.	Ast.	TP	Avg.
1985-86	Indiana	81	516	.515	160	.684	584	79	1192	14.7
1986-87	Indiana	81	458	.513	258	.709	475	117	1174	14.5
	Totals	162	974	.514	418	.699	1059	196	2366	14.6

STEVE STIPANOVICH 26 7-0 250   Center

Okay, so he looks like he should be performing at Disney World, but you can do a lot worst at center... Had his finest season as a pro, improving in every statistical category except scoring... Was second on the club in steals with 106, led the team in blocked shots and shot .503 from the field... Considering he doesn't spend as much time in the paint as a lot of other centers, that's an impressive figure... Has never escaped stigma of being the other player in Ralph Sampson coin flip, chosen second in the 1983 draft out of Missouri, but has come a lot closer to living up to his potential than the Houston multi-millionaire... Born Nov. 17, 1960, in St. Louis... "He's underrated by the public," notes Jack Ramsay, "but the NBA people appreciate him."

Year	Team	G	FG	FG Pct.	FT	FT Pct.	Reb.	Ast.	TP	Avg.
1983-84	Indiana	81	392	.480	183	.753	562	170	970	12.0
1984-85	Indiana	82	414	.475	297	.798	614	199	1126	13.7
1985-86	Indiana	79	416	.470	242	.768	623	206	1076	13.6
1986-87	Indiana	81	382	.503	307	.837	670	180	1072	13.2
	Totals	323	1604	.481	1029	.793	2469	755	4244	13.1

VERN FLEMING 25 6-5 195   Guard

Coming along very nicely, thank you... Third-year point guard continues to make solid progress... Led club in assists for second straight season with 5.8 per game and steals, 1.4 a game... Field-goal percentage climbed to career-best .509... Has twin brother, Victor, who plays for Cincinnati Slammers of CBA... Victor made $7,000 last season, Vern pulled in $210,000 . . . U.S. Olympian in 1984 . . . No. 18 pick overall by Pacers that year . . . Born Feb. 2, 1962, in Long Island City, N.Y. . . . One of better rebounding point guards averaging 4.1 a game . . . Scored 1,777 points at Georgia, replacing Dominique Wilkins as all-time leader.

Year	Team	G	FG	FG Pct.	FT	FT Pct.	Reb.	Ast.	TP	Avg.
1984-85	Indiana	80	433	.470	260	.767	323	247	1126	14.1
1985-86	Indiana	80	436	.506	263	.745	386	505	1136	14.2
1986-87	Indiana	82	370	.509	238	.788	334	473	980	12.0
	Totals	242	1239	.493	761	.766	1043	1225	3242	13.4

CLARK KELLOGG 26 6-7 225   Forward

This "60 Minutes" might be the end of the show . . . That's all Special K played all season because recurring knee problems limited him to the first four games of the season . . . Left knee has undergone surgery three straight seasons . . . Although he was such a vital cog in the past, presence of Chuck Person has made life without Kellogg much easier to swallow . . . Co-captain spent most of the season reading novels and the stock market, and recuperating . . . "If it's not in God's plans to play basketball, then I'll have to be successful in another area," says former Ohio State star . . . Earned $516,000 last season . . . Born July 2, 1961, in Cleveland . . . Pacers made him No. 8 pick overall in 1982 after he had been named Big 10 MVP . . . Seems like a long time ago.

Year	Team	G	FG	FG Pct.	FT	FT Pct.	Reb.	Ast.	TP	Avg.
1982-83	Indiana	81	680	.479	261	.741	860	223	1625	20.1
1983-84	Indiana	79	619	.519	261	.768	719	234	1506	19.1
1984-85	Indiana	77	562	.505	301	.760	724	244	1432	18.6
1985-86	Indiana	19	139	.473	53	.768	168	57	335	17.6
1986-87	Indiana	4	8	.364	3	.750	11	6	20	5.0
	Totals	260	2008	.497	879	.757	2482	764	4918	18.9

CLINT RICHARDSON 31 6-3 195   Guard

Reporters wish he'd play more . . . When he was with the Sixers, he combined with Julius Erving to form one of the best quote combinations in the NBA . . . Arrival of John Long cut his playing time dramatically to 17 minutes a game . . . Shot 46.7 from the field, the second-best mark in his career . . . Has pancake jump shot, dating back to his childhood days in Seattle when he used to practice on a hoop in a basement with a low ceiling . . . Born Aug. 7, 1956, in Seattle . . . Was drafted No.

36 overall by Sixers in 1979 out of the University of Seattle... Came to Pacers Oct. 23, 1985, for two second-round picks after bitter contract squabble... Will earn $275,000 this season... Brightest moment came in '85 playoffs, when he made 24 of 37 shots during Sixer sweep of Bucks... Continues to study criminal justice at his alma mater.

Year	Team	G	FG	FG Pct.	FT	FT Pct.	Reb.	Ast.	TP	Avg.
1979-80	Philadelphia.........	52	159	.457	28	.622	123	107	347	6.7
1980-81	Philadelphia.........	77	227	.489	84	.778	176	152	538	7.0
1981-82	Philadelphia.........	77	140	.452	69	.784	118	109	351	4.6
1982-83	Philadelphia.........	77	259	.463	71	.640	247	168	589	7.6
1983-84	Philadelphia.........	69	221	.467	79	.767	165	155	521	7.6
1984-85	Philadelphia.........	74	183	.453	76	.854	155	157	443	6.0
1985-86	Indiana............	82	335	.455	123	.837	251	372	794	9.7
1986-87	Indiana............	78	218	.467	59	.797	143	241	501	6.4
	Totals............	586	1742	.463	589	.770	1378	1461	4084	7.0

STUART GRAY 24 7-0 245   Center

Played the most minutes of his career (8.3 a game), which isn't saying much... Had no business leaving UCLA after his junior season to become Pacers' second-round pick (29th overall) in 1984... Pacers had no business picking him, much less giving him $647,000 in guaranteed money... Game has not improved... Proves once again, however, that this is a great country if you are a seven-footer and white... Scored 13 points against Nets on March 15, a career high and only his second pro game of double-figure scoring in three years ... Was born in Panama Canal Zone, May 27, 1963... Is often seen (or unseen) in camouflage wardrobe... The way he plays, it's not such a bad idea to hide.

Year	Team	G	FG	FG Pct.	FT	FT Pct.	Reb.	Ast.	TP	Avg.
1984-85	Indiana............	52	35	.380	32	.681	123	15	102	2.0
1985-86	Indiana............	67	54	.500	47	.635	118	15	155	2.3
1986-87	Indiana............	55	41	.406	28	.718	129	26	110	2.0
	Totals............	174	130	.432	107	.669	370	56	367	2.1

KYLE MACY 30 6-3 195   Guard

Hoosier Homecoming... State's former "Mr. Basketball" came back home prior to the season when he was traded by Chicago for two second-round picks... Was coached by his dad in Peru, Ind., as a schoolboy... Born April 9, 1957, in Kendalville, Ind.... Drafted 22nd overall by the Suns in 1979 as a junior eligible out of Kentucky... A bicycling enthusiast, he plans to travel down the California coast on two wheels ... Shot better than 80 percent from the free-throw line for seventh straight season, but shot 48 percent from the field, the lowest mark of his career ... Doesn't get to the line enough because he doesn't drive enough ... Had more steals (59) than turnovers (58) ... Has been to playoffs seven straight years.

Year	Team	G	FG	FG Pct.	FT	FT Pct.	Reb.	Ast.	TP	Avg.
1980-81	Phoenix	82	272	.511	107	.899	132	160	663	8.1
1981-82	Phoenix	82	486	.514	152	.899	261	384	1163	14.2
1982-83	Phoenix	82	328	.517	129	.872	165	278	808	9.9
1983-84	Phoenix	82	357	.501	95	.833	186	353	832	10.1
1984-85	Phoenix	65	282	.485	127	.907	179	380	714	11.0
1985-86	Chicago	82	286	.483	73	.811	178	446	703	8.6
1986-87	Indiana	76	164	.481	34	.829	113	197	376	4.9
	Totals	551	2175	.501	717	.873	1214	2198	5259	9.5

GREG DREILING 23 7-1 250   Center

Is there any way to explain how Dreiling, Stuart Gray and Steve Stipanovich ended up on the same team? ... Dreiling played in 24 games, all in a reserve role, after being taken on the second round, 26th overall, out of Kansas, in the 1986 draft ... Coming out of high school in 1981, he was considered along with Patrick Ewing one of the top two prospects in the country ... Boy, did his star fade ... Played for one year at Wichita State before transferring to Kansas, where Jayhawks went to Final Four in 1986 ... Born Nov. 7, 1963, in Wichita, Kan. ... Took all of 14 shots the second half of the season ... At least he made seven of them ... Could develop into a decent rebounder ... Has good hands ... Expect him to stay in the league and land on an expansion team because of his size.

Year	Team	G	FG	FG Pct.	FT	FT Pct.	Reb.	Ast.	TP	Avg.
1986-87	Indiana	24	16	.432	10	.833	43	7	42	1.8

SCOTT SKILES 23 6-2 190   Guard

This could have been interesting ... World wanted to see how wise guy would do in NBA but a protruding disc in his back shelved him for much of rookie season with Milwaukee, where he played in just 13 games ... Bucks decided to give him up to Pacers for 1989 second-round draft pick ... Second-leading scorer in NCAA I two years ago with 27.4 average ... Taken 22nd overall out of Michigan State in 1986 draft ... Born March 5, 1964, in LaPorte, Ind. ... Has been called

"Jimmy Cagney in shorts." . . . Spent 15 days in jail due to convictions on drug and alcohol-related charges before turning pro.

Year	Team	G	FG	FG Pct.	FT	FT Pct.	Reb.	Ast.	TP	Avg.
1986-87	Milwaukee..........	13	18	.290	10	.833	26	45	49	3.8

RON ANDERSON 29 6-7 215   Forward

Deserves more playing time . . . But where's he going to get it? . . . Backing up Chuck Person is not exactly the way to show your stuff . . . Here's a hint of what he can do . . . Scored 23 of the Pacers' 42 points in the second half vs. New Jersey, on his way to a season-high 27 on April 7 . . . Averaged a point every two minutes . . . A true late bloomer . . . Did not play college ball . . . Was a stock manager in a grocery store in Chicago, then began his college career at age 22 at Santa Barbara . . . Finished at Fresno State . . . Cavs drafted him No. 27 overall in 1984 . . . Pro career began with 27-point explosion against Julius Erving . . . Then he was injured and missed 46 games . . . Sprained a knee last season . . . Born Oct. 15, 1958, in Chicago . . . Needs a rebirth somewhere.

Year	Team	G	FG	FG Pct.	FT	FT Pct.	Reb.	Ast.	TP	Avg.
1984-85	Cleveland..........	36	84	.431	41	.820	88	34	210	5.8
1985-86	Clev.-Ind..........	77	310	.494	85	.669	274	144	707	9.2
1986-87	Indiana............	63	139	.473	85	.787	151	54	363	5.8
	Totals.............	176	533	.477	211	.740	513	232	1280	7.3

TOP ROOKIE

REGGIE MILLER 22 6-7 190   Guard-Forward

Magic man from the outside . . . Was hoping to go to his hometown L.A. Clippers . . . Pacers snagged him with the 11th pick . . . Finished as the second all-time leading scorer for UCLA behind Kareem Abdul-Jabbar with 2,095 points . . . Sister Cheryl was star on 1984 women's Olympic team . . . Born Aug. 24, 1965 in Riverside, Cal. . . . Led Bruins to first Pac-10 championship since 1983, averaging 22.3 points on .543 shooting . . . "I don't put myself in the same category with Kareem and the redhead [Bill Walton]," he says. "They're Hall of Famers. They've been to the mountain top and back. I'm just trying to get there."

COACH JACK RAMSAY: Dr. Jack was given a new lease on coaching last season and made the most of it ...In his first season at the helm in Indiana, he directed the Pacers to their first playoff appearance in six seasons...Playoffs are nothing new for Ramsay, of course...In 19 years as a head coach, his teams have gone to the playoffs 16 times...Drives no one harder than he drives himself...Is an accomplished triathlete...Known as a teacher, Ramsay has coached 1,558 regular season games, an NBA record...He is the second-winningest coach in NBA history, 826-732 record for a winning percentage of .530...Only Red Auerbach has won more games ...In playoffs his record drops to 44-58...Coached 11 years at St. Joseph's in Philadelphia...Born Feb. 21, 1925, in Philadelphia...Played at St. Joseph's and then in the Eastern Basketball League...Named GM of the 76ers in 1966, the season Philly won an NBA championship...Coached the Sixers and brought them to the playoffs three times in four years...Moved to Buffalo Braves as coach in 1972-73 and put them in the playoffs three out of four years...Went out to the Great Northwest and brought a title to the Blazers in 1977...A true coaching legend.

GREATEST COACH

By the numbers you have to go with Bob (Slick) Leonard, who compiled a 529-456 record in 11 years. He won three ABA championships in seven seasons, but in the NBA never did better than a tie for third in four seasons.

The ABA years, of course, were the glory days for this franchise. The heroes were Mel Daniels, George McGinnis and Roger Brown.

A strong case, however, can be made for their present coach, Jack Ramsay. Dr. Jack gets the call not only for his one-season renaissance, but his overall works of beauty in the NBA. Ramsay took a team that averaged 23 victories over the last four seasons and put them into the playoffs with a 41-41 mark.

He took an inexperienced, under-motivated team and molded it into an aggressive, rock-solid squad that will continue to grow as long as Chuck Person is rifling them up.

ALL-TIME PACER LEADERS

SEASON

Points: George McGinnis, 2,353, 1974-75
Assists: Don Buse, 689, 1975-76
Rebounds: Mel Daniels, 1,475, 1970-71

GAME

Points: George McGinnis, 58 vs. Dallas, 11/28/72
Assists: Don Buse, 20 vs. Denver, 3/26/76
Rebounds: George McGinnis, 37 vs. Carolina, 1/12/74

CAREER

Points: Billy Knight, 10,780, 1974-83
Assists: Don Buse, 2,747, 1972-77, 1980-82
Rebounds: Mel Daniels, 7,622, 1968-74

MILWAUKEE BUCKS

TEAM DIRECTORY: Pres.: Herb Kohl; VP-Bus. Oper.: John Steinmiller; Dir. Player Personnel: Stu Inman; Dir. Pub. Rel.: Bill King II; Coach: Del Harris. Arena: Milwaukee Arena (11,052). Colors: Forest green, red and white.

SCOUTING REPORT

SHOOTING: Only two Bucks shot over .500 from the field—Ricky Pierce (.534) and Terry Cummings (.511). Ironically, both missed key baskets down the stretch in Game 7 vs. the Celtics. After a disappointing regular season, Jack Sikma gave the Bucks scoring from the center hole in the playoffs. And that's why he was brought east.

Paul Pressey, point forward extraordinaire, continued his downward shooting slide. In the last three seasons his field-goal percentage has fallen from .517 to .488 to .477. Three-point specialist Craig Hodges really bottomed out—.500 to .462.

Shooting doesn't mean the world to the Bucks, however. After all, it's defense that wins games for this franchise.

PLAYMAKING: Their season was saved when John Lucas was rescued from the cocaine garbage heap. Lucas took a lot of pressure off Pressey and made the Bucks an uptempo, high-scoring team. That different look created problems for the Celtics in the playoffs. All the Bucks are generally good ball-handlers. Execution always has been their trademark.

DEFENSE: This team plays defense so well you'd swear there were six Bucks on the court. Oppressive is the word that best describes their play. Pressey is the most annoying of the bunch, being in two places at once. The Bucks finished fifth in defense, allowing just 106 points per game. Opponents shot .470 from the field as they were badgered into hurried shots.

Pressey was all over Larry Bird in the playoffs, and until he fouled out in Game 7 the Bucks looked like they were going to make it to the Eastern finals. How long this team's overall hustle can continue, however, is a question to ponder. Especially since The Man—Don Nelson—is gone.

REBOUNDING: The Achilles heel. Only the hapless Clippers and Knicks pulled down less rebounds than the Bucks' 3,441. In the playoffs, the Celtics particularly made use of the Bucks' in-

BUCK ROSTER

No.	Veteran	Pos.	Ht.	Wt.	Age	Yrs. Pro	College
45	Randy Breuer	C	7-3	230	27	4	Minnesota
24	Dudley Bradley	G	6-6	195	30	7	North Carolina
34	Terry Cummings	F	6-9	235	26	5	DePaul
40	Jerome Henderson	C	6-11	230	28	1	New Mexico
15	Craig Hodges	G	6-3	190	27	5	Cal-Long Beach
10	John Lucas	G	6-3	185	34	11	Maryland
44	Paul Mokeski	C	7-0	250	30	8	Kansas
4	Sidney Moncrief	G	6-4	190	30	8	Arkansas
22	Ricky Pierce	G-F	6-5	205	28	5	Rice
25	Paul Pressey	G-F	6-5	200	28	5	Tulsa
35	Jerry Reynolds	F	6-9	198	24	2	Louisiana State
43	Jack Sikma	C	6-11	250	31	10	Illinois Wesleyan
11	Keith Smith	G	6-3	193	23	2	Loyola (Cal.)

Rd.	Top Rookies	Sel. No.	Pos.	Ht.	Wt.	College
2	Bob McCann	32	F	6-9	245	Morehead State
2	Winston Garland	40	G	6-2	180	SW Missouri State
3	J.J. Weber	64	F	6-7	230	Wisconsin
4	Darryl Bedford	87	F	6-8	270	Austin Peay
5	Brian Vaughns	110	F	6-8	220	Cal-Santa Barbara

ability to rebound as Kevin McHale and Robert Parish played volleyball on the glass. Sikma pulled down 10 a night to really save the Bucks from total board embarrassment, but Paul Mokeski and Randy Breuer just aren't the answer to this team's woes. Management is hoping that 6-9, 245-pound second-round draft pick Bob McCann (11.3 rpg for Morehead State) can grab his fair share.

OUTLOOK: Is there life after Don Nelson? The heart and the soul of the franchise was driven out by Buck owner Herb Kohl in a bitter battle. Now, it's up to Del Harris to keep the Bucks' winning tradition alive. They had captured six straight Central Division titles before finishing third last season. This is definitely a team in decline.

There will be two straight years with no No. 1 pick and team leader, Sidney Moncrief, is cursed by sore knees. With young turks like the Pistons and Hawks charging through the division, plus the improving Pacers, Bulls and Cavs, it's not going to be easy for Harris. Nelson, always one step ahead of the competition, may have gotten out while the gettin' was good.

Terry Cummings gives Bucks an inside track.

BUCK PROFILES

TERRY CUMMINGS 26 6-9 235   Forward

One of the best forwards—inside or out—he led Bucks in scoring, steals and minutes played while ranking second in rebounds, blocks and field-goal percentage...But there's more to his life than basketball...He's an ordained Pentecostal minister, husband, father, singer, musician, businessman and a true-blue role model...One of 13 kids, he made it out of a ghetto in Chicago, where he was born March 15, 1962...Deadly medium-range jumper who loves to go to the hoop from right to left...Won Rookie-of-the-Year honors in 1982-83...Another Clipper mistake...Taken No. 2 by that sorry ship, out of DePaul, but was dealt away with Craig Hodges and Ricky Pierce for Marques Johnson, Junior Bridgeman and Harvey Catchings prior to 1984-85...Did extremely well against Celtics in playoffs, but one or two clutch baskets in Game 7 would have carried Bucks home...Will earn $1.3 million this season.

Year	Team	G	FG	FG Pct.	FT	FT Pct.	Reb.	Ast.	TP	Avg.
1982-83	San Diego	70	684	.523	292	.709	744	177	1660	23.7
1983-84	San Diego	81	737	.494	380	.720	777	139	1854	22.9
1984-85	Milwaukee	79	759	.495	343	.741	716	228	1861	23.6
1985-86	Milwaukee	82	681	.474	265	.656	694	193	1627	19.8
1986-87	Milwaukee	82	729	.511	249	.662	700	229	1707	20.8
	Totals	394	3590	.499	1529	.700	3631	966	8709	22.1

PAUL PRESSEY 28 6-5 200   Forward-Guard

He is to the Bucks what beer and bratwurst are to Milwaukee...He's so good, Don Nelson invented a new position for him, "point forward."...One of the finest all-around players, he has to be the most invaluable 13.9 ppg scorer in the league...Dislocated his ring finger in January...Without him Bucks were 8-13...When he was in the lineup, record was 42-19...If he had not fouled out against Celtics in final minutes of Game 7, Nelson would have coached at least one more series in Milwaukee...Bucks drafted him 20th overall in 1982 out of Tulsa...Born Christmas Eve, 1958, in Norfolk, Va....Extremely mobile and has tentacles for arms...Two-time first-team All-Defense...Should be on it every year...Improved in all the important categories last season...And to think, he was cut from his high-school team as a soph and couldn't play his senior year because he was too old.

Year	Team	G	FG	FG Pct.	FT	FT Pct.	Reb.	Ast.	TP	Avg.
1982-83	Milwaukee............	79	213	.457	105	.597	281	207	532	6.7
1983-84	Milwaukee............	81	276	.523	120	.600	282	252	674	8.3
1984-85	Milwaukee..........	80	480	.517	317	.758	429	543	1284	16.1
1985-86	Milwaukee..........	80	411	.488	316	.806	399	623	1146	14.3
1986-87	Milwaukee..........	61	294	.477	242	.738	296	441	846	13.9
	Totals.............	381	1674	.495	1100	.727	1687	2066	4482	11.8

RICKY PIERCE 28 6-5 205   Guard-Forward

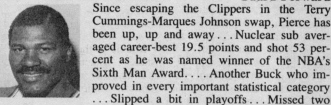

Since escaping the Clippers in the Terry Cummings-Marques Johnson swap, Pierce has been up, up and away... Nuclear sub averaged career-best 19.5 points and shot 53 percent as he was named winner of the NBA's Sixth Man Award.... Another Buck who improved in every important statistical category ... Slipped a bit in playoffs... Missed two big shots down the stretch in Game 7... Born Aug. 19, 1959, in Garland, Tex.... Pistons let · him get away... After picking Rice product 18th in 1982 draft, he was traded to Clippers for a pair of second-round draft picks in 1983... Explosive middle- and long-range jump shooter, although three-pointer is a step out of his range... Wife, Joyce, was a member of the Fifth Dimension.

Year	Team	G	FG	FG Pct.	FT	FT Pct.	Reb.	Ast.	TP	Avg.
1982-83	Detroit.............	39	33	.375	18	.563	35	14	85	2.2
1983-84	San Diego..........	69	268	.470	149	.861	135	60	685	9.9
1984-85	Milwaukee..........	44	165	.537	102	.823	117	94	433	9.8
1985-86	Milwaukee..........	81	429	.538	266	.858	231	177	1127	13.9
1986-87	Milwaukee..........	79	575	.534	387	.880	266	144	1540	19.5
	Totals.............	312	1470	.518	922	.854	784	489	3870	12.4

JOHN LUCAS 34 6-3 185   Guard

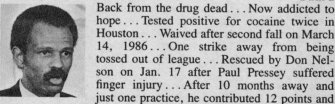

Back from the drug dead... Now addicted to hope... Tested positive for cocaine twice in Houston... Waived after second fall on March 14, 1986... One strike away from being tossed out of league... Rescued by Don Nelson on Jan. 17 after Paul Pressey suffered finger injury... After 10 months away and just one practice, he contributed 12 points and seven assists in 20 minutes of play first game out... A classic coast-to-coast driver who made the Bucks into an up-tempo team ... In addition, his wheeling, free-form drives to the hoop opened up the inside... Great at kicking the ball out to Bucks'

deadly outside shooters... Wound up third on team in scoring (17.5) and added nearly seven assists a night... Born Oct 31, 1953, in Durham, N.C.... Rockets made him No. 1 pick in the 1976 draft out of Maryland... This is his sixth and last NBA stop... Lucas knows it's a battle every day to stay clean.

Year	Team	G	FG	FG Pct.	FT	FT Pct.	Reb.	Ast.	TP	Avg.
1976-77	Houston...........	82	388	.477	135	.789	219	463	911	11.1
1977-78	Houston...........	82	412	.435	193	.772	255	768	1017	12.4
1978-79	Golden State.......	82	530	.462	264	.822	247	762	1324	16.1
1979-80	Golden State.......	80	388	.467	222	.768	220	.602	1010	12.6
1980-81	Golden State.......	66	222	.439	107	.738	154	464	555	8.4
1981-82	Washington.........	79	263	.426	138	.784	166	551	666	8.4
1982-83	Washington.........	35	62	.473	21	.500	29	102	145	4.1
1983-84	San Antonio.........	63	275	.462	120	.764	180	673	689	10.9
1984-85	Houston...........	47	206	.462	103	.798	85	318	536	11.4
1985-86	Houston...........	65	365	.446	231	.775	143	571	1006	15.5
1986-87	Milwaukee..........	43	285	.457	137	.787	125	290	753	17.5
	Totals............	724	3396	.454	1671	.776	1823	5564	8612	11.9

SIDNEY MONCRIEF 30 6-4 190　　　　　Guard

A pro's pro... Played in just 39 games due to recurring knee problems and had the worst year of his career, but came back strong in the playoffs... Scored a career-playoff high 34 points in Game 5 vs. Celtics, the only game the Bucks won in Boston... After averaging 11.8 in regular season, almost seven points under his career average, he came back to score 19.4 a night in postseason... Twice named Defensive Player of the Year... Such a team leader that he traveled with Bucks even when he was on injured list... Entered the NBA as a classic "tweener" with a suspect shooting touch, but worked to become a fine jump-shooter... A tremendous post-up guard... Starts collecting $1.4 million in deferred payments this season ... Bright, articulate... Sits on board of directors for gas company.... Bucks drafted him No. 5 overall in 1979, out of Arkansas... Born Sept. 21, 1957, in Little Rock, Ark.... Active in many charitable organizations.

Year	Team	G	FG	FG Pct.	FT	FT Pct.	Reb.	Ast.	TP	Avg.
1979-80	Milwaukee..........	77	211	.468	232	.795	338	133	654	8.5
1980-81	Milwaukee..........	80	400	.541	320	.804	406	264	1122	14.0
1981-82	Milwaukee..........	80	556	.523	468	.817	534	382	1581	19.8
1982-83	Milwaukee..........	76	606	.524	499	.826	437	300	1712	22.5
1983-84	Milwaukee..........	79	560	.498	529	.848	528	358	1654	20.9
1984-85	Milwaukee..........	73	561	.483	454	.828	391	382	1585	21.7
1985-86	Milwaukee..........	73	470	.489	498	.859	334	357	1471	20.2
1986-87	Milwaukee..........	39	158	.488	136	.840	127	121	460	11.8
	Totals............	577	3522	.504	3136	.829	3095	2297	10239	17.7

JACK SIKMA 31 6-1 250 Center

The big gamble . . . Bucks made monster deal with Sonics prior to the start of last season, giving up Alton Lister and two No. 1 picks for center, in effort to plug hole in the middle . . . Was a disappointment in regular season but did well in playoffs . . . Known for his unique drop-back shot, which hardly ever gets blocked . . . As fate would have it, he did get rejected by Robert Parish in pivotal play of Game 7 . . . Decided to let ball bounce out of bounds and Dennis Johnson flew in and knocked it off his leg . . . Extremely durable, has missed only 23 games in 10 years and has played all 82 seven times . . . Very solid defensive rebounder and one of the better pivot passers of the last decade . . . The steal of the 1977 draft, when Sonics made him No. 8 overall out of Illinois Wesleyan . . . Born Nov. 14, 1955, in Kankakee, Ill. . . . Was foundation of Seattle franchise, where he anchored their championship team . . . Only thing that's changed over the years is his haircut . . . His $1.6-million salary is among league's elite.

Year	Team	G	FG	FG Pct.	FT	FT Pct.	Reb.	Ast.	TP	Avg.
1977-78	Seattle	82	342	.455	192	.777	678	134	876	10.7
1978-79	Seattle	82	476	.460	329	.814	1013	261	1281	15.6
1979-80	Seattle	82	470	.475	235	.805	908	279	1175	14.3
1980-81	Seattle	82	595	.454	340	.823	852	248	1530	18.7
1981-82	Seattle	82	581	.454	447	.855	1038	277	1611	19.6
1982-83	Seattle	75	484	.464	400	.837	858	233	1368	18.2
1983-84	Seattle	82	576	.499	411	.856	911	327	1563	19.1
1984-85	Seattle	68	461	.489	335	.852	723	285	1259	18.5
1985-86	Seattle	80	508	.462	355	.864	748	301	1371	17.1
1986-87	Milwaukee	82	390	.463	265	.847	822	203	1045	12.7
	Totals	797	4883	.470	3309	.837	8551	2548	13079	16.4

CRAIG HODGES 27 6-3 190 Guard

Paid the price when John Lucas arrived on the scene . . . Lost minutes and his role . . . Never complained, never stopped giving 100 percent . . . That's typical of the work and life ethic of this three-point shooting whiz . . . After a Milwaukee teenager was shot and killed last year, he started self-help program Operation Unite: Save Our Youth . . . Points and field-goal percentage (two and three-point) took a tumble last season . . . But made a career-high 85 three-point baskets . . . He personally hit more three-point baskets than seven teams . . . Another one of those quality players plucked away from the Clippers in the infamous 1984 trade . . . A lot of strength in little frame . . . Born June

27, 1960, in Park Forest, Ill. . . . Mother marched with Dr. Martin Luther King . . . Drafted No. 48 overall by Clippers in 1982 out of Cal State-Long Beach . . . Went to the basket more last season and wound up fifth in the league in free-throw percentage.

Year	Team	G	FG	FG Pct.	FT	FT Pct.	Reb.	Ast.	TP	Avg.
1982-83	San Diego	76	318	.452	94	.723	122	275	750	9.9
1983-84	San Diego	76	258	.450	66	.750	86	116	592	7.8
1984-85	Milwaukee	82	359	.490	106	.815	186	349	871	10.6
1985-86	Milwaukee	66	284	.500	75	.872	117	229	716	10.8
1986-87	Milwaukee	78	315	.462	131	.891	140	240	846	10.8
	Totals	378	1534	.471	472	.812	651	1209	3775	10.0

RANDY BREUER 27 7-3 230   Center

What's 7-3 and invisible? . . . Before Don Nelson left town he said he had "lost Breuer . . . his progress stopped this season." . . . That's bad news for the giant who averaged 7.9 points and 4.6 rebounds . . . Hard to believe he started 63 games two years ago . . . Had a 17-point, 13-rebound six-assist game against Houston . . . Slid from 116 blocks in 1985-86 to 76 in only six fewer games last season . . . Bucks were hoping to get second coming or at least a second-class Kevin McHale when they drafted him 18th overall out of Minnesota in 1983 . . . Born Oct. 11, 1960, in Lake City, Minn. . . . Goes home in the offseason to work on the farm.

Year	Team	G	FG	FG Pct.	FT	FT Pct.	Reb.	Ast.	TP	Avg.
1983-84	Milwaukee	57	68	.384	32	.696	109	17	168	2.9
1984-85	Milwaukee	78	162	.511	89	.701	256	40	413	5.3
1985-86	Milwaukee	82	272	.477	141	.712	458	114	685	8.4
1986-87	Milwaukee	76	241	.485	118	.584	350	47	600	7.9
	Totals	293	743	.476	380	.663	1173	218	1866	6.4

PAUL MOKESKI 30 7-0 250   Center

A seven-foot speed bag . . . Worked over his eight years in the league by press and opponents, he had the most difficult season of his career because he was implicated in Phoenix drug probe . . . Tearfully broke down in press conference, saying, "I didn't do anything wrong, I hope you believe me." . . . His two free throws sent Game 3 of Celtic series to overtime . . . Will make $350,000 this season . . . Knee problems severely hampered whatever mobility he had . . . Spent four seasons in Milwaukee after bouncing from Houston to Detroit to

Cleveland in first four seasons . . . Averages a personal foul every 5.6 minutes . . . Drafted 42nd overall by Rockets in 1979 out of Kansas . . . Born Jan. 3, 1957, in Spokane, Wash. . . . Was once guest conductor of Milwaukee symphony . . . Journalism grad . . . Father, Cass, played basketball at University of Detroit and Gonzaga.

Year	Team	G	FG	FG Pct.	FT	FT Pct.	Reb.	Ast.	TP	Avg.
1979-80	Houston.	12	11	.333	7	.778	29	2	29	2.4
1980-81	Detroit.	80	224	.489	120	.600	418	135	568	7.1
1981-82	Det.-Clev.	67	84	.435	48	.762	208	35	216	3.2
1982-83	Clev.-Mil.	73	119	.458	50	.735	260	49	288	3.9
1983-84	Milwaukee.	68	102	.479	50	.694	166	44	255	3.8
1984-85	Milwaukee.	79	205	.478	81	.698	410	99	491	6.2
1985-86	Milwaukee.	45	59	.424	25	.735	139	30	143	3.2
1986-87	Milwaukee.	62	52	.403	46	.719	138	22	150	2.4
	Totals.	486	856	.462	427	.682	1768	416	2140	4.4

JEROME HENDERSON 28 6-11 230   Center

Literally came from nowhere and everywhere . . . One of only two players on league roster at end of season who was not drafted by an NBA or ABA team . . . The other is Dennis Nutt of Dallas . . . Appeared in six games with Bucks after signing on April 3 . . . Averaged 1.8 points and 2.2 rebounds . . . Prior to joining the Bucks he had played only one other NBA game, in 1985-86 with the Lakers . . . Holds the CBA record for blocks in a playoff game with 10 . . . Has seen the world, thanks to basketball . . . Played in the Phillipines, Mexico and Turkey and throughout CBA . . . Born Oct. 5, 1959, in Los Angeles. . . . Played two seasons at University of New Mexico before deciding to skip final year of eligibility.

Year	Team	G	FG	FG Pct.	FT	FT Pct.	Reb.	Ast.	TP	Avg.
1985-86	L.A. Lakers.	1	2	.667	0	.000	1	0	4	4.0
1986-87	Milwaukee.	6	4	.308	4	1.000	7	0	12	2.0
	Totals.	7	6	.375	4	1.000	8	0	16	2.3

DUDLEY BRADLEY 30 6-6 195   Guard

Your basic NBA survivor . . . He's been in the league seven years, so he must be doing something right . . . Defense has been his saving grace . . . At North Carolina he was twice named the Tar Heels' top defensive player and he has carried that piece of luggage known as "D" to Indiana, Phoenix, Chicago, the CBA, Washington and now Milwaukee . . . Played in

68 games for Bucks and averaged 1.5 steals per outing, despite playing just 13 minutes a game...For third straight year he was in select group of players who had more steals (105) than turnovers (34)...Has sociology degree...Brother of former Celtic Charles Bradley...Pacers drafted him 13th overall in 1979...Born March 19, 1957, in Baltimore...Can also shoot the three-pointer, although it took four years for anyone to discover that fact.

Year	Team	G	FG	FG Pct.	FT	FT Pct.	Reb.	Ast.	TP	Avg.
1979-80	Indiana............	82	275	.452	136	.782	223	252	688	8.4
1980-81	Indiana............	82	265	.474	125	.702	193	188	657	8.0
1981-82	Phoenix............	64	125	.445	74	.740	87	80	325	5.1
1982-83	Chicago............	58	82	.516	36	.800	105	106	201	3.5
1984-85	Washington.........	73	142	.475	54	.684	134	173	358	4.9
1985-86	Washington.........	70	73	.349	32	.571	95	107	195	2.8
1986-87	Milwaukee..........	68	76	.357	47	.810	102	66	212	3.1
	Totals............	497	1038	.446	504	.730	939	972	2636	5.3

JERRY REYNOLDS 24 6-8 198   Forward

DNP-CD...That's box score shorthand for "Did not play—coach's decision"...His nickname "Ice" has taken on a whole new meaning...Departure of Don Nelson could bring about a warming trend...Started 21 games during first half of the season, averaging 8.4 points, but then fell into Nelson's doghouse and off the edge of the earth...Was drafted 22nd overall in 1985 out of LSU following junior season ...Streak shooter was All-SEC...Born Dec. 23, 1962, in Brooklyn, N.Y....Played a total of five minutes in playoffs... Will make $180,000 this year, whether he sits out or not...Have to think, though, that somebody could use swingman's talents.

Year	Team	G	FG	FG Pct.	FT	FT Pct.	Reb.	Ast.	TP	Avg.
1985-86	Milwaukee..........	55	72	.444	58	.558	80	86	203	3.7
1986-87	Milwaukee..........	58	140	.393	118	.641	173	106	404	7.0
	Totals............	113	212	.409	176	.611	253	192	607	5.4

TOP ROOKIE

BOB McCANN 23 6-9 245   Forward

A Wayman Tisdale clone...Led Morehead State in scoring (18.6) and rebounding (11.3)...Only player to lead Ohio Valley Conference in rebounding three straight seasons...Taken in second round, 32nd pick overall . . . Born April 22, 1964, in Morristown, N.J. . . . Biggest Morehead State grad since Giants' QB Phil Simms . . . Signed to play at Division III Upsala College in New Jersey after graduating from high school, but grew three inches as a freshman and transferred to Morehead State.

COACH DEL HARRIS: Has big shoes to fill . . . Not to mention how does he look in a fish tie? . . . Signed three-year deal, succeeding Don Nelson in June after Nellie left to become part-owner of the Golden State Warriors following bitter feud with Bucks' owner Herb Kohl . . . Harris coached the Houston Rockets from 1979-83, compiling a 141-187 record . . . His playoff mark was 15-18 and his 1980-81 team set an NBA playoff record for most victories on the road with eight . . . That team won the Western Conference title before losing in the finals to Boston . . . "I would rather follow where success has been established and it can be more easily attained than trying to get some dog to wake up," Harris says . . . He began scouting for the Bucks in 1983 and left in March 1986 to pursue head-coaching jobs . . . Rejoined Bucks prior to start of last season . . . Born June 18, 1937, in Orleans, Ind. . . . Graduated from Milligan (Tenn.) College and went on to earn his master's degree at Indiana . . . Has come up through the ranks . . . Compiled a 176-70 mark at Earlham College in Richmond, Ind. . . . Coached the Bayama Cowboys in Puerto Rico from 1969-75, winning three national titles . . . Will open up the floor with Bucks . . . Did excellent job in Game 5 victory over Philadelphia after Nelson was ejected . . . Possesses a calm, gentlemanly manner.

GREATEST COACH

Milwaukee is the only team Don Nelson has ever coached. And he has been the only coach besides Larry Costello to roam the Buck sideline. Costello won a championship in 1971, but he rode Kareem Abdul-Jabbar to the title.

Irreconcilable differences with owner Herbert Kohl led to Nellie's resignation last May and a new challenge with the Golden State Warriors, but the 6-foot-6 Nelson can stand tall on his record.

In his 10 seasons with the Bucks, he was 540-344 and he won

seven straight division championships. His 50-win season last year made it seven in a row that he won 50 or more games. He reached 500 career wins faster than any coach in NBA history, and his winning percentage of .610 is the sixth best of all time.

A superior strategist and the highest-paid coach in the league at $400,000 annually, Nelson was twice Coach of the Year—1983 and 1985—and he left Milwaukee still yearning for his first NBA championship ring as coach after winning five as a forward with the Boston Celtics.

He proved himself as more than a coach and ex-player. The 47-year-old native of Muskegon, Mich., and Iowa State alumnus became a champion of the farmer in Wisconsin in the summer of 1986 when he organized Nellie's Farm Fund. He raised funds for distressed farmers by getting donors to pledge money for each of the 50 pounds he dropped from a robust 272. And his cross-state tractor ride dramatically increased public awareness of the farm crisis.

ALL-TIME BUCK LEADERS

SEASON

Points: Kareem Abdul-Jabbar, 2,822, 1971-72
Assists: Oscar Robertson, 668, 1970-71
Rebounds: Kareem Abdul-Jabbar, 1,346, 1971-72

GAME

Points: Kareem Abdul-Jabbar, 55 vs. Boston, 12/10/71
Assists: Guy Rodgers, 22 vs. Detroit, 10/31/68
Rebounds: Swen Nater, 33 vs. Atlanta, 12/19/76

CAREER

Points: Kareem Abdul-Jabbar, 14,211, 1969-75
Assists: Brian Winters, 2,479, 1975-83
Rebounds: Kareem Abdul-Jabbar, 7,161, 1969-75

NEW JERSEY NETS

TEAM DIRECTORY: Chairman: Alan Aufzien; Vice Chairman Exec. Committee: David Gerstein; Pres.: Bernie Mann; Exec. VP-Chief Operating Officer: Bob Casciola; Dir. Player Personnel: Al Menendez; Asst. GM: Bob MacKinnon; Dir. Pub. Rel.: Jim Lampariello; Coach: Dave Wohl; Asst. Coaches: Bob Wenzl, Gary St. Jean. Arena: Brendan Byrne Meadowlands Arena (20,149). Colors: Red, white and blue.

Nets expect to rebound behind Buck Williams.

SCOUTING REPORT

SHOOTING: The shooting goes down as the injuries go up. Field-goal percentage dropped for the third straight season, to .476, 12th best in the league. Two of the biggest reasons for the decline were injuries to Darryl Dawkins, who played in only six games, and Otis Birdsong, seven games. Without them the load was put on center Mike Gminski, who physically could not handle it. G-Man went from .517 to .457.

Throw in the continuing decline and fall of Albert King (.426), Leon Wood's horrid performance (.373) and you have big problems from the floor. Only the addition of Orlando Woolridge (.521) and the dramatic improvement of Buck Williams (.523 to .557) kept the Nets from falling to the bottom of the pack. Top pick Dennis Hopson, the Big Ten's all-time leading scorer, will be like manna from heaven for this team.

PLAYMAKING: The backcourt was a fiasco from the start. Rookie Dwayne (Pearl) Washington couldn't find his way to the Meadowlands the day he was introduced to the media and was lost the entire season. Washington spent most of his time sitting around in Dave Wohl's doghouse getting fat.

As for his backup, just three years into his career, Wood is, at best, a journeyman and offers little help. Only six teams in the league totaled less assists than the Nets. Micheal Ray Richardson, please call home.

DEFENSE: This is another area where the loss of Dawkins was crucial. Opponents constantly attacked the soft underbelly of the Nets' interior. At least when the 6-11 Dawkins was around, those who dared drive to the basket took the chance of being driven into the floor.

For years now the Nets have been getting hammered at the small forward position. Mike O'Koren, their only defensive-minded small forward was dealt for Wood, which made it even easier to score against them. Woolridge is an easy touch and swingman King never has played defense. Washington is a defensive gambler and his 92 steals did lead the team by a wide margin.

The bottom line: Opponents shot 48 percent as the Nets sur-

NET ROSTER

No.	Veteran	Pos.	Ht.	Wt.	Age	Yrs. Pro	College
2	James Bailey	F-C	6-9	220	30	8	Rutgers
10	Otis Birdsong	G	6-4	190	31	10	Houston
35	Tony Brown	G	6-6	195	27	3	Arkansas
40	Ben Coleman	F	6-9	235	26	1	Maryland
53	Darryl Dawkins	C	6-11	260	30	12	None
50	Chris Engler	C	7-0	248	28	5	Wyoming
42	Mike Gminski	C	6-11	260	28	7	Duke
55	* Albert King	F-G	6-6	190	27	6	Maryland
12	Kevin McKenna	G-F	6-6	195	28	5	Creighton
30	* Jeff Turner	F	6-9	225	25	3	Vanderbilt
1	Dwayne Washington	G	6-2	205	23	1	Syracuse
52	Buck Williams	F	6-8	215	27	6	Maryland
13	* Ray Williams	G	6-3	195	33	10	Minnesota
33	Leon Wood	G	6-3	190	25	3	Cal-Fullerton
0	Orlando Woolridge	F	6-9	215	27	6	Notre Dame

*Free agent unsigned at press time

Rd.	Top Rookies	Sel. No.	Pos.	Ht.	Wt.	College
1	Dennis Hopson	3	G	6-5	200	Ohio State
2	Jamie Waller	48	G	6-4	210	Virginia Union
4	Andrew Moten	72	G	6-0	175	Florida
5	James Blackmon	94	G	6-3	175	Kentucky
6	Perry Bromwell	118	G	6-1	175	Penn

rendered 113 points a night and only scored 108, a five-point hole.

REBOUNDING: Charles Linwood (Buck) Williams was born to rebound. After falling short of 1,000 rebounds the first time in his career the year before, Williams stormed back to grab 1,023 last season, an average of 12.5 a game. Williams was the third-best rebounder in the league. Gminski (630) and Woolridge (367) held their own up front and Tony Brown gave the Nets a lift from the backcourt, hauling in 219 rebounds.

OUTLOOK: Last season was one for the books, the medical books. There were 252 man-games missed due to injuries as the Nets finished with the second-worst record (24-58) in their history. Washington has to play hard and prove his critics wrong. Hopson, the rookie, has to be his smooth self and, most of all, Dawkins has to avoid slipping in the shower. Then the Nets will climb out of their black hole.

NET PROFILES

DARRYL DAWKINS 30 6-11 260   Center

Slip-slidin' away . . . His career could be over after falling in shower and suffering back injury for third straight season . . . On Nov. 11, two days before the accident, he made seven of eight shots from the field as Nets upset Celtics . . . Played in just six games, averaging 9.5 points and 3.1 rebounds . . . Had second back operation in February . . . Earned $858,000 last season and became a free agent, but if he can play it will be for one final payday . . . Born Jan. 11, 1957, in Orlando, Fla. . . . Nets desperately missed his defensive presence in the middle and simply could not win without him . . . Drafted out of high school as No. 5 pick overall by Philadelphia in 1975 . . . Dealt to Nets for first-round pick and cash prior to 1982-83 season . . . Would someday like to open summer camps for children . . . Says he comes from the planet Lovetron.

Year	Team	G	FG	FG Pct.	FT	FT Pct.	Reb.	Ast.	TP	Avg.
1975-76	Philadelphia	37	41	.500	8	.333	49	3	90	2.4
1976-77	Philadelphia	59	135	.628	40	.506	230	24	310	5.3
1977-78	Philadelphia	70	332	.575	156	.709	555	85	820	11.7
1978-79	Philadelphia	78	430	.517	158	.672	631	128	1018	13.1
1979-80	Philadelphia	80	494	.522	190	.653	693	149	1178	14.7
1980-81	Philadelphia	76	423	.607	219	.720	545	109	1065	14.0
1981-82	Philadelphia	48	207	.564	114	.695	305	55	528	11.0
1982-83	New Jersey	81	401	.599	166	.646	420	114	968	12.0
1983-84	New Jersey	81	507	.593	341	.735	541	123	1357	16.8
1984-85	New Jersey	39	192	.566	143	.711	181	45	527	13.5
1985-86	New Jersey	51	284	.644	210	.707	251	77	778	15.3
1986-87	New Jersey	6	20	.625	17	.708	19	2	57	9.5
	Totals	706	3466	.573	1762	.688	4420	914	8696	12.3

ORLANDO WOOLRIDGE 27 6-9 215   Forward

Soft as Jello . . . Nice stats, but have to see him every night to learn not to appreciate him . . . Nickname is "O", not "D" . . . Nets signed free agent to $900,000-a-year contract last fall after Chicago received 1987 first-round pick and 1988 and 1990 No. 2s as compensation . . . No. 1 pick shifted to 1988 because Nets fell into lottery . . . Obviously Dave Wohl was smart enough to realize Woolridge wouldn't turn Nets around by himself . . . Averaged team-high 20.7 points (same as year before)

and 4.8 rebounds . . . First Net forward to average 20 since Bernard King did it in 1978-79 . . . Should take some lessons in toughness, though, from cousin Willis Reed . . . Born Dec. 16, 1959, in Mansfield, La. . . . Bulls drafted him sixth overall in 1981 after brilliant career at Notre Dame.

Year	Team	G	FG	FG Pct.	FT	FT Pct.	Reb.	Ast.	TP	Avg.
1981-82	Chicago	75	202	.513	144	.699	227	81	548	7.3
1982-83	Chicago	57	361	.580	217	.638	298	97	939	16.5
1983-84	Chicago	75	570	.525	303	.715	369	136	1444	19.3
1984-85	Chicago	77	679	.554	409	.785	435	135	1767	22.9
1985-86	Chicago	70	540	.495	364	.788	350	213	1448	20.7
1986-87	New Jersey	75	556	.521	438	.777	367	261	1551	20.7
	Totals	429	2908	.530	1875	.745	2046	923	7697	17.9

TONY BROWN 27 6-6 195   Guard

I-have-a-dream guy . . . Waived by four NBA teams and spent two years slogging around CBA, Brown has now found a home in the Meadowlands . . . Signed by the Pacers prior to 1984-85 after competing in "Walter Mitty" tryout camp . . . Your typical physical Arkansas guard . . . Tough rebounder . . . Stepped in for Nets after Otis Birdsong went down seven games into season . . . Went on to average 11.3 points, including a 29-point night against Knicks . . . Career high in college was 24 . . . Originally drafted by Jersey in fourth round (No. 82 overall) . . . Waived by Nets, Pistons (twice), Indiana and Chicago . . . Born July 29, 1960, in Chicago . . . A streaky shooter, he is better suited for 15 minutes a night instead of 30 minutes he got last season.

Year	Team	G	FG	FG Pct.	FT	FT Pct.	Reb.	Ast.	TP	Avg.
1984-85	Indiana	82	214	.460	116	.678	288	159	544	6.6
1985-86	Chicago	10	18	.439	9	.692	16	14	45	4.5
1986-87	New Jersey	77	358	.442	152	.738	219	259	873	11.3
	Totals	169	590	.448	277	.710	523	432	1462	8.7

BUCK WILLIAMS 27 6-8 215   Forward

Ultimate party animal on the boards . . . After failing to grab 1,000 rebounds for first time in career two years ago, he came back to haul down 1,023 last season . . . Shooting percentage went from .523 to .557 . . . Averaged 18 points a game . . . A terrible passer . . . Nobody's perfect . . . Contract was redone and now he earns $1.5 million a season . . . Worth every penny... One of the game's classiest individuals... One of few Nets to stay in touch with Micheal Ray Richardson... Brother drowned at an early age and Buck devoted his life to his memory... Born March 8, 1960, in Rocky Mount, N.C.... Only game missed in six seasons was because of league-imposed sanction by Scotty Stirling for fighting... Losing is beginning to wear him down... If he were on a contender, he would be one of best-known players in league.

Year	Team	G	FG	FG Pct.	FT	FT Pct.	Reb.	Ast.	TP	Avg.
1981-82	New Jersey.........	82	513	.582	242	.624	1005	107	1268	15.5
1982-83	New Jersey.........	82	536	.588	324	.620	1027	125	1396	17.0
1983-84	New Jersey.........	81	495	.535	284	.570	1000	130	1274	15.7
1984-85	New Jersey.........	82	577	.530	336	.625	1005	167	1491	18.2
1985-86	New Jersey.........	82	500	.523	301	.676	986	131	1301	15.9
1986-87	New Jersey.........	82	521	.557	430	.731	1023	129	1472	18.0
	Totals............	491	3142	.551	1917	.643	6046	789	8202	16.7

RAY WILLIAMS 33 6-3 195   Guard

Mr. Revolving Door... Second time around with Nets... Has been around Eighth Ave. twice with Knicks... Modeled five different uniforms in last three seasons... Did not join Nets until last third of the season because team said he had back problems... Made immediate impact in backcourt, giving stability and leadership... Why wasn't he signed sooner? ... Shot .452 from field after two straight years of 38 percent ... Loves animals... Has menagerie in his house... Nice kid who has gotten a bad rap... Would have been a great defensive back... Born Oct. 14, 1954, in Mt. Vernon, N.Y.... Drafted 10th overall in 1977 by Knicks out of Minnesota... Along with Micheal Ray Richardson was considered backcourt of the future ... Funny how things work out.

Year	Team	G	FG	FG Pct.	FT	FT Pct.	Reb.	Ast.	TP	Avg.
1977-78	New York..........	81	305	.443	146	.705	209	363	756	9.3
1978-79	New York..........	81	575	.457	251	.802	291	504	1401	17.3
1979-80	New York..........	82	687	.496	333	.787	412	512	1714	20.9
1980-81	New York..........	79	616	.461	312	.817	321	432	1560	19.7
1981-82	New Jersey.........	82	639	.462	387	.832	325	488	1674	20.4
1982-83	Kansas City........	72	419	.392	256	.769	327	569	1109	15.4
1983-84	New York..........	76	418	.445	263	.827	267	449	1124	14.8
1984-85	Boston............	23	55	.385	31	.674	57	90	147	6.4
1985-86	Atl.-S.A.-N.J.......	47	117	.382	115	.913	86	187	355	7.6
1986-87	New Jersey.........	32	131	.452	49	.817	75	185	318	9.9
	Totals............	655	3962	.451	2143	.802	2370	3779	10158	15.5

MIKE GMINSKI 28 6-11 260   Center

After years of abuse, fans have finally taken to him . . . G-Man's point production, 16.4, almost duplicated previous season, but field-goal percentage was worst in five years . . . In second year of two-year $4.6-million contract . . . Great guy to have a beer with . . . Wife, Stacy, is a stockbroker and marketing analyst . . . Gminski says, "She'll be moving into six figures just about time I'm moving out." . . . That won't be for some time because talented white centers can remain in NBA forever . . . Excellent passer . . . Handy off the court, too . . . Owns farm in upstate New York, which he helped rebuild . . . Dawkins' absence hurts him more than anyone because he is not built to be a 35-minute center . . . Born Aug. 3, 1959, in Monroe, Conn. . . . Would love to move across the river and play for Knicks.

Year	Team	G	FG	FG Pct.	FT	FT Pct.	Reb.	Ast.	TP	Avg.
1980-81	New Jersey	56	291	.423	155	.767	419	72	737	13.2
1981-82	New Jersey	64	119	.441	97	.822	186	41	335	5.2
1982-83	New Jersey	80	213	.500	175	.778	382	61	601	7.5
1983-84	New Jersey	82	237	.513	147	.799	433	92	621	7.6
1984-85	New Jersey	81	380	.465	276	.841	633	158	1036	12.8
1985-86	New Jersey	81	491	.517	351	.893	668	133	1333	16.5
1986-87	New Jersey	72	433	.457	313	.846	630	99	1179	16.4
	Totals	516	2164	.475	1514	.832	3351	656	5842	11.3

DWAYNE (PEARL) WASHINGTON 23 6-2 205   Guard

Nickname should be "Costume Jewelry" . . . Played more with knife and fork than ball and rim . . . No. 1 pick (13th overall) was major, major disappointment . . . Nets were duped into giving up Darwin Cook to Washington so Pudgy Pearl could be picked . . . All along, Washington wanted John Williams . . . Immediately entered Dave Wohl's doghouse when he came to camp a blimp . . . Needs to mature . . . Spent one game on the bench wearing a telephone beeper . . . Don't ask why . . . Born Jan. 6, 1964, in Brooklyn, N.Y. . . . Following outstanding career at Syracuse he played just 1,600 minutes for Nets . . . Led club in steals (92) . . . Averaged 8.6 points and 4.1 assists . . . Unofficially led league in getting his shots blocked . . . Has long, tough road ahead of him.

Year	Team	G	FG	FG Pct.	FT	FT Pct.	Reb.	Ast.	TP	Avg.
1986-87	New Jersey	72	257	.478	98	.784	129	301	616	8.6

ALBERT KING 27 6-6 190 Forward-Guard

Living example that nice guys finish last... Has world of talent but isn't tough enough... If he had brother Bernard's angry outlook, he'd be much better player... Was on contract merry-go-round before last season when his five-year, $3.3-million deal was shot down and had to settle for $650,000 for the season ...Four years in a row his shooting percentage has dropped...Not good enough ball-handler to play guard... Averaged career-low 9.5 points over 61 games... Once again nagging injuries cut his season short...Born Dec. 17, 1959, in Brooklyn, N.Y.... One of greatest high-school players in New York history...Nets drafted him 10th out of Maryland in 1981...Knicks wanted him two years ago. Nets hope they still do.

Year	Team	G	FG	FG Pct.	FT	FT Pct.	Reb.	Ast.	TP	Avg.
1981-82	New Jersey	76	391	.482	133	.778	312	142	918	12.1
1982-83	New Jersey	79	582	.475	176	.775	456	291	1346	17.0
1983-84	New Jersey	79	465	.492	232	.786	388	203	1165	14.7
1984-85	New Jersey	42	226	.491	85	.817	159	58	537	12.8
1985-86	New Jersey	73	438	.456	167	.823	366	181	1047	14.3
1986-87	New Jersey	61	244	.426	81	.810	214	103	582	9.5
	Totals	410	2346	.471	874	.795	1895	978	5595	13.6

LEON WOOD 25 6-3 190 Guard

Wrong-Way Wood... Point guard ran wrong play so often throughout season that at one point exasperated Dave Wohl wondered: "How many years would I get for manslaughter?" ...Will make $330,000 this season despite fact he has never shot better than 39 percent ...Drafted 10th overall by Sixers in 1984 but quickly disappointed and was dealt to Bullets for Kenny Green in January 1986...Nets picked him up as Pearl insurance for Mike O'Koren day before season...Born March 25, 1962, in Los Angeles...Starred at Cal State-Fullerton and won gold medal with U.S. Olympic team in 1984...Nice guy but hopefully he has banked much of his three-year contract because gravy train will run out soon.

Year	Team	G	FG	FG Pct.	FT	FT Pct.	Reb.	Ast.	TP	Avg.
1984-85	Philadelphia	38	50	.373	18	.692	18	45	122	3.2
1985-86	Phil.-Wash.	68	184	.395	123	.794	90	182	532	7.8
1986-87	New Jersey	76	187	.373	123	.799	120	370	557	7.3
	Totals	182	421	.382	264	.788	228	597	1211	6.7

OTIS BIRDSONG 31 6-4 190 Guard

Should wear a mask when he picks up his paycheck... Sometimes NBA owners need to have their heads examined... After missing 109 games last five seasons and getting $5 million, Nets re-signed Birdsong to a guaranteed $1.185-million deal over three years with a potential value of $2.25 million... Surprise, surprise, Otis then appeared in just seven games before complaining of leg woes and excusing himself for the season... Upset owners took the matter to court and stopped payment, saying Birdsong hid injury prior to signing... Case was dropped but then went to NBA arbitration... Birdsong does not like fans or most of the media... Kings chose him No. 2 overall in 1977 out of University of Houston... Born Dec. 9, 1955, in Winter Haven, Fla.... Sweet shooter those rare moments he does make it onto the court, unless, of course, he is on the foul line... Career 66 percent from charity stripe, so his misses were nicknamed Birdballs by teammates.

Year	Team	G	FG	FG Pct.	FT	FT Pct.	Reb.	Ast.	TP	Avg.
1977-78	Kansas City	73	470	.492	216	.697	175	174	1156	15.8
1978-79	Kansas City	82	741	.509	296	.725	354	281	1778	21.7
1979-80	Kansas City	82	781	.505	286	.694	331	202	1858	22.7
1980-81	Kansas City	71	710	.544	317	.697	258	233	1747	24.6
1981-82	New Jersey	37	225	.469	74	.583	97	124	524	14.2
1982-83	New Jersey	62	426	.511	82	.566	150	239	936	15.1
1983-84	New Jersey	69	583	.508	194	.608	170	266	1365	19.8
1984-85	New Jersey	56	495	.511	161	.622	148	232	1155	20.6
1985-86	New Jersey	77	542	.513	122	.581	202	261	1214	15.8
1986-87	New Jersey	7	19	.452	6	.667	7	17	44	6.3
	Totals	616	4992	.510	1754	.661	1892	2029	11777	19.1

JEFF TURNER 25 6-9 225 Forward

Bright, polite... Drafted No. 1 (17th overall) in 1984 because glint of his Olympic gold medal blinded Net owners... Management thought so little of him before the start of last season that they refused to pick up the option year on his contract worth $225,000... Allowed him to become a free agent and wound up saving themselves $75,000, signing him for $150,000... Dave Wohl likes his work ethic (you have to figure there is some reason he's playing) but not his production or his penchant for fouls... Beware, hacker at work... Commits a foul every 5.06 minutes... Born April 9, 1962, in Bangor, Me.... Bobby Knight kept him on Olympic team instead of

Charles Barkley...Looks like perfect Minnesota Timberwolf material.

Year	Team	G	FG	FG Pct.	FT	FT Pct.	Reb.	Ast.	TP	Avg.
1984-85	New Jersey.........	72	171	.454	79	.859	218	108	421	5.8
1985-86	New Jersey.........	53	84	.491	58	.744	137	14	226	4.3
1986-87	New Jersey.........	76	151	.465	76	.731	197	60	378	5.0
	Totals............	201	406	.465	213	.777	552	182	1025	5.1

JAMES BAILEY 30 6-9 220   Forward-Center

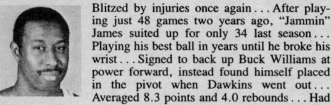

Blitzed by injuries once again...After playing just 48 games two years ago, "Jammin" James suited up for only 34 last season...Playing his best ball in years until he broke his wrist...Signed to back up Buck Williams at power forward, instead found himself placed in the pivot when Dawkins went out...Averaged 8.3 points and 4.0 rebounds...Had 35-point effort vs. Cleveland...Did not get along with Hubie Brown because hard-bitten coach constantly questioned his toughness...Fainted at least three times during his two-year tenure with Hubie...Can you blame him?...Earned $550,000 last season...Born May 25, 1957, in Dublin, Ga....Starred at Rutgers...This is his second go-round with Nets.

Year	Team	G	FG	FG Pct.	FT	FT Pct.	Reb.	Ast.	TP	Avg.
1979-80	Seattle.............	67	122	.450	68	.673	197	28	312	4.7
1980-81	Seattle.............	82	444	.499	256	.709	607	98	1145	14.0
1981-82	Sea.-N.J...........	77	261	.517	137	.612	391	65	659	8.6
1982-83	N.J.-Hou...........	75	385	.497	226	.702	474	67	996	13.3
1983-84	Houston...........	73	254	.491	138	.719	294	79	646	8.8
1984-85	New York...........	74	156	.447	73	.676	344	39	385	5.2
1985-86	New York...........	48	202	.456	129	.772	334	50	533	11.1
1986-87	New Jersey.........	34	112	.469	58	.725	137	20	282	8.3
	Totals............	530	1936	.486	1085	.698	2778	446	4958	9.4

BEN COLEMAN 26 6-9 235   Forward

We're talking mean...Rookie backup to Buck Williams made tremendous progress last season...Figures though—just what the Nets need, another power forward...One of the few bright spots, Coleman played in 68 games, shot 58 percent from the field...Pulled down 4.2 rebounds a night in limited duty...First NBA start scored 19 points, grabbed 12 rebounds vs. Philly...Plays well against quality opponents, especially Kevin McHale, because he is so strong and wide...Born Oct. 14, 1961, in Minneapolis, Minn....Drafted by Chicago in second round (37th overall) of 1984 draft out of Maryland . . . Was not coached well in college and needed to spend two years in Italy sharpening game and elbows . . . Signed as free agent before last season.

Year	Team	G	FG	FG Pct.	FT	FT Pct.	Reb.	Ast.	TP	Avg.
1986-87	New Jersey	68	182	.581	88	.727	288	37	452	6.6

TOP ROOKIE

DENNIS HOPSON 22 6-5 200   **Guard**

Nets think they got second-best player in the draft with third pick . . . Explosive Ohio State scorer, set single-season Big Ten scoring record with 958 points, averaging 29 a game . . . That's second-best in the country . . . Named Big Ten Player of the Year . . . "I've never coached anyone as talented as Dennis," said Buckeye coach Gary Williams . . . Born April 22, 1965, in Toledo, Ohio . . . Has all-around skills, averaging 8.2 rebounds and 3.6 assists.

COACH DAVE WOHL: Extremely intelligent, sometimes he thinks too much . . . Threatened to quit in middle of the season because team was not playing up to potential, a Net tradition . . . Burning desire to succeed under calm exterior . . . Easygoing away from the court . . . Injuries and Micheal Ray Richardson escapades have submarined him . . . Came down very hard on rookie Dwayne Washington, refusing to play him until new GM Harry Weltman ordered Pearl to play . . . Another in a long line of Nellie Worshippers . . . Was assistant for Don Nelson for three years at Milwaukee before becoming Pat Riley's aide in LA . . . Quite a comedown . . . Net owners adore him . . . One-year option was picked up last spring . . . Must win this season after compiling 63-101 mark first two years . . . Takes time to coach in "Special Olympics" during summer . . . Known as Captain Video during his LA days for tireless work with video tapes . . . Local boy makes good . . . Born Nov. 2, 1949, in Flushing, N.Y., then moved to New Jersey . . . Starred at East Brunswick High before moving onto the University of Pennsylvania . . . Has a degree in history . . . Seven-year NBA journeyman, whose playing career ended when he was waived by Nets.

GREATEST COACH

In two years he did more for the team than thought possible, but, some say, he did more harm than good.

One thing you can't dispute is the fact Larry Brown is a teacher of the first degree and for a short while he brought respect to a floundering franchise.

After the Nets posted a 24-58 season in 1980-81, Brown was hired away from UCLA. Motivating young players like Buck Williams and Albert King, Brown gobbled up 44 wins his first season. The next season the Nets were 47-29 and heading for the playoffs when Brown went out to visit Kansas. The moment owner Joe Taub found out, Brown was fired and all he had built was lost in a day.

Dazed and leaderless, the Nets lost four of the last six games and were wiped away in the first round of the playoffs by the Knicks. If Brown had stayed, this would have become one of the NBA's surging franchises.

The most successful season in Net history, however, belongs to Kevin Loughery. In 1973-74 Julius Erving arrived on the scene and the Nets went on to win the ABA championship.

Looking back over Loughery's career, he should have quit while he was ahead.

ALL-TIME NET LEADERS

SEASON

Points: Rick Barry, 2,518, 1971-72
Assists: Kevin Porter, 801, 1977-78
Rebounds: Billy Paultz, 1,035, 1971-72

GAME

Points: Julius Erving, 63 vs. San Diego (4 OT), 2/14/75
Assists: Kevin Porter, 29 vs. Houston, 2/24/78
Rebounds: Billy Paultz, 33 vs. Pittsburgh, 2/17/71

CAREER

Points: Buck Williams, 8,202, 1981-87
Assists: Billy Melchionni, 2,251, 1969-75
Rebounds: Buck Williams, 5,023, 1981-86

NEW YORK KNICKS

TEAM DIRECTORY: Pres.: Richard Evans; VP-GM: Al Bianchi; VP-Administration: Jack Diller; Dir. Administration: Hal Childs; Dir. Scouting Services: Dick McGuire; Dir. Communications: John Cirillo; Dir. Inf.: Carl Martin; Coach: Rick Pitino; Asst. Coach: Stu Jackson. Arena: Madison Square Garden (19,591). Colors: Orange, white and blue.

Bernard King is Knicks' ace in the brace.

KNICK ROSTER

No.	Veteran	Pos.	Ht.	Wt.	Age	Yrs. Pro	College
25	Bill Cartwright	C	7-1	245	30	8	San Francisco
42	Pat Cummings	F	6-9	230	31	8	Cincinnati
33	Patrick Ewing	C	7-0	240	25	2	Georgetown
7	Gerald Henderson	G	6-2	175	31	8	Va. Commonwealth
30	* Bernard King	F	6-7	207	30	10	Tennessee
14	Chris McNealy	F	6-7	215	26	2	San Jose State
44	Jawann Oldham	C	7-1	255	30	7	Seattle
55	Louis Orr	F	6-8	200	29	7	Syracuse
2	* Rory Sparrow	G	6-2	175	29	7	Villanova
23	Bob Thornton	F	6-10	225	25	2	Cal-Irvine
6	* Trent Tucker	G	6-5	190	27	5	Minnesota
34	Kenny Walker	F	6-8	210	23	1	Kentucky
45	Eddie Lee Wilkins	F-C	6-10	220	25	3	Gardner-Webb
21	Gerald Wilkins	G	6-6	185	24	2	Tenn.-Chattanooga
8	* Brad Wright	C	6-11	235	25	1	UCLA

*Free agent unsigned at press time

Rd.	Top Rookies	Sel. No.	Pos.	Ht.	Wt.	College
1	Mark Jackson	18	G	6-3	205	St. John's
2	Ron Moore	25	F	6-10	240	West Virginia State
3	Jerome Batiste	49	F	6-9	215	McNeese State
4	Mike Morgan	71	F	6-6	195	Drake
5	Glen Clem	95	F	6-6	195	Vanderbilt

SCOUTING REPORT

SHOOTING: Yuck! At .474, the sixth-worst in the league. And that contributed mightily to the fact the Knicks were the lowest-scoring team at 103.8. Worst than the numbers is the selection of shots. The Knicks just don't know how to work for a good shot. It's enough to make Bradley, DeBusschere, Reed, Frazier and Monroe burn their uniforms.

After years of being told what to do—and what they couldn't do—by Hubie Brown, they became shooting madmen. One teammate said giving the ball to Patrick Ewing was like sending it up in outer space to the black hole—it never came back.

Ewing (.503) and Bill Cartwright (.531), another shot-happy center, were the only two Knicks over .500. Gerald Wilkins was a very respectable .486 and is an emerging star. Kenny Walker has a suspect jumper and must make his points off the break.

Bernard King came back for the last six games and wound up leading the team in scoring at 22.7. Six games, however, do not a comeback make, but getting the former scoring ace back in the lineup would work wonders for the offense.

PLAYMAKING: A joke. Zero chemistry. That's why the drafting of St. John's point guard Mark Jackson was so important. Gerald Henderson is a nice player but he is not a lead guard. No one on the team passes well. The instincts just aren't there. Numbers backed up what the eyes saw. The Knicks were the second-worst team in the league in total assists.

DEFENSE: Brown was successful in this department because that's all he concentrated on. The ball was slowed to a snail's pace and the Knicks dug in on "D." Given the freedom to run by Bob Hill, defense was all but forgotten as the Knicks allowed 110 points a game.

Ewing does not yet comprehend NBA defense. Too often he gets caught on the perimeter going after jump shots instead of blocking out. Bill Cartwright is the league's worst defensive center and Wilkins does not stop anyone. Only malcontent Jawann Oldham has a concept of what defense is all about.

REBOUNDING: For the second straight year the Knicks were the worst rebounding team in the league. Ewing managed just 8.8 a game. Thirty-million-dollar ballplayers should be expected to get at least double-figure rebounds. He has to forget about the turnaround jumper and crash the boards.

Kenny Walker was supposed to help board up front but was bothered by a nagging back injury. No. 2 pick Ron Moore, who didn't rebound to his potential in college, is being counted on to give assistance.

OUTLOOK: After three straight Titanic seasons, a complete overhaul was done. GM Scotty Stirling and coach Bob Hill were fired the day after the season ended. A new team of GM Al Bianchi and coach Rick Pitino takes over and is expected to bring a stabilizing influence on Team Chaos. They have an overwhelming job to do, but there is talent. The players have to learn to be winners before they can win. Unselfishness must take the place of greed. And all that is easier said than done.

KNICK PROFILES

BILL CARTWRIGHT 30 7-1 245   Center

A hot commodity everywhere but New York ...After two years of being "Invisibill" because of four-time fractured left foot, he returned to play 58 games...However, a long way from being "Incredibill"...Averaged 17.5 points but did not care about any other aspect of the game...Terrible defensive player...Makes James Edwards look like Bill Russell...Can shoot free throws and turnaround jumper... Sulked when he was moved to forward and Patrick Ewing was put in the middle...Too slow, too heavy...On trade block but will earn more than $1 million, which makes him difficult to deal...Born July 30, 1957, in Folsom, Cal....Loves 50s and 60s music and baseball...Third pick overall in 1979 out of San Francisco.

Year	Team	G	FG	FG Pct.	FT	FT Pct.	Reb.	Ast.	TP	Avg.
1979-80	New York...........	82	665	.547	451	.797	726	165	1781	21.7
1980-81	New York...........	82	619	.554	408	.788	613	111	1646	20.1
1981-82	New York...........	72	390	.562	257	.763	421	87	1037	14.4
1982-83	New York...........	82	455	.566	380	.744	590	136	1290	15.7
1983-84	New York...........	77	453	.561	404	.805	649	107	1310	17.0
1984-85	New York...........					Injured				
1985-86	New York...........	2	3	.429	6	.600	10	5	12	6.0
1986-87	New York...........	58	335	.531	346	.790	445	96	1016	17.5
	Totals.............	455	2920	.553	2252	.781	3454	707	8092	17.8

BERNARD KING 30 6-7 207   Forward

Ego is as large as Empire State Building... Played in six games after sitting out two years with knee injury, then declared "I'm terrific" and was looking for new contract for over million a year...Took home $1.6 million two years he was injured...Angered teammates because he stayed away from practice and games...Won them over again when he stepped back on the court...Born Dec. 4, 1956, in Brooklyn, N.Y....Led Knicks in scoring in six games at 22.7...Italian food is his passion off the court...For years has quietly done charity work for parapalegics...Came to Knicks for Micheal Ray Richardson prior to 1982-83...Has meanest game face and quickest release in league...Little brother Albert lost in his shadow with Nets...Ex-scoring champ does not have explosiveness he once possessed and will never be that player again, but can still score mightily.

Year	Team	G	FG	FG Pct.	FT	FT Pct.	Reb.	Ast.	TP	Avg.
1977-78	New Jersey	79	798	.479	313	.677	751	193	1909	24.2
1978-79	New Jersey	82	710	.522	349	.564	669	295	1769	21.6
1979-80	Utah	19	71	.518	34	.540	88	52	176	9.3
1980-81	Golden State	81	731	.588	307	.703	551	287	1771	21.9
1981-82	Golden State	79	740	.566	352	.705	469	282	1833	23.2
1982-83	New York	68	603	.528	280	.722	326	195	1486	21.9
1983-84	New York	77	795	.572	437	.779	394	164	2027	26.3
1984-85	New York	55	691	.530	426	.772	317	204	1809	32.9
1985-86	New York					Injured				
1986-87	New York	6	52	.495	32	.744	32	19	136	22.7
	Totals	546	5191	.538	2530	.698	3597	1691	12916	23.7

PATRICK EWING 25 7-0 240   Center

Not exactly St. Patrick... Ability to withstand pain has to be questioned after missing 51 games first two seasons because of knee injuries... Hubie Brown was fired because he went to war with Patrick and lost... Moved by Brown to center and rebelled, forcing Hubie to put him back in pivot... Overall play a disappointment considering his $30-million contract... Field-goal percentage improved from .474 to .503 as he averaged 21.5 points... Former Rookie of the Year ... Born Aug. 5, 1962, in Kingston, Jamaica... Hates cold weather, loves reggae music... Top pick in 1985 lottery... Rebounding has been a disappointment... May wear prescription goggles this season... Exact opposite of Georgetown reputation ... May be too nice a guy... Needs to get angry on the court... Two years of losing has worn him down mentally... Will be a monster one day.

Year	Team	G	FG	FG Pct.	FT	FT Pct.	Reb.	Ast.	TP	Avg.
1985-86	New York	50	386	.474	226	.739	451	102	998	20.0
1986-87	New York	63	530	.503	296	.713	555	104	1356	21.5
	Totals	113	916	.491	522	.724	1006	206	2354	20.8

GERALD WILKINS 24 6-6 185   Guard

Dominique Who?... Most improved player on team... Increased output in every statistical category... Points went from 12.5 to 19.1, field-goal percentage from .468 to .486, free throws from .557 to .701... Most exciting player in the Garden... Along with brother Dominique of the Hawks, they became most productive single-season brother act in

NBA history... Sleeper in second round of 1985 draft, chosen 47th out of Tennessee-Chattanooga... Born Sept. 11, 1963, in Atlanta... Salary jumped from $70,000 to $300,000. Now wishes he signed for more... Big believer in positive thinking ... Meditates before games... Must learn to play defense... Bright, bright future as long as bright lights of city don't blind him.

Year	Team	G	FG	FG Pct.	FT	FT Pct.	Reb.	Ast.	TP	Avg.
1985-86	New York...........	81	437	.468	132	.557	208	161	1013	12.5
1986-87	New York...........	80	633	.486	235	.701	294	354	1527	19.1
	Totals.............	161	1070	.479	367	.642	502	515	2540	15.8

KENNY WALKER 23 6-8 210   Forward

The sky is falling... Nicknamed "Sky" because of his jumping ability but became so depressed by end of season he wanted to be called "Twilight" because he was stationed much of the time outside shooting zone... Highlight of rookie season was winning a harness race at Monticello Raceway... Born Aug. 18, 1964, in Roberta, Ga.... Back injury forced Kentucky star to miss 14 games and was never really 100 percent after that... Averaged 10.4 points... Production will improve when Knicks learn to run fastbreak... Excellent rebounder who perfected craft while working peach orchards for his father... Wants to get much stronger so he doesn't get pushed around as easily in the paint... Likes to dance... Was fifth selection overall right behind Chuck Person in 1986 draft... Does wonderful Rodney Dangerfield... Didn't get any respect from refs, fans or media.

Year	Team	G	FG	FG Pct.	FT	FT Pct.	Reb.	Ast.	TP	Avg.
1986-87	New York...........	68	285	.491	140	.757	338	75	710	10.4

GERALD HENDERSON 31 6-2 175   Guard

A man's man... After living the good life with Celtics for five years has lived on poor side of town with Sonics and Knicks... Was dealt by Seattle for No. 1 pick seven games into the season... Trade cost GM Scotty Stirling his job... Career highlight was big steal in Game 2 of 1983-84 finals that sent Celtics on their way to 15th title... A leader who figures to help young Knicks much more this season... Sometimes out of control at the point... Led Knicks in diving on the floor for loose balls... Is in partnership with his wife, selling fur coats

. . . Born Jan. 16, 1956, in Richmond, Va., and played at Virginia Commonwealth . . . A third-round draft pick of San Antonio in 1978 . . . Was cut and played in defunct Western Basketball Association before rescued by Red Auerbach.

Year	Team	G	FG	FG Pct.	FT	FT Pct.	Reb.	Ast.	TP	Avg.
1979-80	Boston.............	76	191	.500	89	.690	83	147	473	6.2
1980-81	Boston.............	82	261	.451	113	.720	132	213	636	7.8
1981-82	Boston.............	82	353	.501	125	.727	152	252	833	10.2
1982-83	Boston.............	82	286	.463	96	.722	124	195	671	8.2
1983-84	Boston.............	78	376	.524	136	.768	147	300	908	11.6
1984-85	Seattle............	79	427	.479	199	.780	190	559	1062	13.4
1985-86	Seattle............	82	434	.482	185	.830	187	487	1071	13.1
1986-87	Sea.-N.Y........	74	298	442	190	.826	175	471	805	10.9
	Totals.............	635	2626	.480	1133	.768	1190	2624	6459	10.2

RORY SPARROW 29 6-2 175   Guard

Sulk, sulk, sulk . . . Demoted to reserve point guard once Gerald Henderson arrived and Bob Hill went with uptempo offense . . . Did not take new role well and said he may retire . . . Has come a long way . . . Was 75th pick in 1980 draft . . . Made $500,000 last season and does not figure to see that kind of money again unless he hits the lottery . . . Born July 12, 1958, in Suffolk, Va. . . . Started Rory Sparrow Foundation that has helped thousands of children in a number of ways . . . Tireless charity worker whose off-the-court future seems limitless . . . Has engineering degree from Villanova and plans to get law degree as well.

Year	Team	G	FG	FG Pct.	FT	FT Pct.	Reb.	Ast.	TP	Avg.
1980-81	New Jersey.........	15	22	.349	12	.750	18	32	56	3.7
1981-82	Atlanta............	82	366	.501	124	.838	224	424	857	10.5
1982-83	Atl.-N.Y..........	81	392	.484	147	.739	230	397	936	11.6
1983-84	New York..........	79	350	.474	108	.824	189	539	818	10.4
1984-85	New York..........	79	326	.492	122	.865	169	557	781	9.9
1985-86	New York..........	74	345	.477	101	.795	170	472	796	10.8
1986-87	New York..........	80	263	.446	71	.798	115	432	608	7.6
	Totals.............	490	2064	.478	685	.805	1115	2853	4852	9.9

PAT CUMMINGS 31 6-9 230   Forward

After missing 51 games two years ago, he sat out 33 last season with torn ligament in right ring finger . . . Born July 11, in Johnstown, Pa. . . . Which may explain blue-collar work ethic . . . One of only two Knicks who lives in New York City, he often takes subway to games . . . Was slowed by rehab of foot injury and scoring average dipped from 15.7 to 8.6

...A plodder, does not seem to fit future run-and-gun plans of team...Look for him to wind up in another Hubie Brown-type offense...Huge salary, $630,000, may make a trade impossible ...Fantastic outside shooter...Learned skill because he was bigger than all his friends and they said it was too easy for him to score underneath...Has varied business interests...Fun to be around off the court.

Year	Team	G	FG	FG Pct.	FT	FT Pct.	Reb.	Ast.	TP	Avg.
1979-80	Milwaukee	71	187	.505	94	.764	238	53	468	6.6
1980-81	Milwaukee	74	248	.539	99	.707	292	62	595	8.0
1981-82	Milwaukee	78	219	.509	67	.736	245	99	505	6.5
1982-83	Dallas	81	433	.493	148	.755	668	144	1014	12.5
1983-84	Dallas	80	452	.494	141	.742	658	158	1045	13.1
1984-85	New York	63	410	.514	177	.780	518	109	997	15.8
1985-86	New York	31	195	.478	97	.698	280	47	487	15.7
1986-87	New York	49	172	.450	79	.718	312	38	423	8.6
	Totals	527	2316	.499	902	.742	3211	710	5534	10.5

JAWANN OLDHAM 30 7-1 255　　　　Center-Forward

Brother from another planet...Nicknamed ALF as in the TV show "Alien Life Form"... Overestimates ability, often comparing himself to Kareen Abdul-Jabbar even though he has averaged four points a game over seven-year career...Demands to be traded and did not like playing behind or alongside Patrick Ewing...Believes he is every bit the player Patrick is...Defensively, Oldham is better...One of the best shot-blockers in the league, rejecting 71 last season in just 776 minutes...Strained knee sidelined him last 19 games...Inked five-year, $1.7-million contract at start of season...Traded from Bulls for Denver No. 1 pick...A helicopter pilot, Oldham would like to ferry around business executives in the future... Demands his name be pronounced Old-HAM...Drafted 41st overall out of Seattle by Nuggets in 1980...Spent time in CBA ...A Yankee Doodle Dandy, born July 4, 1957, in Seattle.

Year	Team	G	FG	FG Pct.	FT	FT Pct.	Reb.	Ast.	TP	Avg.
1980-81	Denver	4	2	.333	0	.000	5	0	4	1.0
1981-82	Houston	22	13	.361	8	.571	24	3	34	1.5
1982-83	Chicago	16	31	.534	12	.545	47	5	74	4.6
1983-84	Chicago	64	110	.505	39	.591	233	33	259	4.0
1984-85	Chicago	63	89	.464	34	.680	236	31	212	3.4
1985-86	Chicago	52	167	.517	53	.582	306	37	387	7.4
1986-87	New York	44	71	.408	31	.544	179	19	173	3.9
	Totals	265	483	.480	177	.590	1030	128	1143	4.3

LOUIS ORR 29 6-8 200   Forward

Picture perfect for expansion... Averaged career-low 7.0 points... Field-goal percentage plummeted to .427... Nicknamed "Biafra" by teammates because of his emaciated look... A loveable soul... Team leader in locker room ... Not afraid to speak up to anyone despite his fragile frame... Hit buzzer-beating basket against Celts on Martin Luther King Day... Always suited best for backup role but two years of filling in for Bernard King has taken its toll... Born May 7, 1958, in Cincinnati... Is 3-35 from three-point range during seven-year career... Pacers made him No. 29 pick overall in 1980 out of Syracuse... Rick Pitino recruited Orr while on his honeymoon ... Needs to go to another team for own well being.

Year	Team	G	FG	FG Pct.	FT	FT Pct.	Reb.	Ast.	TP	Avg.
1980-81	Indiana............	82	348	.491	163	.807	361	132	859	10.5
1981-82	Indiana............	80	357	.497	203	.799	331	134	918	11.5
1982-83	New York..........	82	274	.462	140	.800	228	94	688	8.4
1983-84	New York..........	78	262	.458	173	.820	228	61	697	8.9
1984-85	New York..........	79	372	.486	262	.784	391	134	1007	12.7
1985-86	New York..........	74	330	.445	218	.784	312	179	878	11.9
1986-87	New York..........	65	166	.427	125	.727	232	110	458	7.0
	Totals.............	540	2109	.470	1284	.790	2083	844	5505	10.2

BOB THORNTON 25 6-10 225   Forward

Original California kid... May be the only California Angels' fan east of the Rockies... Actually believes Gene Mauch knows how to win the big game... Played in just 33 games because of sprained ankles and L.O.T. (lack of talent)... Never stops trying, though... Fourth-round pick by Knicks and No. 87 overall in 1984 out of California-Irvine... Was sixth among NCAA I shooters with .640 mark his senior year ... Played for Caja, Madrid in Spanish National League... Born July 10, 1962, in Mission Viejo, Cal.... Owns three dogs, but never plays like one... Made $80,000 last season... Fan favorite at the Garden... Another one of those guys headed to expansion team.

Year	Team	G	FG	FG Pct.	FT	FT Pct.	Reb.	Ast.	TP	Avg.
1985-86	New York..........	71	125	.456	86	.531	290	43	336	4.7
1986-87	New York..........	33	29	.433	13	.650	56	8	71	2.2
	Totals.............	104	154	.452	99	.544	346	51	407	3.9

TRENT TUCKER 27 6-5 190   Guard

 Toasted his marshmallow image... One of the few bright spots for team last season, averaging a career-high 11.4 points... Getting away from Hubie Brown was main reason for improvement... Perhaps the smoothest shot in NBA... Celtics and Lakers covet him... Born Dec. 20, 1959, in Tarboro, N.C.... Starred at Minnesota before being drafted sixth overall in 1982... Known for his three-point shooting, Tucker finished fifth in league with .422 percentage last season after coming in second in 1986.... An underrated defensive player ... Still too much a pacifist... Took just 101 free throws but did drive to the hoop more... Wants to become a TV sports producer... Made $325,000 last season.

Year	Team	G	FG	FG Pct.	FT	FT Pct.	Reb.	Ast.	TP	Avg.
1982-83	New York............	78	299	.462	43	.672	216	195	655	8.4
1983-84	New York............	63	225	.500	25	.758	130	138	481	7.6
1984-85	New York............	77	293	.483	38	.792	188	199	653	8.5
1985-86	New York............	77	349	.472	79	.790	169	192	818	10.6
1986-87	New York............	70	325	.470	77	.762	135	166	795	11.4
	Totals.............	365	1491	.476	262	.757	838	890	3402	9.3

TOP ROOKIES

MARK JACKSON 22 6-3 205   Guard

St. John's product is young point guard Knicks sought... Local favorite, Felt Forum draft crowd was chanting "Don't mess up!" as Knicks made him 18th pick... A second-team All-American ... Averaged 18.9 points and 6.4 assists... Finished career as St. John's all-time assist leader with 738... Reminds many of Dennis Johnson... Born April 1, 1965, in Brooklyn, N.Y.... A born leader... While waiting to get picked he said: "It was the hardest five minutes of my life. I felt like Dorothy from the Wizard of Oz. I was sitting there clicking my heels, saying there's no place like home."

RON MOORE 25 6-10 240   Forward

Big beef... Dropped 50 pounds before his senior season at West Virginia State... Diet paid off as he averaged 27.6 points and 11 rebounds and was named small college All-American... Born June 16, 1962, in Brooklyn, N.Y.... Runs the floor well for a big man but has to become more aggressive under the boards... Has to discipline himself in the pros to make it big.

COACH RICK PITINO: After the most extensive search since the kidnapping of the Lindbergh baby, the Knicks finally settled on a coach they could have had from Day 1...The 35-year-old Pitino, courtwise beyond his years, promises to make the sad-sack losers a hustling winner overnight...He did just such a trick in his two years at Providence College, bringing the Friars from the depth of the Big East to the Final Four...Born Sept. 18, 1952, in New York City, just four blocks from the old Madison Square Garden...He was a star guard for St. Dominic High School in Oyster Bay, N.Y., before going to the University of Massachusetts, where he was a teammate of Julius Erving...He started his college coaching career at Boston University, where in five seasons he posted a 153-81 record...He spent two seasons with the Knicks as Hubie Brown's assistant, earning respect from those in the know...At clinics he's considered the second most dynamic speaker on the planet, the first being Brown..."I'm not leaving Providence College—which I consider to be the best coaching job in America—to go through the kind of season the Knicks had last year," said Pitino.

GREATEST COACH

Red Holzman had the brains and street smarts it took to build a champion. He was an oasis in a desert of losing for the Knicks, winning 613 games and two championships in 1970 and 1973.

Holzman, a member of the Basketball Hall of Fame, was the conductor who blended DeBusschere, Bradley, Reed, Frazier and Barnett into champions. "That first championship was my biggest thrill," he says. "That team may have been the best to have ever played the game."

The City Game belonged to Red. A New Yorker who starred at CCNY, he played for the Rochester Royals, NBA champions in 1950-51.

With the Knicks, Holzman introduced a defensive mentality to the game. The Garden chants of "Dee—fense! Dee—fense!" will remain his legacy. A master bench coach, Holzman broke the game down to its simplest form.

"You've got to play good defense," he says. "You've got to hit the open man. You've got to pass and think. And the players still take pride in winning, no matter how much money they make. You try to tap that pride."

He tapped it.

ALL-TIME KNICK LEADERS

SEASON

Points: Richie Guerin, 2,303, 1961-62
Assists: Micheal Ray Richardson, 832, 1979-80
Rebounds: Willis Reed, 1,191, 1968-69

GAME

Points: Bernard King, 60 vs. New Jersey, 12/25/84
Assists: Richie Guerin, 21 vs. St. Louis, 12/12/58
Rebounds: Harry Gallatin, 33 vs. Ft. Wayne, 3/15/53
              Willis Reed, 33 vs. Cincinnati, 2/2/71

CAREER

Points: Walt Frazier, 14,617, 1967-77
Assists: Walt Frazier, 4,791, 1967-77
Rebounds: Willis Reed, 8,414, 1964-74

PHILADELPHIA 76ERS

TEAM DIRECTORY: Owner: Harold Katz; GM: John Nash; Dir. Press Rel.: Harvey Pollack; Coach: Matt Guokas; Asst. Coaches: Jim Lynam, Fred Carter. Arena: The Spectrum (17,967). Colors: Red, white and blue.

SCOUTING REPORT

SHOOTING: Now that Dr. J has retired, it's time Charles Barkley took more shots for the Sixers. The forward's .594 shooting percentage was the third best in the NBA. And no one rams home a dunk, and frees himself for a dunk, like the Human Space Shuttle. As a team, the Sixers shot .491, fifth best in the league.

The other two Sixers who blistered from the field were surprising center Tim McCormick (.545), who helped make up for Jeff Ruland's absence (a career .564 shooter) and do-it-all guard Maurice Cheeks (.527). Roy Hinson took the biggest fall, going from .532 to .478. Andrew Toney made it back to play in 52 games but he wasn't the Android of old. The lifetime .502 shooter dropped to .451.

PLAYMAKING: There's only one better point guard than Maurice Cheeks and he's the best of all time, Magic Johnson. Cheeks is the epitome of the professional athlete. He was 10th in the league in assists (7.9) and third in steals (2.65). There's no one who makes the most of his talent like Cheeks. He'll hit the open man or the open jumper. He is as selfless as Cliff ("It's my ball") Robinson is selfish.

Barkley did pass off for 4.8 assists per game, but sometimes his fullcourt charges—he runs the break like the Packers used to run the sweep—would be more successful if he gave it up.

DEFENSE: Although the Sixers allowed just 106.2 ppg, sixth best in the league, a lot of times too many easy shots were given up. Opponents shot .491. Only five teams allowed the opposition a better percentage. The Sixers were fourth in the league in blocked shots with Hinson's 161 leading the way.

Barkley added another 104 swat-aways, but the most pivotal part of defense is the center position and opponents weren't afraid to go deep against McCormick. Cheeks and David Wingate put some serious defense on the opposition from the backcourt.

REBOUNDING: The Sixers were the third-worst rebounding team in the East and fifth worst in the league. That's one reason

Explosive Charles Barkley carries Sixer hopes.

SIXER ROSTER

No.	Veteran	Pos.	Ht.	Wt.	Age	Yrs. Pro	College
34	Charles Barkley	F	6-6	255	24	3	Auburn
10	Maurice Cheeks	G	6-1	180	31	9	West Texas State
14	Steve Colter	G	6-3	175	25	3	New Mexico State
21	Ken Green	F	6-7	215	23	2	Wake Forest
23	Roy Hinson	F-C	6-9	210	26	4	Rutgers
40	* Tim McCormick	C	6-11	240	25	3	Michigan
31	Mark McNamara	C	6-11	235	29	3	California
4	* Cliff Robinson	F	6-9	230	27	8	USC
22	Andrew Toney	G	6-3	190	29	7	SW Louisiana
25	* David Wingate	G	6-5	185	25	1	Georgetown
20	Danny Vranes	F	6-8	220	29	6	Utah

*Free agent unsigned at press time

Rd.	Top Rookies	Sel. No.	Pos.	Ht.	Wt.	College
1	Chris Welp	16	C	7-0	245	Washington
2	Vincent Askew	39	G	6-6	210	Memphis State
2	Andrew Kennedy	43	F	6-7	205	Virginia
3	Hansi Gnad	57	C	6-10	220	Alaska-Anchorage
3	Eric Riggins	62	F	6-9	210	Rutgers

teams get easy shots. Here is where Moses Malone was missed, thank you Harold Katz. Just imagine where the Sixers would have finished rebounding if Barkley weren't around. He was the No. 1 Charles and No. 1 rebounder in the NBA with 14.6 a game, finishing ahead of Charles Oakley and Charles (Buck) Williams. The No. 1 draft pick, 7-foot center Chris Welp, will give added bulk and scoring capabilities at center . . . eventually.

OUTLOOK: The Julius Erving victory tour is complete. Malone is finishing up his career in Washington. Matt Guokas' Sixers are a team in transition. Again. Better chemistry must be found. Barkley needs to run wild, a bull in the proverbial china shop, but players like Robinson have to be leashed for the Sixers to survive in the East.

The problem with the Sixers isn't always the players or coaches; it's meddlesome owner Harold Katz. There have been too many middle-of-the-night deals by Katz, and even though Barkley and Cheeks are prime-time material, this team is not ready to duel the Celtics, Hawks and Pistons.

76ER PROFILES

CHARLES BARKLEY 24 6-6 255   Forward

Half man, half tractor—trailer... The most incredible physical specimen in the NBA... "He's my guy, I love him," gushes Magic Johnson. "He's the real Mr. Coast to Coast ...He's the only guy in the league I won't stand there and take a charge from—too big" ...Earned his first NBA rebounding crown with 14.6 and was among league leaders in scoring (23.0) and shooting percentage (.594)... Averaged 24 points and 12 rebounds vs. Bucks in playoffs, but could not do it alone... Coaches finally had enough sense to name him to all-star team... Schick Pivotal Player of the Year for the second straight season... A joy to watch... May be the best forward in the game... "I think I'm more talented than Bird," he says, "but I have to learn to play harder than he does"... Signed an eight-year, $13-million contract before last season... Mouth sometimes gets him in trouble, but is vital part of his engaging personality... Born Feb. 20, 1963, in Leeds, Ala.... When he was cut from high-school basketball team, he moved to become a great player and though he was a 5-10, 220-pound blimp he would practice jumping flat-footed over a five-foot high chain-link fence... Drafted No. 5 overall in 1984 by Sixers out of Auburn.

Year	Team	G	FG	FG Pct.	FT	FT Pct.	Reb.	Ast.	TP	Avg.
1984-85	Philadelphia.........	82	427	.545	293	.733	703	155	1148	14.0
1985-86	Philadelphia.........	80	595	.572	396	.685	1026	312	1603	20.0
1986-87	Philadelphia.........	68	557	.594	429	.761	994	331	1564	23.0
	Totals.............	230	1579	.572	1118	.725	2723	798	4315	18.8

MAURICE CHEEKS 31 6-1 180   Guard

Look up underrated in the dictionary and you'll see a picture of Cheeks... Finally getting some respect and was named to the all-star team for third time... Pound for pound is the best pure point guard in the league... Among NBA leaders in steals and assists... Durable, averaged six more minutes a game last season than career average of 33.3... Hardly ever misses an open jumper, shot 53 percent from the field... Totally unselfish, smart and savvy... Where would

Sixers have been if they hadn't drafted him 36th overall, out of West Texas State?... Born Sept. 8, 1956, in Chicago... Got a long overdue raise that gives him $995,000 this season... His 15.6 ppg last season was best of career.

Year	Team	G	FG	FG Pct.	FT	FT Pct.	Reb.	Ast.	TP	Avg.
1978-79	Philadelphia	82	292	.510	101	.721	254	431	685	8.4
1979-80	Philadelphia	79	357	.540	180	.779	274	556	898	11.4
1980-81	Philadelphia	81	310	.534	140	.787	245	560	763	9.4
1981-82	Philadelphia	79	352	.521	171	.777	248	667	881	11.2
1982-83	Philadelphia	79	404	.542	181	.754	209	543	990	12.5
1983-84	Philadelphia	75	386	.550	170	.733	205	478	950	12.7
1984-85	Philadelphia	78	422	.570	175	.879	217	497	1025	13.1
1985-86	Philadelphia	82	490	.537	282	.842	235	753	1266	15.4
1986-87	Philadelphia	68	415	.527	227	.777	215	538	1061	15.6
	Totals	703	3428	.536	1627	.787	2102	5023	8519	12.1

ROY HINSON 26 6-9 210　　　　　　　　Forward-Center

Sure, a lot was expected, but he could have done better... Cost Sixers top pick in the draft and a true center in Brad Daugherty when he was traded from Cavs on June 16, 1986... Harold Katz pocketed $750,000 in the deal, too... Was forced to play center too often... Sixers figured his game would step up a notch being traded to a better team but it really didn't... Did well in playoffs, though, against Bucks... Ninth in the league in blocked shots at 2.12... The best player Rutgers has ever produced, chosen 20th overall by Cavs in 1983... Has hands the size of a catcher's mitt... Dramatic improvement over rookie season... Born May 2, 1961, in Trenton, N.J.

Year	Team	G	FG	FG Pct.	FT	FT Pct.	Reb.	Ast.	TP	Avg.
1983-84	Cleveland	80	184	.496	69	.590	499	69	437	5.5
1984-85	Cleveland	76	465	.503	271	.721	596	68	1201	15.8
1985-86	Cleveland	82	621	.532	364	.719	639	102	1606	19.6
1986-87	Philadelphia	76	393	.478	273	.758	488	60	1059	13.9
	Totals	314	1663	.506	977	.719	2222	299	4303	13.7

CLIFF ROBINSON 27 6-9 230　　　　　　　　Forward

Has never had the ball in his hands for more than six seconds without firing up a shot... Was benched in second half of fifth and final game against Bucks... Despite awesome talents, has no self-control when it comes to offense... Has been with five teams in last seven years... Wears out coaches and welcome... Was bothered by allergy condi-

tion in his eye, which contributed to his missing 27 games ...
Came to Sixers along with Jeff Ruland in Harold Katz' folly,
which sent Moses Malone, Terry Catledge and two No. 1 draft
picks to Washington ... Eight-year veteran left USC at 19 to be
drafted 11th overall by Nets in 1979 ... Can be a great open-
court scorer but still needs coddling ... College nickname was
"Treetop" and it's on his Rolls Royce ... Born March 13, 1960,
in Oakland ... Hopefully, will some day grow up.

Year	Team	G	FG	FG Pct.	FT	FT Pct.	Reb.	Ast.	TP	Avg.
1979-80	New Jersey.........	70	391	.469	168	.694	506	98	951	13.6
1980-81	New Jersey.........	63	525	.491	178	.718	481	105	1229	19.5
1981-82	K.C.-Clev...........	68	518	.453	222	.709	609	120	1258	18.5
1982-83	Cleveland...........	77	587	.477	213	.708	856	145	1387	18.0
1983-84	Cleveland...........	73	533	.450	234	.701	753	185	1301	17.8
1984-85	Washington.........	60	422	.471	158	.742	546	149	1003	16.7
1985-86	Washington.........	78	595	.474	269	.762	680	186	1460	18.7
1986-87	Philadelphia........	55	338	.464	139	.755	307	89	815	14.8
	Totals.............	544	3909	.469	1581	.723	4738	1077	9404	17.3

TIM McCORMICK 25 6-11 240   Center

Life is full of surprises ... Obtained from
Seattle along with Danny Vranes for Clemon
Johnson and a 1989 No. 1 prior to the season
to fill in for Jeff Ruland, he did an admirable
job ... Averaged 12.8 points, 7.5 rebounds
and shot .545 from the floor ... Faded in
playoffs due to intense Milwaukee pressure,
scoring just 5.6 ppg ... Everyone has always
loved his hustle and intelligence, but questioned his raw talent
... Learned to bang and fight in the rugged Big 10, then left
Michigan a year early to enter the NBA draft ... Has shown a
willingness to play inside with the big guys and an assortment of
offensive skills ... Burned the Rockets on March 1, scoring 26
points and grabbing seven rebounds ... Born March 10, 1962, in
Detroit ... The 16th player chosen in the 1984 draft by Cleveland, he wound up in Seattle via a three-way trade ... Was sent to
Washington with Cliff Robinson for Mel Turpin, then went coast-
to-coast with Ricky Sobers in deal for Gus Williams prior to
1984-85 ... Nothing flashy, just solid.

Year	Team	G	FG	FG Pct.	FT	FT Pct.	Reb.	Ast.	TP	Avg.
1984-85	Seattle.............	78	269	.557	188	.715	398	78	726	9.3
1985-86	Seattle.............	77	253	.570	174	.713	403	83	681	8.8
1986-87	Philadelphia........	81	391	.545	251	.719	611	114	1033	12.8
	Totals.............	236	913	.555	613	.716	1412	275	2440	10.3

ANDREW TONEY 29 6-3 190   Guard

Shadow of his former self... Shown occasional flashes when feet were right, but still hampered by injuries, which owner Harold Katz seems to feel are more in his head than his body... After playing but six games the previous season, managed to make 52 appearences last season... Scored in double figures just twice after March 23... Averaged just 5.6 in playoffs... Made $710,000 last season, which makes him nearly impossible to deal... Born Nov. 23, 1957, in Birmingham, Ala.... Was eighth pick overall out of SW Louisiana in 1980, going to Sixers after Nets took Mike Gminski and Mike O'Koren... Onetime "Boston Strangler" is struggling to hold on ... A shame, because he was deadly when healthy.

Year	Team	G	FG	FG Pct.	FT	FT Pct.	Reb.	Ast.	TP	Avg.
1980-81	Philadelphia.........	75	399	.495	161	.712	143	273	968	12.9
1981-82	Philadelphia.........	77	511	.522	227	.742	134	283	1274	16.5
1982-83	Philadelphia.........	81	626	.501	324	.788	225	365	1598	19.7
1983-84	Philadelphia.........	78	593	.527	390	.839	193	373	1588	20.4
1984-85	Philadelphia.........	70	450	.492	306	.862	177	363	1245	17.8
1985-86	Philadelphia.........	6	11	.306	3	.375	5	12	25	4.2
1986-87	Philadelphia.........	52	197	.451	133	.796	85	188	549	10.6
	Totals.............	439	2787	.502	1544	.797	962	1857	7247	16.5

DAVID WINGATE 23 6-5 185   Guard

Literally a steal in the draft... Chosen 44th overall out of Georgetown... Defensive specialist created havoc whenever he was on the floor, flailing his telephone-pole arms... Had 93 steals, good enough for third on the team ... Scored in double figures over 30 times and came on strong at the end... Scored 28 points vs. Chicago on March 11... Excellent passer, racked up 13 assists vs. Dallas on March 23... Outside shot questionable... Ditto free-throw shooting and has to be more careful with the ball... Born Dec. 15, 1963, in Baltimore... Like a colt, he has to be broken, but Georgetown marauder has talent... Former St. John's star Chris Mullin still has nightmares when he thinks of Wingate's defense.

Year	Team	G	FG	FG Pct.	FT	FT Pct.	Reb.	Ast.	TP	Avg.
1986-87	Philadelphia.........	77	259	.430	149	.741	156	155	680	8.8

STEVE COLTER 25 6-3 175   Guard

Take a seat, Steve, and watch... Backing up Maurice Cheeks is tremendous learning experience... Unfortunately, the minutes aren't there to put into use what you've learned... Came to Sixers on New Year's Eve from Chicago in deal for Sedale Threatt... Started when Cheeks was out with injuries and averaged 14.5 ppg and 5.6 assists in those 13 games... Skinny, minny... Doesn't look like much... Maybe that's why so many teams passed on him in 1984 draft and allowed the Blazers to grab him with the No. 33 pick... Needs work on his shot... Mustered just 42 percent from the field... Made 56 steals... Born July 24, 1962, in Phoenix... Had a quietly effective four-year career at New Mexico State... His development at point guard pushed Darnell Valentine out of the picture in Portland... Traded to Bulls from Blazers for Larry Krystkowski and second-round picks in 1987 and 1992.

Year	Team	G	FG	FG Pct.	FT	FT Pct.	Reb.	Ast.	TP	Avg.
1984-85	Portland...........	78	216	.453	98	.754	150	243	556	7.1
1985-86	Portland...........	81	272	.456	135	.823	177	257	706	8.7
1986-87	Chi.-Phil...........	70	169	.426	82	.766	108	210	424	6.1
	Totals.............	229	657	.447	315	.786	435	710	1686	7.4

MARK McNAMARA 29 6-11 235   Center

A handsome Paul Mokeski with much less talent... The only place they'll ever retire his number will be in the Princeton Summer League... Has played with three of the four teams there... Was taken by the Sixers in the first round, 22nd pick overall in the 1982 draft out of the University of California... Then became NBA vagabond, spending time in San Antonio and the last season and a half in Europe... Does have a world championship ring for his troubles... Member of the 1983 championship team... Signed by the Sixers on March 4 to beef up their ailing front line... Played just 11 games and got two minutes of action in the playoffs... Born June 8, 1959, in San Jose, Cal.

Year	Team	G	FG	FG Pct.	FT	FT Pct.	Reb.	Ast.	TP	Avg.
1982-83	Philadelphia.........	36	29	.453	20	.444	76	7	78	2.2
1983-84	San Antonio.........	70	157	.621	74	.471	317	31	388	5.5
1984-85	S.A.-K.C............	45	40	.526	32	.516	74	6	112	2.5
1986-87	Philadelphia.........	11	14	.467	7	.368	36	2	35	3.2
	Totals.............	162	240	.567	133	.470	503	46	613	3.8

DANNY VRANES 29 6-8 220 Forward

Squeaky clean reputation, that's why he appeared in a soap commercial...Who knows why he appears in the NBA?...Made $500,000 last season...That's a lot of suds for his output of 2.4 ppg...In the good old days in Seattle he once averaged eight points ...Then defenses cracked down on him...Known as a defensive specialist...Julius Erving once said he was one of the toughest defensive players he ever faced...Came to Sixers in Tim McCormick trade prior to season that sent Clemon Johnson and the club's No. 1 pick in 1989 to Seattle...Was No. 5 pick overall in the 1981 draft and that's a joke...Born Oct. 29, 1958, in Salt Lake City and starred at the University of Utah...Cousin Jeff Judkins spent time in the NBA with Boston and Utah.

Year	Team	G	FG	FG Pct.	FT	FT Pct.	Reb.	Ast.	TP	Avg.
1981-82	Seattle............	77	143	.546	89	.601	198	56	375	4.9
1982-83	Seattle............	82	226	.527	115	.550	425	120	567	6.9
1983-84	Seattle............	80	258	.521	153	.648	395	132	669	8.4
1984-85	Seattle............	76	186	.463	67	.528	436	152	440	5.8
1985-86	Seattle............	80	131	.461	39	.520	281	68	301	3.8
1986-87	Philadelphia.........	58	59	.428	21	.467	146	30	140	2.4
	Totals............	453	1003	.499	484	.576	1881	558	2492	5.5

TOP ROOKIE

CHRIS WELP 23 7-0 245 Center

Washington's all-time leading scorer (2,073) was snatched with 16th pick...Born Jan. 2, 1964, in Delmenhorst, West Germany ...Like other foreign-born players, he's just touching the surface of his skills...Exploded for 40 points vs. UCLA...Averaged 20 points and nine rebounds as a senior..."Chris has the God-given ability to put the ball in the basket," says his college coach Andy Russo...Russo also coached Utah's Karl Malone and says Welp is much better offensive player coming out of college.

COACH MATT GUOKAS: Into every life a little rain must fall

... His downpour is named Harold Katz... Despite meddlesome owner, Guokas remains a class act... Was given new two-year contract after playoffs when the feeling was he would be axed by Weird Harold... One of his biggest backers is Charles Barkley... After final loss in Milwaukee, Charles scribbled on blackboard, "Harold, Keep Matty."... Team won 45 regular-season games, which is no small accomplishment, considering general chaos that followed Sixers around and fact they lost so many games to injury... Guokas has risen through the ranks... A foot soldier... Was 76ers first-round pick in 1966 and played for six teams in 10 years... Served as Billy Cunningham's assistant and had plenty of doubters when he took over in 1985-86... As Philly as cheese steak... Was All-America at St. Joseph's... Father, Matt Sr., played on 1946-47 NBA champion Philadelphia Warriors and son won ring in 1966-67 with Sixers... A reporter's dream, he remembers his years in broadcast booth with Sixers... Has 99-65 mark over two years.

GREATEST COACH

Alex Hannum was the only coach to break Boston's decade-long stranglehold on the NBA. In 1966-67, the Sixers blew smoke in new GM Red Auerbach's face, winning the NBA championship.

The Sixers rolled up an incredible 68-13 record, an .840 winning percentage, the second-best mark in NBA history. That team was anchored by Wilt Chamberlain and also included Luke Jackson, Billy Cunningham, Wally Jones and Hal Greer.

In an era when coaches refused to play up to players Hannum had a most difficult job. But he had the sense to let Wilt dominate the game physically and at the same time convince Chamberlain he was part of a team. It was a masterful coaching job.

The year before Wilt averaged a league-leading 33.5 points, but the Sixers were knocked out during the Eastern Conference finals by the Celtics in five games. In the championship season, Wilt's scoring average dropped to 24.1 but the team benefitted and the tables were turned on the Celtics as they were eclipsed in five games by Philly.

The following year the Sixers again won the Eastern Division with a 62-20 mark but lost a seven-game war to the Celtics. During his two seasons Hannum rolled up a 130-33 mark, a .797 winning percentage.

ALL-TIME 76ER LEADERS

SEASON

Points: Wilt Chamberlain, 2,649, 1965-66
Assists: Maurice Cheeks, 753, 1985-86
Rebounds: Wilt Chamberlain, 1,957, 1966-67

GAME

Points: Wilt Chamberlain, 68 vs. Chicago, 12/16/67
Assists: Wilt Chamberlain, 21 vs. Detroit, 2/2/68
          Maurice Cheeks, 21 vs. New Jersey, 10/30/82
Rebounds: Wilt Chamberlain, 43 vs. Boston, 3/6/65

CAREER

Points: Hal Greer, 21,586, 1958-73
Assists: Maurice Cheeks, 5,023, 1978-87
Rebounds: Dolph Schayes, 11,256, 1948-64

WASHINGTON BULLETS

TEAM DIRECTORY: Pres.: Abe Pollin; Vice Chairman: Jerry Sachs; Exec. VP: Garnett Flatton; GM: Bob Ferry; Dir. Pub. Rel.: Mark Pray; Coach: Kevin Loughery; Asst. Coaches: Bill Blair, Wes Unseld. Arena: Capital Centre (19,411). Colors: Red, white and blue.

SCOUTING REPORT

SHOOTING: If you ever have to go before a firing squad, let's hope the Bullets are manning the rifles. Kevin Loughery's club was the second-worst shooting team in the NBA, coming in at a sad .454. Only the Clippers were more pitiful from the field. For the seventh straight season, Moses Malone's field-goal percentage dropped. It's no coincidence Moses' mark is the same as the team's .454.

But at least Moses usually gets his own rebound and puts it back in the hole. Not one Bullet shot 50 percent from the field. Washington also was the only team that shot less than .200 from three-point range. Larry Bird (90) made more than twice as many three-pointers as the entire Washington team (43).

Other nasty numbers: For the second straight season Darwin Cook shot .426. Point guard Michael Adams was bricking 'em at a .407 clip. Jeff Malone, their best long-range shooter, completely fell apart in the playoffs for the second straight season.

PLAYMAKING: Here's the definition of desperation. When 5-3 guys are taken with the 12th pick in the draft, this department is in big trouble. Wake Forest's Tyrone (Mugsy) Bogues is talented, but that talented? For the second straight season the Bullets were dead last in assists. It didn't help that Frankie Johnson broke his foot again. Even if Bogues can do the job, pushing the ball upcourt, who is he going to pass to? Multitalented John Williams can help in the ball-handling department, if he is utilized correctly.

DEFENSE: The Bullets not only stop themselves, they can stop other people. A beefed-up Manute Bol—no longer does he look like an elongated malnutrition poster child—was second in the league in blocked shots, averaging 3.68. Washington allowed 107.3 ppg, the eighth-best mark in the league, and held opponents to .473 accuracy. Williams, showing what he is capable of doing, led the Bullets in steals with 128.

Moses Malone focuses on his 14th season.

BULLET ROSTER

No.	Veteran	Pos.	Ht.	Wt.	Age	Yrs. Pro	College
14	* Michael Adams	G	5-11	165	24	2	Boston College
10	Manute Bol	C	7-6	225	25	2	Bridgeport
33	Terry Catledge	F	6-8	230	24	2	South Alabama
12	* Darwin Cook	G	6-3	195	31	7	Portland
15	* Frank Johnson	G	6-3	185	28	6	Wake Forest
23	* Charles Jones	F	6-9	216	30	4	Albany State (Ga.)
24	Jeff Malone	G	6-4	205	26	4	Mississippi State
4	Moses Malone	C	6-10	260	32	13	None
42	Jay Murphy	F	6-9	220	25	2	Boston College
31	Jay Vincent	F	6-7	225	28	6	Michigan State
2	* Ennis Whatley	G	6-3	177	25	4	Alabama
34	John Williams	F-G	6-9	240	21	1	Louisiana State

*Free agent unsigned at press time

Rd.	Top Rookies	Sel. No.	Pos.	Ht.	Wt.	College
1	Tyrone Bogues	12	G	5-3	140	Wake Forest
2	Duane Washington	36	G	6-4	195	Middle Tennessee St.
3	Danny Pearson	59	G	6-6	215	Jacksonville
4	Scott Thompson	81	C	6-11	260	San Diego
5	Patrick Fairs	106	G	6-5	185	Texas

REBOUNDING: Only the Knicks had a lower percentage of defensive rebounds (.634) than the Bullets. The offensive boards are in the good hands of Moses, but Bol doesn't rebound worth a darn and that's one reason the Bullets get wiped off the glass. Now, if only Bogues could stand on Bol's shoulders the Bullets would be on to something.

OUTLOOK: Not good. Wheeling-and-dealing GM Bob Ferry is looking to swing another blockbuster, similar to the Malone deal that saved the Bullets' skins before the 1986-87 season. He nearly stole away Denver's Fat Lever, but the Nuggets backed out the last second.

A big deal is needed to keep the Bullets afloat in the East. Other teams are getting better and Moses is getting older. Jeff Malone has yet to prove he's the answer at shooting guard, but perhaps Bogues can get him untracked. Williams will be a good one. Jay Vincent had better do a lot more damage than last season, his first year of exile from Dallas. Ferry and Loughery took a huge gamble with their Lilliputian point guard. If Bogues doesn't pay off, they will be in big, big trouble.

BULLET PROFILES

MOSES MALONE 32 6-10 260   Center

No miracles this time... Moses was supposed to lead Bullets to the promised land in the playoffs, but the team didn't even win one game in postseason... He came to Washington in a blockbuster on draft day 1986, along with Terry Catledge and a pair of first-round picks in exchange for Jeff Ruland and Cliff Robinson... Only player in NBA to rank in top 10 in scoring (24.1) and rebounding (11.3)... Finished fifth the year before in rebounding after winning five straight titles ... Coming off season in which he broke orbit bone around right eye... Shooting percentage of .454 was worst mark in 11-year career, 0-11 from three-point range... Born March 23, 1955, in Petersburgh, Va.... Began career with Utah of ABA straight out of high school in 1974-75... Will earn $2.125 million this season... Scored 50 on April 8 at Meadowlands and became only third Bullet to hit that mark... Lovely sight to see him holding and playing with his two sons throughout All-Star weekend... Needs help along frontline but old warhorse should have one good bump-and-grind year left in him.

Year	Team	G	FG	FG Pct.	FT	FT Pct.	Reb.	Ast.	TP	Avg.
1974-75	Utah (ABA).........	83	591	.571	375	.635	1209	82	1557	18.8
1975-76	St. Louis (ABA)......	43	251	.512	112	.612	413	58	614	14.3
1976-77	Buf.-Hou............	82	389	.480	305	.693	1072	89	1083	13.2
1977-78	Houston............	59	413	.499	318	718	886	31	1144	19.4
1978-79	Houston............	82	716	.540	599	.739	1444	147	2031	24.8
1979-80	Houston............	82	778	.502	563	.719	1190	147	2119	25.8
1980-81	Houston............	80	806	.522	609	.757	1180	141	2222	27.8
1981-82	Houston............	81	945	.519	630	.762	1188	142	2520	31.1
1982-83	Philadelphia.........	78	654	.501	600	.761	1194	101	1908	24.5
1983-84	Philadelphia.........	71	532	.483	545	.750	950	96	1609	22.7
1984-85	Philadelphia.........	79	602	.469	737	.815	1031	130	1941	24.6
1985-86	Philadelphia.........	74	571	.458	617	.787	872	90	1759	23.8
1986-87	Washington.........	73	595	.454	570	.824	824	120	1760	24.1
	Totals.............	967	7843	.501	6580	.750	13453	1374	22267	23.0

JEFF MALONE 26 6-4 205   Guard

If anyone in Pontiac finds Malone's jump shot, please Federal Express it to Washington... Quickly...A career .472 shooter from the field, Malone hit just 17-46 vs. Detroit... Second straight playoff failure for one of the game's sweetest shooters...Percentage slipped badly in regular season, too... Malone is looking to renegotiate contract to half a million per year...Named to all-star team second straight season...Scored career-high 48 against Knicks on March 4... Born June 28, 1961, in Mobile, Ala....Bullets drafted him 10th overall in 1983 out of Mississippi State...Can streak-shoot with the best, but desperately needs to get on one of those streaks during the playoffs.

Year	Team	G	FG	FG Pct.	FT	FT Pct.	Reb.	Ast.	TP	Avg.
1983-84	Washington.........	81	408	.444	142	.826	155	151	982	12.1
1984-85	Washington.........	76	605	.499	211	.844	206	184	1436	18.9
1985-86	Washington.........	80	735	.483	322	.868	288	191	1795	22.4
1986-87	Washington.........	80	689	.457	376	.885	218	298	1758	22.0
	Totals.............	317	2437	.472	1051	.863	867	824	5971	18.8

TERRY CATLEDGE 24 6-8 230   Forward

A solid performer in his second season...Part of the steal-deal that brought Moses Malone to Bullets for Cliff Robinson and Jeff Ruland... Provided needed inside scoring and rebounding, finishing third on the team in scoring (13.1) and second in rebounding (7.2)...Did not fade in the playoffs, either, averaging 15 points on 56-percent shooting and 8.3 rebounds...Born Aug. 22, 1963, in Houston, Miss....Drafted No. 21 overall out of South Alabama...Earned $150,000... Had difficult rookie season that included bout with chicken pox ...Says he's nicknamed "Cadillac" because he's "long, black and lovely."...But last summer he suffered a neck fracture in a car accident and his status is uncertain.

Year	Team	G	FG	FG Pct.	FT	FT Pct.	Reb.	Ast.	TP	Avg.
1985-86	Philadelphia.........	64	202	.469	90	.647	272	21	494	7.7
1986-87	Washington.........	78	413	.495	199	.594	560	56	1025	13.1
	Totals.............	142	615	.486	289	.610	832	77	1519	10.7

JAY VINCENT 28 6-7 225 — Forward

Escaped Dallas and Mark Aguirre's shadow, but did not perform as expected... "Big Daddy" got too big... Insiders say he did not work hard enough... Tore a tendon in his right ring finger in team's first preseason game, which sidelined him all of training camp and first 30 games of season and, as a result, never really got into shape... Flopped in three-game playoffs, shooting 36 percent and scoring just 10 points... Traded to Washington prior to the start of the season in exchange for Bullets' 1990 first-round draft choice... Born July 10, 1959, in Kalamazoo, Mich.... Will make $315,000 this season... Magic Johnson's teammate in high school and wound up as Magic's teammate on the 1979 NCAA championship team at Michigan State... An entrepreneur, he never goes anywhere without a briefcase... Brother, Sam, was a first-round draft choice of Celtics in 1985.

Year	Team	G	FG	FG Pct.	FT	FT Pct.	Reb.	Ast.	TP	Avg.
1981-82	Dallas	81	719	.497	293	.716	565	176	1732	21.4
1982-83	Dallas	81	622	.489	269	.784	592	212	1513	18.7
1983-84	Dallas	61	252	.435	168	.781	247	114	672	11.0
1984-85	Dallas	79	545	.479	351	.836	704	169	1441	18.2
1985-86	Dallas	80	442	.481	222	.810	368	180	1106	13.8
1986-87	Washington	51	274	.447	130	.769	210	85	678	13.3
	Totals	433	2854	.478	1433	.783	2686	936	7142	16.5

JOHN WILLIAMS 21 6-9 240 — Forward-Guard

Puppy young... Needs good coaching and time to develop awesome talents... Improving jump shot is a must... Also, has to keep weight down... Selected 12th overall in 1986 draft after leaving LSU after sophomore season... College coach, unsinkable Dale Brown, says Williams is an artist. "He reminds me of Baryshnikov and Nureyev."... Born Oct. 16, 1966, in Los Angeles... Was youngest player in the NBA last season... Only played point guard three games last season and experiment was abandoned... His steals (128) led Bullets... Averaged 9.2 points, but that will change... Had 658 points in final year at LSU, joining Pete Maravich and Bob Pettit as only Tigers to top 600 in a season.

Year	Team	G	FG	FG Pct.	FT	FT Pct.	Reb.	Ast.	TP	Avg.
1986-87	Washington	78	283	.454	144	.646	366	191	718	9.2

FRANK JOHNSON 28 6-3 185   Guard

Must have walked under a lot of ladders over the years...Tied Bill Cartwright for NBA broken-feet lead when he snapped left foot for the fourth time on Nov. 19...Bad luck continued when Johnson went on injured list the end of March with tendonitis in his left knee ...Played just 18 games...Saw just 28 minutes of action in the playoffs...Uncanny jumping ability...Obviously his career is in jeopardy...Was chosen 11th overall by Washington in 1981 out of Wake Forest ...Foot problems date all the way back to days with Deacons ...Brother of Seattle guard Eddie Johnson and cousin of Tree Rollins...Born Nov. 23, 1958, in Weirsdale, Fla....Career certainly has been weird.

Year	Team	G	FG	FG Pct.	FT	FT Pct.	Reb.	Ast.	TP	Avg.
1981-82	Washington	79	336	.414	153	.750	147	380	842	10.7
1982-83	Washington	68	321	.408	196	.751	178	549	852	12.5
1983-84	Washington	82	392	.467	187	.742	184	567	982	12.0
1984-85	Washington	46	175	.489	72	.750	63	143	428	9.3
1985-86	Washington	14	69	.448	38	.704	28	76	176	12.6
1986-87	Washington	18	59	.461	35	.714	30	58	153	8.5
	Totals	307	1352	.439	681	.743	630	1773	3433	11.2

MICHAEL ADAMS 24 5-11 165   Guard

Other half of Bullets' Mutt-and-Jeff act... Adams became an important part of Bullet backcourt, which says a lot about the big heart in this little man's body and the big hole in the Washington backcourt...Averaged 21 minutes in 63 games as he became the catalyst for second-team pressing defense...Even got to start a playoff game this season...Signed as a free agent on May 13, 1986...Waived prior to the start of the season and returned to the team on Nov. 21 after Frank Johnson broke his foot...A third-round draft choice of the Sacramento Kings in 1985, out of Boston College...Played in the CBA and USBL (with Manute Bol)...Born Jan. 19, 1963, in Hartford, Conn....Nancy Lieberman is one of his best friends.

Year	Team	G	FG	FG Pct.	FT	FT Pct.	Reb.	Ast.	TP	Avg.
1985-86	Sacramento	18	16	.364	8	.667	6	22	40	2.2
1986-87	Washington	63	160	.407	105	.847	123	244	453	7.2
	Totals	81	176	.403	113	.831	129	266	493	6.1

ENNIS WHATLEY 25 6-3 177 Guard

Travelin' Man... In four years Whatley has been with five teams... This was the point guard's second go-round with the Bullets... Was horrid in Detroit series, with more turnovers (8) than points (6)... Benched in final game... Not a good shooter... A 1983 first-round draft choice of the Kansas City Kings (13th overall), out of Alabama, he was immediately shipped to Chicago Bulls... He played two seasons with the Bulls and was traded to Cleveland on June 18, 1985, along with Keith Lee for Charles Oakley and Calvin Duncan... Signed by Washington on Jan. 2, 1986, to a 10-day contract, he was cut and signed to another 10-day deal by San Antonio... He again signed with the Bullets prior to last season and wound up starting the final 72 games... Born Aug. 11, 1962, in Birmingham, Ala.

Year	Team	G	FG	FG Pct.	FT	FT Pct.	Reb.	Ast.	TP	Avg.
1983-84	Chicago	80	261	.469	146	.730	197	662	668	8.4
1984-85	Chicago	70	140	.447	68	.791	101	381	349	5.0
1985-86	Clev.-Wash.-S.A.	14	15	.429	5	.500	14	23	35	2.5
1986-87	Washington	73	246	.478	126	.764	194	392	618	8.5
	Totals	237	662	.467	345	.748	506	1458	1670	7.0

MANUTE BOL 25 7-6 225 Center

The Sultan of Swat... Washington Monument put on 25 pounds last summer through off-season weight program—he no longer can hide behind Louis Orr—and still blocked an NBA second-best 302 shots... Down 95 from rookie season when he led the league... The Dinka tribesman registered his first-ever triple-double (15 blocks, 19 rebounds and 10 points) vs. Pacers on Feb. 26.... His offense is still quite comical (3.1 points per game), but considering he was the 31st choice in the 1985 draft, out of the University of Bridgeport, Bol has to be considered one of the biggest and tallest draft-day steals in NBA history... "He's the only guy who can stand eight feet away from you and still have his hand in your face," says Boston's Danny Ainge... Born Oct. 16, 1962, in Gogrial, The Sudan... Will make $200,000 this season and double that next year... Like everything else about him, he owns a bizarre hook shot... When he learned to drive, the front seat had to be removed from the car... Owns several hundred acres of African farmland... Living the American Dream.

Year	Team	G	FG	FG Pct.	FT	FT Pct.	Reb.	Ast.	TP	Avg.
1985-86	Washington........	80	128	.460	42	.488	477	23	298	3.7
1986-87	Washington........	82	103	.446	45	.672	362	11	251	3.1
	Totals.............	162	231	.454	87	.569	839	34	549	3.4

DARWIN COOK 31 6-3 195   Guard

GM Bob Ferry pulled a quick one on the Nets, taking Cook in exchange for not drafting Pearl Washington in 1986... Ferry, of course, didn't want Pearl and had his sights set on John Williams all along... Spending six seasons in chaotic Net organization, however, took its toll on Cook, who shot 42 percent from field for the second straight season... Playing behind Jeff Malone, Cook never was able to find rhythm for his high-arcing jumpers, reminiscent of UCLA's Lynn Schackleford... Born Aug. 6, 1956, in Los Angeles... University of Portland star was drafted 70th overall by Pistons in 1980, then was cut and signed by Nets as free agent... Product of Crenshaw High, which spawned Darryl Strawberry, Wendell Tyler and Marques Johnson.

Year	Team	G	FG	FG Pct.	FT	FT Pct.	Reb.	Ast.	TP	Avg.
1980-81	New Jersey.........	81	383	.468	132	.733	236	297	904	11.2
1981-82	New Jersey.........	82	387	.482	118	.728	156	319	899	11.0
1982-83	New Jersey.........	82	446	.449	186	.769	240	448	1080	13.2
1983-84	New Jersey.........	82	304	.443	95	.754	156	356	714	8.7
1984-85	New Jersey.........	58	212	.468	47	.870	92	160	473	8.2
1985-86	New Jersey.........	79	267	.426	84	.757	177	390	629	8.0
1986-87	Washington........	82	265	.426	82	.796	145	151	614	7.5
	Totals.............	546	2264	.453	744	.761	1201	2121	5313	9.7

CHARLES JONES 30 6-9 216   Forward

If at first you don't succeed... Drafted 165th overall by Suns in 1979, out of Albany State, and didn't play his first NBA game until 1983-84... Majored in sociology, Jones did his basketball field work on nearly every court in the world—Italy, France, Florida, Rhode Island—and was given NBA chances by Phoenix, Portland, New York, Philadelphia and Chicago... His best friend is his luggage and the blocked shot... Led CBA in blocked shots three years... Defensive specialist started 64 games for the Bullets and had blocked shots in 68 out of 79 games... Offense is another language... One of the Jones

Boys, brothers Caldwell, Major and Wil all have played in the NBA... Born April 3, 1957, in McGhee, Ark.... Nice guy... Nice story.

Year	Team	G	FG	FG Pct.	FT	FT Pct.	Reb.	Ast.	TP	Avg.
1983-84	Philadelphia.........	1	0	.000	1	250	0	0	1	1.0
1984-85	Chi.-Wash..........	31	67	.528	40	.690	184	26	174	5.6
1985-86	Washington........	81	129	.508	54	.628	321	76	312	3.9
1986-87	Washington........	79	118	.474	48	.632	356	80	284	3.6
	Totals.............	192	314	.498	143	.638	861	182	771	4.0

TOP ROOKIE

TYRONE BOGUES 22 5-3 140   **Guard**

Munchkin point guard was the shock of the draft when Bullets made him 12th pick... Scouts say small man can definitely play in the NBA... Tremendous passing ability... Not afraid to go in among the tall trees... Atlanta's Spud Webb was his inspiration ... Nicknamed Mugsy... Born Jan. 9, 1965, in Baltimore... Wake Forest star finished college career as ACC's all-time leader in assists... Named first-team ACC senior year after averaging 14.8 points and 9.5 assists... Was MVP at Baltimore's Dunbar High School, where he played on same team as Georgetown's Reggie Williams and Northeastern's Reggie Lewis.

COACH KEVIN LOUGHERY: Changed his hairdo but not his luck this season... Has appeared in more sequels than Rocky... Every time you think he's finished, he pops up somewhere else in the league, all the time trying to recapture his glory years with the Nets when he won two titles... You think Dr. J had something to do with Loughery's success?... Great guy to pal around with, that's probably why he will always have a job... After tenures with Nets in two leagues, Hawks and Bulls, he rejoined coaching ranks on March 19, 1986, when another Golden Oldie, Gene Shue, was fired... Reached magic mark (ABA-NBA) of 500 wins last season (501)... Unfortunately, he also has 568 losses... NBA record is 333-484 ... Signed by Bullets by former roommate Bob Ferry, now Bullet GM... There was a conflict between Loughery and Moses Malone last season that bears watching... ... Played 11 NBA seasons, including at least a part of nine seasons with the Bullets . . . Born March 28, 1940, in Brooklyn, N.Y. . . . Was second-round draft choice by Pistons in 1962, out of St. John's.

GREATEST COACH

In 1977-78 he uttered the now famous quote, "The opera ain't over 'till the fat lady sings." For that single sentence Dick Motta should be recognized as the Bullets' greatest coach.

That season Motta brought the Bullets to their one and only championship . . . and he did it with a 6-6 center. It helped, of course, that Wes Unseld was 6-6 vertically and horizontally.

Motta came to the Bullets after eight successful years with the Bulls. He spent four seasons in Washington, compiling a 185-143 record as he fashioned the Bullets into back-alley brawlers. He engineered a second straight drive to the NBA finals in 1978-79, but this time when the fat lady sang, the Bullets were erased, four games to one, by Seattle.

Gene Shue, whom Motta passed last season to become the third winningest coach in NBA history (811 victories), won 512 games with the Bullets. He also lost 505. One other coach of note is K.C. Jones, who finished 155-91 in three seasons before moving on to better things.

ALL-TIME BULLET LEADERS

SEASON

Points: Walt Bellamy, 2,495, 1961-62
Assists: Kevin Porter, 734, 1980-81
Rebounds: Walt Bellamy, 1,500, 1961-62

GAME

Points: Earl Monroe, 56 vs. Los Angeles, 2/3/68
Assists: Kevin Porter, 24 vs. Detroit, 3/23/80
Rebounds: Walt Bellamy, 37 vs. St.Louis, 12/4/64

CAREER

Points: Elvin Hayes, 15,551, 1972-81
Assists: Wes Unseld, 3,822, 1968-81
Rebounds: Wes Unseld, 13,769, 1968-81

DALLAS MAVERICKS

TEAM DIRECTORY: Pres.: Donald Carter; Chief Oper. Off./GM
Norm Sonju; VP Basketball Oper.: Rick Sund; Dir. Communica-
tions: Allen Stone; Dir. Media Services: Kevin Sullivan; Coach:
John MacLeod; Asst. Coaches: Rich Adubato, Garfield Heard.
Arena: Reunion Arena (17,077). Colors: Blue and green.

Is this the breakthrough year for Mark Aguirre?

SCOUTING REPORT

SHOOTING: You've really got to wonder how high this team's field-goal percentage would be if the Mavs were to go out every night and play at the same tempo as the Lakers. They'll run when they have the opportunity. But even doing much of their scoring from a set offense, Dallas is able to connect at a very good clip.

Mark Aguirre, Rolando Blackman, Sam Perkins, Derek Harper and Brad Davis are all players you'd feel comfortable with if they were taking a 15-footer with your life hanging in the balance. Unless, of course, it's the first round of the playoffs against Seattle, in which case you'd be dead.

But seriously, shooting has never been a problem in Dallas and the overall team percentage has been helped in the last couple of seasons by the presence of James Donaldson in the middle. He ranked fourth in the league (.586) in field-goal percentage last season. But that doesn't make him a good shooter, just a guy who doesn't shoot much more than two feet away.

Aguirre, Blackman, Harper and Davis all went down in their shooting last year from the previous season and that is a curious stat to ponder, since the Mavs won a franchise-record 55 games in the league season.

Now Dallas has added first-round draft choice Jim Farmer, who has good range, and that old deadeye from Indiana, Steve Alford, if he can stick to the roster all season. Toss those on top of Detlef Schrempf, a finalist in the NBA Long Distance Shoot-out last season, and there is no shortage of marksmen in Big D.

PLAYMAKING: Why is it that Derek Harper spends six months of the regular season displaying a solid game and enhancing his reputation as a blossoming point guard, then tears it all down in a matter of seconds somewhere in the playoffs? Remember, a couple of years ago he dribbled out the clock with the score tied in a playoff game against the Lakers, and Dallas eventually lost in overtime. Well, last season he threw away an inbounds pass in the final seconds of Game 2 of the playoffs against Seattle. That errant pass led to a Seattle basket and a Sonics' win in Game 2, which led to Seattle winning three in a row and led to the big embarrassment of the Mavs being upset in the first round.

Still, despite the gaffes, you've got to like the way Harper pushes the ball up the floor and dishes it off to his teammates. His assist-turnover ratio is 4-to-1—except in the playoffs. Backup Brad Davis has got a couple of good years left in him and this position is solid.

MAVERICK ROSTER

No.	Veteran	Pos.	Ht.	Wt.	Age	Yrs. Pro	College
24	Mark Aguirre	F	6-6	235	27	6	DePaul
33	Uwe Blab	C	7-1	252	25	2	Indiana
22	Rolando Blackman	G	6-6	194	28	6	Kansas State
15	Brad Davis	G	6-3	180	31	10	Maryland
40	James Donaldson	C	7-2	277	30	7	Washington State
12	Derek Harper	G	6-4	203	26	4	Illinois
21	Dennis Nutt	G	6-2	170	24	1	Texas Christian
41	Sam Perkins	F-C	6-9	235	26	3	North Carolina
32	Detlef Schrempf	F-G	6-10	214	24	2	Washington
42	Roy Tarpley	F-C	6-11	230	22	1	Michigan
23	Bill Wennington	F-C	7-0	240	22	2	St. John's
4	Al Wood	G	6-6	210	29	6	North Carolina

Rd.	Top Rookies	Sel. No.	Pos.	Ht.	Wt.	College
1	Jim Farmer	20	G	6-4	190	Alabama
2	Steve Alford	26	G	6-2	180	Indiana
3	Mike Richmond	66	F	6-9	230	Texas-El Paso
4	David Johnson	89	F	6-8	240	Oklahoma
5	Sam Hill	112	F	6-9	215	Iowa State

DEFENSE: They've got Blackman, who might be one of the league's most underrated big guards defensively, and Harper, who has a reputation for getting in your face. But you can't win big in the NBA if the only guys who are playing first-class defense are the guards.

The Mavs have always been and still are vulnerable in the middle. Donaldson, 7-2 and a half-ton, clogs up the middle somewhat and blocked 136 shots last season. But Sam Perkins still plays too soft on the inside, Roy Tarpley is still too raw and Aguirre has never shown an ounce of interest in playing anything that vaguely resembles defense. To move up a notch, this area must improve.

REBOUNDING: Who would have believed it? You might have thought J.R. Ewing had a better chance of turning communist. But the Mavs—the little team with nothing in the middle—actually finished fifth in the NBA in rebounding last season. They're getting bigger with Donaldson, Tarpley and Perkins and they could become fearsome if second-year man Tarpley gets a lot of playing time under new coach John MacLeod.

OUTLOOK: It will be different around the Mavs' locker room without ol' Dick Motta poor-mouthing his club. Though it caught everybody by surprise, Motta's leaving could be a blessing in disguise. No more Motta vs. Aguirre feuds to disrupt the team. The foundation is there, obviously, based on the 55-27 season. If Tarpley can continue to improve and MacLeod's strict stytem of regulating the minutes played doesn't cause bad feelings, they should be leading the race in the Midwest Division again.

MAVERICK PROFILES

MARK AGUIRRE 27 6-6 235   Forward

Moody... Immature... What you see is what you get... Every year people keep waiting for him to grow up and simply become a full-time superstar... But every year there is always another episode of pouting... Extraordinary offensive talent... Make no mistake about it, he can score a ton of points... May also break your heart in a clutch situation... It happened against Seattle in the upset first-round playoff loss... He disappeared... Born Dec. 10, 1959, in Chicago... Starred at DePaul for three years, but even then there was the developing reputation as a difficult guy to handle... Dallas made him the No. 1 pick in the 1981 draft, passing over Buck Williams and Isiah Thomas... Known early as "the Muffin Man" and the "Pillsbury Doughboy" for his out-of-shape appearance... But tests have proven that he's got a very low percentage of body fat... Great quick release on the jumper... Loves to post up.

Year	Team	G	FG	FG Pct.	FT	FT Pct.	Reb.	Ast.	TP	Avg.
1981-82	Dallas	51	381	.465	168	.680	249	164	955	18.7
1982-83	Dallas	81	767	.483	429	.728	508	332	1979	24.4
1983-84	Dallas	79	925	.524	465	.749	469	358	2330	29.5
1984-85	Dallas	80	794	.506	440	.759	477	249	2055	25.7
1985-86	Dallas	74	668	.503	318	.705	445	339	1670	22.6
1986-87	Dallas	80	787	.495	429	.770	427	254	2056	25.7
	Totals	445	4322	.499	2249	.739	2575	1696	11045	24.8

ROLANDO BLACKMAN 28 6-6 194   Guard

The dependable half of Dallas' all-star leadership tandem with the erratic Mark Aguirre... Did not have the grand reputation coming into the league, but is now regarded as one of the finest off-guards in the game... Can shoot from the outside and take it to the hole... Plays the defense... An all-around threat... Born Feb. 26, 1959, in Panama City,

Panama... Grew up in Brooklyn, N.Y.... Started out playing soccer, but couldn't find enough playmates... Switched to basketball and was cut from school team in seventh, eighth and ninth grades... He showed 'em in the end... Starred at Kansas State, where he became all-time field-goal percentage leader... Member of 1980 U.S. Olympic team that boycotted Moscow Games... In actuality, he was not a U.S. citizen at the time... The No. 9 pick in 1981 draft with pick obtained from Denver for Kiki Vandeweghe... Two-time NBA all-star, should have been MVP of the 1987 game in Seattle.

Year	Team	G	FG	FG Pct.	FT	FT Pct.	Reb.	Ast.	TP	Avg.
1981-82	Dallas	82	439	.513	212	.768	254	105	1091	13.3
1982-83	Dallas	75	513	.492	297	.780	293	185	1326	17.7
1983-84	Dallas	81	721	.546	372	.812	373	288	1815	22.4
1984-85	Dallas	81	625	.508	342	.828	300	289	1598	19.7
1985-86	Dallas	82	677	.514	404	.836	291	271	1762	21.5
1986-87	Dallas	80	626	.495	419	.884	278	266	1676	21.0
	Totals	481	3601	.512	2046	.823	1789	1404	9268	19.3

JAMES DONALDSON 30 7-2 277   Center

The missing link... He arrived in Dallas during the 1985-86 season and finally provided the Mavs with the strength and size in the middle to become a real contender... Many say the Mavs would not have been ousted from the playoffs by Seattle in the first round if he had not suffered a foot injury which severely limited his playing time... One of the game's most accurate shooters, mostly because he doesn't shoot from more than a foot or two from the hoop... Born Aug. 16, 1957, in Meachem, England... A gentle giant off the court, he can be a monster in games... Fourth in league in field-goal percentage ... Was embarrassed to be seen in short pants as a high-school player... Very late bloomer... Played at Washington State... A fourth-round pick of Seattle in 1979... Traded to San Diego in 1983 and came to Dallas in exchange for Kurt Nimphius... Darryl Dawkins nicknamed him "American Tourister." Why? "Because his head is as big as a suitcase," Dawkins explained.

Year	Team	G	FG	FG Pct.	FT	FT Pct.	Reb.	Ast.	TP	Avg.
1980-81	Seattle	68	129	.542	101	.594	309	42	359	5.3
1981-82	Seattle	82	255	.609	151	.629	490	51	661	8.1
1982-83	Seattle	82	289	.583	150	.688	501	97	728	8.9
1983-84	San Diego	82	360	.596	249	.761	649	90	969	11.8
1984-85	L.A. Clippers	82	351	.637	227	.749	668	48	929	11.3
1985-86	LAC-Dal.	83	256	.558	204	.803	795	96	716	8.6
1986-87	Dallas	82	311	.586	267	.812	973	63	889	10.8
	Totals	561	1951	.592	1349	.733	4385	487	5251	9.4

DEREK HARPER 26 6-4 203   Guard

Big mistakes in big games . . . Three years ago he dribbled out the clock with the score tied in Game 4 of the playoff series with the Lakers and it cost his team a win in overtime . . . Last season he threw away an inbounds pass in the final seconds of Game 2 against Seattle that led to a loss and eventually Dallas' early elimination . . . It's a shame, since he's made himself into a good all-around point guard . . . Plays tenacious defense . . . Fourth in the NBA in steals . . . Born Oct. 13, 1961, in New York City, but was raised in West Palm Beach, Fla. . . . Plays tennis, pool, dances . . . A No. 1 pick (11th overall) of the Mavs in 1983 . . . Eventually displaced Brad Davis as the QB . . . A college teammate of Phoenix' Eddie Johnson at Illinois . . . Former Dallas coach Dick Motta could never understand why he wears an earring . . . Funny-looking sideways rotation on jumper, but can stick the three-pointer.

Year	Team	G	FG	FG Pct.	FT	FT Pct.	Reb.	Ast.	TP	Avg.
1983-84	Dallas	82	200	.443	66	.673	172	239	469	5.7
1984-85	Dallas	82	329	.520	111	.721	199	360	790	9.6
1985-86	Dallas	79	390	.534	171	.747	226	416	963	12.2
1986-87	Dallas	77	497	.501	160	.684	199	609	1230	16.0
	Totals	320	1416	.504	508	.710	796	1624	3452	10.8

DETLEF SCHREMPF 24 6-10 214   Forward-Guard

Modern day luftwaffer with deadly outside range . . . Finished second to Larry Bird in the 1987 three-point shoot-out during All-Star weekend in Seattle . . . Has excellent all-around skills . . . Trades of Dale Ellis and Jay Vincent allowed him to show a little more in his second pro season . . . Born Jan. 21, 1963, in Leverkusen, West Germany . . . Attended high school in Centralia, Wash., as part of an exchange program and stayed in the Pacific Northwest where he became a star at the University of Washington . . . Played on the 1984 West German Olympic team . . . Played in all but one game last season for the Mavs . . . An outstanding open-court player . . . Big things are projected for him down the road.

Year	Team	G	FG	FG Pct.	FT	FT Pct.	Reb.	Ast.	TP	Avg.
1985-86	Dallas	64	142	.451	110	.724	198	88	397	6.2
1986-87	Dallas	81	265	.472	193	.742	303	161	756	9.3
	Totals	145	407	.465	303	.735	501	249	1153	8.0

SAM PERKINS 26 6-9 235   Forward-Center

Smooth Sam... Slick Sam... Quiet Sam... People want to know when he's going to become Wham Bam, Thank You Sam... Needs to develop a mean streak to take advantage of all those physical tools and make the most of his NBA career... Has the outside shot and has a 77-inch wingspan on his 6-9 body that could make him a terror... Needs to assert himself more at the power forward spot... Born June 14, 1961, in New York City... Grew up in Brooklyn under the watchful eye of Herb Crossman, his legal guardian... Dean Smith molded him into an All-American at North Carolina... The No. 4 overall pick of the Mavs in 1984... Usually destroys Ralph Sampson in head-to-head matchups in college and pros, but doesn't like to talk about it... Strange... It's time he turned off the cruise control and put his career into overdrive.

Year	Team	G	FG	FG Pct.	FT	FT Pct.	Reb.	Ast.	TP	Avg.
1984-85	Dallas	82	347	.471	200	.820	605	135	903	11.0
1985-86	Dallas	80	458	.503	307	.814	685	153	1234	15.4
1986-87	Dallas	80	461	.482	245	.828	616	146	1186	14.8
	Totals	242	1266	.486	752	.820	1906	434	3323	13.7

AL WOOD 29 6-6 210   Guard

Oops!... Mavericks traded Dale Ellis to Seattle to get him and guess who burned them in the 1987 playoffs? Yes, Dale Ellis... It's hard to believe they wanted this guy... He's been overrated ever since Atlanta made him the No. 4 pick overall in the 1981 draft... Supposed to be an above-average defensive player. He's not... Last time he was something special was in 1981 when he set an NCAA semifinal record for North Carolina with 39 points in a game against Virginia... He's been with four teams in six NBA seasons... No way he was worth half of his $500,000 salary last season... Born June 2, 1958, in Gray, Ga.... Made the 1980 U.S. Olympic team that never got to Moscow... Is a 5-handicap golfer... Lives in Seattle in offseason.

Year	Team	G	FG	FG Pct.	FT	FT Pct.	Reb.	Ast.	TP	Avg.
1981-82	Atl.-S.D.	48	179	.470	93	.782	134	58	454	9.5
1982-83	San Diego	76	343	.464	124	.770	236	134	825	10.9
1983-84	Seattle	81	467	.494	223	.823	275	166	1160	14.3
1984-85	Seattle	80	515	.485	166	.776	279	236	1203	15.0
1985-86	Seattle	78	355	.435	187	.782	244	114	902	11.6
1986-87	Dallas	54	121	.390	109	.784	94	34	358	6.6
	Totals	417	1980	.465	902	.789	1262	742	4902	11.8

ROY TARPLEY 22 6-11 230   Forward-Center

Aggressive, hard-working defender . . . His rebound and blocked-shot averages per minute were higher than starting center James Donaldson's last season . . . Often played like a rookie and made his share of mistakes . . . But his willingness to get in there and mix it up is what a "soft" Dallas team needs . . . A good outside shot for a big man . . . Was tossed into the breach in Game 4 of the playoff series against Seattle when Donaldson was hurt and failed miserably . . . Born Nov. 22, 1964, in Detroit . . . Stayed close to home for college at Michigan and wound up as the school's sixth-leading scorer of all time . . . Dallas got him with the No. 7 pick in the 1986 draft.

Year	Team	G	FG	FG Pct.	FT	FT Pct.	Reb.	Ast.	TP	Avg.
1986-87	Dallas.............	75	233	.467	94	.676	533	52	561	7.5

BRAD DAVIS 31 6-3 180   Guard

Hanging on . . . The years go by, younger players come in, but he holds onto a job for one reason—he's dependable . . . A very capable backup point guard, he started a half-dozen games after assorted injuries and illnesses to Derek Harper last year . . . Can run the offense and stick the outside shot . . . Also not afraid to take the ball to the hole . . . A survivor . . . He had to be . . . Born Dec. 17, 1955, in Rochester, Pa. . . . One of Lefty Driesell's boys at Maryland . . . Lakers made him the 15th pick—ahead of Norm Nixon—in the 1977 draft . . . Was shuffled off to Indiana and Utah and then made the CBA circuit with the Anchorage Northern Knights . . . Dallas brought him in from the cold as a free agent in 1980 and he's been there ever since . . . Once had a baseball tryout with the Pittsburgh Pirates . . . Curly perm has been gone for a couple of years.

Year	Team	G	FG	FG Pct.	FT	FT Pct.	Reb.	Ast.	TP	Avg.
1977-78	Los Angeles.........	33	30	.417	22	.759	35	83	82	2.5
1978-79	L.A.-Ind.............	27	31	.564	16	.696	17	52	78	2.9
1979-80	Ind.-Utah...........	18	35	.556	13	.813	17	50	83	4.6
1980-81	Dallas.............	56	230	.561	163	.799	151	385	626	11.2
1981-82	Dallas.............	82	397	.515	185	.804	226	509	993	12.1
1982-83	Dallas.............	79	359	.572	186	.845	198	565	915	11.6
1983-84	Dallas.............	81	345	.530	199	.836	187	561	896	11.1
1984-85	Dallas.............	82	310	.505	158	.888	193	581	825	10.1
1985-86	Dallas.............	82	267	.532	198	.868	146	467	764	9.3
1986-87	Dallas.............	82	199	.456	147	.860	114	373	577	7.0
	Totals.............	622	2203	.524	1287	.837	1284	3626	5839	9.4

BILL WENNINGTON 22 7-0 240   Center-Forward

We send Canada acid rain and they send us this guy... Maybe we deserve it... Born Dec. 26, 1964, in Montreal... Attended high school in Brookville, N.Y., at Long Island Lutheran... Went on to St. John's, where his reputation became blown way out of proportion... Dallas made him the No. 16 pick in the 1985 draft and all he's done since then is try to whip the Reunion Arena crowd into a frenzy by waving his towel on the end of the bench... A shooter who can't shoot and a big man who can't rebound... The perfect combination... Should have stayed in Canada and become the world's biggest hockey goalie.

Year	Team	G	FG	FG Pct.	FT	FT Pct.	Reb.	Ast.	TP	Avg.
1985-86	Dallas.............	56	72	.471	45	.726	132	21	189	3.4
1986-87	Dallas.............	58	56	.424	45	.750	129	24	157	2.7
	Totals.............	114	128	.449	90	.738	261	45	346	3.0

DENNIS NUTT 24 6-2 170   Guard

Pride of the TCU Horned Frogs... Practice fodder... A hustling, solid citizen who will sit on the end of the bench and not complain... Born March 25, 1963, in Little Rock, Ark. ... Was a starter at TCU, but not drafted by the NBA... Hooked on with La Crosse (Wis.) of the CBA, where he played the 1985-86 season... Wasn't even a first-round draft choice in the CBA... But he came to the Dallas rookie camp and hustled his way to a second look in the fall... A cult favorite at Reunion Arena... If he got into the game, you knew the Mavs were either way ahead or way behind.

Year	Team	G	FG	FG Pct.	FT	FT Pct.	Reb.	Ast.	TP	Avg.
1986-87	Dallas.............	25	16	.400	20	.909	8	16	57	2.3

UWE BLAB 25 7-1 252   Center

Blab the Blob... He's been nothing but a big blotch on the Mavs' drafting record for the last two years... Hasn't contributed a thing, except to give teammate Detlef Schrempf somebody to talk to in his native tongue... No. 17 pick in 1985, just behind teammate Bill Wennington... Born March 26, 1962, in Munich, West Germany... Got just 160 minutes of playing time all of last season... Came to U.S. in an exchange program and played high-school ball in Effingham, Ill. ...Bob Knight got the most out of his hulking size at Indiana...But has neither the speed or the heart to make it in the NBA...Used to sport a rat-tail haircut...Plays like a rodent.

Year	Team	G	FG	FG Pct.	FT	FT Pct.	Reb.	Ast.	TP	Avg.
1985-86	Dallas............	48	44	.468	36	.537	91	17	124	2.6
1986-87	Dallas............	30	20	.392	13	.464	36	13	53	1.8
	Totals............	78	64	.441	49	.516	127	30	177	2.3

TOP ROOKIE

JIM FARMER 23 6-4 190   **Guard**
Solid, but not spectacular...You've got to wonder if he has the foot speed to be a standout in the NBA...Became a regular as a junior at Alabama and was the team floor leader as a senior...Born Sept. 23, 1964, in Dothan, Ala....The No. 20 pick on the first round...Had a strong showing in front of the scouts at the Aloha Classic.

COACH JOHN MacLEOD: Talk about landing on your feet ...He was fired after 13½ seasons with the Phoenix Suns and winds up with this plum job as boss of the Mavericks after contractual problems forced Don Nelson to turn it down ...He's moving in after Dick Motta's surprising retirement announcement following the playoffs...MacLeod's got it all set up in front of him, taking over a team that won 55 games in the regular season, despite the first-round playoff loss to Seattle...Born Oct. 3, 1937, in New Albany, Ind....A product of Bellarmine College...Was one who led the flow of college coaches in jumping to the NBA...Took Oklahoma University to consecutive NIT berths in 1973 and 1974 before moving to Phoenix...Led the Suns to the NBA finals in 1976...His wardrobe comes right out of *Gentlemen's Quarterly*...Once was a sparring partner for boxer Jimmy Ellis...Had a baseball career cut short when he suffered an arm injury tossing balls at an Altoona, Pa., amusement park...It will be interesting to see how his system of tightly monitoring minutes played goes over with Dallas veterans like Mark Aguirre...Mavs owner Donald Carter says he'll be on the hot seat to produce immediately.

GREATEST COACH

OK, who was in charge of this election, Ferdinand Marcos?

Put away the pretzels and sit down those beers, folks. There's no argument here.

Let's see, was the best coach in Mavericks' history Dick Motta, who led the expansion team to a 15-67 mark in 1980-81? Or maybe it was Dick Motta, who produced Dallas' first winning season ever (43-39) in 1983-84 and the Mavs' first trip to the playoffs. It could have been in 1985-86 when Dick Motta steered Dallas to a 44-38 mark and then threw a scare into the big, bad LA Lakers in the playoffs. Or was it in 1986-87, when the Mavs under Dick Motta won a franchise-record 55 games in the regular season and then were ambushed by Seattle in the first round of the playoffs?

The choices are clear. It's either Motta, Motta, Motta, Motta, Motta, Motta or Motta, the only coach the Mavs have had—until this year.

The results are in and the vote is unanimous for the greatest coach in the history of the Dallas franchise. Bar none. Congratulations, Dick.

ALL-TIME MAVERICK LEADERS

SEASON

Points: Mark Aguirre, 2,330, 1983-84
Assists: Derek Harper, 609, 1986-87
Rebounds: James Donaldson, 973, 1986-87

GAME

Points: Mark Aguirre, 49 vs. Philadelphia, 1/28/85
Assists: Brad Davis, 17 vs. Cleveland, 3/16/85 (OT)
Rebounds: James Donaldson, 22 vs. Denver, 12/14/85

CAREER

Points: Mark Aguirre, 11,045, 1981-87
Assists: Brad Davis, 3,441, 1980-87
Rebounds: Mark Aguirre, 2,575, 1981-87

DENVER NUGGETS

TEAM DIRECTORY: Owner: Sidney Shlenker; Pres.: Vince Boryla; VP Basketball Oper.: Pete Babcock; Dir. Communications: Harv Kirkpatrick; Coach: Doug Moe; Asst. Coaches: Allan Bristow, Dr. Irwin Vinnik; Arena: McNichols Sports Arena (17,022). Colors: White, blue, green, yellow, red, purple and orange.

SCOUTING REPORT

SHOOTING: It wasn't too long ago that the only thing higher than the Rockies was the Nuggets' field-goal percentage. But all of a sudden you get the feeling that Doug Moe's troops couldn't hit Pike's Peak with a snowball. Alex English (.503) is the only starter who made half his shots last season and the Nuggets wound up as the fifth-worst shooting club in the entire league.

With Calvin Natt on the shelf all of last year, and questionable this season following Achilles tendon surgery, the Nuggets don't get many of those high-percentage inside shots. Too often, they come down the floor and settle for the perimeter jumper. That's no way to contend for the division title. But then, the Nuggets aren't even close to doing that anyway.

PLAYMAKING: Is that any way to say thanks? Point guard Lafayette Lever leads the club in rebounding and rings up almost as many triple-doubles as Magic Johnson and his reward was to be put on the trading block the moment the season ended. Well, it's nothing personal. Just that Lever lacks the speed to push the ball up the floor and get the Nuggets into the kind of fastbreak game that Doug Moe wants to play.

They had expected last year's first-round draft choice, Maurice Martin, to challenge Lever for the quarterback job. But all he challenged was former Nugget Rob Williams' record for having the most insults thrown at him by Moe. This is a gaping hole in the Nuggets' attack and will likely again be a reason Denver sinks in the standings.

DEFENSE: A couple of years ago it was fashionable to say that the Nuggets had one of the most underrated defenses in the league. Now it's fashionable—and accurate—to say that the Nuggets are the worst. Moe still embraces the all-out pressure game and the scrambling into the passing lanes. Without Natt and with Wayne Cooper (fat and happy with a new contract?) falling off, the Nuggets were a team that didn't stop anybody.

You can't play defense in the NBA without a formidable

Nuggets leave it to Lever to run the offense.

frontline and the Nuggets wouldn't scare a Cub Scout team. The Denver defense comes from the hustle plays of people like Bill Hanzlik and T.R. Dunn. But hustle only takes you so far. What the Nuggets need is defensive talent in a hurry.

NUGGET ROSTER

No.	Veteran	Pos.	Ht.	Wt.	Age	Yrs. Pro	College
32	Mark Alarie	F	6-8	217	23	1	Duke
42	Wayne Cooper	C	6-10	220	31	9	New Orleans
23	T.R. Dunn	G	6-4	193	32	10	Alabama
2	Alex English	F	6-7	190	33	11	South Carolina
5	Mike Evans	G	6-1	170	32	8	Kansas State
24	Bill Hanzlik	G-F-C	6-7	200	29	7	Notre Dame
12	Lafayette Lever	G	6-3	175	27	5	Arizona State
11	Maurice Martin	G	6-6	200	23	1	St. Joseph's (Pa.)
33	Calvin Natt	F	6-6	220	30	8	NE Louisiana
41	Blair Rasmussen	C	7-0	250	24	2	Oregon
34	Danny Schayes	C	6-11	245	28	6	Syracuse
22	Otis Smith	G	6-5	210	23	1	Jacksonville
4	* Darrell Walker	G	6-4	180	26	4	Arkansas

*Free agent unsigned at press time

Rd.	Top Rookies	Sel. No.	Pos.	Ht.	Wt.	College
2	Andre Moore	31	F	6-9	215	Loyola (Ill.)
3	Tom Schafer	54	F	6-7	210	Iowa State
4	David Boone	77	F	6-6	220	Marquette
5	Ronnie Grandison	100	F	6-8	225	New Orleans
6	Kelvin Scarborough	123	G	6-1	175	New Mexico

REBOUNDING: What does it say for your rebounding ability when a 6-3 guard like Lever is tops on the team at getting the ball off the boards? It says that your big men ought to hang their heads in shame, come dressed in disguises and return a major portion of their paychecks.

Cooper complained of nagging injuries all year, but showed up for 69 games and just looked like a guy going through the motions. It certainly didn't help that the Nuggets lacked a first-round draft choice to go out and get a big man. If Natt is unable to return at full strength, the Nuggets will be wiped out on the boards by everybody again this year.

OUTLOOK: It seems incredible that less than three years ago the Nuggets were the Midwest Division champs. Now they've been passed in the title department by both Houston and Dallas and will likely be passed by every other team in the standings this time around. English can't carry the offensive burden all by himself, and the defense and rebounding debits all add up to no Rocky Mountain high for the Nuggets again this season.

NUGGET PROFILES

ALEX ENGLISH 33 6-7 190   Forward

Light, delicate, baby soft...That's his touch on those off-balance jumpers that he banks gently off the glass and through the net... Silky smooth...Poetry in motion...Doesn't have the great open-court speed, but possesses an excellent first step and always seems to find a way to get open for his shot...Is working on a contract that now pays him over $1-million a year and he's worth it to this franchise...The top gun... NBA's third-leading scorer last year with 28.6 ppg...Born Jan. 5, 1954, in Columbia, S.C....A late bloomer as a superstar...Quiet college career at South Carolina...Drafted No. 23 by Milwaukee in 1976...Went to Indiana and then arrived in the Rockies in 1980 in exchange for George McGinnis ...Has published poetry books...Has worked for Ethiopian famine relief...Starred in an anti-nuclear arms film with Gregory Peck and Jamie Lee Curtis called *Amazing Grace and Chuck.* He played a member of the Boston Celtics, of all things.

Year	Team	G	FG	FG Pct.	FT	FT Pct.	Reb.	Ast.	TP	Avg.
1976-77	Milwaukee	60	132	.477	46	.767	168	25	310	5.2
1977-78	Milwaukee	82	343	.542	104	.727	395	129	790	9.6
1978-79	Indiana	81	563	.511	173	.752	655	271	1299	16.0
1979-80	Ind.-Den.	78	553	.501	210	.789	605	224	1318	16.9
1980-81	Denver	81	768	.494	390	.850	646	290	1929	23.8
1981-82	Denver	82	855	.551	372	.840	558	433	2082	25.4
1982-83	Denver	82	959	.516	406	.829	601	397	2326	28.4
1983-84	Denver	82	907	.529	352	.824	464	406	2167	26.4
1984-85	Denver	81	939	.518	383	.829	458	344	2262	27.9
1985-86	Denver	81	951	.504	511	.862	405	320	2414	29.8
1986-87	Denver	82	965	.503	411	.844	344	422	2345	28.6
	Totals	872	7935	.514	3358	.827	5299	3261	19242	22.1

LAFAYETTE LEVER 27 6-3 175   Guard

Who spiked this guy's Gatorade?...In one season he went from being an above-average point guard to the NBA's newest triple-double threat...A miniature version of Magic Johnson last season as he did it all for the slumping Nuggets...At just 6-3, he was the runaway team leader in rebounding with more than 700 ...Born Aug. 18, 1960, in Pine Bluff, Ark., but grew up in Tucson, Ariz. . . . Played at Arizona State, where five members of the starting lineup—Alton Lister, Byron Scott, Sam Williams and Kurt Nimphius—made it to the NBA . . . Portland made him the No. 11 pick in 1982 draft . . . Could not beat out Darnell Valentine and Blazers mistakenly shipped him with Wayne Cooper and Calvin Natt and two draft picks to Denver for Kiki Vandeweghe in 1984 . . . Solid defender, finished sixth in the league in steals . . . Got nickname "Fat" because his younger brothers and sisters could not pronounce his full name.

Year	Team	G	FG	FG Pct.	FT	FT Pct.	Reb.	Ast.	TP	Avg.
1982-83	Portland	81	256	.431	116	.730	225	426	633	7.8
1983-84	Portland	81	313	.447	159	.743	218	372	788	9.7
1984-85	Denver	82	424	.430	197	.770	411	613	1051	12.8
1985-86	Denver	78	468	.441	132	.725	420	584	1080	13.8
1986-87	Denver	82	643	.469	244	.782	729	654	1552	18.9
	Totals	404	2104	.447	848	.755	2003	2649	5104	12.6

BILL HANZLIK 29 6-7 200   Guard-Forward-Center

A junkyard dog . . . That is meant in the complimentary way . . . He is not the most talented player in the NBA, but there probably isn't any player in the league who works harder . . . This wiry tough guy has played every position in the Denver lineup—including center—over the last couple of seasons . . . All-Defensive team selection . . . In short, he's a pest . . . The bigger opponents hate him. Just ask Ralph Sampson . . . Born Dec. 6, 1957, in Middletown, Ohio . . . Played at Notre Dame under Digger Phelps and nobody pegged him for a long-termer in the NBA . . . Drafted No. 20 by Seattle in 1980 . . . Traded to Denver in 1982 with a first-round draft choice for David Thompson . . . Member of the 1980 U.S. Olympic team that boycotted Moscow . . . Terms of his three-year, $1-million contract were reached during a marathon gin rummy game . . . Always seems to be down on the floor going for a loose ball . . . Doug Moe loves to ride him. Moe also loves to play him.

Year	Team	G	FG	FG Pct.	FT	FT Pct.	Reb.	Ast.	TP	Avg.
1980-81	Seattle	74	138	.478	119	.793	153	111	396	5.4
1981-82	Seattle	81	167	.468	138	.784	266	183	472	5.8
1982-83	Denver	82	187	.428	125	.781	236	268	500	6.1
1983-84	Denver	80	132	.431	167	.807	205	252	434	5.4
1984-85	Denver	80	220	.421	180	.756	207	210	621	7.8
1985-86	Denver	79	331	.447	318	.785	264	316	988	12.5
1986-87	Denver	73	307	.412	316	.786	256	280	952	13.0
	Totals	549	1482	.436	1363	.784	1587	1620	4363	7.9

DARRELL WALKER 26 6-4 180   Guard

Out of the doghouse...Finally escaped the wrath of Hubie Brown in New York when he was shipped to Denver for a draft choice before last season...A mercurial talent who has the defensive skills and quickness to stand out in the league...One of those guys who could come to flourish under Doug Moe...Born March 6, 1961, in Chicago...Played under Eddie Sutton at Arkansas...Knicks made him the No. 12 pick in 1983, but he never got along with Brown in the Big Apple... Not much of a shooter, but he could get by with the other aspects of his game.

Year	Team	G	FG	FG Pct.	FT	FT Pct.	Reb.	Ast.	TP	Avg.
1983-84	New York	82	216	.417	208	.791	167	284	644	7.9
1984-85	New York	82	430	.435	243	.700	278	408	1103	13.5
1985-86	New York	81	324	.430	190	.686	220	337	838	10.3
1986-87	Denver	81	358	.482	272	.745	327	282	988	12.2
	Totals	326	1328	.442	913	.729	992	1311	3573	11.0

MIKE EVANS 32 6-1 170   Guard

King of the threes...He's definitely not the best shooter from three-point territory in the NBA. But he's a threat to jack one up at anytime during a game...A Mad Bomber...- He can take the wind right out of an opponent's sails by going on a hot streak...Born April 19, 1955, in Goldsboro, N.C....Played at Kansas State under Jack Hartman...An original first-round draft pick of Denver in 1978...But he bounced around to San Antonio, Milwaukee and Cleveland before coming back to the Rockies and catching on in 1982... Barely makes above the NBA minimum salary of $75,000...A couple of years ago, when a salary survey was released, his considerate teammates left a can of dog food in his locker...Nice.

Year	Team	G	FG	FG Pct.	FT	FT Pct.	Reb.	Ast.	TP	Avg.
1979-80	San Antonio	79	208	.448	58	.682	107	230	486	6.2
1980-81	Milwaukee	71	134	.460	50	.781	87	167	320	4.5
1981-82	Mil.-Clev.	22	35	.407	13	.650	22	42	83	3.8
1982-83	Denver	42	115	.473	33	.805	58	113	263	6.3
1983-84	Denver	78	243	.431	111	.847	138	288	629	8.1
1984-85	Denver	81	323	.489	113	.863	119	231	816	10.1
1985-86	Denver	81	304	.425	126	.846	101	177	773	9.5
1986-87	Denver	81	334	.458	96	.780	128	185	817	10.1
	Totals	535	1696	.452	600	.806	760	1433	4187	7.8

CALVIN NATT 30 6-6 220   Forward

Career in jeopardy...Already bothered by a pair of arthritic knees that he said could shorten his career, he tore an Achilles tendon in the opening game of the 1986-87 season and was out for the year...It's questionable whether he can come back...Without his hustle and muscle, the Nuggets suffered badly ...Call him Old Blood and Guts...Always a candidate to be diving into the stands for a loose ball...Says that he enjoys the sight of his own blood and feeling the pain from diving on the floor...Born Jan. 8, 1957, in Bastrop, La....Played college ball at Northeastern, La....The No. 8 pick in the 1979 draft by New Jersey...Traded to Portland for Maurice Lucas...Came to Denver in 1984 as part of 5-for-1 package with Wayne Cooper and Fat Lever and two draft choices for Kiki Vandeweghe...Hardly plays like the son of a Baptist minister ...Brother Kenny had a brief NBA career.

Year	Team	G	FG	FG Pct.	FT	FT Pct.	Reb.	Ast.	TP	Avg.
1979-80	N.J.-Port.	78	622	.479	306	.730	691	169	1553	19.9
1980-81	Portland	74	395	.497	200	.707	431	159	994	13.4
1981-82	Portland	75	515	.576	294	.750	613	150	1326	17.7
1982-83	Portland	80	644	.543	339	.792	599	171	1630	20.4
1983-84	Portland	79	500	.583	275	.797	476	179	1277	16.2
1984-85	Denver	78	685	.546	447	.793	610	238	1817	23.3
1985-86	Denver	69	469	.504	278	.801	436	164	1218	17.7
1986-87	Denver	1	4	.400	2	1.000	5	2	10	10.0
	Totals	534	3834	.531	2141	.770	3861	1232	9825	18.4

MARK ALARIE 23 6-8 217   Forward

A project...Does not have good speed, but a few years under Doug Moe's motion offense and he could find a niche...A better-than-average shooter...Big star in college at Duke, where he used his smarts to get himself open and burned zone defenses...Played with San Antonio's Johnny Dawkins on Blue Devil team that lost to Louisville in 1986 NCAA title game...Born Dec. 11, 1963, in Phoenix...Denver was delighted that he was available in the No. 18 slot in the 1986 draft ...Should be part of the Nuggets' future...Has a degree in economics.

Year	Team	G	FG	FG Pct.	FT	FT Pct.	Reb.	Ast.	TP	Avg.
1986-87	Denver	64	217	.490	67	.663	214	74	503	7.9

BLAIR RASMUSSEN 24 7-0 250   Center

Not pretty, but he's managing to get the job done... After saying originally that the Nuggets made a mistake by making him a first-round draft choice in 1985, a lot of clubs have shown interest... Good outside shooter for a big man... Looks gawky at times, but gets rebounds... Born Nov. 13, 1952, in Auburn, Wash.... Became an All-Pac 10 performer at Oregon and fourth-leading scorer in school history... Raised his stock dramatically after his senior year at the postseason Aloha Classic... Last season he stole some of the minutes away from fellow backup big man Danny Schayes... Down the line, he could turn out to be a very valuable asset.

Year	Team	G	FG	FG Pct.	FT	FT Pct.	Reb.	Ast.	TP	Avg.
1985-86	Denver.............	48	61	.407	31	.795	97	16	153	3.2
1986-87	Denver.............	74	268	.470	169	.732	465	60	705	9.5
	Totals.............	122	329	.457	200	.741	562	76	858	7.0

DANNY SCHAYES 28 6-11 245   Center

A late bloomer... Had to overcome the burden of being the son of Hall of Famer Dolph Schayes... That's a lot to live up to... Was easily pushed around and developed a reputation as a crybaby when he entered the league ... Has been working to improve his game and succeeded somewhat... A good outside shooter for a big man... Was miscast as a starter last season when Wayne Cooper was injured... A decent enough backup... Born May 10, 1959, in Syracuse, N.Y., while dad was playing for the old Syracuse Nats... The No. 13 pick in the 1981 draft by Utah... He was traded to Denver in 1983 for Rich Kelley... Dad once came out of the stands at the Palestra in Philly during one of his college games for Syracuse when Danny Boy was getting roughed up.

Year	Team	G	FG	FG Pct.	FT	FT Pct.	Reb.	Ast.	TP	Avg.
1981-82	Utah.............	82	252	.481	140	.757	427	146	644	7.9
1982-83	Utah-Den.............	82	342	.457	228	.773	635	205	912	11.1
1983-84	Denver.............	82	183	.493	215	.790	433	91	581	7.1
1984-85	Denver.............	56	60	.465	79	.814	144	38	199	3.6
1985-86	Denver.............	80	221	.502	216	.777	439	79	658	8.2
1986-87	Denver.............	76	210	.519	229	.779	380	85	649	8.5
	Totals.............	458	1268	.484	1107	.779	2458	644	3643	8.0

WAYNE COOPER 31 6-10 220   Center

Was he hurt or just fat and happy?... When a string of nagging injuries caused him to miss games or play just part-time last season, people wondered if it wasn't because he had just signed a new multi-year, guaranteed contract ... Does he still have the hunger and desire now that he's finally gotten his respect and money?... Born Sept. 16, 1956, in Milan, Ga.... Butch van Breda Kolff was his college coach at New Orleans... Another blown draft pick by Golden State... Warriors made him the No. 40 pick in 1978 and let him get away... Went to Utah, Dallas and Portland before finally blossoming in Denver... An excellent shot-blocker, despite not having great leaping ability... Not a good shooter... Started late, did not play organized ball until his senior year in high school ... Has to show that he still wants it.

Year	Team	G	FG	FG Pct.	FT	FT Pct.	Reb.	Ast.	TP	Avg.
1978-79	Golden State	65	128	.437	41	.672	280	21	297	4.6
1979-80	Golden State	79	367	.489	136	.751	507	42	871	11.0
1980-81	Utah	71	213	.452	62	.689	440	52	489	6.9
1981-82	Dallas	76	281	.420	119	.744	550	115	682	9.0
1982-83	Portland	80	320	.443	135	.685	611	116	775	9.7
1983-84	Portland	81	304	.459	185	.804	476	76	793	9.8
1984-85	Denver	80	404	.472	161	.685	631	86	969	12.1
1985-86	Denver	78	422	.466	174	.795	610	81	1021	13.1
1986-87	Denver	69	235	.448	79	.725	473	68	549	8.0
	Totals	679	2674	.457	1092	.737	4578	657	6446	9.5

T.R. DUNN 32 6-4 193   Guard

Mr. Anonymous... Can do everything except score... Nuggets have always looked for an excuse to put him on the bench, but he does the dirty work so well that he keeps working his way back into the starting lineup... The lowest scoring average of any regular starter in the NBA, maybe in the history of the league ... Born Feb. 1, 1955, in Birmingham, Ala. ... Played college ball at Alabama and was the 41st pick of the 1977 draft by Portland... Spent three years with the Blazers... Traded to Denver for a second-round draft choice in 1980 and was well worth the price... Named after Theodore Roosevelt, he walks softly and carries a big stick... His body looks like a piece of classic sculpture . . . Unfortunately, there are statues who could score more.

Year	Team	G	FG	FG Pct.	FT	FT Pct.	Reb.	Ast.	TP	Avg.
1977-78	Portland	63	100	.417	37	.661	147	45	237	3.8
1978-79	Portland	80	246	.448	122	.772	344	103	614	7.7
1979-80	Portland	82	240	.436	84	.757	324	147	564	6.9
1980-81	Denver	82	146	.412	79	.653	301	81	371	4.5
1981-82	Denver	82	258	.512	153	.712	559	188	669	8.2
1982-83	Denver	82	254	.482	119	.730	615	189	627	7.6
1983-84	Denver	80	174	.470	106	.731	574	228	454	5.7
1984-85	Denver	81	175	.489	84	.724	385	153	434	5.4
1985-86	Denver	82	172	.454	68	.773	377	171	412	5.0
1986-87	Denver	81	118	.428	36	.655	265	147	272	3.4
	Totals	795	1883	.458	888	.723	3891	1452	4654	5.9

MAURICE MARTIN 23 6-6 200   Guard

The reincarnation of Rob Williams? . . . Almost from the moment he arrived in Denver, coach Doug Moe was on his back . . . Was labeled fat and lazy and spent most of the season riding the bench . . . When he did get on the floor, he rarely produced . . . The off-season acquisition of Darrell Walker pushed him farther down in the rotation . . . Has a lot of work to do to return from the depths of the lineup . . . Born July 2, 1964, in Liberty, N.Y. . . . Tied for third on St. Joseph's University all-time scoring list and was highly regarded . . . Nuggets wanted him badly and took him No. 16, ahead of Mark Alarie, in the 1986 draft . . . MVP in the Atlantic 10 in his senior year in college.

Year	Team	G	FG	FG Pct.	FT	FT Pct.	Reb.	Ast.	TP	Avg.
1986-87	Denver	43	51	.378	42	.636	41	35	147	3.4

TOP ROOKIE

ANDRE MOORE 23 6-9 215   Forward

A longshot . . . The Nuggets tried to trade up, but failed and settled for this darkhorse candidate at the No. 31 spot on the second round . . . Transferred to Loyola of Chicago after starting out at Illinois-Chicago . . . Was the Midwestern City Conference Player of the Year as a senior, scoring more than 20 points a game . . . Born July 2, 1964, in Chicago.

COACH DOUG MOE: Here's a guy with a sense of humor...

Here's a guy who definitely needed a sense of humor last season as his former Midwest Division contenders fell apart... Even his motion offense could not cover up for the loss of Calvin Natt and an injury that bothered Wayne Cooper for most of the year... Doesn't get a lot of respect because he's a nonconformist... But he can get people to play for him... When he's got the horses, he can make them run... Born Sept. 21, 1938, in New York City... He's still got the accent ... Went to North Carolina, where he played under Dean Smith ... He calls his old coach "El Deano"... Irreverence is what he's all about... Doesn't take himself too seriously... A three-time ABA all-star during a five-year playing career... Made the San Antonio Spurs into a run-and-shoot power team... Lost his job, moved to Denver and usually has had the Nuggets contending ... His teams are fun to watch and he is fun to be around... There's only one... They broke the mold.

GREATEST COACH

It was a different time and a different league, even a different basketball with red-white-and-blue stripes. But the game and the franchise were the same and they were undisputably the glory days of the Denver Nuggets.

Larry (The Traveler) Brown actually stayed around the Mile High City for nearly five years and produced some of the finest teams that Denver has ever seen. They had players like Mack Calvin, Fatty Taylor, David Thompson and Monty Towe and they rung up records of 65-19 in 1974-75 and 60-24 in 1975-76 in the ABA. But they could never get over the playoff hump and were beaten by the N.Y. Nets and a young Dr. J in the memorable 1976 finals.

The following season, the Nuggets joined the NBA and Brown kept them rolling right along with a pair of first-place finishes in the Midwest Division and quickly established the Nuggets as a legitimate force in the established league.

Doug Moe took the torch in 1981 and has done an excellent job. But so far, nobody in Denver has been able to match Larry Brown.

ALL-TIME NUGGET LEADERS

SEASON

Points: Spencer Haywood, 2,519, 1969-70
Assists: Lafayette Lever, 654, 1986-87
Rebounds: Spencer Haywood, 1,637, 1969-70

GAME

Points: David Thompson, 73 vs. Detroit, 4/9/78
Assists: Larry Brown, 23 vs. Pittsburgh, 2/20/72
Rebounds: Spencer Haywood, 31 vs. Kentucky, 11/13/69

CAREER

Points: Dan Issel, 16,589, 1975-85
Assists: Alex English, 2,694, 1979-87
Rebounds: Dan Issel, 6,630, 1975-85

GOLDEN STATE WARRIORS

TEAM DIRECTORY: Owner: Jim Fitzgerald; Pres.: Daniel Finnane; Exec. VP: Don Nelson; Dir. Player Personnel: Jack McMahon; Dir. Pub. Rel.: Cheri White, Coach: George Karl; Asst. Coaches: Herman Kull, Ed Gregory. Arena: Oakland Coliseum (15,025). Colors: Gold and blue.

SCOUTING REPORT

SHOOTING: Often the only thing foggier in the Bay Area than the twin spires of the Golden Gate Bridge is the Warriors' shot selection. George Karl simply has himself a collection of players who have never met a shot they didn't like. Of the regulars, only Larry Smith (.546) and Chris Mullin (.514) were able to coax half their shots into the hoop last season. In the case of Smith, five feet away in the paint is out of his range, so he barely counts as a marksman.

Sleepy Floyd is a tremendous streak shooter, but that means that he has some bad streaks. If center Joe Barry Carroll would take the ball inside more, he'd have a higher percentage, too. They've got to work on the power game more, get better shots and drive up those shooting numbers. Rookie Tellis Frank should help up front with a nice medium-range touch on the jumper.

As for Purvis Short, the fifth-leading scorer in the league in 1985-86, injuries limited him to 34 games last year.

PLAYMAKING: It's been a wild and crazy, highly improbable ride, but Floyd seems to have successfully made the transition from off guard to quarterback. Oh, he can still pour in the points —as his 51 against the Lakers in the playoffs will testify—but he's truly happy now dishing the ball off, as well. He ranked second in the league in assists, trailing only Magic Johnson. The problem here is with depth. Mullin doesn't handle the ball very well and there is too great a burden on Sleepy to be in the ballgame for the full 48 minutes.

DEFENSE: Only four teams in the league allowed their opponents to shoot a higher percentage from the field than the Warriors. Three of those teams—San Antonio, Phoenix and the LA Clippers—wound up in the draft lottery. So you can see that the Warriors aren't going very far in the playoffs if they don't change.

Sleepy Floyd averaged eye-opening 10.3 assists per game.

WARRIOR ROSTER

No.	Veteran	Pos.	Ht.	Wt.	Age	Yrs. Pro	College
2	Joe Barry Carroll	C	7-0	253	29	6	Purdue
21	Eric Floyd	G	6-4	178	27	5	Georgetown
22	* Rod Higgins	F	6-7	205	27	5	Fresno State
30	Ben McDonald	F	6-8	210	25	2	Cal-Irvine
10	* Perry Moss	G	6-2	185	28	2	Northeastern
17	Chris Mullin	G	6-6	205	24	2	St. John's
11	Clinton Smith	G	6-6	210	23	2	Cleveland State
13	Larry Smith	F	6-8	225	29	7	Alcorn State
20	* Terry Teagle	G	6-5	195	27	5	Baylor
8	Chris Washburn	C	6-11	254	22	1	North Carolina St.
33	Jerome Whitehead	C	6-10	234	31	9	Marquette

*Free agent unsigned at press time

Rd.	Top Rookies	Sel. No.	Pos.	Ht.	Wt.	College
1	Tellis Frank	14	F	6-10	225	Western Kentucky
3	Darryl Johnson	58	G	6-2	170	Michigan State
4	Bennie Bolton	83	F	6-8	220	North Carolina St.
5	Terry Williams	105	F	6-9	230	SMU

Carroll is where the whole thing begins and he is likely to be the one who gets the most "unofficial" help from new Warriors' minority owner Don Nelson. Remember, Nellie tried to get Carroll with an offer sheet two summers ago in Milwaukee, so he believes there is potential in that 7-foot body.

Smith, of course, is the bellwether on the boards for the Warriors, pound-for-pound the hungriest rebounder in the league. But they said they were going to draft some upfront help for Smith and then settled for the 6-10 Frank of Western Kentucky. He's tall, but not physical. The boost here could come from Chris Washburn, a washout as a rookie, who has the tools, but might lack the desire.

OUTLOOK: You can go up and down the roster and find plenty of holes that need filling. But this is an up-and-coming team that a lot of people wouldn't mind owning about five years from now. Jim Fitzgerald and Don Nelson give them stability in the front office and Karl is a good, young taskmaster on the sidelines.

They made their first playoff appearance in a decade last season and were routed by the Lakers in the first round. They might make more noise this year. If Nelson and Karl can find the way to light a fire under Carroll, the Warriors could be the surprise team of the season.

WARRIOR PROFILES

ERIC FLOYD 27 6-4 178   Guard

Sleepy . . . There was nothing drowsy about his performance in Game 4 of the playoff series against the Lakers last spring when he erupted for an NBA-record 29 points in the fourth quarter and finished with 51 to lead his team to a brilliant comeback win . . . Has always been a potent offensive performer . . . More importantly for the team, he has worked to become one of the league's top point guards . . . Second in the NBA in assists, trailing only Magic Johnson . . . A gambling defender who plays the passing lanes . . . Born March 6, 1960, in Gastonia, N.C. . . . Led Georgetown in scoring for four straight seasons and played in NCAA title game in 1982 which went to North Carolina . . . New Jersey made him No. 13 pick of 1982 draft . . . Warriors obtained him and Mickey Johnson for Micheal Ray Richardson on Feb. 6, 1963 . . . A real steal.

Year	Team	G	FG	FG Pct.	FT	FT Pct.	Reb.	Ast.	TP	Avg.
1982-83	N.J.-G.S............	76	226	.429	150	.833	137	138	612	8.1
1983-84	Golden State........	77	484	.463	315	.816	271	269	1291	16.8
1984-85	Golden State........	82	610	.445	336	.810	202	406	1598	19.5
1985-86	Golden State........	82	510	.506	351	.796	297	746	1410	17.2
1986-87	Golden State........	82	503	.488	462	.860	268	848	1541	18.8
	Totals.............	399	2333	.468	1614	.824	1175	2407	6452	16.2

JOE BARRY CARROLL 29 7-0 253   Center

He talks . . . After years of being the NBA's version of the reclusive Howard Hughes, J.B. is now sharing his thoughts with the outside world . . . He also seems to have finally gotten with the program and made an effort to fit into George Karl's system . . . Not the best defensive player, but he's trying now . . . Conflict of egos with Karl never materialized as he led the club in scoring . . . Born July 24, 1958, in Pine Bluff, Ark., also the birthplace of Denver's Fat Lever . . . Was an All-American at Purdue, where he earned a degree in economics . . . The No. 2 pick in the 1980 draft, ahead of Darrell Griffith and Kevin McHale . . . Warriors paid too dear a price of Robert Parish and the No. 3 spot (McHale) to get him . . . Contract dispute sent him to Italy for the 1984-85 season ... Now in the third year of five-year contract that will pay him $1.325-million this season.

Year	Team	G	FG	FG Pct.	FT	FT Pct.	Reb.	Ast.	TP	Avg.
1980-81	Golden State........	82	616	.491	315	.716	759	117	1547	18.9
1981-82	Golden State........	76	527	.519	235	.728	633	64	1289	17.0
1982-83	Golden State........	79	785	.513	337	.719	688	169	1907	24.1
1983-84	Golden State........	80	663	.477	313	.723	636	198	1639	20.5
1985-86	Golden State........	79	650	.463	377	.752	670	176	1677	21.2
1986-87	Golden State........	81	690	.472	340	.787	589	214	1720	21.2
	Totals.............	477	3931	.488	1917	.738	3975	938	9779	20.5

CHRIS MULLIN 24 6-6 205   Guard

On the way back ... Off to a bad start in rookie year due to contract hassle ... Then missed an offseason meeting with George Karl ... And showed up to camp very overweight ... He went to work, dropped the pounds and became a solid contributor by the end of the year ... Does not have the speed, so he must use his smarts to get open for his shots ... Deadly from medium range ... Needs plenty of work on his defense ... Born July 30, 1963, in Brooklyn, N.Y.... Became a legend during college career at St. John's ... All-American and winner of the 1985 John Wooden Award as the best college player in the country ... A gym rat, who can often be found working on his game late at night ... Warriors made him the No. 7 pick in the 1985 draft.

Year	Team	G	FG	FG Pct.	FT	FT Pct.	Reb.	Ast.	TP	Avg.
1985-86	Golden State........	55	287	.463	189	.896	F115	105	768	14.0
1986-87	Golden State........	82	477	.514	269	.825	181	261	1242	15.1
	Totals.............	137	764	.494	458	.853	296	366	2010	14.7

PURVIS SHORT 30 6-7 215   Forward

Just his luck ... The team finally has a good year and he spends most of it on the injured list with a bad left knee ... Still was delighted to make the playoffs for the first time in his nine-year pro career ... The Warriors' top gun ... He could still get along on one good leg and fire in that high-arching rainbow jumper ... One of the best pure shooters in the game today ... Not much at the defensive end, though ... Born July 2,

1957, in Hattiesburg, Miss.... Somehow the Warriors managed to hold onto this guy after making him the No. 5 selection in the 1978 draft... Played college ball at Jackson State... Has never played in the All-Star Game despite four straight seasons of averaging more than 20 points a game... Career high was 59 vs. New Jersey on Nov. 17, 1984... Brother Eugene played briefly for the Knicks.

Year	Team	G	FG	FG Pct.	FT	FT Pct.	Reb.	Ast.	TP	Avg.
1978-79	Golden State........	75	369	.479	57	.671	347	97	795	10.6
1979-80	Golden State........	62	461	.503	134	.812	316	123	1056	17.0
1980-81	Golden State........	79	549	.475	168	.820	391	249	1269	16.1
1981-82	Golden State........	76	456	.488	177	.801	266	209	1095	14.4
1982-83	Golden State........	67	589	.487	255	.828	354	228	1437	21.4
1983-84	Golden State........	79	714	.473	353	.793	438	246	1803	22.8
1984-85	Golden State........	78	819	.460	501	.817	398	234	2186	28.0
1985-86	Golden State........	64	633	.482	351	.865	329	237	1632	25.5
1986-87	Golden State........	34	240	.479	137	.856	137	86	621	18.3
	Totals............	614	4830	.479	2133	.818	2976	1709	11894	19.4

TERRY TEAGLE 27 6-5 195   Guard

Best return from the dead this side of Count Dracula... Looked like a wasted draft pick after two years with the Houston Rockets... But signed on as a free agent with Golden State and has turned into a valuable reserve ... Seems to have overcome his initial fear of playing at the NBA level... Has extraordinary leaping ability and can stick the outside shot ... What took him so long? Who knows?... Had the credentials when he came out of Baylor as the all-time scoring leader in the Southwest Conference... Houston had made him the No. 16 selection in the 1982 draft... Was cut by Rockets in 1984, played briefly with Detroit and was resurrected in the Bay Area ... Born April 10, 1960, in tiny Broaddus, Tex.... Exceptional physical talent.

Year	Team	G	FG	FG Pct.	FT	FT Pct.	Reb.	Ast.	TP	Avg.
1982-83	Houston...........	73	332	.428	87	.696	194	150	761	10.4
1983-84	Houston...........	68	148	.470	37	.841	78	63	340	5.0
1984-85	Det.-G.S...........	21	74	.540	25	.714	43	14	175	8.3
1985-86	Golden State........	82	475	.496	211	.796	235	115	1165	14.2
1986-87	Golden State........	82	370	.458	182	.778	175	105	922	11.2
	Totals............	326	1399	.467	542	.771	725	447	3363	10.3

LARRY SMITH 29 6-8 225   Forward

The Unknown Foot Soldier...Mr. Mean gets very little publicity for grabbing all of the big rebounds for the Warriors...His offensive game is nonexistent, except for layups he gets on offensive rebounds, but his work ethic is invaluable...Born Jan. 18, 1958, in Rolling Fork, Miss....Led the nation in rebounding as a senior, but was overlooked in the draft because he played at tiny Alcorn State...Warriors got a steal on the second round in 1980 and he's been a fixture on the front line ever since...As if this incredible hulk needs it, he loves to work out on the Nautilus machine during the offseason...An avid pool player...Probably eats cue balls for snacks...One tough hombre.

Year	Team	G	FG	FG Pct.	FT	FT Pct.	Reb.	Ast.	TP	Avg.
1980-81	Golden State........	82	304	.512	177	.588	994	93	785	9.6
1981-82	Golden State........	74	220	.534	88	.553	813	83	528	7.1
1982-83	Golden State........	49	180	.588	53	.535	485	46	413	8.4
1983-84	Golden State........	75	244	.560	94	.560	672	72	582	7.8
1984-85	Golden State........	80	366	.530	155	.605	869	96	887	11.1
1985-86	Golden State........	77	314	.536	112	.493	856	95	740	9.6
1986-87	Golden State........	80	297	.546	113	.574	917	95	707	8.8
	Totals.............	517	1925	.540	792	.563	5606	580	4642	9.0

CHRIS WASHBURN 22 6-11 254   Center

Wasted talent...Showed absolutely nothing as a rookie and then wound up entering a rehab program after admitting that he had a cocaine problem...Prior to that, he had become noteworthy only for missing busses, planes, practices and being late for games...Immense raw talent, but no brain to go with it...Passed up his last two years at North Carolina State to turn pro...George Karl's old coach, Dean Smith, warned him not to draft this guy...Warriors took him with the No. 3 pick and may live to regret it...Had off-the-court problems in college when he was prosecuted for stealing a stereo out of a dorm...Born May 13, 1965, in Hickory, N.C....He could stick around the league for years due to his size and strength and provide nothing more than a ton of headaches.

Year	Team	G	FG	FG Pct.	FT	FT Pct.	Reb.	Ast.	TP	Avg.
1986-87	Golden State........	35	57	.393	18	.353	101	16	132	3.8

ROD HIGGINS 27 6-7 205   Forward

The real Comeback Kid... He keeps coming back and coming back and coming back... Refused to quit after being cut by four different teams in the 1985-86 season... Set an NBA record by making appearances that year for Seattle, San Antonio, New Jersey and Chicago... Signed with the Warriors as a free agent and impressed with his hustle... Even started 28 games last season... Born Jan. 31, 1960, in Monroe, La.... Chicago made him a second-round pick out of Fresno State in 1982... Has long arms and can play good defense... Was one of only three Warriors to shoot 50 percent from the field... Will always be scrapping for a job.

Year	Team	G	FG	FG Pct.	FT	FT Pct.	Reb.	Ast.	TP	Avg.
1982-83	Chicago............	82	313	.448	209	.792	366	175	848	10.3
1983-84	Chicago............	78	193	.447	113	.724	206	116	500	6.4
1984-85	Chicago............	68	119	.441	60	.667	147	73	308	4.5
1985-86	Sea.-S.A.-N.J.-Chi...	30	39	.368	19	.704	51	24	98	3.3
1986-87	Golden State........	73	214	.519	200	.833	237	96	631	8.6
	Totals.............	331	878	.458	601	.773	1007	484	2385	7.2

JEROME WHITEHEAD 31 6-10 234   Center

Wears goggles like Kareem Abdul-Jabbar... Plays in the NBA like Kareem Abdul-Jabbar ...But that's where the similarity ends... He's got to work for every minute on the court... Spends his summers at Pete Newell's camp for big men and that has probably kept his career alive... Can be a useful backup center off the bench... He'll knock people down... Hardly an offensive threat... Born Sept. 30, 1956, in Waukegan, Ill.... Member of Al McGuire's NCAA title team at Marquette in 1977... Tapped in game-winning shot in semifinals to beat UNC-Charlotte at the buzzer... Father is a minister... He's had enough faith in himself to stick with it after bouncing from Buffalo to Utah to Dallas to Cleveland before landing with the Warriors in 1984... A second-round pick of the Buffalo Braves in 1978.

Year	Team	G	FG	FG Pct.	FT	FT Pct.	Reb.	Ast.	TP	Avg.
1978-79	San Diego.........	31	15	.441	8	.444	50	7	38	1.2
1979-80	S.D.-Utah.........	50	58	.509	10	.286	167	24	126	2.5
1980-81	Dal.-Clev.-S.D.......	48	83	.461	28	.500	214	26	194	4.0
1981-82	San Diego.........	72	406	.559	184	.763	664	102	996	13.8
1982-83	San Diego.........	46	164	.536	72	.828	261	42	400	8.7
1983-84	San Diego.........	70	144	.490	88	.822	245	19	376	5.0
1984-85	Golden State........	79	421	.510	184	.783	622	53	1026	13.0
1985-86	Golden State........	81	126	.429	60	.619	328	19	312	3.9
1986-87	Golden State........	73	147	.450	79	.699	262	24	373	5.1
	Totals.............	550	1564	.505	713	.721	2813	316	3841	7.0

PERRY MOSS 28 6-2 185   Guard

In just two seasons, he's already been in and out of more camps than a dozen boy scouts... Drafted No. 6 overall by Boston in 1985... Cut by Celtics and started rookie season in Washington... Lasted just 12 games and was cut... Failed tryout with New Jersey... Signed by Philly for rest of the year and was cut in camp in fall of 1986... Played for three different CBA teams and signed with Warriors as a free agent... Born Nov. 11, 1958, in Tucson, Ariz.... Played college ball at Northeastern... Will be back in the CBA before long... A very marginal talent.

Year	Team	G	FG	FG Pct.	FT	FT Pct.	Reb.	Ast.	TP	Avg.
1985-86	Wash.-Phil...........	72	116	.397	65	.730	115	108	304	4.2
1986-87	Golden State........	64	91	.440	49	.710	95	90	232	3.6
	Totals.............	136	207	.415	114	.722	210	198	536	3.9

BEN McDONALD 25 6-8 210   Forward

A hustler and a leaper... Filled in for 34 games as a starter in the spot of the injured Purvis Short... Couldn't make up for the offense, but he worked hard... Born July 20, 1962, in Torrance, Cal.... Stayed at home to play college ball at Cal-Irvine, where he developed reputation as a solid, but unspectacular player... A third-round (50th overall) draft pick of Cleveland in 1984 . . . He didn't hook on with the Cavs until signing as a free agent in 1985-86 season . . . George Karl remembered him from the Cleveland days and gave him a shot to win a job at Golden State . . . He made the most of the opportunity.

Year	Team	G	FG	FG Pct.	FT	FT Pct.	Reb.	Ast.	TP	Avg.
1985-86	Cleveland	21	28	.483	5	.625	38	9	61	2.9
1986-87	Golden State	63	164	.456	24	.632	183	84	353	5.6
	Totals	84	192	.459	29	.630	221	93	414	4.9

TOP ROOKIE

TELLIS FRANK 22 6-10 225　　　　　　　　　　**Forward**
A small forward trapped inside a big man's body . . . His game does not match up with what the Warriors said they were going after—a strong rebounder . . . Born April 26, 1965, in Gary, Ind. . . . Played little in his first two years at Western Kentucky . . . Got high marks at the postseason Aloha Classic . . . Has a good outside shot . . . The No. 14 selection on the first round.

COACH GEORGE KARL: He showed them in Cleveland . . . Just one season after he was run out of town by the lowly Cavaliers, he straightened out a sinking Warrior ship and took them to the playoffs for the first time in more than a decade . . . He's a rising star in the coaching ranks and should have received more votes in the Coach-of-the-Year balloting . . . He's young, but he's capable . . . Did an excellent job turning around a bad situation in his first year in Cleveland, then was fired the next year . . . Born May 12, 1952, in Penn Hills, Pa. . . . A scrapper who turned himself into an All-American at North Carolina . . . Carved out a five-year pro career in San Antonio and had to retire after a knee injury . . . Spent two years as Doug Moe's assistant with the Spurs and was twice named CBA Coach of the Year with Montana Golden Nuggets . . . Milwaukee's Don Nelson recommended him for the Warrior job . . . He's a no-nonsense coach . . . Believes in a tough defense and he gets results . . . Watch him . . . He's going places.

GREATEST COACH

A little-known fact: outside of the Celtics and Lakers, no NBA franchise in history has won more championships than the Warriors.

Another little known fact: the Warriors won the very first NBA championship in 1946-47.

So, we're talking about a franchise with a long and storied history and also the only one to make a coast-to-coast move from Philadelphia to the San Francisco Bay Area.

It was the legendary Eddie Gottlieb who led the Philly Warriors to that first title back in the 1940s and it was George Senesky who coached them to their second crown in 1955-56.

But we're looking for the best coaching job here and it's hard to look past those 1974-75 Warriors led by Rick Barry and under the direction of former defensive star Al Attles. That club hustled to a 48-34 regular-season mark, bulled its way through the playoffs and then shocked everybody by knocking off the heavily-favored Washington Bullets in a 4-0 sweep for the title.

The Warriors have had plenty of coaches in their day, but nobody has ever done a better job in one season than Al Attles.

ALL-TIME WARRIOR LEADERS

SEASON

Points: Wilt Chamberlain, 4,029, 1961-62
Assists: Eric Floyd, 848, 1986-87
Rebounds: Wilt Chamberlain, 2,149, 1960-61

GAME

Points: Wilt Chamberlain, 100 vs. New York, 3/2/62
Assists: Guy Rodgers, 28 vs. St. Louis, 3/14/63
Rebounds: Wilt Chamberlain, 55 vs. Boston, 11/24/60

CAREER

Points: Wilt Chamberlain, 17,783, 1959-65
Assists: Guy Rodgers, 4,845, 1958-70
Rebounds: Nate Thurmond, 12,771, 1963-74

HOUSTON ROCKETS

TEAM DIRECTORY: Chairman: Charlie Thomas; Pres./GM: Ray Patterson; Dir. Pub. Rel.: Jim Foley; Coach Bill Fitch; Asst. Coaches: Carroll Dawson, Rudy Tomjanovich. Arena: The Summit (16,279). Colors: Red and gold.

Where there's Akeem, there's usually a way for Rockets.

SCOUTING REPORT

SHOOTING: The Rockets' high shooting percentage in the previous few seasons was always due to the number of easy shots that they converted on the fastbreak and the dozens of alley-oops and power dunks that were rammed home by the Twin Towers of Akeem Olajuwon and Ralph Sampson. But the Houston running game ground to a halt last season when Lewis Lloyd and Mitchell Wiggins were booted out of the league for using cocaine and when Sampson, Olajuwon and seemingly everybody else on the team went down for stretches with injuries.

The Rockets had to slow down the tempo and lack of a consistent outside threat became a glaring weakness. Rodney McCray (.552) is among the best percentage shooters in the league, but is still not confident from the perimeter, while Robert Reid and Allen Leavell are strictly streaky. Steve Harris was a bust and Sampson struggled all year due to injuries. The best shooters on the team by the end were Olajuwon on his turnaround and reserve forward Jim Petersen from down on the baseline.

PLAYMAKING: The play that surely lived in the mind's eye of Rockets' fans all summer was the sight of Dirk Minniefield stripped of the ball at midcourt by Nate McMillan and Seattle going on to wipe out a five-point lead in the last 55 seconds of regulation to win the playoff series in Game 6.

The Rockets' point guards are strictly from hunger—Minniefield and Leavell—and, in fact, the team functions best when McCray handles the ball. The Rockets passed on Duke's Tommy Amaker in the draft and went for 6-6 Doug Lee of Purdue. To have the Twin Towers playing with these imposters in the backcourt is a crime.

DEFENSE: When you score a basket against the Rockets, you can feel good, because you had to work for it. Even when Sampson was shelved with a knee injury for 27 games, they still had what it took up front to shut down opponents' attempts to bring the ball into the middle. With Olajuwon, Sampson and McCray, they've got as awesome a shot-blocking frontline as you'll see in the game. They can stop you.

ROCKET ROSTER

No.	Veteran	Pos.	Ht.	Wt.	Age	Yrs. Pro	College
40	* Richard Anderson	F	6-10	243	27	3	Cal-Santa Barbara
5	Dave Feitl	C	7-0	240	25	1	Texas-El Paso
20	Steve Harris	G	6-5	195	24	2	Tulsa
1	Buck Johnson	F	6-7	190	23	1	Alabama
30	Allen Leavell	G	6-2	190	30	8	Oklahoma City
18	Cedric Maxwell	F	6-8	215	31	10	NC-Charlotte
22	* Rodney McCray	F	6-8	235	26	4	Louisville
10	* Dirk Minniefield	G	6-3	180	26	4	Kentucky
34	Akeem Olajuwon	C	7-0	250	24	3	Houston
43	Jim Petersen	C	6-10	236	25	3	Minnesota
33	* Robert Reid	G-F	6-8	215	32	9	St. Mary's (Tex.)
50	* Ralph Sampson	F-C	7-4	230	27	4	Virginia

*Free agent unsigned at press time

Rd.	Top Rookies	Sel. No.	Pos.	Ht.	Wt.	College
2	Doug Lee	35	G	6-6	220	Purdue
4	Joe Niego	82	G	6-6	205	Lewis (Ill.)
5	Andre LaFleur	104	G	6-3	190	Northeastern
6	Fred Jenkins	129	G	6-4	205	Tennessee
7	Clarence Grier	151	F	6-7	190	Campbell

REBOUNDING: This is the area where they were affected most by the absence of Sampson for most of last season, yet they still managed to finish fifth in the league in rebounding. Bill Fitch wants the big men to rip people's heads off for every rebound and he usually gets that kind of effort from the likes of Olajuwon, Petersen and McCray. Sampson is often criticized for not carrying his weight. But in the three seasons before last, he could always be counted on to pull down double-figure boards on an average night. When these guys are healthy, they clean the glass better than Windex.

OUTLOOK: Just a year ago they were being touted as the league's blossoming dynasty. But the Lakers bounced back, the Rockets were hit by injuries and drug suspensions and The Little Dynasty That Couldn't finished way up the track. The frontline is top quality, but the backcourt is dogmeat. They didn't have a first-round draft choice, so it's going to take a major trade to bolster the backcourt and make the Rockets serious contenders again. They might even be two years away from being considered a legitimate threat to return to the NBA finals. How quickly dynasties crumble.

ROCKET PROFILES

AKEEM OLAJUWON 24 7-0 250   Center

A dream or a nightmare? . . . Well, it depends which side of the fence you're on . . . In just his third NBA season, the torch has already been passed . . . He is clearly the best all-around center in the game today . . . Was voted to the starting Western Conference team for the 1987 NBA All-Star Game . . . He can do it all. Was 12th in the league in scoring, eighth in rebounding and third in blocked shots . . . Has developed an incredible fadeaway jump shot that almost hits the ceiling and he can use it effectively out to about 19 feet . . . Born Jan. 23, 1963, in Lagos, Nigeria . . . Wonderful success story . . . Came to U.S. sight-unseen by University of Houston coach Guy Lewis . . . Could barely dribble the ball, but was soon leading Cougars to three straight Final Four appearances . . . Left school early and Rockets won his rights in coin flip with Portland . . . Missed seven games last year with a knee injury . . . Heroic 49-point, 25-rebound effort could not save Rockets in Game 6 playoff loss to Seattle . . . Signed 10-year contract extension worth $20 million and worth every penny.

Year	Team	G	FG	FG Pct.	FT	FT Pct.	Reb.	Ast.	TP	Avg.
1984-85	Houston............	82	677	.538	338	.613	974	111	1692	20.6
1985-86	Houston............	68	625	.526	347	.645	781	137	1597	23.5
1986-87	Houston............	75	677	.508	400	.702	858	220	1755	23.4
	Totals.............	225	1979	.524	1085	.654	2613	468	5044	22.4

RALPH SAMPSON 27 7-4 230   Forward-Center

Maybe he'll wake up over the summer like Bobby Ewing of "Dallas" and discover it was all just a bad dream . . . Began the season on the injured list with a sprained ankle . . . Came back too soon and sprained the other ankle . . . Later missed seven weeks of the season due to arthroscopic knee surgery . . . Played only 43 games . . . Came back for the playoffs and averaged 18 points and 9 rebounds . . . But his 7-for-22 shooting performance and a missed jumper from the foul line in Game 6 vs. Seattle made him the object of fans' scorn again . . . Born July 7, 1960, in Harrisonburg, Va. . . . Stayed at home and received degree from the University of Virginia, but never won an NCAA title . . . You either love him or you hate him . . . Probably suffers from playing out of position at forward . . . No. 1 pick of the Rockets in 1983 after winning coin flip with Indiana . . . Earned $1,363,500 last season in the final year of a four-year contract . . . Became a free agent in the offseason . . . He'll win an NBA title—somewhere—before it's all over. Believe it.

Year	Team	G	FG	FG Pct.	FT	FT Pct.	Reb.	Ast.	TP	Avg.
1983-84	Houston...........	82	716	.523	287	.661	913	163	1720	21.0
1984-85	Houston...........	82	753	.502	303	.676	853	224	1809	22.1
1985-86	Houston...........	79	624	.488	241	.641	879	283	1491	18.9
1986-87	Houston...........	43	277	.489	118	.624	372	120	672	15.6
	Totals.............	286	2370	.503	949	.656	3017	790	5692	19.9

RODNEY McCRAY 26 6-8 235   Forward

Mr. Consistency . . . Rumor has it that Bogart learned his tough-guy routine from McCray . . . The Sphinx is like a backyard gossip compared to this guy . . . Doesn't toot his own horn, just goes out and plays hard every night . . . Great quickness and leaping ability make him one of the best in the league at finishing off the fastbreak . . . Can also be a terrific rebounder and added the duties of ball-handler last season . . . Born Aug. 29, 1961, in Mt. Vernon, N.Y. . . . Learned the game on the same playgrounds as Earl Tatum, Gus and Ray Williams and older brother Scooter . . . Became a starter as a freshman at Louisville when Scooter was injured and helped Cards to the 1980 NCAA title . . . Rockets made him No. 3 pick in 1983 draft . . . Finished ninth in the NBA in field-goal percentage (.552) and should have more of a role in the Houston offense . . . Earned $565,000 last season and became a free agent over the summer.

Year	Team	G	FG	FG Pct.	FT	FT Pct.	Reb.	Ast.	TP	Avg.
1983-84	Houston...........	79	335	.499	182	.731	450	176	853	10.8
1984-85	Houston...........	82	476	.535	231	.738	539	355	1183	14.4
1985-86	Houston...........	82	338	.537	171	.770	520	292	847	10.3
1986-87	Houston...........	81	432	.552	306	.779	578	434	1170	14.4
	Totals.............	324	1581	.536	890	.756	2087	1257	4053	12.5

ROBERT REID 32 6-8 215   Guard-Forward

The Entrepreneur... After the march to the NBA finals in 1986, he became the most familiar face in Houston. Had his own TV show, opened a nightclub and did everything but kiss babies on the street... Some thought the outside distractions hurt his game... Missed seven games in December after arthroscopic knee surgery and that slowed him considerably... Was not up to the task of being the point guard on a full-time basis... Born Sept. 30, 1955, in Atlanta... A military brat, he lived in Crete and Hawaii before settling in Schertz, Tex.... His mother is a pentecostal minister and he left the NBA in the 1982-83 season to pursue strict religious beliefs. Now he runs a bar. You figure it out... Rockets plucked him out of tiny St. Mary's University in San Antonio as the No. 40 pick in 1977 ... Jumper can be a work of art when it's on. But he shot just 30 of 89 (.337) in the playoff loss to Seattle... Earned $400,000 and became a free agent.

Year	Team	G	FG	FG Pct.	FT	FT Pct.	Reb.	Ast.	TP	Avg.
1977-78	Houston	80	261	.455	63	.656	359	121	585	7.3
1978-79	Houston	82	382	.492	131	.704	483	230	895	10.9
1979-80	Houston	76	419	.487	153	.736	441	244	991	13.0
1980-81	Houston	82	536	.482	229	.756	583	344	1301	15.9
1981-82	Houston	77	437	.456	160	.748	511	314	1035	13.4
1983-84	Houston	64	406	.474	81	.659	341	217	895	14.0
1984-85	Houston	82	312	.481	88	.698	273	171	713	8.7
1985-86	Houston	82	409	.464	162	.757	301	222	986	12.0
1986-87	Houston	75	420	.417	136	.768	289	323	1029	13.7
	Totals	700	3582	.467	1203	.730	3581	2186	8430	12.0

JIM PETERSEN 25 6-10 236   Center

Has had the women at The Summit swooning since he first arrived in the NBA... But he's not just another pretty face... A hard worker and a real banger who'll knock your head off going for a rebound... Has worked hard to develop a good medium-range jump shot and became much more of an offensive force last season... Born Feb. 22, 1962, in Minneapolis... Now people talk about him as the latest off the factory line at the University of Minnesota behind Kevin McHale and Mychal Thompson... But you'd have never known that in college... An excellent third-round draft choice by Houston (No. 51) in 1984. He went into the weight room and made himself into a bonafide NBA player... Friendly, an engaging talker ... Only Robert Reid makes more off-court personal appearances among the Rockets... Will get even better.

Year	Team	G	FG	FG Pct.	FT	FT Pct.	Reb.	Ast.	TP	Avg.
1984-85	Houston..........	60	70	.486	50	.758	147	29	190	3.2
1985-86	Houston..........	82	196	.477	113	.706	396	85	505	6.2
1986-87	Houston..........	82	386	.511	152	.727	557	127	924	11.3
	Totals.............	224	652	.498	315	.724	1100	241	1619	7.2

CEDRIC MAXWELL 31 6-8 215   Forward

Mad Max... The Mouth... The luckiest man alive... One morning in January he woke up and found himself traded from the lowly LA Clippers to the young and talented Rockets in exchange for a first-round draft choice... "I felt like I died and went to heaven," he said ... Born Nov. 21, 1955, in Kingston, N.C.... Made his name when he led UNC-Charlotte to the NCAA Final Four in 1977... But don't call him "Cornbread," as he was known in the college days... One of the most colorful players in the game... Has a funny line for every occasion... Spent eight seasons in Boston, after Celtics made him their first-round draft choice (12th overall) in 1977... Was the MVP of the 1981 NBA finals, when Boston beat Houston, and led the way again in 1984 in Game 7 when Boston downed LA... Had a $505,000 salary adjusted downward so he could fit under Rockets' salary cap... Likes to pull up to a construction site in his car with the air-conditioner running in the summer "and watch other people work."

Year	Team	G	FG	FG Pct.	FT	FT Pct.	Reb.	Ast.	TP	Avg.
1977-78	Boston.............	72	170	.538	188	.752	379	68	528	7.3
1978-79	Boston.............	80	472	.584	574	.802	791	228	1518	19.0
1979-80	Boston.............	80	457	.609	436	.787	704	199	1350	16.9
1980-81	Boston.............	81	441	.588	352	.782	525	219	1234	15.2
1981-82	Boston.............	78	397	.548	357	.747	499	183	1151	14.8
1982-83	Boston.............	79	331	.499	280	.812	422	186	942	11.9
1983-84	Boston.............	80	317	.532	320	.753	461	205	955	11.9
1984-85	Boston.............	57	201	.533	231	.831	242	102	633	11.1
1985-86	L.A. Clippers.......	76	314	.475	447	.795	624	215	1075	14.1
1986-87	LAC-Hou...........	81	253	.530	303	.775	435	197	809	10.0
	Totals.............	764	3353	.548	3488	.784	5082	1802	10195	13.3

ALLEN LEAVELL 30 6-2 190   Guard

He's like crabgrass. You can't get rid of him ... Mr. Roller Coaster was finally cut after seven seasons in the backcourt in November of last season ... None of the other 22 NBA teams showed an interest ... But he was re-signed in January when Lewis Lloyd and Mitchell Wiggins were booted out of the league for drug use ... Scrapped and hustled his way to a decent second half of the season ... Played well in the first round of the playoffs against Portland, then flamed out (15 of 51, .294) against Seattle ... Born May 27, 1957, in Muncie, Ind. ... Houston made him 104th pick of the 1979 draft out of Oklahoma City College ... A rare bone disease locked his right elbow and produced the weird form on his jumper ... A very streaky shooter who is too often out of control ... As long as he is starting, you know Houston has backcourt problems.

Year	Team	G	FG	FG Pct.	FT	FT Pct.	Reb.	Ast.	TP	Avg.
1979-80	Houston...........	77	330	.503	180	.814	184	417	843	10.9
1980-81	Houston...........	79	258	.471	124	.832	134	384	642	8.1
1981-82	Houston...........	79	370	.467	115	.852	168	457	864	10.9
1982-83	Houston...........	79	439	.415	247	.832	195	530	1167	14.8
1983-84	Houston...........	82	349	.477	238	.832	117	459	947	11.5
1984-85	Houston...........	42	88	.421	44	772	37	102	228	5.4
1985-86	Houston...........	74	212	.463	135	.854	67	234	583	7.9
1986-87	Houston...........	53	147	.411	100	.840	61	224	412	7.8
	Totals............	565	2193	.456	1183	.832	963	2807	5686	10.1

BUCK JOHNSON 23 6-7 190   Forward

The Buck stops here ... If only that were true ... Came to the Rockets with the reputation as a good inside performer who could take the ball to the hole against taller players ... But that was in college and this is a different ballgame ... He spent most of his rookie year on the bench ... Born Jan. 3, 1964, in Birmingham, Ala. ... Led University of Alabama to four straight NCAA appearances and was regarded by many as the sleeper of the 1986 draft. Instead, the Rockets might just have been asleep when they took him at the No. 20 spot. In need of guards, they could have selected Seattle's Nate McMillan or Philly's David Wingate ... Rockets say he's a young Alex English. The real Alex English should be insulted.

Year	Team	G	FG	FG Pct.	FT	FT Pct.	Reb.	Ast.	TP	Avg.
1986-87	Houston...........	60	94	.468	40	.690	88	40	228	3.8

DIRK MINNIEFIELD 26 6-3 180   Guard

Mini-talent . . . Rockets picked him up off the scrap heap from Cleveland for a third-round draft choice in December when Robert Reid had knee surgery . . . He was the answer to the point-guard problem for about a week and then his many weaknesses became exposed . . . Born Jan. 17, 1961, in Lexington, Ky. . . . Was Kentucky's Mr. Basketball in 1979 as a schoolboy and starred at the University of Kentucky . . . Named the team co-MVP three straight years . . . Drafted on second round by Dallas in 1983 and traded away to New Jersey less than a month later . . . Waived by the Nets, Chicago and Cleveland . . . He'll be back in the CBA before long.

Year	Team	G	FG	FG Pct.	FT	FT Pct.	Reb.	Ast.	TP	Avg.
1985-86	Cleveland	76	167	.481	73	.785	131	269	417	5.5
1986-87	Clev.-Hou	74	218	.452	62	.689	140	348	509	6.9
	Totals	150	385	.464	135	.738	271	617	926	6.2

DAVE FEITL 25 7-0 240   Center

You can't coach height . . . That's what Frank Layden keeps telling us and that's why guys like this keep getting drafted . . . Born June 8, 1962, in Butler, Pa., he was raised in Tucson, Ariz. . . . One of 10 children, has four sisters and five brothers. If they're all as big as he is it must have been a huge house . . . First-team All-WAC as a senior at UTEP . . . A decent outside shot, still needs plenty of polish . . . Rockets made him No. 43 pick in the 1986 draft . . . Sports a new-wavish spiked haircut.

Year	Team	G	FG	FG Pct.	FT	FT Pct.	Reb.	Ast.	TP	Avg.
1986-87	Houston	62	88	.436	53	.746	117	22	229	3.7

STEVE HARRIS 24 6-5 195   Guard

Somebody take his pulse . . . Is he alive or dead? . . . That's what Houston fans were asking after his second year in the league . . . Was supposed to blossom last season, but rarely got off the bench . . . Has a good medium-range jumper, but is not long outside threat . . . Also shows an unwillingness to penetrate, which annoys Bill Fitch . . . Born Oct. 15, 1963, in

Kansas City, Mo. . . . Played under Nolan Richardson at Tulsa and developed reputation as a pure shooter . . . All-time Tulsa scoring leader . . . No. 19 pick in the 1985 draft . . . Very up and down . . . Had 18 points in Game 5 of playoff series vs. Seattle, then shot 2-for-12 in Game 6 . . . It's time for him to start producing . . . He'll make a guaranteed $180,000 this season . . . At times looks frightened on the court . . . Barely says a word.

Year	Team	G	FG	FG Pct.	FT	FT Pct.	Reb.	Ast.	TP	Avg.
1985-86	Houston.	57	103	.442	50	.926	57	50	257	4.5
1986-87	Houston.	74	251	.419	111	.854	170	100	613	8.3
	Totals.	131	354	.425	161	.875	227	150	870	6.6

RICHARD ANDERSON 27 6-10 243   Forward

Who? . . . That's right, any questions about Houston's lack of depth last season can begin and end with this guy . . . Returned from Europe and oblivion to get in one more year toward an NBA pension . . . Incredibly, he's now fooled three different NBA teams—San Diego, Denver and Houston—long enough to collect a year's pay . . . Born Nov. 19, 1960, in Anaheim, Cal. . . . A sociology major at Santa Barbara . . . Second-round pick of the Clippers in 1982 . . . Traded to Denver for Billy McKinney . . . Waived by the Nuggets . . . Biggest contribution to Rockets was an airball in the last seconds of the final playoff loss to Seattle.

Year	Team	G	FG	FG Pct.	FT	FT Pct.	Reb.	Ast.	TP	Avg.
1982-83	San Diego.	78	174	.404	48	.696	272	120	403	5.2
1983-84	Denver.	78	272	.426	116	.773	406	193	663	8.5
1986-87	Houston.	51	59	.424	22	.759	79	33	144	2.8
	Totals.	207	505	.418	186	.750	757	346	1210	5.8

TOP ROOKIE

DOUG LEE 23 6-6 218   Guard

Who's he? . . . That's what Houston fans were asking when the Rockets plucked this guy with the No. 35 pick on the second round . . . Was not on any of the postseason scouting lists, though he had a decent showing in Chicago pre-draft camp . . . Born Oct. 24, 1964, in Peoria, Ill. . . . Began college career at Texas A&M and transferred to Purdue . . . He'll have to justify his selection.

COACH BILL FITCH: Just call him SOB—Same Old Bill . . .

Nothing ever changes except his hair color. Last season he became a redhead . . . Still is probably the single largest user of videotape in the country . . . Also uses cracks about his Irish ancestry and all sorts of jokes as tools . . . He needed that sense of humor last season as the defending Western Conference champs fell off their pedestal and were beaten by Seattle in the second round of the playoffs . . . He lost players to injury and drugs and also suffered from charges of tanking games . . . He tried to dance around the criticism, but the fact remains that a couple of poor first-round draft choices, hand-picked by him, hurt the Rockets' depth and chances to recover late in the season . . . Born May 19, 1934, in Davenport, Iowa . . . Became the fifth member of the NBA 700-win club (718-678) . . . Coaching career began at Coe College (Iowa), then on to Bowling Green and Minnesota before jumping to the NBA with expansionist Cleveland Cavs . . . Spent four years with Boston Celtics and never won fewer than 56 games . . . Only coach in NBA history to win titles in three different divisions . . . Received a three-year contract extension that will carry through 1991.

GREATEST COACH

It tells you something about the stability of a franchise when in his fourth season on the job Bill Fitch becomes the coach with the most longevity in the history of the Rockets' franchise.

Incredible as it may seem, in the 20-year history of this club in San Diego and Houston, Fitch is also only the second coach to have a career winning percentage better than the .500 mark.

Tom Nissalke (.504) took the Rockets on their earliest run to glory in the 1976-77 season. They won the Central Division title and gave the Philadelphia 76ers a real scare in the Eastern Conference finals.

Nissalke was followed by Del Harris, who, behind Moses Malone, led the Rockets on a Cinderella ride to the NBA finals in 1981, where they lost to—guess who?—Bill Fitch and Boston.

Fitch, a two-time NBA Coach of the Year in Boston and Cleveland, started over in Houston in 1983. He hasn't yet produced the championship Houston was promised, but he's fifth on the all-time NBA coaching list and is clearly the best that the Rockets have ever seen.

ALL-TIME ROCKET LEADERS

SEASON

Points: Moses Malone, 2,520, 1980-81
Assists: John Lucas, 768, 1977-78
Rebounds: Moses Malone, 1,444, 1978-79

GAME

Points: Calvin Murphy, 57 vs. New Jersey, 3/18/78
Assists: Art Williams, 22 vs. San Francisco, 2/14/70
    Art Williams, 22 vs. Phoenix, 12/28/68
Rebounds: Moses Malone, 37 vs. New Orleans, 2/9/79

CAREER

Points: Calvin Murphy, 17,949, 1970-83
Assists: Calvin Murphy, 4,402, 1970-83
Rebounds: Elvin Hayes, 6,974, 1968-72, 1981-84

LOS ANGELES CLIPPERS

TEAM DIRECTORY: Owner Donald T. Sterling: Pres.: Alan I. Rothenberg; Exec. VP/GM: Elgin Baylor; Exec. VP/Bus. Oper.: Andy Roeser; Dir. Pub. Rel.: Todd Parker; Dir. Inf.: Jack Gallagher; Coach: Gene Shue; Asst. Coach: Don Casey. Arena: Los Angeles Sports Arena (15,371). Colors: Red, white and blue.

Michael Cage rebounded into solid two-way performer.

SCOUTING REPORT

SHOOTING: You've heard of the Gang That Couldn't Shoot Straight? Well, meet their West Coast office. They couldn't hit the proverbial bull in the backside with a bass fiddle. Heck, based on the shooting percentages, they probably couldn't see either the bull or the fiddle.

Only Michael Cage, who shook off two seasons of playing like a wimp, was able to consistently put the ball in the hole (.515). The rest of the Clippers looked like they were trying to fit a medicine ball through a keyhole. There was Mike Woodson (.437), Larry Drew (.432), Benoit Benjamin (.449), Darnell Valentine (.410) and Quintin Dailey (.407) and even Marques Johnson (.439), prior to being sidelined after 10 games due to a leg injury.

It was downright dangerous to sit in the front row when the Clippers were playing. Top draft choice Reggie Williams should help, but this is an offense that needs a complete overhaul.

PLAYMAKING: In terms of numbers, this is like saying that the Rockettes don't have anybody who can dance. They went into last season with Norm Nixon, Drew and Valentine on the roster. But Nixon was on the injured list after tearing up his knee playing softball and Drew turned out to be a big (or is that little?) bust after coming south with Woodson as part of the deal that sent Derek Smith to Sacramento.

Drew has barely a 2-to-1 assist-turnover ratio and is more interested in getting his own points than dishing the ball off. Then there's Valentine, who was correctly dumped two seasons ago by Jack Ramsay when he was still in Portland. They'd better hope Nixon is completely healed this time around. He's their only hope.

DEFENSE: This is a team that thinks de-fense is something that goes around de-yard. They don't give up a lot of points because they play at a fast tempo. They give up points because their defense stinks. The center is the key to any defense and so you can look right to Benjamin for causing the foulest of odors. Until he decides that he wants to play in this league and be a shot-blocking force, the Clippers aren't going anywhere without a trade.

The hope here lies in the trio of rookies that were plucked on the first round. Reggie Williams certainly learned to play defense under John Thompson at Georgetown and Joe Wolf is an unspectacular, but solid player. Toss in Ken Norman and you've got a

CLIPPER ROSTER

No.	Veteran	Pos.	Ht.	Wt.	Age	Yrs. Pro	College
00	Benoit Benjamin	C	7-0	245	22	2	Creighton
44	* Michael Cage	F	6-9	230	25	3	San Diego State
25	* Earl Cureton	F-C	6-9	215	30	7	Detroit
20	Quintin Dailey	G	6-3	190	26	5	San Francisco
2	Larry Drew	G	6-2	190	29	7	Missouri
54	* Kenny Fields	F	6-7	225	25	3	UCLA
4	Lancaster Gordon	G	6-3	190	25	3	Louisville
8	Marques Johnson	F-G	6-7	220	31	10	UCLA
31	* Steffond Johnson	F	6-8	225	22	1	San Diego State
41	* Tim Kempton	F-C	6-10	245	23	1	Notre Dame
10	Norm Nixon	G	6-2	175	32	9	Duquesne
1	Darnell Valentine	G	6-2	185	28	6	Kansas
42	Mike Woodson	G	6-5	198	29	7	Indiana

*Free agent unsigned at press time

Rd.	Top Rookies	Sel. No.	Pos.	Ht.	Wt.	College
1	Reggie Williams	4	G-F	6-7	180	Georgetown
1	Joe Wolf	13	F-C	6-10	230	North Carolina
1	Ken Norman	19	F	6-8	215	Illinois
2	Norris Coleman	38	F	6-8	210	Kansas
3	Tim McCalister	47	G	6-3	200	Oklahoma

young nucleus around which to start over, which the Clippers have to do. They allowed opponents to make an ungodly .518 from the field last season.

REBOUNDING: We keep coming back to Benjamin, but it is so obvious that he is the key to this team doing anything. He's got the body and the talent, but has never shown the brains and rarely the desire to justify his selection as the No. 3 pick in the 1985 draft. Cage improved dramatically under the boards last year and should continue to be a consistent force. Williams averaged eight rebounds a game as a guard-forward at Georgetown and around here he's going to have to pitch in.

OUTLOOK: This graveyard of coaches has finally resurrected a ghost from its past. Gene Shue is back for a second try with this sad-sack franchise. This time he's got more talent on hand. The biggest obstacle he faces is a mental one of getting some of the veterans to believe in themselves again and to put out every night. The rookie choices of Williams, Wolf and Norman were good ones. All come from winning programs. It's rebuilding time from the ground floor with this club and it will be a couple of years, at least, before they can even dream of the playoffs.

CLIPPER PROFILES

MIKE WOODSON 29 6-5 198 Guard

Maybe it was the smog in Southern California ...Or maybe it was just a case of being infected by the Clippers...Whatever the reason, one of the best shooters in the game fell way off his mark last season...This is a guy who can usually start to drill jumpers the moment he steps off the bus...The Houston Rockets will never forget his incredible 22-for-24 performance from the field in 1983 when he was playing in Kansas City...Born March 24, 1958, in Indianapolis... Stayed close to home and attended Indiana University and learned what it's like to sweat under Bob Knight...The No. 12 pick overall in the 1980 draft, he's been moving ever since... Started in New York, then New Jersey, KC, Sacramento and now LA...Came to the Clippers with Larry Drew in exchange for Derek Smith, Franklin Edwards and Junior Bridgeman.

Year	Team	G	FG	FG Pct.	FT	FT Pct.	Reb.	Ast.	TP	Avg.
1980-81	New York	81	165	.442	49	.766	97	75	380	4.7
1981-82	N.J.-K.C.	83	538	.503	221	.773	247	222	1304	15.7
1982-83	Kansas City	81	584	.506	298	.790	248	254	1473	18.2
1983-84	Kansas City	71	389	.477	247	.818	175	175	1027	14.5
1984-85	Kansas City	78	530	.496	264	.800	198	143	1329	17.0
1985-86	Sacramento	81	510	.475	242	.837	226	197	1264	15.6
1986-87	L.A. Clippers	74	494	.437	240	.828	162	196	1262	17.1
	Totals	549	3210	.480	1561	.805	1353	1262	8039	14.6

MARQUES JOHNSON 31 6-7 220 Guard-Forward

Comeback II?...After all, sequels are the in thing nowadays...Having already won the Comeback Player of the Year Award in 1985-86, he's a candidate again after missing all but 10 games last season due to a ruptured cervical disc in his neck, suffered in a game against Dallas...Born Feb. 8, 1956, in Natchitoches, La., he was raised in Los Angeles...Named after Marques Haynes, the ball-handling wizard of the Harlem Globetrotters...Starred at UCLA...The No. 3 overall pick of the 1977 draft by Milwaukee...Spent seven years with the Bucks before returning to hometown with Harvey Catchings and Junior Bridgeman in trade for Terry Cummings, Ricky Pierce and Craig Hodges...At $1.3 million, he's one of the league's highest-paid players...Has shifted to the backcourt in LA...He deserves a fate better than to have to play for the

Clippers . . . Hit by tragedy in the offseason when his infant son fell into a swimming pool and drowned.

Year	Team	G	FG	FG Pct.	FT	FT Pct.	Reb.	Ast.	TP	Avg.
1977-78	Milwaukee..........	80	628	.522	301	.736	874	190	1557	19.5
1978-79	Milwaukee..........	77	820	.550	332	.760	586	234	1972	25.6
1979-80	Milwaukee..........	77	689	.544	291	.791	566	273	1671	21.7
1980-81	Milwaukee..........	76	636	.552	269	.706	518	346	1541	20.3
1981-82	Milwaukee..........	60	404	.532	182	.700	364	213	990	16.5
1982-83	Milwaukee..........	80	723	.509	264	.735	562	363	1714	21.4
1983-84	Milwaukee..........	74	646	.502	241	.709	480	315	1535	20.7
1984-85	L.A. Clippers........	72	494	.452	190	.731	428	248	1181	16.4
1985-86	L.A. Clippers........	75	613	.510	298	.760	416	283	1525	20.3
1986-87	L.A. Clippers........	10	68	.439	30	.714	33	28	166	16.6
	Totals............	681	5721	.519	2398	.738	4800	2493	13852	20.3

BENOIT BENJAMIN 22 7-0 245   Center

You've heard of people who can't walk and chew gum at the same time? . . . Here's one who has trouble doing those things separately . . . What an incredible waste of a big body on this under-motivated stiff . . . He can rebound when he wants to, is an offensive force occasionally . . . The only thing he's consistent about is getting his coaches and teammates mad and frustrated over his performances . . . Showed signs of coming on at the end of the 1985-86 season, but dogged it again in second year . . . Born Nov. 22, 1964, in Monroe La. . . . Left Creighton University early and Clippers made him the No. 3 pick in the 1985 draft, against the advice of his Creighton coach, former NBA great Willis Reed . . . First name is Lenard . . . Known for oversleeping and missing team busses and practices.

Year	Team	G	FG	FG Pct.	FT	FT Pct.	Reb.	Ast.	TP	Avg.
1985-86	L.A. Clippers........	79	324	.490	229	.746	600	79	878	11.1
1986-87	L.A. Clippers........	72	320	.449	188	.715	586	135	828	11.5
	Totals............	151	644	.469	417	.730	1186	214	1706	11.3

MICHAEL CAGE 25 6-9 230   Forward

Finally . . . Was motivated by a description of himself in this very handbook last year that called him a wimp . . . Said he took that personally and wanted to show he could be a real NBA force . . . He succeeded . . . Used his Greek god's body to become a strong inside player and ranked sixth in the league in rebounding . . . That earned him a role as a regular starter . . . If he continues, to work with the same dedication, he could become a star . . . Born Jan. 28, 1965, in West

Memphis, Ark.... A prep teammate of Keith Lee... A big scorer and rebounder at San Diego State... Most scouts shied away because of his lack of hustle and desire... Fact is, he played like a wimp in LA for the first two NBA seasons... Now he's shown signs of turning it around.

Year	Team	G	FG	FG Pct.	FT	FT Pct.	Reb.	Ast.	TP	Avg.
1984-85	L.A. Clippers	75	216	.543	101	.737	392	51	533	7.1
1985-86	L.A. Clippers	78	204	.479	113	.649	417	81	521	6.7
1986-87	L.A. Clippers	80	457	.521	341	.730	922	131	1255	15.7
	Totals	223	877	.515	555	.713	1731	263	2309	10.4

LARRY DREW 29 6-2 190   Guard

Talk about your flashes in the pan... This guy had one big season (1982-83) in Kansas City and turned that into untold free-agent riches ... The owners of the Kings paid him $700,000 per season and gave him big real estate holdings to keep him... He lasted just one season with the club in Sacramento and was shipped south with Mike Woodson in the deal for Derek Smith, Franklin Edwards and Junior Bridgeman ... Born April 2, 1958, in Kansas City, Kan.... No. 17 overall pick in the 1980 draft by Detroit... He's water-bug quick, but is an undependable shot... Cashing those big checks is like stealing money.

Year	Team	G	FG	FG Pct.	FT	FT Pct.	Reb.	Ast.	TP	Avg.
1980-81	Detroit	76	197	.407	106	.797	120	249	504	6.6
1981-82	Kansas City	81	358	.473	150	.794	149	419	874	10.8
1982-83	Kansas City	75	599	.492	310	.820	207	610	1510	20.1
1983-84	Kansas City	73	474	.462	243	.776	146	558	1194	16.4
1984-85	Kansas City	72	457	.501	154	.794	164	484	1075	14.9
1985-86	Sacramento	75	376	.485	128	.795	125	338	890	11.9
1986-87	L.A. Clippers	60	295	.432	139	.837	103	326	741	12.4
	Totals	512	2756	.471	1230	.802	1014	2984	6788	13.3

NORM NIXON 32 6-2 175   Guard

Savoir faire... That's what the Lakers used to call this slick operator back in the old days... The good old days... Since being shipped across town to the Clippers for Swen Nater and Byron Scott prior to the 1983-84 season, it's been all downhill... Had a contract hassle two seasons ago and missed all of the 1986-87 campaign with a knee injury suffered in a softball game... Born Oct. 11, 1955, in Macon, Ga.... Played prep ball under well-known motivator Don Richardson at Macon Southwest High... Not a high-percentage shooter, but he'll knock in the big jumper when you need... Shoots off-balance, leaning to one side... Married to singer Debbie Allen.

Year	Team	G	FG	FG Pct.	FT	FT Pct.	Reb.	Ast.	TP	Avg.
1977-78	Los Angeles	81	496	.497	115	.714	239	553	1107	13.7
1978-79	Los Angeles	82	623	.542	158	.775	231	737	1404	17.1
1979-80	Los Angeles	82	624	.516	197	.779	229	642	1446	17.6
1980-81	Los Angeles	79	576	.476	196	.778	232	696	1350	17.1
1981-82	Los Angeles	82	628	.493	181	.808	176	652	1440	17.6
1982-83	Los Angeles	79	533	.475	125	.744	205	566	1191	15.1
1983-84	San Diego	82	587	.462	206	.760	203	914	1391	17.0
1984-85	L.A. Clippers	81	596	.465	170	.780	218	711	1395	17.2
1985-86	L.A. Clippers	67	403	.438	131	.809	180	576	979	14.6
1986-87	L.A. Clippers					Injured				
Totals		715	5066	.485	1479	.773	1913	6047	11703	16.4

EARL CURETON 30 6-9 215   Forward-Center

The consummate journeyman... Shows just enough flashes to make you think he could be a real star, but can't do it on a consistent basis ... Born Sept. 3, 1957, in Detroit... Stayed home to play for the University of Detroit, and the Philadelphia 76ers made him a third-round pick in 1979... Was a reserve on Philly's championship team in 1983... Traded to Chicago before last season, he came to Clippers after All-Star Game break for 1989 draft pick... He'll stick around strictly on hustle for another year or two.

Year	Team	G	FG	FG Pct.	FT	FT Pct.	Reb.	Ast.	TP	Avg.
1980-81	Philadelphia	52	93	.454	33	.516	155	25	219	4.2
1981-82	Philadelphia	66	149	.487	51	.543	270	32	349	5.3
1982-83	Philadelphia	73	108	.419	33	.493	269	43	249	3.4
1983-84	Detroit	73	81	.458	31	.525	287	36	193	2.6
1984-85	Detroit	81	207	.484	82	.569	419	83	496	6.1
1985-86	Detroit	80	285	.505	117	.555	504	137	687	8.6
1986-87	Chi.-LAC	78	243	.476	82	.539	452	122	568	7.3
Totals		503	1166	.476	429	.542	2356	478	2761	5.5

LANCASTER GORDON 25 6-3 190   Guard

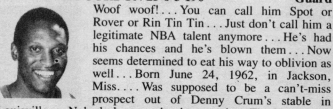

Woof woof!... You can call him Spot or Rover or Rin Tin Tin... Just don't call him a legitimate NBA talent anymore... He's had his chances and he's blown them... Now seems determined to eat his way to oblivion as well... Born June 24, 1962, in Jackson, Miss.... Was supposed to be a can't-miss prospect out of Denny Crum's stable in Louisville... Nobody knows what happened... The No. 8 pick overall in 1984 by LA, he has not produced at all... His

.406 shooting percentage last year was the best of his three-year career . . . Here, Lancaster, go chase the bone.

Year	Team	G	FG	FG Pct.	FT	FT Pct.	Reb.	Ast.	TP	Avg.
1984-85	L.A. Clippers	63	110	.383	37	.755	61	88	259	4.1
1985-86	L.A. Clippers	60	130	.377	45	.804	68	60	312	5.2
1986-87	L.A. Clippers	70	221	.406	70	.737	126	139	526	7.5
	Totals	193	461	.392	152	.760	255	287	1097	5.7

KENNY FIELDS 25 6-7 225   Forward

Staying alive . . . But barely . . . After Milwaukee made him the 21st pick overall in the 1984 draft, he showed nothing in spot duty for Don Nelson . . . Bucks waived him early last season and he was signed as a free agent by the Clippers . . . Born Feb. 9, 1962, in Iowa City, Iowa . . . Made a name for himself at UCLA, but also developed a reputation as being lazy . . . Take a good look. He won't be around much longer.

Year	Team	G	FG	FG Pct.	FT	FT Pct.	Reb.	Ast.	TP	Avg.
1984-85	Milwaukee	51	84	.440	27	.750	84	38	195	3.8
1985-86	Milwaukee	78	204	.513	91	.689	203	79	499	6.4
1986-87	Mil.-LAC	48	159	.452	73	.777	148	61	394	8.2
	Totals	177	447	.475	191	.729	435	178	1088	6.1

RORY WHITE 28 6-8 215   Forward

The Invisible Man . . . Every year you think he's gone from the NBA and every year he seems to turn up with a job . . . In five seasons, he's been with three teams . . . He's strong and has good leaping ability . . . But he continues to collect NBA paychecks because of his willingness to hustle and scrap . . . Born Aug. 16, 1959, in Tuskegee, Ala. . . . A fourth-round draft choice of Phoenix out of South Alabama . . . Has also played briefly in Milwaukee . . . Was out of the league, played with the Albuquerque Silvers of the CBA and returned to the bigs with the Clippers in 1983 . . . One of those guys who plays for the minimum salary.

Year	Team	G	FG	FG Pct.	FT	FT Pct.	Reb.	Ast.	TP	Avg.
1982-83	Phoenix	65	127	.543	70	.642	105	30	324	5.0
1983-84	Phoe.-Mil.-S.D.	36	80	.471	26	.553	74	15	186	5.2
1984-85	L.A. Clippers	80	144	.516	90	.692	195	34	378	4.7
1985-86	L.A. Clippers	75	355	.519	164	.739	181	74	875	11.7
1986-87	L.A. Clippers	68	265	.480	94	.653	194	79	624	9.2
	Totals	324	971	.506	444	.681	749	232	2387	7.4

QUINTIN DAILEY 26 6-3 190 Guard

The Q-Man...San Quintin...Off-court problems have followed him everywhere...Had to turn to the woeful Clippers for another —perhaps his last—shot at the NBA after entering a drug rehab program twice in his career at Chicago...Clips signed him midway through the season and he was perfectly dreadful...Now he's fat, too...Born Jan. 22, 1961, in Baltimore...Bulls made him the No. 7 pick in 1982 draft, despite a much-publicized sexual assault charge while at the University of San Francisco...When he's hot, he can hit the long-range shot...But the feeling is he's wasted a potential big career.

Year	Team	G	FG	FG Pct.	FT	FT Pct.	Reb.	Ast.	TP	Avg.
1982-83	Chicago	76	470	.466	206	.730	260	280	1151	15.1
1983-84	Chicago	82	583	.474	321	.811	235	254	1491	18.2
1984-85	Chicago	79	525	.473	205	.817	208	191	1262	16.0
1985-86	Chicago	35	203	.432	163	.823	68	67	569	16.3
1986-87	L.A. Clippers	49	200	.407	119	.768	83	79	520	10.6
	Totals	321	1981	.460	1014	.791	854	871	4993	15.6

DARNELL VALENTINE 28 6-2 185 Guard

What happened?...He came into the league with such promise and just hasn't made much progress since...Spent four-and-a-half seasons in Portland before falling into then-coach Jack Ramsay's doghouse...Blazers had made him No. 16th pick overall in 1980 draft...Clippers got him in a bad deal that sent a first-round pick up to Portland...Born Feb. 3, 1959, in Chicago...Developed big reputation at Kansas and was named to the 1980 U.S. Olympic team that boycotted the Games...A horrible offensive player, he's just adequate now as a point guard and defender...Has thighs that look like tree trunks...A perfect Clipper—overrated and washed up.

Year	Team	G	FG	FG Pct.	FT	FT Pct.	Reb.	Ast.	TP	Avg.
1981-82	Portland	82	187	413	152	.760	149	270	526	6.4
1982-83	Portland	47	209	.454	169	.793	117	293	587	12.5
1983-84	Portland	68	251	.447	194	.789	127	395	696	10.2
1984-85	Portland	75	321	.473	230	.793	219	522	872	11.6
1985-86	Port.-LAC	62	161	.415	130	.743	125	246	456	7.4
1986-87	L.A. Clippers	65	275	.410	163	.815	150	447	726	11.2
	Totals	399	1404	.437	1038	.784	887	2173	3863	9.7

TOP ROOKIES

REGGIE WILLIAMS 23 6-7 180   Guard-Forward
A winner, plain and simple... He's got the shot, the ball-handling ability, plays defense and goes to the boards... Did it all for Georgetown last season... The Hoyas averaged 24 wins a season during his college career... Born March 5, 1964, in Baltimore... Georgetown's all-time single-season scoring leader... Big East Player of the Year in 1987... No. 4 pick in the first round.

JOE WOLF 22 6-11 230   Center-Forward
Comes from family of athletes... An excellent shooter and a solid performer on the boards... Received college training at North Carolina under Dean Smith... Born Dec. 17, 1964, in Kohler, Wis.... A great competitor who improved every season with the Tar Heels... The No. 13 pick on the first round, a selection the Clippers received from Houston in a trade for Cedric Maxwell... The second of three first-round picks for the Clips.

KEN NORMAN 23 6-8 215   Forward
Snake... Got the nickname for his slithery moves around the basket... A proven scorer who was All-Big Ten in both his junior and senior seasons... Born Sept. 5, 1964, in Chicago... Started career at Wabash (Ill.) Valley College, then transferred to Illinois... The No. 19 selection on the first round, a pick the Clippers obtained from Detroit.

COACH GENE SHUE: Second time around... He guided this mismanaged Clipper franchise back in the days in San Diego... It is a match made in heaven, because he's made a career out of getting the most from problem players... Despite 20 years of mostly rebuilding teams, he is currently the fourth-winningest coach (757 victories) in NBA history, trailing only Red Auerbach, Jack Ramsay and Dick Motta... If he can whip this team into shape, then he's a real miracle worker... Born Dec. 18, 1931, in Baltimore... A star performer at the University of Maryland... The third player taken in the 1954 draft... Had a 10-year NBA playing career... Started coaching with Baltimore Bullets, then went to Philly, San Diego and back to Washington... Was fired by the Bullets late in the 1985-86 season... Spent the interim as a color commentator on Philly TV crew... Coach of the Year in 1969 and 1982... This is his

roughest challenge yet... Always youthful looking...
According to Dr. J, that's because he dyes his hair with shoe
polish.

GREATEST COACH

Best coach in the history of the Clippers? As they used to say
in those old cop movies, just round up all of the usual suspects.

We are definitely talking suspects here, since the Clippers are
barely conversant in the language of winning basketball games.

This franchise sucks coaches down like a bog of quicksand.
Since being founded in 1972 in Buffalo, there have been 11 different coaches of the Braves/Clippers and not a single one has a
career percentage of .500.

If you want the best, you've probably got to go back to the
first—Jack Ramsay, who led the Braves in Buffalo for four seasons before fleeing to Portland and took the franchise to its only
three trips to the playoffs, the last in 1976.

They have been the Clippers of San Diego and LA since mov-
ing to the West Coast in 1978 and have barely seen the light of a
Southern California day under Gene Shue, Paul Silas, Jim
Lynam, Don Chaney. And now Shue is back.

The greatest coach of the Clippers has yet to be found.

ALL-TIME CLIPPER LEADERS

SEASON

Points: Bob McAdoo, 2,831, 1974-75
Assists: Norm Nixon, 914, 1983-84
Rebounds: Elmore Smith, 1,184, 1971-72

GAME

Points: Bob McAdoo, 52 vs. Seattle, 3/17/76
Bob McAdoo, 52 vs. Boston, 2/22/74
Assists: Ernie DiGregorio, 25 vs. Portland, 1/1/74
Rebounds: Swen Nater, 32 vs. Denver, 12/14/79

CAREER

Points: Randy Smith, 12,735, 1971-79, 1982-83
Assists: Randy Smith, 3,498, 1971-79, 1982-83
Rebounds: Bob McAdoo, 4,229, 1972-76

LOS ANGELES LAKERS

TEAM DIRECTORY: Owner: Jerry Buss; Pres.: Bill Sharman; GM: Jerry West; Dir. Pub. Rel.: Josh Rosenfeld; Coach: Pat Riley; Asst. Coaches: Bill Bertka, Randy Pfund. Arena: The Forum (17,505). Colors: Royal purple and gold.

SCOUTING REPORT

SHOOTING: The name of the game is putting the ball into the hole. The guys that do it the most win. Therefore, it should come as no surprise that the team that did it more efficiently than anybody else won the championship last season. Actually, for the first time in recent memory, the Lakers finished second (.516 to Boston's .517) in field-goal percentage, but still possess the most potent offense in the game.

It's like walking into Howard Johnson's with 31 different flavors. How do you want your points—Kareem Abdul-Jabbar's skyhook (.564), James Worthy's inside moves (.539), A.C. Green on offensive rebounds (.538), Magic Johnson from anywhere (.522) or Mychal Thompson from medium range (.480)? When it comes to shooting the ball, the Lakers are the best.

PLAYMAKING: Magic. The nickname makes it all sound so deceiving, as if it happens with a simple wave of a hand or a wand. But playmaking begins and ends with Magic, the best in the game today, and perhaps the best—along with Oscar Robertson—ever to lace up his sneakers in the NBA. The peek-a-boo over-the-shoulder backdoor pass, the bullet-through-a-crowd on the fastbreak or the simple bounce pass to Kareem for the sky-hook. He's the best there is at setting up the bucket.

As long as his knees hold up, the Lakers don't have a worry in the world in this department. There are a lot of other teams in the league who would be content to have Magic's backup at the point position, Michael Cooper, running their offense.

DEFENSE: Yeah, yeah, yeah, we've heard it all before. The Lakers are glitz and glitter and Showtime and fastbreak dunks. They rank at the top of the league in offensive stats and somewhere in the middle on defense. But those defensive numbers are a product of their fastbreak style of play. These guys can throw down some ferocious defense. Don't believe it? Ask the Boston Celtics, who had the clamps put on them (30-12) in the third quarter of the clinching Game 6 of the NBA finals last year.

The Lakers trapped and smothered and put the Celtics in a

James Worthy and Lakers set sights on two in a row.

defensive vice that eventually squeezed out their fourth world championship in eight years. Just look at the point-differential numbers. LA outscored its opponents by an astounding 9.3 points a game last season. Now that's defense.

REBOUNDING: They may not be in the best rebounders in the NBA, but they are fairly efficient. Instead of getting bigger, bulk-

LAKER ROSTER

No.	Veteran	Pos.	Ht.	Wt.	Age	Yrs. Pro	College
33	Kareem Abdul-Jabbar	C	7-2	235	40	18	UCLA
24	* Adrian Branch	F	6-8	185	23	1	Maryland
21	Michael Cooper	G	6-7	170	31	9	New Mexico State
45	A.C. Green	F	6-9	220	24	2	Oregon State
32	Earvin Johnson	G	6-9	215	28	8	Michigan State
1	* Wes Matthews	G	6-1	170	28	7	Wisconsin
31	Kurt Rambis	F	6-8	220	29	6	Santa Clara
4	* Byron Scott	G	6-4	202	26	4	Arizona State
52	* Mike Smrek	C	7-0	250	25	2	Canisius
55	Billy Thompson	F	6-7	195	23	1	Louisville
43	Mychal Thompson	C-F	6-10	226	32	9	Minnesota
42	James Worthy	F	6-9	219	26	5	North Carolina

*Free agent unsigned at press time

Rd.	Top Rookies	Sel. No.	Pos.	Ht.	Wt.	College
3	Willie Glass	69	F	6-6	210	St. John's
4	Ralph Tally	92	G	6-1	170	Norfolk State
5	Kenny Travis	115	G	6-2	175	New Mexico State
6	Frank Ford	138	G	6-4	220	Auburn
7	Ron Vanderschaaf	161	F	6-8	215	Central Washington

ier bodies following their upset playoff loss to Houston two years ago, the Lakers got leaner and faster and it produced a title. Nevertheless, this is still a chink in their armor and if they fail to repeat, this will likely be the reason. They are still vulnerable to a tall team with speed, such as Houston. A frontline of Abdul-Jabbar, Worthy, Green and Mychal Thompson doesn't really scare anybody when it comes to rebounding.

OUTLOOK: Based on their regular-season and playoff performance, the inclination is to say that if any team is going to repeat as champions, Pat Riley's Lakers can do it. But we've been saying that about defending champs for the last 18 years and not since the 1969 Celtics has any team been able to win back-to-back.

Will it be injuries, complacency or lack of rebounding strength? Surely, the Lakers are capable of repeating and surely they will be in the hunt all the way. But history says, when it comes time to fit the 1988 champ for rings, it won't be the team in the purple and gold.

LAKER PROFILES

EARVIN (MAGIC) JOHNSON 28 6-9 215   Guard

The main man... The MVP.... Finally... After seven seasons of setting the table for the Lakers, he finally got the individual recognition he deserved... Pat Riley made him the focus of the offense and he responded by winning both the regular-season and NBA finals MVP awards... Shooting, passing, rebounding, he can do it all... Boston's Larry Bird calls him "the only player in the NBA I'd pay to watch."... Born Aug. 14, 1959, in Lansing, Mich... Won the NCAA title as a sophomore at Michigan State and then jumped to the NBA, where he led Lakers to the title as a rookie... He's already won four championships as a pro... Led the NBA in assists and is considered by many the best passer who ever played the game ... The term "triple-double" was invented specifically for him ... Twenty assists is just another Magic night... Reputation as a Hollywood star, but is actually very quiet and loner off the floor ... Bothered by chronic tendinitis, but offseason workouts have reduced the pain... The best in the game right now.

Year	Team	G	FG	FG Pct.	FT	FT Pct.	Reb.	Ast.	TP	Avg.
1979-80	Los Angeles..........	77	503	.530	374	.810	596	563	1387	18.0
1980-81	Los Angeles..........	37	312	.532	171	.760	320	317	798	21.6
1981-82	Los Angeles..........	78	556	.537	329	.760	751	743	1447	18.6
1982-83	Los Angeles..........	79	511	.548	304	.800	683	829	1326	16.8
1983-84	Los Angeles..........	67	441	.565	290	.810	491	875	1178	17.6
1984-85	L.A. Lakers..........	77	504	.561	391	.843	476	968	1406	18.3
1985-86	L.A. Lakers..........	72	483	.526	378	.871	426	907	1354	18.8
1986-87	L.A. Lakers..........	80	683	.522	535	.848	504	977	1909	23.9
	Totals.............	567	3993	.539	2772	.818	4247	6179	10805	19.1

JAMES WORTHY 26 6-9 219   Forward

The newest superstar... Finally came out of the shadows of the other big-name Lakers and established himself as a virtually unstoppable force last season... Only low points came during the three games at Boston Garden in the NBA finals when he couldn't buy a basket and became tentative... Returned to LA for Game 6 and made a big hustle play, diving to save a loose ball in the third quarter, that sent the Lakers on the way to the title... Born Feb. 27, 1961, in Gastonia, N.C.... Won an NCAA title under Dean Smith at North Carolina in 1982... Lakers made him the No. 1 pick in the 1982 draft with a choice they obtained from Cleveland for Don Ford... Explosive leaper, great first step, awesome on the fastbreak and he can post up, too... Wears the Abdul-Jabbar-style goggles... All-time playoff leader in field-goal percentage.

Year	Team	G	FG	FG Pct.	FT	FT Pct.	Reb.	Ast.	TP	Avg.
1982-83	Los Angeles	77	447	.579	138	.624	399	132	1033	13.4
1983-84	Los Angeles	82	495	.556	195	.759	515	207	1185	14.5
1984-85	L.A. Lakers	80	610	.572	190	.776	511	201	1410	17.6
1985-86	L.A. Lakers	75	629	.579	242	.771	387	201	1500	20.0
1986-87	L.A. Lakers	82	651	.539	292	.751	466	226	1594	19.4
	Totals	396	2832	.564	1057	.741	2278	967	6722	17.0

MICHAEL COOPER 31 6-7 170   Guard

Mr. Do-It-All... Let's see, he's the defensive specialist, the sparkplug off the bench, the awesome fastbreak dunker and the three-point shot artist... Did we leave out selling popcorn at halftime? Simply a great athlete, who is also a keen student of the game and has made himself into a wonderful offensive and defensive weapon... Named the league's Defensive Player of the Year last season, he also set record in NBA finals with 6-of-7 three pointers in Game 2 vs. Boston... Brings the Forum crowd to its feet when he hooks up with Magic Johnson for one of his Coop-a-Loop dunks... Born April 15, 1956, in Los Angeles... Another great draft choice by the Lakers as the No. 60 player in the 1978 draft... Played at New Mexico State and wants to return to New Mexico to live at the end of his career... High-strung, excitable... Colorful and quotable... What's not to love about him?

Year	Team	G	FG	FG Pct.	FT	FT Pct.	Reb.	Ast.	TP	Avg.
1978-79	Los Angeles	3	3	.500	0	.000	0	0	6	2.0
1979-80	Los Angeles	82	303	.524	111	.776	229	221	722	8.8
1980-81	Los Angeles	81	321	.491	117	.785	336	232	763	9.4
1981-82	Los Angeles	76	383	.517	139	.813	269	230	907	11.9
1982-83	Los Angeles	82	266	.535	102	.785	274	315	639	7.8
1983-84	Los Angeles	82	273	.497	155	.838	262	482	739	9.0
1984-85	L.A. Lakers	82	276	.465	115	.865	255	429	702	8.6
1985-86	L.A. Lakers	82	274	.452	147	.865	244	466	758	9.2
1986-87	L.A. Lakers	82	322	.438	126	.851	254	373	859	10.5
	Totals	652	2421	.488	1012	.823	2123	2848	6095	9.3

MYCHAL THOMPSON 32 6-10 226   Center-Forward

Died and went to heaven... At midseason, he was toiling for the San Antonio Spurs, the second-worst team in the Western Conference... But one of those incredible trades that the Lakers always seem to pull off brought him to LA in exchange for Frank Brickowski, Petur Gudmundsson and a couple of draft picks... What a steal!... He gave the Lakers the depth up front they needed to win it all... Did an excellent job in the clincher over Boston... Born Jan. 30, 1955, in Nassau, The Bahamas... Says he wants to be Prime Minister there someday... Grew up in Miami, where he played cricket, softball and soccer... Starred in basketball at the University of Minnesota and became first foreign-born player drafted No. 1 overall when Blazers tabbed him in 1978... Spent eight seasons in Portland claiming he was a power forward, not a center... Sent to San Antonio in June 1986 for Larry Krystowiak and Steve Johnson... One of the most glib players in the league... He's got a one-liner for every occasion... Good perimeter shooter as well.

Year	Team	G	FG	FG Pct.	FT	FT Pct.	Reb.	Ast.	TP	Avg.
1978-79	Portland..........	73	460	.490	154	.572	604	176	1074	14.7
1979-80	Portland..........					Injured				
1980-81	Portland..........	79	569	.494	207	.641	686	284	1345	17.0
1981-82	Portland..........	79	681	.523	280	.628	921	319	1642	20.8
1982-83	Portland..........	80	505	.489	249	.621	753	380	1259	15.7
1983-84	Portland..........	79	487	.524	266	.667	688	308	1240	15.7
1984-85	Portland..........	79	572	.515	307	.684	618	205	1451	18.4
1985-86	Portland..........	82	503	.498	198	.641	608	176	1204	14.7
1986-87	S.A.-LAL..........	82	359	.450	219	.737	412	115	938	11.4
	Totals.............	633	4136	.500	1880	.650	5290	1963	10153	16.0

KAREEM ABDUL-JABBAR 40 7-2 235   Center

His Royal Baldness... The hair keeps getting thinner and shorter, but there has not been much diminishing of his game... Played a lesser role in the Laker offense last season as Magic Johnson took center stage and was still very productive and instrumental in season-long run to the title... He's already climbed every mountain and now has proven he can be a great complementary player as well... Scored 32 points in the Game 6 title-clincher over the Boston Celtics... Has six MVP awards and five world championship rings to show for one of the all-time great careers... Became the NBA's all-time scoring leader on April 5, 1984, when he passed Wilt Chamberlain with a skyhook from the baseline in Las Vegas against the Utah Jazz ... Has signed a contract with the Lakers that will pay him $4 million to continue for two more seasons ... Born April 16, 1947, in New York City as Lewis Ferdinand Alcindor ... No. 1 pick out of UCLA in 1969 draft by Milwaukee ... Led Bucks to title in 1971 ... Traded to Lakers in 1975 with Walt Wesley for Elmore Smith, Brian Winters, David Meyers and Junior Bridgeman ... He's done it all.

Year	Team	G	FG	FG Pct.	FT	FT Pct.	Reb.	Ast.	TP	Avg.
1969-70	Milwaukee	82	938	.518	485	.653	1190	337	2361	28.8
1970-71	Milwaukee	82	1063	.577	470	.690	1311	272	2596	31.7
1971-72	Milwaukee	81	1159	.574	504	.689	1346	370	2822	34.8
1972-73	Milwaukee	76	982	.554	328	.713	1224	379	2292	30.2
1973-74	Milwaukee	81	948	.539	295	.702	1178	386	2191	27.0
1974-75	Milwaukee	65	812	.513	325	.763	912	264	1949	30.0
1975-76	Los Angeles	82	914	.529	447	.703	1383	413	2275	27.7
1976-77	Los Angeles	82	888	.579	376	.701	1091	319	2152	26.2
1977-78	Los Angeles	62	663	.550	274	.783	801	269	1600	25.8
1978-79	Los Angeles	80	777	.577	349	.736	1025	431	1903	23.8
1979-80	Los Angeles	82	835	.604	364	.765	886	371	2034	24.8
1980-81	Los Angeles	80	836	.574	423	.766	821	272	2095	26.2
1981-82	Los Angeles	76	753	.579	312	.706	659	225	1818	23.9
1982-83	Los Angeles	79	722	.588	278	.749	592	200	1722	21.8
1983-84	Los Angeles	80	716	.578	285	.723	587	211	1717	21.5
1984-85	L.A. Lakers	79	723	.599	289	.732	622	249	1735	22.0
1985-86	L.A. Lakers	79	755	.564	336	.765	478	280	1846	23.4
1986-87	L.A. Lakers	78	560	.564	245	.714	523	203	1366	17.5
	Totals	1406	15044	.562	6385	.720	16628	5451	36474	25.9

A.C. GREEN 24 6-9 220   Forward

The initials stand for—what else?—A.C. They're his given name ... He was also given the starting power-forward job last season and at times looked like he was a superstar about to burst forth ... But by the end of the playoffs, he had many people wondering if he wasn't just a bigger version of Byron Scott—coming up empty in the clutch ... He's got the size, speed and leaping ability ... The only question is about his heart ... Born Oct. 10, 1963, in Portland, Ore. ... Has the body of a Greek god ... Starred at Oregon State, where he wound up the school's third-leading scorer behind Mel Counts and Steve Johnson ... Majored in speech communications and says he wants to pursue a career as a minister when he's done playing

. . . Lakers plunked him down in the No. 23 spot in the 1985 draft, a shrewd selection.

Year	Team	G	FG	FG Pct.	FT	FT Pct.	Reb.	Ast.	TP	Avg.
1985-86	L.A. Lakers.........	82	209	.539	102	.611	381	54	521	6.4
1986-87	L.A. Lakers.........	79	316	.538	220	.780	615	84	852	10.8
	Totals.............	161	525	.538	322	.717	996	138	1373	8.5

BYRON SCOTT 26 6-4 202   Guard

Excess baggage on the Laker Express . . . Did nothing during the NBA finals against the Boston Celtics to disprove the theory that he disappears in big games . . . He's a deadly shooter from 20 feet or more on the wings or the baseline when the pressure is off . . . But he'll never be nicknamed "Mr. Clutch" . . . In the three games in Boston, he was often confused with one of the famous dead spots on the Garden floor . . . Born March 28, 1961, in Ogden, Utah, but was raised down the street from the Forum in Inglewood, Cal. . . . Played three years at Arizona State and left early for the NBA . . . The No. 4 pick in the 1983 draft by the San Diego Clippers, but he never signed and was traded to the Lakers with Swen Nater for Norm Nixon, Eddie Jordan and two second-round draft picks. . . . Some think he'll still blossom.

Year	Team	G	FG	FG Pct.	FT	FT Pct.	Reb.	Ast.	TP	Avg.
1983-84	Los Angeles.........	74	334	.484	112	.806	164	177	788	10.6
1984-85	L.A. Lakers.........	81	541	.539	187	.820	210	244	1295	16.0
1985-86	L.A. Lakers.........	76	507	.513	138	.784	189	164	1174	15.4
1986-87	L.A. Lakers.........	82	554	.489	224	.892	286	281	1397	17.0
	Totals.............	313	1936	.507	661	.832	849	866	4654	14.9

WES MATTHEWS 28 6-1 170   Guard

He got the game ball from the Lakers' Game 6 title-clincher against Boston . . . No, he didn't earn it. He just happened to grab the game ball in garbage time when the clock expired . . . The way he hugged it in the locker room, you'd have thought he made a contribution to the title . . . A nomad . . . LA was his sixth team in seven NBA seasons—also in Washington, Atlanta, Philadelphia, Chicago and San Antonio . . . Reputation as a trouble-maker . . . The fact that he is an individual-type player and can't even spell "defense" explains his constant movement...Quick and erratic...Born Aug. 24, 1959, in Sarasota, Fla....Attended Wisconsin and was booted off the club just before an NIT appearance...Strictly a deep sub for the Lakers...Likely just passing through.

Year	Team	G	FG	FG Pct.	FT	FT Pct.	Reb.	Ast.	TP	Avg.
1980-81	Wash.-Atl.	79	385	.494	202	.802	139	411	977	12.4
1981-82	Atlanta	47	131	.440	60	.759	58	139	324	6.9
1982-83	Atlanta	64	171	.403	86	.768	91	249	442	6.9
1983-84	Atl.-Phil.	20	61	.466	27	.750	27	83	150	7.5
1984-85	Chicago	78	191	.495	59	.694	67	354	443	5.7
1985-86	San Antonio	75	320	.531	173	.820	131	476	817	10.9
1986-87	L.A. Lakers	50	89	.476	29	.806	47	100	208	4.2
	Totals	413	1348	.480	636	.784	560	1812	3361	8.1

BILLY THOMPSON 23 6-7 195   Forward

A trivia answer...Became only the fourth player, following Magic Johnson, Henry Bibby and Bill Russell, to win NCAA and NBA titles in consecutive seasons...All he did for the Lakers was to warm a spot on the bench last season...But he's projected as a contributor down the line...Can play the transition game and has some silky-smooth moves...Underwent arthroscopic knee surgery right after the playoffs...Born Dec. 1, 1963, in Camden, N.J....Played for Denny Crum at Louisville and was instrumental in the Cardinals' title march in 1986...The No. 19 pick in the 1986 draft by Atlanta...Sent to the Lakers in exchange for Mike McGee and Ken Barlow...A project.

Year	Team	G	FG	FG Pct.	FT	FT Pct.	Reb.	Ast.	TP	Avg.
1986-87	L.A. Lakers	59	142	.544	48	.649	171	60	332	5.6

KURT RAMBIS 29 6-8 220   Forward

A relic from the past...Remember back in 1981-82 when he was the starting power forward on the Lakers championship team?...Started a trend of slow, bulky, white guys on NBA frontlines...But now he's an idea whose time has come and gone...He's strictly in a reserve role, having been passed by the younger, faster A.C. Green...Born Feb. 25, 1958, in Cupertino, Cal....Played at Santa Clara...Drafted No. 58 overall by the New York Knicks in 1980, but cut in camp . . . Played pro ball in Greece, where he learned all the dirty tricks of the trade and how to use his body . . . Gets the most out of his talent, which is very little . . . Hustles and bangs . . . Kurt is middle name, Darrell his first name . . . When he puts on those thick-framed glasses he looks like Clark Kent and used to play like Superman . . . But not anymore.

Year	Team	G	FG	FG Pct.	FT	FT Pct.	Reb.	Ast.	TP	Avg.
1981-82	Los Angeles.........	64	118	.518	59	.504	348	56	295	4.6
1982-83	Los Angeles.........	78	235	.569	114	.687	531	90	584	7.5
1983-84	Los Angeles.........	47	63	.558	42	.636	266	34	168	3.6
1984-85	L.A. Lakers.........	82	181	.554	68	.660	528	69	430	5.2
1985-86	L.A. Lakers.........	74	160	.595	88	.721	517	69	408	5.5
1986-87	L.A. Lakers.........	78	163	.521	120	.764	453	63	446	5.7
	Totals.............	423	920	.553	491	.672	2643	381	2331	5.5

MIKE SMREK 25 7-0 250   Center

He's tall . . . Well, that about wraps up the entire list of positive attributes on this guy . . . If he were four inches shorter, he'd have to buy a ticket to get into an NBA game . . . But big bodies are always helpful in practice, so he's likely got several more years of raking in a nice salary for sitting on the bench . . . Originally a second-round pick of Portland in 1985, he was quickly traded to Chicago . . . Born Aug. 31, 1962 at Welland, Ontario . . . Played at Canisius . . . Appeared in just 35 games and played 233 minutes for the Lakers last season . . . But he started three games due to injuries to Kareem Abdul-Jabbar . . . Says his name rhymes with "Wreck" . . . That's appropriate.

Year	Team	G	FG	FG Pct.	FT	FT Pct.	Reb.	Ast.	TP	Avg.
1985-86	Chicago............	38	46	.377	16	.552	110	19	108	2.8
1986-87	L.A. Lakers.........	35	30	.500	16	.640	37	5	76	2.2
	Totals.............	73	76	.418	32	.593	147	24	184	2.5

ADRIAN BRANCH 23 6-8 185   Forward

Another guy who hitched a ride to an NBA championship ring . . . He came out of the CBA to take Larry Spriggs' spot as the designated body-banger in practice . . . Born Nov. 17, 1963, in Washington, D.C. . . . Played at Maryland, where he had a decent career . . . Was a second-round draft choice (No. 46 overall) of Chicago in 1985 . . . He was cut in camp and spent his first pro season with Baltimore of the CBA . . . Got into just 32 games last season, but he's strictly a body to throw on the floor at garbage time.

Year	Team	G	FG	FG Pct.	FT	FT Pct.	Reb.	Ast.	TP	Avg.
1986-87	L.A. Lakers	32	48	.500	42	.778	53	16	138	4.3

TOP ROOKIE

WILLIE GLASS 22 6-6 210   Forward

Another Laker steal? . . . They have a knack for getting talent despite always picking at the bottom of the barrel . . . St. John's second leading scorer and rebounder as a senior . . . Expected to blossom in the wide-open pro game . . . Born Jan. 19, 1965, in Atlantic City, N.J. . . . Fittingly enough, his nickname is "Hollywood" . . . The No. 69 pick in the draft on the third round.

COACH PAT RILEY: Not just another pretty face . . . When you

dig beneath the slicked-back hair, designer suits and fancy Italian shoes, you find an old-fashioned, hard-working coach . . . Has taken his team to the NBA finals five times in six seasons and won three championships . . . Reached the 100-, 200- and 300-win plateaus faster than any coach in NBA history . . . His playoff percentage of .713 (72-29) is the best of all time . . . Also has six straight Pacific Division titles to his credit . . . Comes off as your classic laid-back Southern Californian, but in truth is a relentless, driven performer . . . Born March 20, 1945, in Rome, N.Y. . . . Grew up as self-described "street punk." . . . Can be emotional and uptight . . . A big college star under Adolph Rupp at Kentucky . . . The No. 1 draft pick of the San Diego Rockets expansion franchise in 1967 . . . Had a journeyman career with the Lakers and Phoenix . . . Worked as the color commentator on Laker games until then-coach Jack McKinney was injured in a bicycle accident . . . Became assistant to Paul Westhead and then took over top job in November 1981.

GREATEST COACH

To those who really know, Pat Riley does more than just decorate the sidelines at the Forum and provide the male answer to the Laker Girls.

You can point to a roster that is filled with big-name, talented players. But there have been plenty of other coaches through the years who have managed to mess up talented teams.

Riley took over the head coaching post in 1981 and immediately guided the Lakers to the NBA championship. He's won two more since then and his six-year regular-season winning percentage of .730 (351-130) is the best in the history of the NBA.

Though his appearance and demeanor in public belie it, he is a strong-willed, fiery leader who is totally immersed in the game and plays as much a role in the Lakers' success as Magic Johnson, Kareem Abdul-Jabbar and James Worthy.

John Kundla led the Minneapolis Lakers to five titles from 1948 to 1959, but that was a different game then. Today Pat Riley is tops for the Lakers.

ALL-TIME LAKER LEADERS

SEASON

Points: Elgin Baylor, 2,538, 1960-61
Assists: Earvin (Magic) Johnson, 977, 1986-87
Rebounds: Wilt Chamberlain, 1,712, 1968-69

GAME

Points: Elgin Baylor, 71 vs. New York, 11/15/60
Assists: Jerry West, 23 vs. Philadelphia, 2/1/67
  Earvin (Magic) Johnson, 23 vs. Seattle, 2/21/84
Rebounds: Wilt Chamberlain, 42 vs. Boston, 3/7/69

CAREER

Points: Jerry West, 25,192, 1960-74
Assists: Jerry West, 6,238, 1960-74
Rebounds: Elgin Baylor, 11,463, 1958-72

PHOENIX SUNS

TEAM DIRECTORY: Chairman: Richard Bloch; Pres.: Donald Pitt; VPs: Donald Diamond, Marvin Meyer, Lawrence Kartiganer; Exec. VP/GM: Jerry Colangelo; Dir. Player Personnel: Cotton Fitzsimmons; Dir. Pub. Rel.: Tom Ambrose; Coach: John Wetzel; Asst. Coach: Herb Brown. Arena: Veterans Memorial Coliseum (14,471). Colors: Purple, orange and copper.

SCOUTING REPORT

SHOOTING: Putting the ball into the basket was not a problem with the Suns last year. That might be the only area that wasn't a problem. But the cast of characters is sure to be vastly different this time around as this franchise starts rebuilding almost from the ground floor.

Gone is field-goal percentage leader Ed Pinckney (.584), sent off to Sacramento for Eddie Johnson (.463). Also out—if they can find anybody to take him—will likely be Walter Davis, after finding himself embroiled in a drug investigation.

The Suns can still pack a punch, though, with Larry Nance (.551) and now rookie Armon Gilliam up front. But starting off the season, those two names might be the only two everyday players that Phoenix fans can count on.

PLAYMAKING: This problem could be thornier than one of the cacti that grows in the desert. Jay Humphries, the young guard, was progressing nicely and was being groomed as the quarterback of the future for this team until he—and so many others on this roster—found himself snared in the drug investigation. If Humphries can stay free of any legal problems and put this episode behind him, the picture will look bright in the backcourt for new head coach John Wetzel. Humphries is a solid ball-handler, has a 3-to-1 assist-turnover ratio and has excellent speed to run the break.

DEFENSE: Ah yes, there's the rub. It's one thing to score points, but another one entirely to stop your opponents. The Suns are a perfect case in point to prove that you do have to play defense to win in the NBA. They allowed opponents to shoot at a .494 clip and average 113 points a game last year. They've got speed and quickness on the perimeter, but have always lacked that monster in the middle to stop penetration for the easy baskets.

James Edwards, quite obviously, was not the answer and nei-

Not even stalwart Larry Nance could eclipse Suns' woes.

SUN ROSTER

No.	Veteran	Pos.	Ht.	Wt.	Age	Yrs. Pro	College
33	Alvan Adams	C	6-9	218	33	12	Oklahoma
6	Walter Davis	G	6-6	200	33	10	North Carolina
53	James Edwards	C	7-1	250	31	10	Washington
44	Kenny Gattison	F	6-8	240	23	1	Old Dominion
3	Grant Gondrezick	G	6-4	205	24	1	Pepperdine
14	Jeff Hornacek	G	6-3	195	24	1	Iowa State
24	Jay Humphries	G	6-3	182	25	3	Colorado
8	Eddie Johnson	F	6-7	210	28	6	Illinois
22	Larry Nance	F	6-10	217	28	6	Clemson
11	Mike Sanders	F	6-6	210	27	5	UCLA
7	Bernard Thompson	G	6-6	211	25	3	Fresno State
32	Joe Ward	G	6-6	210	24	1	Georgia

Rd.	Top Rookies	Sel. No.	Pos.	Ht.	Wt.	College
1	Armon Gilliam	2	F	6-9	230	Nevada-Las Vegas
2	Bruce Dalrymple	46	G	6-4	210	Georgia Tech
3	Winston Crite	53	F	6-7	220	Texas A&M
4	Steve Beck	76	G	6-3	185	Arizona State
5	Brent Counts	99	F	6-9	215	Pacific

ther was William Bedford. Now they've got rookie Gilliam inside to throw around some muscle, but at 6-9 he's still not the stopper that is needed. Johnson, obtained from Sacramento in the trade for Pinckney, has never attracted any attention for his defense and isn't likely to help shore up what is a big, big problem.

If you're a 7-footer and can walk and chew gum at the same time, phone the Suns. They have a job for you at decent pay.

REBOUNDING: You almost have to try hard to be as bad at rebounding the ball as the Suns. They ranked 20th out of 23 last season and, if anything, they've gotten smaller in the off season.

What could change though is the attitude, if the veterans decide they want to follow the muscling, hustling lead of "The Hammer" Gilliam, who knocked people down to get rebounds at Nevada-Las Vegas. He's a bull out of the Buck Williams mold, but has a better offensive game to go with it. If Gilliam uses his strength on one side and Nance his great leaping ability on the other side, the Suns could have one of the best rebounding sets of forwards in the league.

The problem, of course, will be that big hole in the middle.

Alvan Adams never was a good rebounder and he's certainly not improving with age.

On the saddest note, 7-2 Nick Vanos, who lost his chance to prove himself, is gone, the victim of a plane crash in Detroit.

OUTLOOK: Would you believe another trip back to the draft lottery? Well, maybe if the Suns get involved enough times, they will eventually come away as winners. Back in 1969, they lost out on Kareem Abdul-Jabbar (then Lew Alcindor) and had to settle for Neal Walk, and last spring they finished second to San Antonio for the rights to David Robinson. Big problems have forced this team to almost rebuild like an expansion franchise and it's going to be a couple of years before any of the efforts bear fruit.

SUN PROFILES

LARRY NANCE 28 6-10 217 Forward

A whirlybird...A jumping jack...The High-Atollah of Slamola...That's what he was called when he won the NBA Slam Dunk title in 1984...Didn't like being regarded as one-dimensional, so he shied away from the spotlight...How they've left him off the all-star team the last two years is a mystery... He's one of the few rays of hope in a bleak Suns' picture...Ranked 17th in the league in scoring...One of the top power forwards in the game...Has the speed, leaping ability and the strength to dominate...Born Feb. 12, 1959, in Anderson, S.C....Unheralded at Clemson, the Suns made out like bandits when they got him at the No. 20 spot in the 1981 draft...One of the top percentage shooters in the league... Collects automobiles...Wouldn't it be great to see him challenge the reigning slam dunk king, Michael Jordan, this year?...Will make $625,000 this season.

Year	Team	G	FG	FG Pct.	FT	FT Pct.	Reb.	Ast.	TP	Avg.
1981-82	Phoenix	80	227	.521	75	.641	256	82	529	6.6
1982-83	Phoenix	82	588	.550	193	.672	710	197	1370	16.7
1983-84	Phoenix	82	601	.576	249	.707	678	214	1451	17.7
1984-85	Phoenix	61	515	.587	180	.709	536	159	1211	19.9
1985-86	Phoenix	73	582	.581	310	.698	618	240	1474	20.2
1986-87	Phoenix	69	585	.551	381	.773	599	233	1552	22.5
	Totals	447	3098	.564	1388	.713	3397	1125	7587	17.0

MIKE SANDERS 27 6-6 210   Forward

Mr. Everything . . . He'll never be a star in this league, but he'll always have a job as long as he's willing to make the sacrifices and do the dirty work . . . Starred at UCLA, yet has turned himself into a real lunch-pail carrier in the NBA . . . Played in every one of the 82 games last season and was a bargain at $110,000 . . . born May 7, 1960, in Vilidia, La. . . . Teamed with Suns' teammate Rod Foster and Portland's Kiki Vandeweghe at UCLA on the 1980 team that lost to Louisville in the NCAA finals . . . A 1982 fourth-round pick of the Kings, who could use him now . . . Went to the CBA, was signed and released by San Antonio and has been a fixture in Phoenix since 1983.

Year	Team	G	FG	FG Pct.	FT	FT Pct.	Reb.	Ast.	TP	Avg.
1982-83	San Antonio.........	26	76	.484	31	.721	94	19	183	7.0
1983-84	Phoenix.............	50	97	.478	29	.690	103	44	223	4.5
1984-85	Phoenix.............	21	85	.486	45	.763	89	29	215	10.2
1985-86	Phoenix.............	82	347	.513	208	.809	273	150	905	11.0
1986-87	Phoenix.............	82	357	.494	143	.781	271	126	859	10.5
	Totals.............	261	962	.498	456	.781	830	368	2385	9.1

JAY HUMPHRIES 25 6-3 182   Guard

Perhaps a fallen star . . . Was blooming into a solid backcourt performer when his name came up in the grand jury investigation into drug use among the Suns . . . Excellent speed . . . Has shown the ability to run the offense . . . Has improved his shooting since entering the league three years ago . . . Born Oct. 17, 1962, in Inglewood, Cal., just a bounce pass from where Magic and the boys operate at the Forum . . . Was a big question mark during a so-so senior year at Colorado and the Suns made him their lucky No. 13 pick on the first round of the 1984 draft . . . Opened some eyes at the 1984 Olympic trials . . . Played in the World University Games in 1983 . . . Has started 164 straight regular-season games over the last two years and has played in 244 of 246 since joining the club.

Year	Team	G	FG	FG Pct.	FT	FT Pct.	Reb.	Ast.	TP	Avg.
1984-85	Phoenix.............	80	279	.446	141	.829	164	350	703	8.8
1985-86	Phoenix.............	82	352	.479	197	.767	260	526	905	11.0
1986-87	Phoenix.............	82	359	.477	200	.769	260	632	923	11.3
	Totals.............	244	990	.468	538	.783	684	1508	2531	10.4

WALTER DAVIS 33 6-6 200   Guard

Down to his last chance . . . As surprised as the NBA was in December 1985, when he admitted to a drug problem and checked into a rehab center, it was even more shocking when he re-entered the rehab center in April 1987 . . . It seemed like he had licked his drug problems . . . Now, according to the league rules, he's got just one more chance to straighten out or else be banned from the league for good . . . Born Sept. 9, 1954, in Pineville, N.C. . . . Was nurtured at North Carolina by Dean Smith and blossomed into a potent offensive weapon in the NBA . . . Suns made him the No. 5 pick in the 1977 draft . . . He flourished as a forward with his great speed and then made the successful shift to the backcourt . . . A real greyhound . . . Played on the 1976 U.S. Olympic team . . . Had played in all 79 games and was league's 11th leading scorer when he admitted to drug problems again . . . Testified to a grand jury about teammates' drug involvement as well.

Year	Team	G	FG	FG Pct.	FT	FT Pct.	Reb.	Ast.	TP	Avg.
1977-78	Phoenix	81	786	.526	387	.830	484	273	1959	24.2
1978-79	Phoenix	79	764	.561	340	.831	373	339	1868	23.6
1979-80	Phoenix	75	657	.563	299	.819	272	337	1613	21.5
1980-81	Phoenix	78	593	.539	209	.836	200	302	1402	18.0
1981-82	Phoenix	55	350	.523	91	.820	103	162	794	14.4
1982-83	Phoenix	80	665	.516	184	.818	197	397	1521	19.0
1983-84	Phoenix	78	652	.512	233	.863	202	429	1557	20.0
1984-85	Phoenix	23	139	.450	64	.877	35	98	345	15.0
1985-86	Phoenix	70	624	.485	257	.843	203	361	1523	21.8
1986-87	Phoenix	79	779	.514	288	.862	244	364	1867	23.6
	Totals	698	6009	.524	2352	.838	2313	3062	14449	20.7

EDDIE JOHNSON 28 6-7 210   Forward

Steady Eddie takes it to Phoenix in trade that sent Ed Pinckney to the Kings . . . His game slipped a bit last year and then-coach Phil Johnson decided to bring him off the bench . . . Settled into the role eventually and became an explosive reserve . . . He's never been one to rock the boat, even though his offensive skills have long been overlooked . . . Born May 1, 1959, in Chicago . . . A high-school teammate of Dallas' Mark Aguirre and a college teammate of Dallas' Derek Harper

... Played in the Big 10 at Illinois ... Not drafted until the second round in 1981 by KC Kings. A lot of scouts should have had to do a lot of explaining for taking a pass on this guy ... Defense not his strong suit ... He's hard-nosed and gets a lot of tough, offensive-rebound hoops.

Year	Team	G	FG	FG Pct.	FT	FT Pct.	Reb.	Ast.	TP	Avg.
1981-82	Kansas City	74	295	.459	99	.664	322	109	690	9.3
1982-83	Kansas City	82	677	.494	247	.779	501	216	1621	19.8
1983-84	Kansas City	82	753	.485	268	.810	455	296	1794	21.9
1984-85	Kansas City	82	769	.491	325	.871	407	273	1876	22.9
1985-86	Sacramento	82	623	.475	280	.816	419	214	1530	18.7
1986-87	Sacramento	81	606	.463	267	.829	353	251	1516	18.7
	Totals	483	3723	.480	1486	.810	2457	1359	9027	18.7

JAMES EDWARDS 31 7-1 250   Center

Just what the Suns needed ... He's played like a dog ever since he showed up in Phoenix and now he's been named in a grand jury investigation into drugs and gambling ... Last year he played only 14 games before suffering a season-ending Achilles injury ... He's a big stiff who prefers to shoot the outside jumper to taking the ball inside ... Should get down on his knees every night and thank the lucky stars for Ted Stepien, the former wacko Cleveland owner who gave him an outrageous contract ... The Suns are still paying to the tune of $600,000 this season ... Born Nov. 22, 1955, in Seattle ... After a less than spectacular career at the University of Washington, he was the 46th pick in the 1977 draft by the Lakers ... Bounced to Indiana and Cleveland before becoming the disgrace in the desert ... Suns gave up Jeff Cook and a third-round draft choice to get him ... That was too much ... Way too much.

Year	Team	G	FG	FG Pct.	FT	FT Pct.	Reb.	Ast.	TP	Avg.
1977-78	L.A.-Ind.	83	495	.453	272	.646	615	85	1252	15.2
1978-79	Indiana	82	534	.501	298	.676	693	92	1366	16.7
1979-80	Indiana	82	528	.512	231	.681	578	127	1287	15.7
1980-81	Indiana	81	511	.509	244	.703	571	212	1266	15.6
1981-82	Cleveland	77	528	.511	232	.684	581	123	1288	16.7
1982-83	Clev.-Phoe.	31	128	.487	69	.639	155	40	325	10.5
1983-84	Phoenix	72	438	.536	183	.720	348	184	1059	14.7
1984-85	Phoenix	70	384	.501	276	.746	387	153	1044	14.9
1985-86	Phoenix	52	318	.542	212	.702	301	74	848	16.3
1986-87	Phoenix	14	57	.518	54	.771	60	19	168	12.0
	Totals	644	3921	.505	2071	.692	4289	1109	9913	15.4

ALVAN ADAMS 33 6-9 218 — Center

A.A.... Do the initials stand for Adams Anonymous?... The Suns are definitely hooked on this guy... Every year when it seems like he's getting up in age and should be thinking about turning in his sneakers, he's got to go back into the starting lineup and bail the club out of another jam in the middle... Of course, he was pinch-hitting for the injured James Edwards again last season... Scoring punch is diminishing and he's not much of a threat on the boards. But he remains one of the best passing big men in the game... Definite member of the All-White-Dunkers Club, though takeoffs are limited these days... Born July 19, 1954, in Lawrence, Kan.... Played under former Phoenix coach John MacLeod at Oklahoma and was No. 4 pick of the Suns in 1975... A student of architecture, he seemed to lose interest and made noises about retiring a few years ago... Now in the last year of a contract that will pay him $675,000... Twelve years with Suns is the longest string of continuous service of a current player in the NBA.

Year	Team	G	FG	FG Pct.	FT	FT Pct.	Reb.	Ast.	TP	Avg.
1975-76	Phoenix............	80	629	.469	261	.735	727	450	1519	19.0
1976-77	Phoenix............	72	522	.474	252	.754	652	322	1296	18.0
1977-78	Phoenix............	70	434	.485	214	.730	565	225	1082	15.5
1978-79	Phoenix............	77	569	.530	231	.799	705	360	1369	17.8
1979-80	Phoenix............	75	465	.531	188	.797	609	322	1118	14.9
1980-81	Phoenix............	75	458	.526	199	.768	546	344	1115	14.9
1981-82	Phoenix............	79	507	.494	182	.781	586	356	1196	15.1
1982-83	Phoenix............	80	477	.486	180	.829	548	376	1135	14.2
1983-84	Phoenix............	70	269	.462	132	.825	319	219	670	9.6
1984-85	Phoenix............	82	476	.520	250	.883	500	308	1202	14.7
1985-86	Phoenix............	78	341	.502	159	.783	477	324	841	10.8
1986-87	Phoenix............	68	311	.503	134	.788	338	223	756	11.1
	Totals............	906	5458	.498	2382	.786	6572	3829	13299	14.7

KENNY GATTISON 23 6-8 240 — Forward

A banger... A hustler... A strong man... No wonder this guy drew attention from college football recruiters at Notre Dame, North Carolina, UCLA and Clemson... He played tight end and one look at his solid body tells you he was the one dealing out the punishment... Born May 23, 1964, in Wilmington, N.C.... Attended Old Dominion University and wound up as the Sun Belt Conference all-time leading rebounder... His college team never won fewer than 19 games in his four seasons... A third-round draft choice (55th overall) of the Suns, who made him one of five rookies on their 1986-87 roster.

Year	Team	G	FG	FG Pct.	FT	FT Pct.	Reb.	Ast.	TP	Avg.
1986-87	Phoenix...........	77	148	.476	108	.632	270	36	404	5.2

GRANT GONDREZICK 24 6-4 205   Guard

Gondo... If the name sounds familiar, it's because he's the brother of former NBA player Glen Gondrezick, who spent time with Denver and New York before going overseas to Europe... Scrapped and hustled his way to a roster spot... But was also named in the grand jury investigation into drug use by members of the Suns... Born Jan. 19, 1963, in Boulder, Colo.... First player in Colorado prep history to average a triple-double for an entire season in his senior year... Starred in college at Pepperdine... Phoenix made him a fourth-round (77th overall) draft choice and he clawed out a job... Question is how long he can hold it.

Year	Team	G	FG	FG Pct.	FT	FT Pct.	Reb.	Ast.	TP	Avg.
1986-87	Phoenix...........	64	135	.450	75	.701	110	81	349	5.5

JEFF HORNACEK 24 6-3 195   Guard

Boy-faced bomber... First turned heads at the NBA pre-draft camp in Chicago in May 1986... Suns made him their second-round (46th overall) pick... A decent shooter and a fine passer in college at Iowa State... Broke Darnell Valentine's old Big Eight career-assists mark by dealing out 665 in four years... Born May 3, 1963, in Elmhurst, Ill.... An All-State prep player, he went on to co-captain the Iowa State team as a junior and senior... A hard worker with good defensive skills... Turned out to be a decent three-point bomber as a rookie... Has a degree in accounting... Brother Jay is in the LA Dodgers' farm system.

Year	Team	G	FG	FG Pct.	FT	FT Pct.	Reb.	Ast.	TP	Avg.
1986-87	Phoenix...........	80	159	.454	94	.777	184	361	424	5.3

TOP ROOKIE

ARMON GILLIAM 23 6-9 230   **Forward**
The Hammer... UNLV Coach Jerry Tarkanian called him the best power forward in the country last year... Who's to argue? ... Has a powerful body and a nice, soft touch on the jumper... Born May 28, 1964, in Pittsburgh... Began athletic career as a football player... Would make an excellent NFL tight end... The No. 2 pick on the first round.

COACH JOHN WETZEL: A company man... A long-time Suns' employee, he was given the job as the new bench boss to replace John MacLeod, fired after 13½ seasons... He had remained as an assistant under interim coach Dick Van Arsdale last season... Spent over seven years as MacLeod's chief aide and in the way the Suns' organization works, it was only logical that he move up to the top spot... Now he's on the hot seat, trying to put the pieces back together after a horrible season that had the Suns charged with drug involvement, gambling and all-around bad play... Born Oct. 22, 1944, in Waynesboro, Va.... Played college ball at Virginia Tech and was an eighth-round pick of the Lakers in 1966... An expansion pick of the Suns in 1968, he spent two years in Phoenix, one in Atlanta, and finished his career back in Phoenix in 1976... First coaching experience was with the Washington Lumberjacks of the old Western Basketball Association... An avid runner and a long-ball hitter on the golf course.

GREATEST COACH

Do you like white bread or rye? Is the beer less filling or does it taste great? Do you judge coaches on the regular season or the playoffs? On how well they've done in a short period of time or do you give credit for longevity? Well, that's why we have bars to hold discussions such as who is the best coach in the history of the Phoenix Suns.

Yes, and before you leap ahead and say that it is without question John MacLeod, consider this: Cotton Fitzsimmons spent two seasons in Phoenix (1970-72), compiled records of 48-34 and 49-33 and did not make the playoffs. Is it Cotton's fault that not as many teams made the playoffs in those days or that the Western Conference was loaded with powerful teams in LA, San Francisco, Milwaukee and Chicago?

On the other hand, MacLeod gave the Suns stability for 13½ seasons, made the playoffs five times and took Phoenix on that dream march to the NBA finals in 1976, which produced the incredible triple-overtime game in Boston.

Less filling or tastes great? White bread or rye?

Give the nod to John MacLeod, but don't forget the Cotton Man.

Something new under the Sun—Eddie Johnson, ex-King.

ALL-TIME SUN LEADERS

SEASON

Points: Charlie Scott, 2,048, 1972-73
Assists: Jay Humphries, 632, 1986-87
Rebounds: Paul Silas, 1,015, 1970-71

GAME

Points: Paul Westphal, 49 vs. Detroit, 2/21/80
Assists: Gail Goodrich, 19 vs. Philadelphia, 10/22/69
Rebounds: Paul Silas, 27 vs. Cincinnati, 1/18/71

CAREER

Points: Walter Davis, 14,449, 1977-87
Assists: Alvan Adams, 3,829, 1975-87
Rebounds: Alvan Adams, 6,572, 1975-87

PORTLAND TRAIL BLAZERS

TEAM DIRECTORY: Chairman: Lawrence Weinberg; Pres.: Harry Glickman; Dir. Pub. Rel.: John Lashway; Coach: Mike Schuler; Asst. Coaches: Rick Adelman, Jack Schalow. Arena: Memorial Coliseum (12,666). Colors: Red, black and white.

SCOUTING REPORT

SHOOTING: All of the stereotypes about offense that some people try to apply to the Lakers definitely fit here in Portland. They can score points as fast and effortlessly as any team in the league—a classic Western Conference outfit—but don't stop anybody, either. If you can't shoot in Portland, then you pack up your gear and get out of town.

There's Steve Johnson (.556), Kiki Vandeweghe (.523), Jerome Kersey (.509) and Clyde Drexler (.502). And their fast-break is already as good as any team in the league, save the Lakers. They traded Jim Paxson (.460) for Cleveland's Keith Lee (.455), but the Blazers called off the deal over concern for Lee's alleged knee problems.

PLAYMAKING: It was a big gamble a couple of seasons ago when Portland decided to let go of veterans like Fat Lever and Darnell Valentine and give the reins to an untested young player named Terry Porter. But the roll of the dice seems to have paid off as the point guard out of Wisconsin-Stevens Point has shown he can do the job. He ranked fifth (8.9) in the league in assists last season and helps the fastbreak run smoothly.

But in truth there are a lot of good passers on this club and that's why the Blazers overall ranked third in the league in assists. It wouldn't hurt, though, to pick up a good backup quarterback. There's uncertainty about first-round draft choice Ronnie Murphy of Jacksonville.

DEFENSE: The defense in Portland is just like the weather—consistently terrible. The Blazers gave up more points per game (114.8) than any other playoff team in the league last season and that goes a long way toward explaining why they were on the sidelines after the first round.

In their defense, the two stoppers—Sam Bowie and Kenny Carr—were on the sidelines with injuries during the playoffs. If the Blazers can ever keep Bowie healthy and available all year, part of the problem will be solved. Carr's ongoing problems caused him to announce his retirement after a 10-year career.

Kiki Vandeweghe led NBA in 3-point accuracy (.481).

REBOUNDING: The rebounding figures reflect most accurately the Blazers' overall ranking in the NBA. They're right in the middle of the pack and that's why nobody can take them seri-

TRAIL BLAZER ROSTER

No.	Veteran	Pos.	Ht.	Wt.	Age	Yrs. Pro	College
31	Sam Bowie	C	7-2	235	26	3	Kentucky
22	Clyde Drexler	G	6-7	215	25	4	Houston
00	Kevin Duckworth	C	6-11	280	23	1	Eastern Illinois
6	Michael Holton	G	6-4	195	26	3	UCLA
40	Ken Johnson	F	6-8	250	24	2	Michigan State
33	Steve Johnson	F-C	6-10	235	29	6	Oregon State
27	* Caldwell Jones	C	6-11	225	37	14	Albany State (Ga.)
8	Charles Jones	F	6-8	230	25	3	Louisville
25	Jerome Kersey	F	6-7	220	25	3	Longwood (Va.)
10	Fernando Martin	F	6-10	238	25	1	Madrid
4	Jim Paxson	G	6-6	210	30	8	Dayton
30	Terry Porter	G	6-3	195	24	2	Wis.-Stevens Pt.
11	Ron Rowan	G	6-5	200	23	1	St. John's
55	Kiki Vandeweghe	F	6-8	220	29	7	UCLA

*Free agent unsigned at press time

Rd.	Top Rookies	Sel. No.	Pos.	Ht.	Wt.	College
1	Ronnie Murphy	17	G-F	6-5	235	Jacksonville
2	Lester Fonville	29	C	7-0	250	Jackson State
2	Nikita Wilson	30	F	6-8	200	Louisiana State
3	Kevin Gamble	63	G	6-6	215	Iowa
5	Pee Wee Barber	109	G	6-1	175	Florida State

ously as a legitimate playoff contender, despite whatever kind of overinflated regular-season record they manage to hang on the board again this season.

So much of their success on the boards depends on Bowie and that is just too much to expect. When it gets down to nut-cutting time in the playoffs again next spring, they'll be hurt by a lack of size and strength on the glass again. That's what happened against Houston last year.

OUTLOOK: We've heard it all before. The Blazers were 49-33 last year during the regular season, they had an impressive string of consecutive home sellouts and a pretty fastbreak. But don't you want to take that Coach-of-the-Year Award away from Mike Schuler after the way his club played so abysmally in the playoff loss to Houston? This team is like cotton candy. It's so light and delicate and it melts in your mouth. Look for them to be bounced in the first round again this season. It's as certain as the rain in Portland.

TRAIL BLAZER PROFILES

CLYDE DREXLER 25 6-7 215 Guard

Clyde the Glide... The nickname says it all ...A thing of beauty is a joy forever and you could go on watching him run, swoop and soar until the end of time... He's the spark in the fastbreak, the ignition key in the Blazers' running game... Excellent in the open court, he's also a harassing defensive player, finishing fifth in the league in steals... Born June 22, 1962, in New Orleans... Grew up in Houston and was not a sought-after prep player... But everyone knew who he was when he was finished with his three-year career as a member of Phi Slama Jama at the University of Houston... Wanted to stay at home and play for the Rockets, but was the No. 13 pick in the first round of 1983 draft... Displaced Jim Paxson as a starter ...Outside shot is getting better.

Year	Team	G	FG	FG Pct.	FT	FT Pct.	Reb.	Ast.	TP	Avg.
1983-84	Portland............	82	252	.451	123	.728	235	153	628	7.7
1984-85	Portland............	80	573	.494	223	.759	476	441	1377	17.2
1985-86	Portland............	75	542	.475	293	.769	421	600	1389	18.5
1986-87	Portland............	82	707	.502	357	.760	518	566	1782	21.7
	Totals.............	319	2074	.486	996	.758	1650	1760	5176	16.2

KIKI VANDEWEGHE 29 6-8 220 Forward

The shooting machine... Wind him up and watch him stick the 20-footer all night long ...He's had plenty of practice from spending hours working on his game... "The sun doesn't shine in the gym," he once said... That explains his pale complexion despite being raised in Southern California... Born Aug. 1, 1958, in Weisbaden, West Germany ...The son of former NY Knick great Ernie Vandeweghe and a former Miss America, he has a sister who played volleyball on the 1976 U.S. Olympic team... Does not have pure speed, but has a very quick first step that gets him open for the jumper... Plays no defense and will never go down as a great passer... Starred at UCLA and was the first-ever pick of the Dallas expansion team... Wouldn't sign and was traded to Denver... Spent four years in the Rockies and came to Portland in 5-for-1 deal that cost Blazers Wayne Cooper, Calvin, Natt, Fat Lever and two draft choices . . . Works as a TV sports commentator in LA in the offseason . . . Collects antique cars.

Year	Team	G	FG	FG Pct.	FT	FT Pct.	Reb.	Ast.	TP	Avg.
1980-81	Denver	51	229	.426	130	.818	270	94	588	11.5
1981-82	Denver	82	706	.560	347	.857	461	247	1760	21.5
1982-83	Denver	82	841	.547	489	.875	437	203	2186	26.7
1983-84	Denver	78	895	.558	494	.852	373	238	2295	29.4
1984-85	Portland	72	618	.534	369	.896	228	106	1616	22.4
1985-86	Portland	79	719	.540	523	.869	216	187	1962	24.8
1986-87	Portland	79	808	.523	467	.886	251	220	2122	26.9
	Totals	523	4816	.537	2819	.869	2236	1295	12529	24.0

SAM BOWIE 26 7-2 235   Center

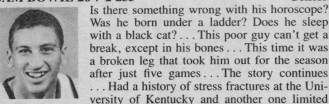

Is there something wrong with his horoscope? Was he born under a ladder? Does he sleep with a black cat? . . . This poor guy can't get a break, except in his bones . . . This time it was a broken leg that took him out for the season after just five games . . . The story continues . . . Had a history of stress fractures at the University of Kentucky and another one limited him to just 38 games in the 1985-86 season . . . Born March 17, 1961, in Lebanon, Pa. . . . One of the most recruited prep players in history . . . Stayed at Kentucky for five years to get his degree . . . An excellent shooter, fine passer and adequate rebounder . . . He could help if he could stay healthy . . . The Blazers will never be able to forget that they passed over Michael Jordan to make him the No. 2 pick in the 1984 draft.

Year	Team	G	FG	FG Pct.	FT	FT Pct.	Reb.	Ast.	TP	Avg.
1984-85	Portland	76	299	.537	160	.711	656	215	758	10.0
1985-86	Portland	38	167	.484	114	.708	327	99	448	11.8
1986-87	Portland	5	30	.455	20	.667	33	9	80	16.0
	Totals	119	496	.512	294	.707	1016	323	1286	10.8

STEVE JOHNSON 29 6-10 235   Forward-Center

Could shoot the wing off a fly at 100 yards . . . Don't believe it? . . . Consider that his .556 field-goal percentage last season was the second-worst of his six-year career . . . Probably slumped a bit because he had to carry so much of the burden in the middle when Sam Bowie went down with a broken leg . . . Excellent offensive moves . . . Major factor in the Blazers' 49-33 season . . . Born Nov. 3, 1957, in San Bernadino, Cal. . . .

Real first name is Clarence, but is known by his middle name ...Family's religious beliefs prevented him from playing games on Friday and Saturday nights in high school, so he left home ...Played college ball at Oregon State...A 1981 first-round draft pick of the KC Kings, he has also made stops in Chicago and San Antonio...Came over from the Spurs in June 1986 in exchange for Mychal Thompson and Larry Krystowiak...Wife Janice is the daughter of Milwaukee player personnel director Stu Inman...Holds NBA mark for most fouls in a season at 325 as a rookie.

Year	Team	G	FG	FG Pct.	FT	FT Pct.	Reb.	Ast.	TP	Avg.
1981-82	Kansas City.........	78	395	.613	212	.642	459	91	1002	12.8
1982-83	Kansas City.........	79	371	.624	186	.574	398	95	928	11.7
1983-84	K.C.-Chi............	81	302	.559	165	.575	418	81	769	9.5
1984-85	Chicago............	74	281	.545	181	.718	437	64	743	10.0
1985-86	San Antonio.........	71	362	.632	259	.694	462	95	983	13.8
1986-87	Portland...........	79	494	.556	342	.698	566	155	1330	16.8
	Totals.............	462	2205	.587	1345	.654	2740	581	5755	12.5

Clyde Drexler is always ablaze.

TERRY PORTER 24 6-3 195   Guard

Solid . . . That describes his physique and his game . . . Came into league with an excellent defensive reputation, but has since developed into a fine all-around point guard . . . Came from tiny NAIA school, Wisconsin-Stevens Point . . . First attracted attention at the 1984 Olympic Trials when he impressed taskmaster Bobby Knight . . . Born April 8, 1963, in Milwaukee . . . The 24th pick overall in the 1985 draft . . . It was originally thought that he was going to be a long-range project. But in just two seasons, he's already paying dividends . . . He'll take your arm off to get the ball . . . A modern-day Quinn Buckner.

Year	Team	G	FG	FG Pct.	FT	FT Pct.	Reb.	Ast.	TP	Avg.
1985-86	Portland	79	212	.474	125	.806	117	198	562	7.1
1986-87	Portland	80	376	.488	280	.838	337	715	1045	13.1
	Totals	159	588	.483	405	.828	454	913	1607	10.1

JIM PAXSON 30 6-6 210   Guard

How time flies . . . Wasn't it just a couple of years ago that NY Knicks were falling over themselves trying to lure this guy away with free-agent millions? . . . Yes, and in just a couple of years, he went from being a star to just another reserve on the Blazer bench . . . And last June he was traded to Cleveland for Keith Lee, but Portland subsequently called it off because the Blazers' doctor didn't like Lee's knees . . . He's solid, but doesn't have the all-around skills . . . Born July 9, 1957, in Kettering, Ohio . . . Father, Jim, played with Minneapolis and Cleveland in the 1950s . . . Brother, John, was a star at Notre Dame and now plays in Chicago . . . No. 1 pick in 1979 out of Dayton . . . His scoring average has dropped in each of the last four seasons . . . Will be paid a salary of $950,000 this season and $1 million per season in the next two years.

Year	Team	G	FG	FG Pct.	FT	FT Pct.	Reb.	Ast.	TP	Avg.
1979-80	Portland	72	189	.411	64	.711	109	144	443	6.2
1980-81	Portland	79	585	.536	182	.734	211	299	1354	17.1
1981-82	Portland	82	662	.526	220	.767	221	276	1552	18.9
1982-83	Portland	81	682	.515	388	.812	174	231	1756	21.7
1983-84	Portland	81	680	.514	345	.841	173	251	1722	21.3
1984-85	Portland	68	508	.514	196	.790	222	264	1218	17.9
1985-86	Portland	75	372	.470	217	.889	148	278	981	13.1
1986-87	Portland	72	337	.460	174	.806	139	237	874	12.1
	Totals	610	4015	.504	1786	.804	1397	1980	9900	16.2

JEROME KERSEY 25 6-7 220   Forward

Who was the runnerup to Michael Jordan at the 1987 NBA Slam Dunk Contest?... That's right, the best leaper and dunker that nobody's ever heard of—Jerome Kersey... A raw talent, who is steadily refining his game and improving... Born June 26, 1962, in Clarksville, Va.... A second-round pick (46th overall) of the Blazers in 1984 out of Longwood (Va.) College... He's hustled and scrapped his way to an NBA career and could still blossom into a star... Has a high field-goal percentage because he works in so close... Not much of a shooter.

Year	Team	G	FG	FG Pct.	FT	FT Pct.	Reb.	Ast.	TP	Avg.
1984-85	Portland	77	178	.478	117	.646	206	63	473	6.1
1985-86	Portland	79	258	.549	156	.681	293	83	672	8.5
1986-87	Portland	82	373	.509	262	.720	496	194	1009	12.3
	Totals	238	809	.514	535	.691	995	340	2154	9.1

KEVIN DUCKWORTH 23 6-11 280   Center

What's a duck worth?... Not much if you want him to do anything more than stand around in the middle and take up space... Obtained early in the season from San Antonio for Walter Berry... He could become the answer to a trivia question if Berry ever reaches his full potential and turns into a star... This guy will have eaten himself out of the league by then... Born April 1, 1964, in Dolton, Ill.... A second-round draft choice of the Spurs out of Eastern Illinois... The NBA's answer to "Refrigerator" Perry... Nicknames are "Sir Duck" and "Freezer"... Once worked at Burger King, so now you know how he got so big.

Year	Team	G	FG	FG Pct.	FT	FT Pct.	Reb.	Ast.	TP	Avg.
1986-87	S.A.-Port	65	130	.476	92	.687	223	29	352	5.4

CALDWELL JONES 37 6-11 225   Center

The moving company's delight... He's played with seven different teams in 14-year career... To look at his skinny frame, you'd think he hasn't gained an ounce over his long career... No offensive threat, he'll block some shots and get some rebounds... Has not been a double-figure scorer since the 1975-76 season in the old ABA... Born July 4, 1950, in

McGhee, Ark. . . . Playing ball runs in the family. Brothers Wil, Charles and Major have all played in the NBA . . . Played college ball at Albany (Ga.) State . . . A second-round draft choice of Philadelphia in 1973, he chose the ABA and played with the San Diego Conquistadors, Kentucky Colonels and the Spirits of St. Louis before that league folded . . . Spent six years in Philly, then moved to Houston, Chicago and Portland . . . He was the center in Houston between the reigns of Moses Malone and Akeem Olajuwon . . . Likes to watch "The Flintstones" . . . Once said his best friends were named Miller and Michelob.

Year	Team	G	FG	FG Pct.	FT	FT Pct.	Reb.	Ast.	TP	Avg.
1973-74	San Diego (ABA)	79	507	.465	171	.743	1095	144	1187	15.0
1974-75	San Diego (ABA)	76	606	.489	264	.788	1074	162	1479	19.5
1975-76	SD-Ky.-St.L. (ABA)	76	423	.470	140	.753	853	147	986	13.0
1976-77	Philadelphia	82	215	.507	64	.552	666	92	494	6.0
1977-78	Philadelphia	80	169	.471	96	.627	570	92	434	5.4
1978-79	Philadelphia	78	302	.474	121	.747	747	151	725	9.3
1979-80	Philadelphia	80	232	.436	124	.697	950	164	588	7.4
1980-81	Philadelphia	81	218	.449	148	.767	813	122	584	7.2
1981-82	Philadelphia	81	231	.497	179	.817	708	100	641	7.9
1982-83	Houston	82	307	.453	162	.786	668	138	776	9.5
1983-84	Houston	81	318	.502	164	.837	582	156	801	9.9
1984-85	Chicago	42	53	.461	36	.766	211	34	142	3.4
1985-86	Portland	80	126	.496	124	.827	355	74	376	4.7
1986-87	Portland	78	111	.496	97	.782	455	64	319	4.1
	Totals	1076	3818	.475	1890	.758	9747	1640	9532	8.9

MICHAEL HOLTON 26 6-4 195   Guard

A basketball gypsy . . . He's not good enough to crack anybody's lineup as an everyday player, but he'll always have a job filling in somewhere . . . In three seasons, he's already played with three different NBA teams . . . Born Aug. 4, 1961, in Seattle, he grew up in Pasadena, Cal. . . . An unspectacular career in UCLA translated into a third-round draft choice by Golden State in 1984 . . . Waived by the Warriors, he was picked up by Phoenix, released and finished the 1985-86 season in Chicago . . . Portland traded a second-round pick in 1992 to the Bulls to get him . . . He's also spent time in the CBA with the Puerto Rico Coquis, Tampa Bay Thrillers and Florida Stingers.

Year	Team	G	FG	FG Pct.	FT	FT Pct.	Reb.	Ast.	TP	Avg.
1984-85	Phoenix	74	257	.446	96	.814	132	198	624	8.4
1985-86	Phoe.-Chi.	28	77	.440	28	.636	33	55	183	6.5
1986-87	Portland	58	70	.409	44	.800	38	73	191	3.3
	Totals	160	404	.438	168	.774	203	326	998	6.2

FERNANDO MARTIN 25 6-10 238   Forward

An international star, he was a big nobody for Portland as a rookie...A member of the Spanish National Team, he's a hero in his native country. Supposedly has the same kind of celebrity that Mickey Mantle enjoyed in the U.S. in the 1950s and 1960s...Born March 25, 1962, in Madrid...He led Real Madrid to the Spanish league title in 1982, 1984, 1985 and 1986...Signed by the Blazers as a free agent on May 6, 1986...Has done a number of modeling assignments at home in Spain...Attended Pete Newell's camp for big men in the summer of 1986, but saw little playing time last season.

Year	Team	G	FG	FG Pct.	FT	FT Pct.	Reb.	Ast.	TP	Avg.
1986-87	Portland............	24	9	.290	4	.364	28	9	22	0.9

TOP ROOKIE

RONNIE MURPHY 23 6-5 235   Guard-Forward

All-Sun Belt Conference four years in a row...Was a big scorer at Jacksonville, second all-time in points (1,937)...A high-percentage long-range shooter...Some question the wisdom of this selection...Born July 29, 1964, in Oviedo, Fla....Can be an explosive performer on the inside...The No. 17 pick on the first round.

COACH MIKE SCHULER: What a debut! First he slipped off

his chair and fell to the floor at the press conference to announce he'd been hired. He picked himself up and wound up as NBA Coach of the Year for leading his club to a 49-33 record...A natty dresser, this guy showed that he deserved the chance as a head coach after serving apprenticeships under Don Nelson and Larry Brown...Had been a head coach on the college level at VMI and Rice...Born Sept. 22, 1940, in Portsmouth, Ohio...Attended Ohio University... Started out on the high-school level, then joined Bobby Knight for a year at Army as an assistant...During his four years at Rice, he was named Southwest Conference Coach of the Year in 1980, leading the Owls to their only winning season in a decade ...Nelson called him the best assistant he's ever had at Milwaukee...Managed to keep the Blazers winning despite the early-season loss of Sam Bowie due to injury...His club was soundly whipped, though, by Houston in the first round of the playoffs.

GREATEST COACH

He wore those wild plaid pants and the outrageous sport coats that sort of matched. He had those big, bushy eyebrows and a temper that could erupt like Mount St. Helens at any second.

Yes, Jack Ramsay was a stalking, whirling dervish on the sidelines at Portland Memorial Coliseum. But for 10 years he was also the man who made the Blazers one of the most consistent winners in the NBA.

In his first season in the Northwest, Ramsay produced a 49-33 regular-season mark. He not only took them to the playoffs for the first time, but all the way to a stunning upset win over Philadelphia for the NBA championship. The following year, his Blazers were 50-10 and clearly the class of the league when Bill Walton went down with a broken foot.

In a decade in Portland, Ramsay produced eight teams with winning records and nine appearances in the playoffs. If you classify the great coaches by their consistency, you've got to rank Jack Ramsay high on the list.

ALL-TIME TRAIL BLAZER LEADERS

SEASON

Points: Kiki Vandeweghe, 2,122, 1986-87
Assists: Terry Porter, 715, 1986-87
Rebounds: Lloyd Neal, 967, 1972-73

GAME

Points: Geoff Petrie, 51 vs. Houston, 2/16/73
          Geoff Petrie, 51 vs. Houston, 1/20/73
Assists: Terry Porter, 18 vs Sacramento, 1/23/87
Rebounds: Sidney Wicks, 27 vs. Los Angeles, 2/26/75

CAREER

Points: Jim Paxson, 9,900, 1979-87
Assists: Geoff Petrie, 2,057, 1970-76
Rebounds: Mychal Thompson, 4,878, 1978-86

SACRAMENTO KINGS

TEAM DIRECTORY: Pres./GM: Joe Axelson; Dir. Pub. Rel.: Julie Fie; Coach: Bill Russell; Asst. Coaches: Willis Reed, Jerry Reynolds. Arena: Sacramento Arena (10,333). Colors: Red, white and blue.

Reggie Theus led Kings in scoring with 20.3 ppg.

SCOUTING REPORT

SHOOTING: If nothing else, their shooting percentage should go up with the addition of Ed Pinckney (.584), obtained for Eddie Johnson in the trade with Phoenix. He can team with Otis Thorpe (.540) as guys the Kings can go to for the tough inside baskets. But unless new coach Bill Russell can make the trade for the big man he so desperately wants and needs, this offense will go nowhere again.

LaSalle Thompson—doesn't this sound like a broken record by now?—will make some club an excellent power forward some day and Joe Kleine will always be able to thumb through his scrapbook and reminisce about the good old days at Arkansas. Reggie Theus has gotten a little better in his shot selection, though, and a healthy Derek Smith for a whole year will help. Still, they rely too much on the perimeter game.

PLAYMAKING: That's just the thanks that Reggie Theus gets. He spends the last two seasons toning down some of his 1-on-1 antics and becoming a playmaker. And what do the Kings draft? A playmaker, of course, in North Carolina's Kenny Smith. Actually, it was a good move, because despite ranking in the Top 10 in assists the last two seasons, Theus was not real comfortable in the QB role. Smith is a good one who should start as a rookie, and now Theus can take over the duties in spots and go back to being more of a big-time scorer.

DEFENSE: If there is one thing that you would expect any team coached by Bill Russell to learn, it's defense, defense, defense. OK, so that's three things. But Russell always played defense three times harder than anybody else. The problem is going to be whether Russell can get lesser talents like Thompson and Kleine to play in the middle the way he did 20 years ago.

You can't coach height, as Frank Layden likes to say, and that's why Russell has spent a great deal of time since getting the job trying to swing a deal for a big man.

REBOUNDING: This was a deceptively effective area last season as the Kings ranked fourth in the league in cleaning off the

KING ROSTER

No.	Veteran	Pos.	Ht.	Wt.	Age	Yrs. Pro	College
10	Franklin Edwards	G	6-1	170	28	6	Cleveland State
35	Joe Kleine	C	6-11	255	25	2	Arkansas
53	* Mark Olberding	F	6-9	230	31	12	Minnesota
54	Ed Pinckney	F	6-9	215	24	2	Villanova
21	Harold Pressley	G-F	6-7	210	24	1	Villanova
32	Johnny Rogers	F	6-11	231	23	1	Cal-Irvine
43	Derek Smith	G	6-6	210	26	5	Louisville
24	Reggie Theus	G	6-7	205	30	9	Nevada-Las Vegas
41	LaSalle Thompson	C	6-10	250	25	5	Texas
33	Otis Thorpe	F	6-10	235	25	3	Providence
40	Terry Tyler	F	6-7	220	30	9	Detroit

*Free agent unsigned at press time

Rd.	Top Rookies	Sel. No.	Pos.	Ht.	Wt.	College
1	Kenny Smith	6	G	6-3	170	North Carolina
3	Sven Meyer	51	C	6-11	235	Oregon
4	Joe Arlauckas	74	F	6-8	230	Niagara
5	Vernon Carr	97	G	6-6	190	Michigan State
6	Darryl Thomas	120	F	6-7	220	Indiana

glass. With the exception of Thorpe—who bounced back after having a bad second year in the league—there is nobody you'd nominate to the All-Rebounding team. No 7-footers and no leapers.

People like Thompson and Thorpe get rebounds the way Russell used to—by hustling for them. Terry Tyler helps in this department with his leaping ability, but he hasn't helped enough to justify the big money, free-agent contract the Kings gave him two years ago. It just goes to show that it doesn't help to rebound the ball if you can't do anything with it.

OUTLOOK: The yahoos in Sacramento have ended the honeymoon with their club early. There were boos being heard throughout Arco Arena last season when the team plummeted out of the playoff picture. Russell says he's in it for the long haul, but the picture will not get any brighter unless they can latch onto a big man. Most of the other necessary parts for a playoff team are already in place.

KING PROFILES

REGGIE THEUS 30 6-7 205   Guard

Mr. Flash goes unnoticed... Ever since he's taken his act to the capital city of California with the Kings, his all-around game has improved, but his frequency in the headlines has gone down... Was snubbed again by Western Conference coaches for spot on the all-star team... Led the Kings again in scoring and assists... Sixth-best assist man in the NBA ... Born Oct. 13, 1957, in Inglewood, Cal., he would always have been right at home in the old neighborhood with the glitzy Lakers... But after starring at UNLV, he was No. 9 pick in 1978 of Chicago and had nothing but problems in the conservative Midwest... Traded to KC Kings in 1984 for Steve Johnson and three second-round picks... Reputation as a ball-hog is no longer deserved... Should get more respect... Handsome and a flamboyant dresser, he modeled for fashion layouts... Had a couple of teeth knocked out in collision with Houston's Rodney McCray last season.

Year	Team	G	FG	FG Pct.	FT	FT Pct.	Reb.	Ast.	TP	Avg.
1978-79	Chicago.............	82	537	.480	264	.761	228	429	1338	16.3
1979-80	Chicago.............	82	566	.483	500	.838	329	515	1660	20.2
1980-81	Chicago.............	82	543	.495	445	.809	287	426	1549	18.9
1981-82	Chicago.............	82	560	.469	363	.808	312	476	1508	18.4
1982-83	Chicago.............	82	749	.478	434	.801	300	484	1953	23.8
1983-84	Chi.-K.C.............	61	262	.419	214	.762	129	352	745	12.2
1984-85	Kansas City.........	82	501	.487	334	.863	270	656	1341	16.4
1985-86	Sacramento.........	82	546	.480	405	.827	304	788	1503	18.3
1986-87	Sacramento.........	79	577	.472	429	.867	266	692	1600	20.3
	Totals.............	714	4841	.476	3388	.819	2425	4818	13197	18.5

OTIS THORPE 25 6-10 235   Forward

Solid and dependable... Bounced back from a bad second year in the league to become one of the veterans that the Kings could count on every night... The only player on the roster to start in all 82 regular-season games... Born Aug. 5, 1962, in Boynton, Fla.... He was a consensus All-Big East pick at Providence, but not widely known elsewhere... Kings got him with the No. 9 pick in the 1984 draft and he was on the all-underrated team in his rookie season when the club was in KC

. . . Knee injury slowed him in his sophomore pro season . . . But he shed the knee brace and the problems last year . . . A fierce rebounder and tough inside scorer, he's developing an all-around game . . . Played just a season and a half of high-school ball . . . Third youngest in a family of 12 children, that's probably where he learned to hustle . . . Will earn all of his $302,500 this season.

Year	Team	G	FG	FG Pct.	FT	FT Pct.	Reb.	Ast.	TP	Avg.
1984-85	Kansas City	82	411	.600	230	.620	556	111	1052	12.8
1985-86	Sacramento	75	289	.587	164	.661	420	84	742	9.9
1986-87	Sacramento	82	567	.540	413	.761	819	201	1547	18.9
	Totals	239	1267	.569	807	.694	1795	396	3341	14.0

ED PINCKNEY 24 6-9 215   Forward

Was beginning to get comfortable with the Suns, and now he's a King, traded for Eddie Johnson in June . . . Came into the NBA as a rookie on the crest of the wave that carried him to the MVP award as Villanova toppled mighty Georgetown for the NCAA title in 1985 . . . Had it rough in the pros . . . Worried people with his laid-back attitude and back-to-basket game . . . Born March 27, 1963, in the Bronx, N.Y. . . . A consensus prep All-American at Adlai Stevensen H.S., where he shot an incredible 75 percent as a senior . . . Smooth and slinky, he became a leader at Villanova . . . E-Z Ed rose to the occasion and outscored Pat Ewing, 16-14, and outrebounded him, 6-5, in the big upset . . . Picked No. 10 by Suns in 1985 draft . . . He should be a solid, but unspectacular pro . . . Can get the tough rebounds.

Year	Team	G	FG	FG Pct.	FT	FT Pct.	Reb.	Ast.	TP	Avg.
1985-86	Phoenix	80	255	.558	171	.673	308	90	681	8.5
1986-87	Phoenix	80	290	.584	257	.739	580	116	837	10.5
	Totals	160	545	.571	428	.711	888	206	1518	9.5

DEREK SMITH 26 6-6 210   Guard

Problems, problems . . . Came to Sacramento prior to last season along with Franklin Edwards and Junior Bridgeman in a deal for Larry Drew and Mike Woodson . . . Was supposed to provide top-flight play in the backcourt, but had problems with injuries (knee) and personality conflicts that made it a lost season . . . Born Oct. 1, 1961, in LaGrange,

Ga.... One of the horses you never heard about in Denny Crum's stable that won the 1980 NCAA title for Louisville... A second-round pick of Golden State in 1982, the Warriors blew it when they cut him... Hooked on with Clippers in San Diego and blossomed into one of the game's best big guards in 1984-85 in LA... Knee injury and mononucleosis sidelined him for much of 1985-86 season... Free agent wanted out of Clippers nuthouse in the worst way... Got a five-year, $2.5 million deal from Kings ... If healthy, he can still be one of the best in the league.

Year	Team	G	FG	FG Pct.	FT	FT Pct.	Reb.	Ast.	TP	Avg.
1982-83	Golden State	27	21	.412	17	.680	38	2	59	2.2
1983-84	San Diego	61	238	.546	123	.755	170	82	600	9.8
1984-85	L.A. Clippers	80	682	.537	400	.794	427	216	1767	22.1
1985-86	L.A. Clippers	11	100	.552	58	.690	41	31	259	23.5
1986-87	Sacramento	52	338	.447	178	.781	182	204	863	16.6
	Totals	231	1379	.511	776	.773	858	535	3548	15.4

LaSALLE THOMPSON 25 6-10 250   Center

The king of the Kings... They treat him like royalty in Sacramento... That's because they love his hustling, aggressive style of play... Who wouldn't?... He gives up several inches to the tall towers of the NBA, but The Tank never gives ground... If he could ever play alongside a bonafide NBA center, he might set the power-forward position on its ear... Born June 23, 1961, in Cincinnati... Played at the University of Texas under good ol' boy Abe Lemons... When the wise-cracking Lemons was canned, Thompson left school early... Center-less Dallas passed on him in the draft and took Bill (Are you kidding?) Garnett instead... Kings got him at No. 5 in 1982... Relentless offensive rebounder... He's got a nice touch on the short jumper... Clint Eastwood is his favorite actor... It shows when he acts like Dirty Harry under the boards.

Year	Team	G	FG	FG Pct.	FT	FT Pct.	Reb.	Ast.	TP	Avg.
1982-83	Kansas City	71	147	.512	89	.650	375	33	383	5.4
1983-84	Kansas City	80	333	.523	160	.717	709	86	826	10.3
1984-85	Kansas City	82	369	.531	227	.721	854	130	965	11.8
1985-86	Sacramento	80	411	.500	202	.732	770	168	1024	12.8
1986-87	Sacramento	82	362	.481	188	.737	687	122	912	11.1
	Totals	395	1622	.512	866	.718	3395	539	4110	10.4

FRANKLIN EDWARDS 28 6-1 170   Guard

Needed a break and it turned out to be a bad one... After signing a two-year, $500,000 offer sheet with the Kings and getting sent north from the LA Clippers in an offseason trade, he promptly broke his foot and missed all but eight games last year... Small, but quick... Drafted on the first round by Philadelphia in 1981 as a shooting guard... He's worked to become a point guard and can do the job quite well ... Born Feb. 2, 1959, in New York City... Big scorer in college at Cleveland State... Played a very limited role on Philly's NBA title team in 1983... He's drifted around the league... But if he stays healthy and somebody gives him a chance, all the guard-poor clubs that passed him by will wish they hadn't... Name is Franklin Delano, after President Roosevelt.

Year	Team	G	FG	FG Pct.	FT	FT Pct.	Reb.	Ast.	TP	Avg.
1981-82	Philadelphia.........	42	65	.433	20	.741	27	45	150	3.6
1982-83	Philadelphia.........	81	228	.472	86	.761	85	221	542	6.7
1983-84	Philadelphia.........	60	84	.380	34	.708	59	90	202	3.4
1984-85	L.A. Clippers........	16	36	.545	19	.792	14	38	91	5.7
1985-86	L.A. Clippers........	73	262	.454	132	.874	86	259	657	9.0
1986-87	Sacramento..........	8	9	.281	10	.714	10	29	28	3.5
	Totals.............	280	684	.447	301	.798	281	682	1670	6.0

HAROLD PRESSLEY 24 6-7 210   Guard-Forward

Elvis might have been talking about this Pressley when he sang, "You ain't nothin' but a hound dog."... After being taken No. 17 overall in the 1986 draft, he didn't show the Kings a whole lot as a rookie... Except, of course, a whole lot of missed shots ...Born July 14, 1963, in Uncasville, Conn.... Played every position in college at Villanova and was a member of the Wildcats' "miracle" team that won the NCAA title in 1985... Mostly used as a big man by Villanova, he had trouble making the shift to the backcourt in the pros... Has the physical tools to be an excellent all-around player... Will do the dirty work... Must produce better than he did as a rookie.

Year	Team	G	FG	FG Pct.	FT	FT Pct.	Reb.	Ast.	TP	Avg.
1986-87	Sacramento.........	67	134	.423	35	.729	176	120	310	4.6

MARK OLBERDING 31 6-9 230 Forward

Can all the banging he's done in a dozen seasons have taken its toll?...Shot just .418 from the field last season and had the lowest offensive output of his career...Seems like he should have a head full of gray hair since he's been around so long...He left the University of Minnesota early to become a first-round draft choice of San Diego in the ABA in 1975 draft...Moved over to San Antonio and was a member of the Spurs' original "Bruise Brothers"...Born April 21, 1956, in Melrose, Minn....Traded to Chicago with Dave Corzine for Artis Gilmore...Then Bulls sent him to the Kings with Larry Micheaux for Ennis Whatley and Chris McNealy...Until last season, he'd always gotten the job done off the bench for the Kings...Could be at the end of the line.

Year	Team	G	FG	FG Pct.	FT	FT Pct.	Reb.	Ast.	TP	Avg.
1975-76	S.D.-S.A. (ABA)	81	302	.498	191	.773	530	142	795	9.8
1976-77	San Antonio	82	301	.503	251	.794	449	119	853	10.4
1977-78	San Antonio	79	231	.481	184	.811	373	131	646	8.2
1978-79	San Antonio	80	261	.474	233	.803	429	211	755	9.4
1979-80	San Antonio	75	291	.478	210	.795	418	327	792	10.6
1980-81	San Antonio	82	348	.508	315	.829	471	277	1012	12.3
1981-82	San Antonio	68	333	.472	273	.808	439	202	941	13.8
1982-83	Chicago	80	251	.481	194	.782	358	131	698	8.7
1983-84	Kansas City	81	249	.494	261	.821	445	192	759	9.4
1984-85	Kansas City	81	265	.502	293	.832	513	243	823	10.2
1985-86	Sacramento	81	225	.558	162	.771	423	266	612	7.6
1986-87	Sacramento	76	69	.418	116	.885	185	91	254	3.3
	Totals	946	3126	.492	2683	.808	5033	2332	8940	9.5

TERRY TYLER 30 6-7 220 Forward

Much ado about nothing...Kings made a lot of noise by signing this free agent to an offer sheet in 1985-86 season and eventually working out a deal with Detroit...He has not paid off the big dividends...Was named the Kings' team captain last season for his work habits...Just doesn't produce enough offense consistently...Born Oct. 30, 1956, in Detroit...Stayed at home to attend the University of Detroit and was drafted (No. 28) by the Pistons in 1978...A real leaper, he had his vertical jump measured at 45 inches...A good shooter of the 15-foot baseline shot...Just hasn't been worth the big investment.

Year	Team	G	FG	FG Pct.	FT	FT Pct.	Reb.	Ast.	TP	Avg.
1978-79	Detroit	82	456	.482	144	.658	648	89	1056	12.9
1979-80	Detroit	82	430	.465	143	.765	627	129	1005	12.3
1980-81	Detroit	82	476	.532	148	.592	567	136	1100	13.4
1981-82	Detroit	82	336	.523	142	.740	493	126	815	9.9
1982-83	Detroit	82	421	.478	146	.745	540	157	990	12.1
1983-84	Detroit	82	313	.453	94	.712	285	76	722	8.8
1984-85	Detroit	82	422	.494	106	.716	423	63	950	11.6
1985-86	Sacramento	71	295	.455	84	.750	313	94	674	9.5
1986-87	Sacramento	82	329	.495	101	.721	328	73	760	9.3
	Totals	727	3478	.487	1108	.703	4224	943	8072	11.1

JOE KLEINE 25 6-11 255 — Center

As good as he's going to get...People keep expecting him to blossom into the next Dave Cowens, but that's strictly dreaming...He's a scrapper and a fighter with very limited skills ...A decent medium-range shooter, he doesn't have the speed or quickness in the first step to get his shot off in the NBA...Born Jan. 4, 1962, in Colorado Springs, Colo.... Raised in Missouri....Signed letter of intent with Notre Dame, then left after one season for Arkansas, where he became an All-American under Eddie Sutton...Fourth-leading scorer in Razorback history...Taken with the No. 6 pick in the 1985 draft by the Kings and given a big, big contract. Will get $575,000 this season. Hardly worth it...Played on the 1984 U.S. Olympic team that won the gold medal in LA.

Year	Team	G	FG	FG Pct.	FT	FT Pct.	Reb.	Ast.	TP	Avg.
1985-86	Sacramento	80	160	.465	94	.723	373	46	414	5.2
1986-87	Sacramento	79	256	.471	110	.786	483	71	622	7.9
	Totals	159	416	.469	204	.756	856	117	1036	6.5

TOP ROOKIE

KENNY SMITH 22 6-3 170 — Guard

Pure point guard...Consensus first team All-American after running the attack for Dean Smith at North Carolina...Excellent penetrator, great passer, can shoot the ball as well . . . Born March 8, 1965, in New York . . . Became a starter at UNC as a freshman . . . The No. 6 pick on the first round, he should get a chance to start right away for the Kings.

COACH BILL RUSSELL: If nothing else, the Kings' move to hire the former NBA great as head coach got his ridiculous cackle and mumbling voice off the WTBS telecasts . . . He is making a return to the sidelines for the first time since 1977 . . . Spent four years as the boss of the Seattle SuperSonics, leading them to a pair of second-place finishes in the Pacific Division . . . Nobody questions his background as one of the true all-time greats and his track record as player-coach of the Boston Celtics at the end of his career . . . The question is whether he can communicate and get his point across with the young players who make up the game today . . . Born Feb. 12, 1934, in Monroe, La. . . . Grew up in the Bay Area of California . . . Led the University of San Francisco to NCAA titles in 1955 and 1956 and the U.S. Olympic team to a gold medal in Melbourne in 1956 . . . Drafted No. 3 in 1956 by Boston with pick obtained from St. Louis . . . Won 11 NBA titles in 13 seasons . . . Named greatest player in the history of the league in 1980 . . . "I know what it takes to win," he says now . . . We'll see . . . Will move up to GM post in two or three years.

GREATEST COACH

You know how it is with little guys. They always have to fight harder, scrap a little bit longer and hustle to gain that extra edge anywhere they can.

That's Cotton Fitzsimmons, the dapper little ex-Kings' coach, who used to buy his clothes at the finest boys' shops in Kansas City.

Fitzsimmons already had successful stints in Phoenix and Atlanta and an aborted stop in Buffalo when he touched down in Kansas City. In his first season on the job, the Kings won the

Midwest Division title at 48-34, still the third-best record in the history of this vagabond franchise.

But it was in the 1980-81 season when Fitzsimmons was at his Cotton-pickin' best, hustling a mediocre team into the playoffs with a 40-42 mark and making it all the way to the Western Conference finals against Houston, where the magic finally ran out.

In six seasons on the job, Fitzsimmons gave the Kings a solid defense, respectability and a little piece of himself. The team may be in Sacramento now, but the best coaching job was done by the tiny guy in KC.

ALL-TIME KING LEADERS

SEASON

Points: Nate Archibald, 2,719, 1972-73
Assists: Nate Archibald, 910, 1972-73
Rebounds: Jerry Lucas, 1,688, 1965-66

GAME

Points: Jack Twyman, 59 vs. Minneapolis, 1/15/60
Assists: Phil Ford, 22 vs. Milwaukee, 2/21/79
　　　　Oscar Robertson, 22 vs. New York, 3/5/66
　　　　Oscar Robertson, 22 vs. Syracuse, 10/29/61
Rebounds: Jerry Lucas, 40 vs. Philadelphia, 2/29/64

CAREER

Points: Oscar Robertson, 22,009, 1960-70
Assists: Oscar Robertson, 7,721, 1960-70
Rebounds: Jerry Lucas, 8,831, 1963-69

SAN ANTONIO SPURS

TEAM DIRECTORY: Pres.: Angelo Drossos; GM: Bob Bass; Dir. Pub. Rel.: Wayne Witt; Coach: Bob Weiss; Asst. Coach: Lee Rose. Arena: HemisFair Arena (15,782). Colors; Silver, black and white.

SCOUTING REPORT

SHOOTING: What was already a poor shooting club is set to take a turn for the worse with the subtraction of center Artis Gilmore. The A-Train was slow and running out of gas, but was also one of the NBA's all-time leaders in field-goal percentage.

Of course, the Spurs are already looking two years down the line when they hope to have this year's No. 1 draft choice, David Robinson, stationed in the middle. For now, Robinson is stationed at a submarine base in Georgia and the forecast for this season is bleak. Another first-round draft choice, Greg Anderson of the University of Houston, will likely get a trial by fire in his rookie season and wind up as the starting center.

Walter Berry (.531) is the most dependable offensive weapon in coach Bob Weiss' arsenal. The backcourt of Alvin Robertson (.466) and Johnny Dawkins (.437) has to improve if the Spurs are to do anything.

PLAYMAKING: There are plenty of players on this roster who fit the quarterback description. There's Dawkins and Johnny Moore and Jon Sundvold and even Robertson, to some extent. What the Spurs need is for one of them—namely Dawkins—to step forward and grab the bull by the horns. He's had his rookie year for adjustment. Now it's time for Dawkins to play with the poise and confidence he showed in college at Duke.

DEFENSE: The team that ranked 21st in the league in blocked shots with only 325 all last season has just traded away Gilmore, who accounted for 95 of them. Next in line was Mychal Thompson and he was gone in the midseason trade last year to the Lakers. It's probably being unfair to rookie Anderson—regarded as a project-type player—to have to step in and control the middle.

But unfair or not, that's the way it's going to be as the Spurs will find the wait for Robinson getting longer and longer. The backcourt defense should be better than it was last year with Robertson and Dawkins. Robertson has to stop playing only the

Johnny Dawkins showed he had the makings as a rookie.

SPUR ROSTER

No.	Veteran	Pos.	Ht.	Wt.	Age	Yrs. Pro	College
6	Walter Berry	F	6-8	215	23	1	St. John's
43	* Frank Brickowski	C-F	6-10	240	28	3	Penn State
24	Johnny Dawkins	G	6-2	165	24	1	Duke
10	* David Greenwood	F	6-9	220	30	8	UCLA
35	Petur Gudmundsson	C	7-2	270	29	3	Washington
11	* Anthony Jones	G	6-6	195	24	1	Nevada-Las Vegas
42	Larry Krystowiak	F	6-10	240	23	1	Montana
34	Mike Mitchell	F	6-7	215	31	9	Auburn
00	Johnny Moore	G	6-3	185	29	6	Texas
32	Ed Nealy	F	6-7	240	27	4	Kansas State
21	Alvin Robertson	G	6-4	195	25	3	Arkansas
20	Jon Sundvold	G	6-1	170	26	4	Missouri

*Free agent unsigned at press time

Rd.	Top Rookies	Sel. No.	Pos.	Ht.	Wt.	College
1	**David Robinson	1	C	7-1	235	Navy
1	Greg Anderson	23	C-F	6-10	230	Houston
2	Nate Blackwell	27	G	6-4	170	Temple
3	Phil Zevenbergen	50	F	6-10	235	Washington
4	Todd May	73	F	6-8½	225	Pikeville

**In U.S. Navy for two years

passing lanes and going for the steals, and fit better into the team concept.

REBOUNDING: David? David? Where are you David Robinson? While the No. 1 draft pick is in Georgia shuffling papers at a Navy desk job, the Spurs will be shuffling everybody in and out of the lineup in a desperate attempt to get rebounds. The big board man here will be David Greenwood, who had a rare healthy season last year and now will be forced to shoulder much of the burden on the boards.

OUTLOOK: Two years from now, it's as hot and spicy as a San Antonio taco, if Robinson can be roped into the fold. But in the meantime, the Spurs could be in for a siege worse than the Alamo. Gilmore is gone, Mike Mitchell (drug problems) is likely on his way out and Anderson is too young and too raw to help stem the tide. On the bright side, when the Spurs finish at the bottom of the standings again, they'll be back in the draft lottery and could really accumulate some supporting talent for Robinson.

SPUR PROFILES

ALVIN ROBERTSON 25 6-4 195   Guard

Slipped a bit... After making the all-star team and being named the league's most improved player in his second year, he took a step or two backwards last season... Some thought that he read too many of his press clippings and began trying to do too much by himself... If he stays within the confines of the game plan, he can be a great one... Excellent quickness ...Plays the passing lanes and led the league in steals for second year in a row...A tough, gritty competitor, who once asked the Spurs for permission to attend a military boot camp in the summer. He was denied...Born July 22, 1962, in Cleveland... Started at Crowder JC in Missouri and then played under Eddie Sutton at Arkansas, which spawned Sidney Moncrief and Darrell Walker...Played on 1984 U.S. Olympic team that won gold in LA...No. 7 pick overall in 1984 draft...Has a weekly radio show where he acts as a DJ and plays Jamaican music... Underpaid at $307,500.

Year	Team	G	FG	FG Pct.	FT	FT Pct.	Reb.	Ast.	TP	Avg.
1984-85	San Antonio.........	79	299	.498	124	.734	265	275	726	9.2
1985-86	San Antonio.........	82	562	.514	260	.795	516	448	1392	17.0
1986-87	San Antonio.........	81	589	.466	244	.753	424	421	1435	17.7
	Totals.............	242	1450	.490	628	.766	1205	1144	3553	14.7

JOHNNY DAWKINS 24 6-2 165   Guard

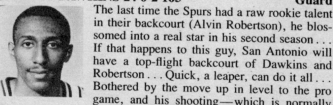

The last time the Spurs had a raw rookie talent in their backcourt (Alvin Robertson), he blossomed into a real star in his second season... If that happens to this guy, San Antonio will have a top-flight backcourt of Dawkins and Robertson...Quick, a leaper, can do it all... Bothered by the move up in level to the pro game, and his shooting—which is normally good—suffered...Born Sept. 28, 1963, in Washington, D.C....The top scorer in Duke history...Led the Blue Devils to the NCAA title game in 1986, where they lost to Louisville ...Spurs plucked him at No. 10 slot in 1986 draft...He should still be regarded as a can't-miss prospect...Runs like a cheetah on the fastbreak.

Year	Team	G	FG	FG Pct.	FT	FT Pct.	Reb.	Ast.	TP	Avg.
1986-87	San Antonio.........	81	334	.437	153	.801	169	290	835	10.3

WALTER BERRY 23 6-8 215   Forward

The Truth . . . That's his nickname and it's also what everybody is trying to find out about this prospect/suspect . . . The 1985-86 College Player of the Year . . . Taken by Portland as the 14th overall pick in the 1986 draft . . . Had contract problems, then all kinds of individual personality clashes with management in Portland . . . Played in just seven games with Blazers and was traded on Dec. 18 to Spurs for fat boy Kevin Duckworth . . . It could be one of the greatest steals of all times if Berry lives up to his potential . . . Of course, he promptly missed his flight to San Antonio . . . Born May 14, 1964, in the Bronx, N.Y. . . . Unstoppable inside player, must develop game facing the basket . . . Should do a better job of rebounding . . . Spent one year at San Jacinto (Tex.) JC, then two years at St. John's . . . Left school a year early against the advice of most experts.

Year	Team	G	FG	FG Pct.	FT	FT Pct.	Reb.	Ast.	TP	Avg.
1986-87	Port.-S.A.	63	407	.531	187	.649	309	105	1001	15.9

DAVID GREENWOOD 30 6-9 220   Forward

Another guy whose best days are past . . . He can still explode for big numbers in scoring and rebounding occasionally, but bad wheels prevent him from being productive every night . . . Will never live down the fact that he's the one the Spurs got in the deal when George Gervin was traded to Chicago . . . Born May 27, 1957, in Lynwood, Cal. . . . Big star at UCLA . . . Bulls made him the No. 2 pick in the 1979 college draft . . . He's one of those guys who has never lived up to his reputation and usually gets coaches fired . . . It is awfully tough to justify the fully guaranteed salary of $1 million that he's got coming this season . . . Strictly excess baggage on any team that is trying to rebuild.

Year	Team	G	FG	FG Pct.	FT	FT Pct.	Reb.	Ast.	TP	Avg.
1979-80	Chicago	82	498	.474	337	.810	773	182	1334	16.3
1980-81	Chicago	82	481	.486	217	.748	724	218	1179	14.4
1981-82	Chicago	82	480	.473	240	.825	786	262	1200	14.6
1982-83	Chicago	79	312	.455	165	.708	765	151	789	10.0
1983-84	Chicago	78	369	.490	213	.737	786	139	951	12.2
1984-85	Chicago	61	152	.458	67	.713	388	78	371	6.1
1985-86	San Antonio	68	198	.510	142	.772	531	90	538	7.9
1986-87	San Antonio	79	336	.513	241	.785	783	237	916	11.6
	Totals	611	2826	.482	1622	.771	5536	1357	7278	11.9

MIKE MITCHELL 31 6-7 215   Forward

Nearing the end...He's been wearing down over the last several seasons and has been plagued by bad knees and ankles...Then late in the 1986-87 season, he turned himself into the NBA's drug rehabilitation program for cocaine abuse...He might make it back to the NBA, but will never be the top-level performer who carried the Spurs for several years ...Born Jan. 1, 1956, in Atlanta...The 15th player drafted overall in 1978 by Cleveland...Unappreciated by the Cavs, he came to San Antonio with his old coach Stan Albeck, shooting rainbow jumpers and getting tough rebounds to lead Spurs to Western Conference finals twice...Had 20 points a game in seven straight seasons before last year...Played in only 40 games, started only 18...Played in college at Auburn, where he set school scoring and rebounding marks...Traded to Spurs in December 1981 with Roger Phegley for Ron Brewer and Reggie Johnson...Sews his own clothes as a hobby.

Year	Team	G	FG	FG Pct.	FT	FT Pct.	Reb.	Ast.	TP	Avg.
1978-79	Cleveland	80	362	.513	131	.736	329	60	855	10.7
1979-80	Cleveland	82	775	.523	270	.787	591	93	1820	22.2
1980-81	Cleveland	82	853	.476	302	.784	502	139	2012	24.5
1981-82	Clev.-S.A.	84	753	.510	220	.728	540	82	1726	20.5
1982-83	San Antonio	80	686	.511	219	.758	537	98	1591	19.9
1983-84	San Antonio	79	779	.488	275	.779	570	93	1839	23.3
1984-85	San Antonio	82	775	.497	269	.777	417	151	1824	22.2
1985-86	San Antonio	82	802	.473	317	.809	409	188	1921	23.4
1986-87	San Antonio	40	208	.435	92	.821	103	38	509	12.7
	Totals	691	5993	.494	2095	.776	4048	942	14097	20.4

JOHNNY MOORE 29 6-3 185   Guard

Nothing comes easy for him...Had to fight his way into the NBA in the first place and now is fighting off the effects of "Desert Fever," a life-threatening illness...Required neuro-surgery to combat the infection during the 1985-86 season...Made it back to the lineup by the start of the 1986-87 campaign, but his game was affected...May have lost the hard mental edge...Late in the season, he was finally able to be weaned from his regular dose of medication...Still not the player he once was...Born March 3, 1958, in Altoona, Pa., but he's a full-fledged Texan now...Played under Abe Lemons on the University of Texas team that won the NIT in 1978...Drafted on the second round by Seattle and cut...Signed as a free agent by Spurs and was cut by then-coach Doug Moe...

Went back to Austin, worked on his game, developed an outside shot and returned to become the Spurs' floor leader. Team's all-time assist leader . . . Adversity just seems to stalk him.

Year	Team	G	FG	FG Pct.	FT	FT Pct.	Reb.	Ast.	TP	Avg.
1980-81	San Antonio.........	82	249	.479	105	.610	196	373	604	7.4
1981-82	San Antonio.........	79	309	.463	122	.670	275	762	741	9.4
1982-83	San Antonio.........	77	394	.468	148	.744	277	753	941	12.2
1983-84	San Antonio.........	59	231	.446	105	.755	178	566	595	10.1
1984-85	San Antonio.........	82	416	.457	189	.762	378	816	1046	12.8
1985-86	San Antonio.........	28	150	.495	59	.686	86	252	363	13.0
1986-87	San Antonio.........	55	198	.442	56	.800	100	250	474	8.6
	Totals.............	462	1947	.463	784	.715	1490	3772	4764	10.3

JON SUNDVOLD 26 6-1 170   Guard

Sunny one so true, they used to love you . . . That was back in the days as a college hero at Mizzou . . . Now he's just one of those journeyman pros who will be hanging around for years and never really getting anything accomplished . . . Put him in a category with Mike Bratz and Roger Phegley . . . Born July 2, 1961, in Sioux Falls, S.D. . . . Raised in Missouri and stayed at home to become school's No. 2 all-time leading scorer . . . Reputation as a pure shooter . . . Treats the lane as if it were quicksand and avoids it at all costs . . . Hardly a tough guy . . . He once passed out at the sight of his own blood . . . For guy who is supposed to be a shooter, it's curious that his .486 percentage last season was the best of a four-year career . . . A first-round pick of Seattle in 1983 . . . Traded to San Antonio in 1986 for a second-round pick.

Year	Team	G	FG	FG Pct.	FT	FT Pct.	Reb.	Ast.	TP	Avg.
1983-84	Seattle.............	73	217	.445	64	.889	91	239	507	6.9
1984-85	Seattle.............	73	170	.425	48	.814	70	206	400	5.5
1985-86	San Antonio.........	70	220	.462	39	.813	80	261	500	7.1
1986-87	San Antonio.........	76	365	.486	70	.833	98	315	850	11.2
	Totals.............	292	972	.460	221	.840	339	1021	2257	7.7

FRANK BRICKOWSKI 28 6-10 240   Center-Forward

Well, he's big . . . That's about all you can say for the basketball talents of this walking concrete block . . . Most notable thing he did last season—in fact, in his whole career—was being part of the bargain-basement package that the LA Lakers shipped to San Antonio in midseason to get Mychal Thompson. Mark it down. It was Brickowski, Petur Gudmundsson, a 1987 first-round choice, a 1990 second-round choice and cash for Thompson... Born Aug. 14, 1959, in Glen Cove, N.Y... Played college ball under Dick Harter at Penn State... Tough guy was drafted on third round by Knicks in 1981... Spent three years in Europe and then caught on with Seattle... Very physical.

Year	Team	G	FG	FG Pct.	FT	FT Pct.	Reb.	Ast.	TP	Avg.
1984-85	Seattle............	78	150	.492	85	.669	260	100	385	4.9
1985-86	Seattle............	40	30	.517	18	.667	54	21	78	2.0
1986-87	LAL-S.A...........	44	63	.508	50	.714	116	17	176	4.0
	Totals.............	162	243	.499	153	.683	430	138	639	3.9

LARRY KRYSTKOWIAK 23 6-10 240   Forward

Nothing fancy here... He's a bull who makes his living by knocking people down to get rebounds... Honorable mention All-American three times at Montana, where he became the school's all-time leader in points and rebounds... Born Sept. 23, 1964, in Shelby, Mont.... Came from a tiny high school in Missoula, Mont., that had just 200 students ... Came to San Antonio the long way... Drafted No. 28 overall by Chicago in 1986 and quickly traded to Portland for guard Steve Colter... He was then shipped by the Blazers along with Mychal Thompson to the Spurs for Steve Johnson.

Year	Team	G	FG	FG Pct.	FT	FT Pct.	Reb.	Ast.	TP	Avg.
1986-87	San Antonio.........	68	170	.456	110	.743	239	85	451	6.6

ED NEALY 27 6-7 240   Forward

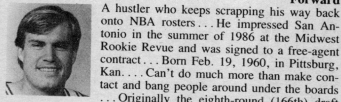

A hustler who keeps scrapping his way back onto NBA rosters... He impressed San Antonio in the summer of 1986 at the Midwest Rookie Revue and was signed to a free-agent contract... Born Feb. 19, 1960, in Pittsburg, Kan.... Can't do much more than make contact and bang people around under the boards ... Originally the eighth-round (166th) draft pick of KC Kings... In those days, his father used to drive him to practice... Stayed with Kings for three seasons... Has also played for Sarasota of the CBA... Played college ball at Kansas State.

Year	Team	G	FG	FG Pct.	FT	FT Pct.	Reb.	Ast.	TP	Avg.
1982-83	Kansas City.........	82	147	.595	70	.614	485	62	364	4.4
1983-84	Kansas City.........	71	63	.500	48	.800	222	50	174	2.5
1984-85	Kansas City.........	22	26	.591	10	.526	44	18	62	2.8
1986-87	San Antonio.........	60	84	.438	51	.739	284	83	223	3.7
	Totals.............	235	320	.525	179	.683	1035	213	823	3.5

TOP ROOKIES

DAVID ROBINSON 22 7-1 235   Center

The aircraft carrier... The main man... The player who can make or break the franchise in San Antonio... Taken No. 1 in the 1987 draft... Has to fulfill a two-year military commitment and the question is whether he'll want to sign with the Spurs before then... Born Aug. 1965, in Woodbridge, Va.... College Player of the Year at Navy... Averaged 28.2 ppg in final season, 21 over four years... Had career-high 50 points in opening-round loss to Michigan in NCAA tournament... Well worth the two-year wait... A franchise player.

GREG ANDERSON 23 6-10 230   Center-Forward

The Cadillac... Received the nickname because he used to ride around the University of Houston campus on his bicycle... A project-type player who must still learn the game... He's got great raw talent and could be a solid power forward by the time David Robinson arrives, if he does, in two years... Born June 22, 1964, in Houston... Followed Akeem Olajuwon as the University of Houston center... The No. 23 pick on the first round.

COACH BOB WEISS: Finally got the chance to be the boss. Was it worth it? You bet it was if he can hang on long enough to get 1987 lottery prize David Robinson in two years... After six years as Dick Motta's assistant in Dallas, he decided to strike out on his own... Just didn't have the horses to do better than last in the Midwest... Born May 7, 1942, in Nazareth, Pa.... A third-round draft choice of Philadelphia 76ers in 1965, he played for six different clubs in 12-year career... Survived the hard way, scrapping, hustling and using his head... May not have a lot of hair on top of it, but inside that head is a sound basketball mind... Given the chance, he'll get the job done... Had his best playing days under Motta in Chicago and Washington... Broke into coaching as Gene Shue's assistant in San Diego... Was named head coach of the Spurs on the same day Mike Schuler got the Portland job. "My biggest mistake was not falling off my chair at the press conference," he said. "That way, everybody knew who Mike was, but nobody heard about me."... After last season, maybe it was better that way.

GREATEST COACH

Should we call it tag-team coaching? Or was it more like a relay race in track and field?

The wild and crazy Doug Moe led this loose and easy team that could run like the wind and pile up points on the scoreboard into the NBA after the merger with the ABA in 1976 and instantly made the Spurs a force in the league.

Moe spent four years in the Alamo City, taking the Spurs to two division titles and to the Eastern Conference finals in 1979.

The following season, when the Spurs switched over to the Western Conference, they also switched coaches to Stan Albeck and the running, the scoring and the winning continued (153-93, .622). Albeck wore his frizzy hairdo and western-cut jackets to three straight division titles and took the Spurs to the Western Conference finals in 1982 and 1983, where they lost to the powerful LA Lakers.

Call it a toss-up. Both were cut from similar bolts of cloth. But give the edge to Albeck when you hoist a margarita in the name of the greatest coach in Spurs' history.

ALL-TIME SPUR LEADERS

SEASON

Points: George Gervin, 2,585, 1979-80
Assists: Johnny Moore, 816, 1984-85
Rebounds: Swen Nater, 1,279, 1974-75

GAME

Points: George Gervin, 63 vs. New Orleans, 4/9/78
Assists: John Lucas, 24 vs. Denver, 4/15/84
Rebounds: Manny Leaks, 35 vs. Kentucky, 11/27/70

CAREER

Points: George Gervin, 23,602, 1974-85
Assists: Johnny Moore, 3,663, 1980-87
Rebounds: George Gervin, 4,841, 1974-85

SEATTLE SUPERSONICS

TEAM DIRECTORY: Chairman: Barry Ackerley; Pres.: Bob Whitsitt; Dir. Pub. Rel.: Jim Rupp; Coach: Bernie Bickerstaff; Asst. Coaches: Bob Klopperburg, Tom Newell. Arena: Seattle Center Coliseum (14,200). Colors: Green and yellow.

SCOUTING REPORT

SHOOTING: Think one man can't make a difference? Think again. The Sonics made the trade of Al Wood for Dale Ellis just prior to last season and changed the face of the entire team. All of a sudden, coach Bernie Bickerstaff had a weapon who could come off screens and fire in 20-foot (and longer) jumpers as though they were hooked up to radar.

In the playoffs, Ellis became the top gun that was not shot down until the Sonics ran into the Lakers in the Western Conference finals. There is plenty of firepower in the likes of Tom Chambers and Xavier McDaniel as well. Now they've added rookies Olden Polynice and Derrick McKey and you've got to wonder if there are going to be enough balls to go around.

PLAYMAKING: Oh boy, look what the Sonics found down on the second round (30th pick) of the 1986 draft. A 6-5 point guard named Nate McMillan. All he did was step in and give the Seattle offense stability and dealt out a season-high 25 assists in one game against the Clippers. Danny Young was able to come in and perform spot relief duty.

Now the Sonics may have pulled off another coup on the fourth round of the 1987 draft if heady Tommy Amaker out of Duke can stick around and provide bench strength.

DEFENSE: Based on the regular-season statistics that showed the Sonics giving up 113 points a game, you wouldn't think they'd heard of defense. But things began to jell late in the season and you can ask the Houston Rockets and Dallas Mavericks about the defense the Sonics played in the playoffs. Alton Lister is a good shot-blocker in the middle, Maurice Lucas uses all of the old and dirty tricks to play it up front and McMillan has the height to be effective in the backcourt.

And don't forget backup guard Kevin Williams, a one-man SWAT team who simply assaults the offensive player. Polynice is a bruising, enforcer type who will make the Sonics even more fearsome up front this season.

Dale Ellis was Sonic boon with team-leading 24.9 ppg.

SONIC ROSTER

No.	Veteran	Pos.	Ht.	Wt.	Age	Yrs. Pro	College
24	Tom Chambers	F	6-10	230	28	6	Utah
3	Dale Ellis	G	6-7	215	27	4	Tennessee
45	Clemon Johnson	C-F	6-10	240	31	9	Florida A&M
15	* Eddie Johnson	G	6-2	190	32	9	Auburn
42	* Curtis Kitchen	C-F	6-9	235	23	1	South Florida
53	* Alton Lister	C	7-0	240	29	6	Arizona State
20	* Maurice Lucas	F	6-9	238	35	13	Marquette
34	Xavier McDaniel	F	6-7	205	23	2	Wichita State
10	Nate McMillan	G	6-5	197	23	1	North Carolina St.
25	Michael Phelps	G	6-4	185	26	2	Alcorn State
40	Russ Schoene	F	6-10	215	27	2	Tenn.-Chattanooga
44	Terence Stansbury	G	6-4	178	26	3	Temple
30	* Kevin Williams	G	6-2	180	26	3	St. John's
22	Danny Young	G	6-4	175	25	3	Wake Forest

*Free agent unsigned at press time

Rd.	Top Rookies	Sel. No.	Pos.	Ht.	Wt.	College
1	**Olden Polynice	8	C	6-11	220	Virginia
1	Derrick McKey	9	F	6-9	205	Alabama
3	Tommy Amaker	55	G	6-0	155	Duke
4	Todd Linder	78	F	6-7	205	Tampa
5	Michael Tait	101	G	6-2	170	Clemson

**Drafted by Chicago and traded to Seattle

REBOUNDING: Has any team ever improved as much in one season in this department as the Sonics? They went from ranking 22nd in 1985-86 to being No. 3 in rebounds in 1986-87. Now the prospects look even brighter. Lister will get help on the inside from Polynice and McKey. McDaniel can be devastating going to the offensive boards and Chambers, with a new attitude, hit the defensive glass in the playoffs. No more pushovers on the boards in Seattle.

OUTLOOK: When Bob Whitsitt took the job as the Sonics' GM two years ago, people around the league openly laughed. They said it was a dying franchise. Well, look who came back to life. Whitsitt has the best young coach in the league in Bickerstaff, a pile of talent on the roster and four more No. 1 draft choices in the next two years.

They were regarded as the Cinderella team in the playoffs last year, but will get attention right from the start this time around. This is a team that is going places—and fast.

SUPERSONIC PROFILES

DALE ELLIS 27 6-7 215   Guard

A late bloomer or a stifled star?... He found it quite ironic that he was named the NBA's Most Improved Player of the 1986-87 season... Says he's always been this good, but never had a chance to show it in Dallas... After three years of riding the pine with the Mavericks, he was set free to Seattle in a trade for Al Wood ... One of the worst trades in NBA history, if you're Dallas... He raised his scoring average 18 points a game —an NBA record—and was a big gun in the Sonics' playoff upsets of the Mavs and Houston... A deadly outside shooter off of screens... Made the switch into the backcourt... One of three Sonics—Xavier McDaniel and Tom Chambers—to average more than 20 points a game... Born Aug. 6, 1960, in Marietta, Ga.... Dallas made him the No. 9 pick in the 1983 draft... Once shaved his head as a result of losing a bet to a female friend.

Year	Team	G	FG	FG Pct.	FT	FT Pct.	Reb.	Ast.	TP	Avg.
1983-84	Dallas............	67	225	.456	87	.719	250	56	549	8.2
1984-85	Dallas............	72	274	.454	77	.740	238	56	667	9.3
1985-86	Dallas............	72	193	.411	59	.720	168	37	508	7.1
1986-87	Seattle............	82	785	.516	385	.787	447	238	2041	24.9
	Totals............	293	1477	.479	608	.764	1103	387	3765	12.8

TOM CHAMBERS 28 6-10 230   Forward

Looks are so deceiving... You'd think that butter would melt in his mouth, but in truth he's a guy with a reputation for being dirty inside... An elbow swinger... Also known as a selfish player who has had teammates griping, even during last year's fantasy ride through the playoffs... An excellent outside shooter for a big man, he can also handle the ball and go to the hoop... One of the league's best white dunkers... Named as a last-minute replacement for the injured Ralph Sampson and went on to be named MVP of the 1987 All-Star Game in Seattle... Born June 21, 1959, in Ogden, Utah... Taken on the No. 8 slot in the 1981 draft by the San Diego Clippers... Shipped north in 1983 along with Al Wood for James Donaldson, Greg Kelser and Mark Radford... He de-

voured Houston's Sampson in the head-to-head playoff matchup
... Will earn a cool $893,366 this season.

Year	Team	G	FG	FG Pct.	FT	FT Pct.	Reb.	Ast.	TP	Avg.
1981-82	San Diego	81	554	.525	284	.620	561	146	1392	17.2
1982-83	San Diego	79	519	.472	353	.723	519	192	1391	17.6
1983-84	Seattle	82	554	.499	375	.800	532	133	1483	18.1
1984-85	Seattle	81	629	.483	475	.832	579	209	1739	21.5
1985-86	Seattle	66	432	.466	346	.836	431	132	1223	18.5
1986-87	Seattle	82	660	.456	535	.849	545	245	1909	23.3
	Totals	471	3348	.482	2368	.782	3167	1057	9137	19.4

XAVIER McDANIEL 23 6-7 205   Forward

X marks the spot... Actually this guy can
score from just about any spot on the court...
He's a ferocious inside player who can kill you
off the glass... But he can also heat it up from
the outside and then he's virtually unstoppable
... Shaves his head... An imposing figure,
he'll stand and fight at the drop of a hat... In
two years in the NBA, he's fought with just
about everybody except the mayor of Seattle... Had a celebrated
scuffle with his wife that had to be broken up by the police...
How fearless is he? Consider that his wife Sylvia is the niece of
Leroy and Lucious Selmon, former All-American football players
at Oklahoma... Born June 4, 1963, in Columbia, S.C....
Wichita State All-American became the first player in NCAA
history to lead the nation in scoring (27.2) and rebounding (14.8)
in his senior season... The No. 4 pick in the 1985 draft by
Seattle... Started all 82 games last season and 162 of 164 since
entering the league... An all-star of the future... Got nickname
X when grandmother couldn't pronounce Xavier... Was called
"Mountain Man" in high school.

Year	Team	G	FG	FG Pct.	FT	FT Pct.	Reb.	Ast.	TP	Avg.
1985-86	Seattle	82	576	.490	250	.687	655	193	1404	17.1
1986-87	Seattle	82	806	.509	275	.696	705	207	1890	23.0
	Totals	164	1382	.501	525	.692	1360	400	3294	20.1

EDDIE JOHNSON 32 6-2 190   Guard

A ghost from the past... Retrieved from the
scrap heap of the CBA by Bernie Bickerstaff
late in the year, he played a bit role in the
Sonics' Cinderella march through the playoffs
... Has the veteran knowledge and skills to
perform in the clutch... But time has robbed
him of his speed... Born Feb. 24, 1955, in
Ocala, Fla.... Played with San Antonio's

Mike Mitchell at Auburn... Drafted No. 49 by Atlanta in 1977 and a star on Hubie Brown's hard-nosed Hawk teams that contended in the Central Division for a couple of seasons... Was MVP of the 1987 CBA All-Star Game... Brother Frank Johnson plays for the Washington Bullets... At the end of a decent career.

Year	Team	G	FG	FG Pct.	FT	FT Pct.	Reb.	Ast.	TP	Avg.
1977-78	Atlanta..........	79	332	.484	164	.816	153	235	828	10.5
1978-79	Atlanta..........	78	501	.510	243	.832	170	360	1245	16.0
1979-80	Atlanta..........	79	590	.487	280	.828	200	370	1465	18.5
1980-81	Atlanta..........	75	573	.504	279	.784	179	407	1431	19.1
1981-82	Atlanta..........	68	455	.450	294	.764	191	358	1211	17.8
1982-83	Atlanta..........	61	389	.453	186	.785	124	318	978	16.0
1983-84	Atlanta..........	67	353	.442	164	.770	146	374	886	13.2
1984-85	Atlanta..........	73	453	.479	265	.798	192	566	1193	16.3
1985-86	Atl.-Clev........	71	284	.457	112	.723	121	333	709	10.0
1986-87	Seattle..........	24	85	.457	42	.764	46	115	217	9.0
	Totals............	675	4015	.476	2029	.791	1522	3436	10163	15.1

ALTON LISTER 29 7-0 240   Center

Proof that hard work pays off... Made himself into a bonafide NBA center by working at it... Attends Pete Newell's summer camp for big men every year... Was under big pressure to produce when he arrived in Seattle from Milwaukee in exchange for Jack Sikma... He produced and quieted the critics of the deal ... Born Oct. 1, 1958, in Dallas... Nothing special in college at Arizona State... Played on same Sun Devil starting five with Byron Scott, Sam Williams, Kurt Nimphius and Fat Lever—all made it to the NBA... A first-round draft choice by Milwaukee in 1981... Was always a backup with the Bucks, first to Bob Lanier, then to Randy Breuer... His intensity was questioned... Bernie Bickerstaff is getting the most out of him, which is mainly defense... Any offense is a bonus... Member of the 1980 U.S. Olympic team that boycotted Moscow ... Broken foot kept him sidelined for all of Dallas series and first two games against Houston in the playoffs.

Year	Team	G	FG	FG Pct.	FT	FT Pct.	Reb.	Ast.	TP	Avg.
1981-82	Milwaukee..........	80	149	.519	64	.520	387	84	362	4.5
1982-83	Milwaukee..........	80	272	.529	130	.537	568	111	674	8.4
1983-84	Milwaukee..........	82	256	.500	114	.626	603	110	626	7.6
1984-85	Milwaukee..........	81	322	.538	154	.588	647	127	798	9.9
1985-86	Milwaukee..........	81	318	.551	160	.602	592	101	796	9.8
1986-87	Seattle............	75	346	.504	179	.675	705	110	871	11.6
	Totals............	479	1663	.524	801	.598	3502	643	4127	8.6

MAURICE LUCAS 35 6-9 238 — Forward

Who me?... That's what the innocent look on his face seems to be saying every time a scuffle breaks out on the court... Big Mo... The Enforcer... A cagey veteran who knows every trick in the book—elbows, slaps, grabs —to provoke his opponent to lose control... Particularly effective in the playoffs against Dallas and Houston... Acquired off the waiver wire after a one-year stay in LA, where he did not provide the expected muscle for the Lakers... Born Feb. 18, 1952, in Pittsburgh... Played college ball at Marquette, left early to sign with St. Louis of the ABA... Also played with Kentucky Colonels before merger delivered him to Portland... Played with Bill Walton Gang that won NBA title in 1977... Has bounced to New Jersey, New York, Phoenix and LA... Has a great scowling game-face... Off the court, he's a big talker... Intelligent, funny... Still can stick the 15-footer... And can still get under your skin.

Year	Team	G	FG	FG Pct.	FT	FT Pct.	Reb.	Ast.	TP	Avg.
1974-75	St. Louis (ABA)	80	438	.467	180	.786	816	287	1058	13.2
1975-76	St. L.-Ky. (ABA)	86	620	.461	217	.767	970	224	1460	17.0
1976-77	Portland	79	632	.466	335	.765	899	229	1599	20.2
1977-78	Portland	68	453	.458	207	.767	621	173	1113	16.4
1978-79	Portland	69	568	.470	270	.783	716	215	1406	20.4
1979-80	Port.-N.J.	63	371	.456	179	.749	537	208	923	14.7
1980-81	New Jersey	68	404	.484	191	.752	575	173	999	14.7
1981-82	New York	80	505	.504	253	.725	903	179	1263	15.8
1982-83	Phoenix	77	495	.474	278	.781	799	219	1269	16.5
1983-84	Phoenix	75	451	.497	293	.765	725	203	1195	15.9
1984-85	Phoenix	63	346	.476	150	.750	557	145	842	13.4
1985-86	L.A. Lakers	77	302	.462	180	.783	566	84	785	10.2
1986-87	Seattle	63	175	.451	150	.802	307	65	500	7.9
	Totals	948	5760	.472	2883	.766	8991	2404	14412	15.2

NATE McMILLAN 23 6-5 197 — Guard

Diamond in the rough... Who would have thought he'd be one of the starting point guards in the Western Conference finals when Sonics made him a second-round (No. 30 overall) draft pick in 1986?... A rookie who blossomed quickly... Has good size to play defense... An excellent passer who finished seventh in the league in assists... Had an NBA season-high 25 assists against the LA Clippers on Feb. 23, 1987... Born Aug. 3, 1964, in Raleigh, N.C.... Became a Juco All-American at Chowan (N.C.), then played for two years under Jim Valvano at North Carolina State... Very down-to-earth person...Could be a big name in years to come...Several teams in need of point guards made a big mistake in letting this guy get away.

Year	Team	G	FG	FG Pct.	FT	FT Pct.	Reb.	Ast.	TP	Avg.
1986-87	Seattle	71	143	.475	87	.617	331	583	373	5.3

CLEMON JOHNSON 31 6-10 240   Center-Forward

A survivor...Has never been given the proper amount of respect...He'll fill the gaps and do a competent job anytime he's asked...Pinch-hit for injured starting center Alton Lister during the first two rounds of the 1987 playoffs after being a backup during the regular season...Has veteran smarts and plenty of experience...Played behind Moses Malone on Philadelphia's championship team in 1983...Born Sept. 12, 1956, in Monticello, Fla....The 44th player chosen in the 1977 draft by Portland...Spent a year with Blazers and then moved on to Indiana and Philly...Sonics acquired him prior to last season along with the first-round draft choice from the Sixers for Tim McCormick and Danny Vranes.

Year	Team	G	FG	FG Pct.	FT	FT Pct.	Reb.	Ast.	TP	Avg.
1978-79	Portland	74	102	.470	36	.486	226	78	240	3.2
1979-80	Indiana	79	199	.503	74	.632	394	115	472	6.0
1980-81	Indiana	81	235	.504	112	.593	468	144	582	7.2
1981-82	Indiana	79	312	.487	123	.651	571	127	747	9.5
1982-83	Ind.-Phil.	83	299	.515	111	.617	524	139	709	8.5
1983-84	Philadelphia	80	193	.468	69	.611	398	55	455	5.7
1984-85	Philadelphia	58	117	.498	36	.735	221	33	270	4.7
1985-86	Philadelphia	75	105	.471	51	.630	255	15	261	3.5
1986-87	Seattle	78	88	.494	70	.636	277	21	246	3.2
	Totals	687	1650	.493	682	.619	3334	727	3982	5.8

KEVIN WILLIAMS 26 6-2 180   Guard

A scrapper...A street hustler...He'll do whatever it takes to get the job done on the floor and to keep a job in the NBA...One of the most aggressive defenders you'll see anywhere...Gave Houston guards fits in the playoffs last spring...Born Sept. 11, 1961, in New York City...Played college ball at St. John's and was a second-round draft choice (No. 45 overall) of San Antonio in the 1983 draft...Spent parts of two seasons with Spurs and Cleveland Cavaliers...Played for three different CBA teams in Massachusetts, Ohio and Florida and finally got another chance, thanks to Bernie Bickerstaff...A miniature Maurice Lucas, a tiny hit man...Was arrested along with teammate Dale Ellis in incident at a Houston bar during 1987 playoffs and drew a fine of $400 and a year's probation ... Charges were dropped against Ellis.

Year	Team	G	FG	FG Pct.	FT	FT Pct.	Reb.	Ast.	TP	Avg.
1983-84	San Antonio	19	25	.431	25	.781	13	43	75	3.9
1984-85	Cleveland	46	58	.433	47	.734	63	61	163	3.5
1986-87	Seattle	65	132	.446	55	.833	83	66	319	4.9
	Totals	130	215	.441	127	.784	159	170	557	4.3

DANNY YOUNG 25 6-4 175 Guard

Wouldn't quit ... After being cut three games into the 1984-85 season, he's fought his way back to a reserve role on the club ... A decent perimeter shooter, the Sonics used him the last two years as a three-point threat ... Born July 26, 1962, in Raleigh, N.C. ... Played college ball at Wake Forest ... Seattle made him a second-round draft choice (No. 39 overall) ... Nicknamed "Cool Breeze" in college for ability to play under pressure ... He played backup on the point to Nate McMillan ... Played most of the 1984-85 season with the Wyoming Wildcatters of the CBA ... Always must hustle to keep his job ... A minimum-wage earner.

Year	Team	G	FG	FG Pct.	FT	FT Pct.	Reb.	Ast.	TP	Avg.
1984-85	Seattle	3	2	.200	0	.000	3	2	4	1.3
1985-86	Seattle	82	227	.506	90	.849	120	303	568	6.9
1986-87	Seattle	73	132	.458	59	.831	113	353	352	4.8
	Totals	158	361	.483	149	.842	236	658	924	5.8

RUSS SCHOENE 27 6-10 215 Forward

Crabgrass ... He came back ... Out of the NBA since 1983, he was signed as a free agent by Seattle ... Had played three previous seasons in Italy, where he teamed with Joe Barry Carroll on Simac team that won Italian League championship ... A very good outside shooter for a big man ... Born April 16, 1960, in Trenton, Ill. ... Drafted on the second round in 1982 by Philadelphia out of Tennessee-Chattanooga ... Split time in rookie season between Philly and Indiana ... Back surgery put him on the sidelines ... Fighting his way back.

Year	Team	G	FG	FG Pct.	FT	FT Pct.	Reb.	Ast.	TP	Avg.
1982-83	Phil.-Ind	77	207	.476	61	.735	255	59	476	6.2
1986-87	Seattle	63	71	.374	29	.630	117	27	173	2.7
	Totals	140	278	.445	90	.698	372	86	649	4.6

TOP ROOKIES

OLDEN POLYNICE 22 6-11 220   **Center**
Rough, tough and a gamble . . . Had to leave University of Virginia due to cheating and stealing incidents . . . Spent last season with Rimini in the Italian League and has learned to bang under the boards . . . Born Nov. 21, 1964, in New York . . . Won't back down . . . Followed Ralph Sampson as the Cavs' center . . . Taken with No. 8 pick on the first round by Chicago and traded to Seattle for No. 5 pick Scottie Pippen.

DERRICK McKEY 21 6-9 205   **Forward**
Southeastern Conference Player of the Year . . . Early entry to the NBA after it was learned he accepted money from an agent . . . There were questions about his maturity . . . No question about his talent and potent scoring ability . . . Can take the ball inside and score over the top . . . Born Oct. 10, 1966, in Meridian, Miss. . . . The No. 9 pick on the first round by Seattle . . . Could be a steal.

COACH BERNIE BICKERSTAFF: Bernie and the Jets . . . Such was the Sonics' sudden and rapid rise through the 1987 playoffs . . . He took a team that struggled to a 39-43 regular-season record and molded them into Western Conference finalists, upsetting both Dallas and Houston along the way . . . A stylish dresser, but nothing flashy about the way he handles himself . . . He knows his personnel and knows his X's and O's . . . Completely rebuilt the Seattle team he took over just two years ago . . . Only three players remained from his first year on the job . . . Coaches an aggressive, frantic defense that does not give an inch . . . Born Nov. 3, 1943, in Benham, Ky. . . . He was long overdue for this job . . . Had starred in college at the University of San Diego . . . Took over as the head coach at his alma mater at the age of 25, inheriting the job from Phil Woolpert . . . Broke into the NBA as the league's youngest assistant coach at age 29 in Washington, staying with Bullets through a dozen years and bosses Dick Motta and Gene Shue . . . An excellent scout and good evaluator of talent . . . He once turned down an offer to play with the Harlem Globetrotters . . . A shining star on the rise.

GREATEST COACH

As a player, he wasn't the flashiest or most flamboyant, and as a coach he was never one of those guys who made like a flamenco dancer on the sidelines.

But in nearly eight full seasons on the job, Lenny Wilkens brought stability and a touch of class to a Seattle SuperSonics' organization that desperately needed direction.

Just look at the results. He took over the Sonics' job 23 games into the 1977-78 season and took a 5-17 ballclub all the way to the NBA finals, where the Sonics were beaten by the Washington Bullets. The following season, Wilkens guided the Sonics to a 52-30 mark, their only Pacific Division title in history, and all the way to the championship, where Seattle got revenge against the Bullets in a five-game series.

Only twice in Wilkens' eight seasons did the Sonics finish below third place in the Pacific.

For now, the choice is clearly Lenny Wilkens. But keep your eye on the new guy, Bernie Bickerstaff, who did such a great job in last year's playoffs.

ALL-TIME SUPERSONIC LEADERS

SEASON

Points: Spencer Haywood, 2,251, 1972-73
Assists: Lenny Wilkens, 766, 1971-72
Rebounds: Jack Sikma, 1,038, 1981-82

GAME

Points: Fred Brown, 58 vs. Golden State, 3/23/74
Assists: Nate McMillan, 25 vs. LA Clippers, 2/23/87
Rebounds: Jim Fox, 30 vs. Los Angeles, 12/26/73

CAREER

Points: Fred Brown, 14,018, 1971-84
Assists: Fred Brown, 3,160, 1971-84
Rebounds: Jack Sikma, 7,729, 1977-86

UTAH JAZZ

TEAM DIRECTORY: Owner: Larry H. Miller; Vice Chairman: Sam Battistone; Pres./GM: Dave Checketts; VP Basketball Oper./Coach: Frank Layden; Dir. Pub. Rel.: Bill Kreifeldt; Asst. Coaches: Jerry Sloan, Scott Layden. Arena: Salt Lake Palace (12,212). Colors; Purple, gold and green.

SCOUTING REPORT

SHOOTING: You've got to wonder if Commissioner David Stern would consider letting the Jazz take the court this season with seeing-eye dogs. Yes, they are that bad as a collection of shooters. Heck, when they hit the rim, they expect to be awarded one point. The only guy on the entire roster who hits more than half his shots from the field is Karl Malone (.512) and he only makes .598 from the foul line.

You figure it out. Utah is simply so tall that coach Frank Layden's troops have been able to overcome their myopic shooting by getting their own rebounds and putting the ball in. Rookie draft choice Jose Ortiz is said to have a nice touch on the medium-range shot and that would be a welcome addition here.

PLAYMAKING: The Jazz are blessed in this department with veteran Rickey Green and heir apparent John Stockton. Though reportedly on the trading block last summer, the lightning-quick Green remains the starter. Stockton, too, is one of the fastest players to lace up a pair of hightops in the NBA and is a huge plus coming off the bench. He's a good passer, can run the break and also take the ball to the hole.

DEFENSE: Mark Eaton. Call him the Great Wall of Utah. He just stands there in the middle and rejects anybody who dares try to take the ball into the paint. He can't jump an inch, but he clogs the middle better than anybody else in the game. Eaton reclaimed his blocked shot title from Manute Bol last season.

The defensive problems that the Jazz have are elsewhere in the lineup. Try looking in the direction of Darrell Griffith, who has yet to guard anybody during his NBA career, or at Kelly Tripucka, who probably thinks Griffith is a good defensive player. This is a club that has to develop more of an overall team concept to playing at the defensive end, rather than just funneling it all inside to Eaton. Still, opponents shot just .456 against the Jazz, the second-best figure in the NBA last season.

Utah foes often get Eaton alive inside the paint.

JAZZ ROSTER

No.	Veteran	Pos.	Ht.	Wt.	Age	Yrs. Pro	College
41	Thurl Bailey	F	6-11	222	26	4	North Carolina St.
54	Kent Benson	C	6-10	245	32	10	Indiana
30	Dell Curry	G	6-5	195	23	1	Virginia Tech
53	Mark Eaton	C	7-4	290	30	5	UCLA
14	Rickey Green	G	6-0	172	33	9	Michigan
35	Darrell Griffith	G	6-4	190	29	7	Louisville
20	Bob Hansen	G	6-6	195	26	4	Iowa
43	Marc Iavaroni	F	6-10	225	31	5	Virginia
32	Karl Malone	F	6-9	256	24	2	Louisiana Tech.
22	Carey Scurry	G-F	6-7	188	24	2	Long Island U.
12	John Stockton	G	6-1	175	25	3	Gonzaga
4	Kelly Tripucka	G-F	6-6	220	28	6	Notre Dame

Rd.	Top Rookies	Sel. No.	Pos.	Ht.	Wt.	College
1	Jose Ortiz	15	F	6-10	225	Oregon State
3	Clarence Martin	61	F	6-8	225	Western Kentucky
3	Billy Donovan	68	G	6-0	170	Providence
4	Reuben Holmes	84	F	6-11	205	Alabama State
5	Bart Kofoed	107	G	6-5	225	Kearney State

REBOUNDING: For a team with so many tall players, the Jazz are only mediocre at getting the ball off the boards. Malone works his tail off on the glass, but the rest of them play too passively underneath. Eaton gets everything that bounces in his direction, but does not have the mobility to chase other rebounds down.

They could use a better effort on the boards from Thurl Bailey, who likes to jack up 18-foot jumpers and play outside; from the leaping Griffith, and from the incredible shrinking man, 6-11 Kent Benson. They really need rebounding help, but drafted Ortiz, a slender 6-10 out of Oregon State. He'll get crushed on the inside in the NBA unless he adds 30 pounds.

OUTLOOK: Layden has lifted this team up from the dregs of the league and made them an average NBA ballclub that will contend annually for the Midwest Division title. It's time to take that next step up the ladder and challenge for the Western Conference finals. To do that, they'll have to rebound the ball better and play better all-around defense.

It was a stunning blow to their credibility to lose in the first round of playoffs to Golden State after taking a 2-0 lead in the best-of-five series. The rest of the Western Conference is improving, but it looks like the Jazz are stuck in a rut. Middle of the pack and an early playoff exit again is in store.

JAZZ PROFILES

RICKEY GREEN 33 6-0 172   Guard

Jesse Owens may have once outrun a horse, but this guy can keep pace with an Indy race car... Flat-out blazing speed... Is at his best zipping through traffic down the lane or finishing off a fastbreak... He can also pull up and bury his slingshot jumper from 18 to 20 feet... A cool floor general who reclaimed his starting job from John Stockton last season ... Born Aug. 18, 1954, in Chicago... Took the long route to NBA stardom... Was a can't-miss prospect when he took Michigan to the Final Four in 1976 and drafted No. 1 by Golden State in 1977... As usual, Warriors let a good man go... He traveled to Detroit, then Hawaii and Billings, Mont., of the CBA before finding a home in Utah... Was once a big scorer... Broke Bob McAdoo's scoring marks at Vincennes JC... Started 80 games.

Year	Team	G	FG	FG Pct.	FT	FT Pct.	Reb.	Ast.	TP	Avg.
1977-78	Golden State........	76	143	.381	54	.600	116	149	340	4.5
1978-79	Detroit.............	27	67	.379	45	.672	40	63	179	6.6
1980-81	Utah.............	47	176	.481	70	.722	116	235	422	9.0
1981-82	Utah.............	81	500	.493	202	.765	243	630	1202	14.8
1982-83	Utah.............	78	464	.493	185	.797	223	697	1115	14.3
1983-84	Utah.............	81	439	.486	192	.821	230	748	1072	13.2
1984-85	Utah.............	77	381	.477	232	.869	189	597	1000	13.0
1985-86	Utah.............	80	357	.471	213	.852	135	411	932	11.7
1986-87	Utah.............	81	301	.467	172	.827	163	541	781	9.6
	Totals.............	628	2828	.473	1365	.799	1455	4071	7043	11.2

KARL MALONE 24 6-9 256   Forward

The Mailman... He'll stamp your letter for you... He'll send it special delivery right down your throat... This guy never played like a rookie... He's rough and he's tough and in two years has established himself as one bad dude... Some claim he's dirty... You tell him... Does have a penchant for swinging his elbows... Born July 24, 1963, in Summerfield, La.... Didn't play senior year, but still finished as the third-leading scorer in Louisiana Tech history... A powerful inside player... The Incredible Hulk... Also has a decent medium-range jumper . . . Improved his free-throw percentage to .598 . . . Jazz got a steal when they took him in the No. 13 spot in the 1985 draft . . . The Mailman delivers every day.

Year	Team	G	FG	FG Pct.	FT	FT Pct.	Reb.	Ast.	TP	Avg.
1885-86	Utah	81	504	.496	195	.481	718	236	1203	14.9
1986-87	Utah	82	728	.512	323	.598	855	158	1779	21.7
	Totals	163	1232	.505	518	.548	1573	394	2982	18.3

BOB HANSEN 26 6-6 195   Guard

Coach's pet? . . . There are those who would say he's definitely the favorite of Frank Layden . . . But other coaches like his hardworking attitude, too . . . Dallas' Dick Motta voted him to his All-Defensive team . . . Not a big scorer, but he started at the off-guard position ahead of Darrell Griffith all year long . . . Born Jan. 18, 1961, in Des Moines, Iowa . . . Jazz picked him up at the No. 84 spot in the 1983 draft and he's been a fixture ever since . . . A bargain, he plays for under $100,000 . . . He's a terror in the Utah summer leagues, averaging 40 points a game. But in those games he's posting up the Osmond brothers . . . He's a plugger and he's a hustler and as long as Layden has the coaching post, he's probably got an NBA job.

Year	Team	G	FG	FG Pct.	FT	FT Pct.	Reb.	Ast.	TP	Avg.
1983-84	Utah	55	65	.448	18	.643	48	44	148	2.7
1984-85	Utah	54	110	.489	40	.556	70	75	261	4.8
1985-86	Utah	82	299	.476	95	.720	244	193	710	8.7
1986-87	Utah	72	272	.453	136	.760	203	102	696	9.7
	Totals	263	746	.467	289	.703	565	414	1815	6.9

DARRELL GRIFFITH 29 6-4 190   Guard

Lost his rhythm . . . Returned to the lineup after missing all of the 1985-86 season with a stress fracture in his foot . . . Also could not attract a big free-agent offer sheet . . . Came back to find that things had changed. Adrian Dantley was gone and the focus of the offense was more balanced . . . Scoring average dropped to a six-year NBA low and his shot was usually way off the mark . . . The former "Dr. Dunkenstein" at Louisville, where he led the Cardinals to the 1980 NCAA championship . . . Born June 1, 1958, in Louisville . . . After big prep career at well-known Male H.S., he stayed right at home to play under Danny Crum in college . . . The No. 2 pick in the 1980 draft—after Joe Barry Carroll and ahead of Kevin McHale . . . Still a phenomenal dunker . . . Gripes that he doesn't get enough credit by being in Utah . . . But then again, he hasn't played an ounce of defense since he got there.

Year	Team	G	FG	FG Pct.	FT	FT Pct.	Reb.	Ast.	TP	Avg.
1980-81	Utah.............	81	716	.464	229	.716	288	194	1671	20.6
1981-82	Utah.............	80	689	.482	189	.697	305	187	1582	19.8
1982-83	Utah.............	77	752	.484	167	.679	304	270	1709	22.2
1983-84	Utah.............	82	697	.490	151	.696	338	283	1636	20.0
1984-85	Utah.............	78	728	.457	216	.725	344	243	1764	22.6
1985-86	Utah.............					Injured				
1986-87	Utah.............	76	463	.446	149	.703	227	129	1142	15.0
	Totals.............	474	4045	.471	1101	.704	1806	1306	9504	20.1

THURL BAILEY 26 6-11 222   Forward

The forgotten man . . . You always think of Malone and Eaton and Griffith and Green on the Utah Jazz . . . But for four seasons, he's provided the big punch off the bench . . . Has excellent outside shooting range for a big man and is also willing to go inside and rebound . . . Also very valuable in being able to check opposing centers in a pinch . . . Born April 7, 1961, in Washington, D.C. . . . Taken No. 7 in the 1983 draft after winning NCAA title at North Carolina State . . . Ate Ralph Sampson's lunch in college . . . Very, very, very underrated . . . Worked as a congressional page one summer in college . . . Wants someday to be a radio-TV announcer.

Year	Team	G	FG	FG Pct.	FT	FT Pct.	Reb.	Ast.	TP	Avg.
1983-84	Utah.............	81	302	.512	88	.752	464	129	692	8.5
1984-85	Utah.............	80	507	.490	197	.842	525	138	1212	15.2
1985-86	Utah.............	82	483	.448	230	.830	493	153	1196	14.6
1986-87	Utah.............	81	463	.447	190	.805	432	102	1116	13.8
	Totals.............	324	1755	.470	705	.816	1914	522	4216	13.0

KELLY TRIPUCKA 28 6-6 220   Guard-Forward

What's a Jersey boy doing in Utah? . . . That's what he wants to know after a lost season . . . Was sent to the Jazz along with Kent Benson in the deal that put Adrian Dantley in Detroit . . . Ran into problems with Frank Layden right away when it was clear he would not be a big gun in the offense . . . After never averaging less than 20 points a game in his first five years, he barely reached double figures with the Jazz and is unhappy . . . He wants out . . . Born Feb. 16, 1959, in Bloomfield, N.J. . . . Father, Frank, was former Notre Dame quarterback of note . . . Will never win any unselfishness awards and doesn't play defense . . . The No. 12 pick in the 1981 draft by Detroit . . . Two-time all-state prep soccer player, also set school marks in high jump (6-6) and javelin (211) . . . Starred under Digger Phelps at Notre Dame . . . An Irish teammate of New Jersey's Orlando Woolridge.

Year	Team	G	FG	FG Pct.	FT	FT Pct.	Reb.	Ast.	TP	Avg.
1981-82	Detroit.............	82	636	.496	495	.797	443	270	1772	21.6
1982-83	Detroit.............	58	565	.489	392	.845	264	237	1536	26.5
1983-84	Detroit.............	76	595	.459	426	.815	306	228	1618	21.3
1984-85	Detroit.............	55	396	.477	255	.885	218	135	1049	19.1
1985-86	Detroit.............	81	615	.498	380	.856	348	265	1622	20.0
1986-87	Utah.............	79	291	.469	197	.872	242	243	798	10.1
	Totals.............	431	3098	.482	2145	.836	1821	1378	8395	19.5

MARK EATON 30 7-4 290   **Center**

Is he a center or one of the mountains that everybody skis on in Utah? . . . The Great White Wall . . . The Pale-Skinned Monster . . . Go ahead, crack the jokes. As Frank Layden says, you can't coach height . . . It's no coincidence that the Jazz' rise as a real NBA threat matches the time that Eaton arrived in the middle . . . Reclaimed his NBA shot-blocking title from Manute Bol last season . . . The most intimidating defender in the league . . . Born Jan. 24, 1957, in Inglewood, Cal., he never dreamed of playing there for the Lakers . . . After going to Cypress JC, he warmed the UCLA bench for two years . . . Was embarking on a career as the world's tallest auto mechanic before Layden came to his rescue, making him the 72nd pick in the 1982 draft . . . Can't jump an inch and can't shoot from two feet away . . . But is overpowering with a flat hook and flat-footed dunks . . . Now he's the world's best-paid auto mechanic at $645,000 for this season.

Year	Team	G	FG	FG Pct.	FT	FT Pct.	Reb.	Ast.	TP	Avg.
1982-83	Utah.............	81	146	.414	59	.656	462	112	351	4.3
1983-84	Utah.............	82	194	.466	73	.593	595	113	461	5.6
1984-85	Utah.............	82	302	.449	190	.712	927	124	794	9.7
1985-86	Utah.............	80	277	.470	122	.604	675	101	676	8.5
1986-87	Utah.............	79	234	.400	140	.657	697	105	608	7.7
	Totals.............	404	1153	.441	584	.653	3356	555	2890	7.2

JOHN STOCKTON 25 6-1 175   Guard

He who laughs last...Nobody's chuckling anymore, since this whippet has proven to be one of the steadiest point guards in the league ...A lot of people were going to have Frank Layden committed back in 1984 when he made him the No. 16 pick in the draft...The real hoop addicts knew. The kid had turned heads at the Olympic trials...Born March 26, 1962, in Spokane, Wash....He stayed local to attend college at Gonzaga...Took over Rickey Green's starting job two years ago, but was back in a reserve role last season...No matter, he still produced...Finished eighth in the league in assists... Might be·the only guy in the NBA who can stay step-for-step with the lightning-fast Green in a foot race...A fearless driver, he's becoming a decent outside shot..."He's Irish-Catholic, laughs at my jokes and his father owns a bar," says Layden... He can also play the game.

Year	Team	G	FG	FG Pct.	FT	FT Pct.	Reb.	Ast.	TP	Avg.
1984-85	Utah	82	157	.471	142	.736	105	415	458	5.6
1985-86	Utah	82	228	.489	172	.839	179	610	630	7.7
1986-87	Utah	82	231	.499	179	.782	151	670	648	7.9
	Totals	246	616	.488	493	.786	435	1695	1736	7.1

MARC IAVARONI 31 6-10 225   Forward

A banger...A hustler...Sound like Kurt Rambis?...He's the clone that Philadelphia pulled off the scrap heap the year after the Sixers were whipped by Rambis and the Lakers in the 1982 NBA finals...He came in as a rookie and started with Dr. J and Moses Malone on the frontline as Philly won it all in 1983...His talents quickly wore thin in Philly...Was shipped to San Antonio, where he spent a year and arrived in Utah in 1986 for Jeff Wilkins...Born Sept. 15, 1956, in Bethpage, N.Y....The answer to the trivia question: Who was the center at Virginia before Ralph Sampson?...The 55th pick in the 1978 draft by New York, the Knicks cut him twice... Played in Italy for three years.

Year	Team	G	FG	FG Pct.	FT	FT Pct.	Reb.	Ast.	TP	Avg.
1982-83	Philadelphia	80	163	.462	78	.690	329	83	404	5.1
1983-84	Philadelphia	78	149	.463	97	.740	310	95	395	5.1
1984-85	Phil.-S.A.	69	162	.458	87	.680	304	119	411	6.0
1985-86	S.A.-Utah	68	110	.451	76	.661	209	82	296	4.4
1986-87	Utah	78	100	.465	78	.672	173	36	278	3.6
	Totals	373	684	.460	416	.690	1325	415	1784	4.8

CAREY SCURRY 24 6-7 188   Guard-Forward

A greyhound of an athlete . . . You can do much worse than to have him in the 11th spot on your roster . . . In two seasons has produced in spots for the Jazz . . . Born Dec. 4, 1962, in Brooklyn, N.Y. . . . Spent a year at Northeast Oklahoma A&M, then returned home to Long Island University . . . An excellent leaper who tied Akeem Olajuwon for the NCAA rebounding title in his junior season . . . Attracted attention at the postseason all-star games and the Jazz made him the 37th player drafted in 1985 . . . Great raw athletic ability has kept him in Salt Lake City . . . If he can harness the talent, it could translate into a productive career . . . Received his degree in communications . . . Dr. J is his idol . . . Nickname is Dog.

Year	Team	G	FG	FG Pct.	FT	FT Pct.	Reb.	Ast.	TP	Avg.
1985-86	Utah	78	142	.472	78	.619	242	85	363	4.7
1986-87	Utah	69	123	.498	94	.701	198	57	344	5.0
	Totals	147	265	.484	172	.662	440	142	707	4.8

KENT BENSON 32 6-10 245   Center

A journeyman, at best . . . It's hard to believe that he was the man in the middle on Bobby Knight's awesome undefeated Indiana championship team of 1976 . . . Strictly a backup to Mark Eaton last season in Utah after Jazz got him along with Kelly Tripucka in the deal that sent Adrian Dantley to Detroit . . . Is wimpish for a guy so big . . . Would prefer to stand out on the wings and shoot the baseline jumper . . . Born Dec. 27, 1954, in New Castle, Ind. . . . He was the No. 1 pick in the draft of 1977 by Milwaukee . . . Was traded with a first-round pick to Detroit for Bob Lanier in February 1980 . . . Earned $345,000 last season and became a free agent . . . He'll stick around a few more years because he's tall.

Year	Team	G	FG	FG Pct.	FT	FT Pct.	Reb.	Ast.	TP	Avg.
1977-78	Milwaukee	69	220	.465	92	.652	295	99	532	7.7
1978-79	Milwaukee	82	413	.518	180	.735	584	204	1006	12.3
1979-80	Mil.-Det.	73	299	.484	99	.702	453	178	698	9.6
1980-81	Detroit	59	364	.473	196	.772	400	172	924	15.7
1981-82	Detroit	75	405	.505	127	.804	653	159	940	12.5
1982-83	Detroit	21	85	.467	38	.760	155	49	208	9.9
1983-84	Detroit	82	248	.550	83	.822	409	130	579	7.1
1984-85	Detroit	72	201	.506	76	.809	324	93	478	6.6
1985-86	Detroit	72	201	.484	66	.795	376	80	469	6.5
1986-87	Utah	73	140	.443	47	.810	231	39	329	4.5
	Totals	678	2576	.493	1004	.758	3880	1203	6163	9.1

DELL CURRY 23 6-5 195   Guard

A jittery rookie... Came into the league with the reputation as another Otis Birdsong with a soft, accurate jumper, but did not turn any heads... Darrell Griffith doesn't have to worry about this guy stealing his job for now ... Did hit 17 of 60 from three-point territory ... Born June 25, 1964, in Grottoes, Va.... The No. 2 all-time leading scorer in the Metro Conference, where he starred for Virginia Tech... Jazz made him the No. 15 pick in the first round of the 1986 draft... Is supposed to be a decent rebounder for a guard, but didn't show much of that either... Seems to have the physical tools... Maybe it was just rookie nerves... The Baltimore Orioles also drafted him to play baseball.

Year	Team	G	FG	FG Pct.	FT	FT Pct.	Reb.	Ast.	TP	Avg.
1986-87	Utah..............	67	139	.426	30	.789	78	58	325	4.9

TOP ROOKIE

JOSE ORTIZ 22 6-10 225   Forward

Pac-10 Player of the Year... Scored in double figures in all 30 games as a senior at Oregon State... Has a nice shooting touch ... Will need to bulk up and learn to bang more in the NBA... A native of Puerto Rico... Will have a tough time cracking Jazz' solid frontcourt rotation... The No. 15 pick on the first round.

COACH FRANK LAYDEN: Fat Frank... The Stand-up Comic

... Jokes 'R Us... All anybody ever wants to talk about are his one-liners... What is often overlooked is that this man is a solid basketball coach and has kept the Jazz franchise on a firm foundation... Make no mistake, he wasn't at all happy about blowing a 2-0 lead and losing their first-round playoff series to Golden State last spring... Nevertheless, the Jazz have finished at .500 or better for four straight seasons and that's saying something considering how bad off this franchise was at one time... Joked that he lost 230 pounds during the off-season—"Yeah, we traded [Adrian] Dantley"... Layden got rid of a headache, but didn't get much in return... Now Kelly Tripucka is unhappy with his role and wants out... Born Jan. 5, 1932, in Brooklyn, N.Y., he's a New Yorker all the way...

Roomed with Hubie Brown at Niagara and coached Calvin Murphy there years later . . . Joined Jazz in 1979 in New Orleans . . . NBA Coach of the Year in 1983-84.

GREATEST COACH

He's the Irish version of Henny Youngman, the poster boy for Omar the Tentmaker, the best customer at Two Guys From Italy Restaurant in Salt Lake City.

He's Frank Layden and it's been clear for the last several seasons that the jokester deserves to be taken seriously as a head coach.

When he was named to the post in December 1981, Jazz guard Rickey Green asked, seriously, "Has Frank ever coached before?" Of course, he did. Layden spent 10 years at Niagara, coached Calvin Murphy there, and has brought his ability to motivate and draw X's and O's to the Jazz.

After Scotty Robertson, Bill van Breda Kolff, Elgin Baylor and Tom Nissalke, Jazz fans barely knew the playoffs existed. But Layden has now taken the Jazz to postseason play four straight seasons.

He might be the funny man, but it's no joke that Frank Layden is the best coach and ambassador the Jazz have ever had.

ALL-TIME JAZZ LEADERS

SEASON

Points: Adrian Dantley, 2,457, 1981-82
Assists: Rickey Green, 748, 1983-84
Rebounds: Len Robinson, 1,288, 1977-78

GAME

Points: Pete Maravich, 68 vs. New York, 2/25/77
Assists: John Stockton, 22 vs. LA Lakers, 1/8/87
Rebounds: Len Robinson, 27 vs. Los Angeles, 11/11/77

CAREER

Points: Adrian Dantley, 13,545, 1979-86
Assists: Rickey Green, 3,859, 1980-87
Rebounds: Rich Kelley, 3,972, 1974-79, 1982-85

1987 NBA COLLEGE DRAFT

Sel. No.	Team	Name	College	Ht.
	FIRST ROUND			
1.	San Antonio	David Robinson	Navy	7-1
2.	Phoenix	Armon Gilliam	Nevada-Las Vegas	6-9
3.	New Jersey	Dennis Hopson	Ohio State	6-5
4.	LA Clippers	Reggie Williams	Georgetown	6-7
5.	Seattle (from New York)	Scott Pippen	Central Arkansas	6-7½
6.	Sacramento	Kenny Smith	North Carolina	6-3
7.	Cleveland	Kevin Johnson	California	6-1
8.	Chicago (from Denver via New York)	Olden Polynice	Virginia	6-11
9.	Seattle	Derrick McKey	Alabama	6-9
10.	Chicago	Horace Grant	Clemson	6-10
11.	Indiana	Reggie Miller	UCLA	6-6
12.	Washington	Tyrone Bogues	Wake Forest	5-3
13.	LA Clippers (from Houston)	Joe Wolf	North Carolina	6-10
14.	Golden State	Tellis Frank	Western Kentucky	6-10
15.	Utah	Jose Ortiz	Oregon State	6-10
16.	Philadelphia	Christian Welp	Washington	7-0
17.	Portland	Ronnie Murphy	Jacksonville	6-4
18.	New York (from Milwaukee via Seattle)	Mark Jackson	St. John's	6-3
19.	LA Clippers (from Detroit)	Ken Norman	Illinois	6-8
20.	Dallas	Jim Farmer	Alabama	6-4
21.	Atlanta	Dallas Comegys	DePaul	6-9
22.	Boston	Reggie Lewis	Northeastern	6-6
23.	San Antonio (from LA Lakers)	Greg Anderson	Houston	6-9
	SECOND ROUND			
24.	Detroit (from LA Clippers via Seattle)	Freddie Banks	Nevada-Las Vegas	6-2
25.	New York	Ron Moore	West Virginia State	6-10
26.	Dallas (from New Jersey)	Steve Alford	Indiana	6-2
27.	San Antonio	Nate Blackwell	Temple	6-4
28.	Chicago (from Sacramento via Detroit)	Ricky Winslow	Houston	6-8
29.	Portland (from Cleveland)	Lester Fonville	Jackson State	7-2
30.	Portland (from Phoenix)	Nikita Wilson	Louisiana State	6-7½
31.	Denver	Andre Moore	Chicago-Loyola	6-8
32.	Milwaukee (from Seattle)	Bob McCann	Morehead State	6-6½
33.	Chicago	Tony White	Tennessee	6-2
34.	Indiana	Brian Rowsom	UNC-Wilmington	6-9
35.	Houston	Doug Lee	Purdue	6-5
36.	Washington (from Golden State)	Duane Washington	Mid. Tennessee State	6-4
37.	Washington	Derrick Dowell	Southern California	6-6
38.	LA Clippers (from Utah via Detroit)	Norris Coleman	Kansas State	6-8
39.	Philadelphia	Vincent Askew	Memphis State	6-6
40.	Milwaukee (from Portland)	Winston Garland	SW Missouri State	6-2
41.	Cleveland (from Milwaukee)	Kannard Johnson	Western Kentucky	6-9
42.	Atlanta (from Detroit)	Terrence Bailey	Wagner	6-2
43.	Philadelphia (from Dallas via New Jersey)	Andrew Kennedy	Virginia	6-7
44.	Atlanta	Terry Coner	Alabama	6-3

Spurs made David Robinson (he's in the Navy now) No. 1.

UNLV's Armon Gilliam got Suns' call as No. 2.

Ohio State's Dennis Hopson, third pick, is a Net.

Sel. No.	Team	Name	College	Ht.
45.	Boston	Brad Lohaus	Iowa	7-0
46.	Phoenix (from LA Lakers via LA Clippers & Detroit)	Bruce Dalrymple	Georgia Tech	6-3

THIRD ROUND

Sel. No.	Team	Name	College	Ht.
47.	LA Clippers	Tim McCalister	Oklahoma	6-3
48.	New Jersey	Jamie Waller	Virginia Union	6-4
49.	New York	Jerome Batiste	McNeese State	6-8
50.	San Antonio	Phil Zevenbergen	Washington	6-10
51.	Sacramento	Sven Meyer	Oregon	6-10
52.	Cleveland	Donald Royal	Notre Dame	6-7
53.	Phoenix	Winston Crite	Texas A&M	6-6
54.	Denver	Tom Schafer	Iowa State	6-7
55.	Seattle	Tommy Amaker	Duke	6-0
56.	Chicago	John Fox	Millersville State	6-8
57.	Philadelphia (from Indiana)	Hansi Gnad	Alaska-Anchorage	6-10
58.	Golden State	Darryl Johnson	Michigan State	6-1
59.	Washington	Danny Pearson	Jacksonville	6-5
60.	Indiana (from Houston)	Sean Couch	Columbia	6-1
61.	Utah	Clarence Martin	Western Kentucky	6-8
62.	Philadelphia	Eric Riggins	Rutgers	6-9
63.	Portland	Kevin Gamble	Iowa	6-6
64.	Milwaukee	J.J. Weber	Wisconsin	6-7
65.	Detroit	Eric White	Pepperdine	6-0
66.	Dallas	Mike Richmond	Texas-El Paso	6-7
67.	Atlanta	Song Tao	Chinese National Team	6-10
68.	Utah (from Boston)	Billy Donovan	Providence	6-0
69.	LA Lakers	Willie Glass	St. John's	6-6

FOURTH ROUND

Sel. No.	Team	Name	College	Ht.
70.	Boston (from LA Clippers)	Tom Sheehey	Virginia	6-9
71.	New York	Mike Morgan	Drake	6-6
72.	New Jersey	Andrew Moten	Florida	6-0
73.	San Antonio	Todd May	Pikeville	6-9
74.	Sacramento	Joe Arlauckas	Niagara	6-9
75.	Cleveland	Chris Dudley	Yale	6-11
76.	Phoenix	Steve Beck	Arizona State	6-3
77.	Denver	David Boone	Marquette	6-6
78.	Seattle	Todd Linder	Tampa	6-7
79.	Chicago	Jack Haley	UCLA	6-10
80.	Cleveland (from Indiana)	Carven Holcomb	TCU	6-4
81.	Washington	Scott Thompson	San Diego	7-0
82.	Houston	Joe Niego	Lewis	6-6
83.	Golden State	Benny Bolton	North Carolina State	6-7
84.	Utah	Reuben Holmes	Alabama State	6-11
85.	Philadelphia	Brian Rahilly	Tulsa	6-11
86.	Portland	Norwood "Pee Wee" Barber	Florida State	6-1
87.	Milwaukee	Darryl Bedford	Austin Peay	6-8
88.	Detroit	David Popson	North Carolina	6-10
89.	Dallas	David Johnson	Oklahoma	6-6
90.	Atlanta	Theofanis Christodoulou	Greek National Team	6-8
91.	Boston	Darryl Kennedy	Oklahoma	6-5
92.	LA Lakers	Ralph Tally	Norfolk State	6-1

Wake Forest's Tyrone Bogues, No. 12, is 5-3 Bullet.

Sel. No.	Team	Name	College	Ht.
	FIFTH ROUND			
93.	LA Clippers	Chad Kessler	Georgia	6-8
94.	New Jersey	James Blackmon	Georgia	6-3
95.	New York	Glenn Clem	Vanderbilt	6-6
96.	San Antonio	Dennis Williams	Georgia	6-3
97.	Sacramento	Vernon Carr	Michigan State	6-6
98.	Cleveland	Carl Lott	TCU	6-4
99.	Phoenix	Brent Counts	Pacific	6-9
100.	Denver	Ronnie Grandison	New Orleans	6-7
101.	Seattle	Michael Tait	Clemson	6-2
102.	Chicago	Anthony Wilson	Louisiana State	6-4
103.	Indiana	Mike Milling	UNC-Charlotte	6-6
104.	Houston	Andre LaFleur	Northeastern	6-3
105.	Golden State	Terry Williams	Southern Methodist	6-9
106.	Washington	Patrick Fairs	Texas	6-5
107.	Utah	Bart Kofoed	Kearney State	6-5
108.	Philadelphia	Frank Ross	American	6-2
109.	Portland	David Moss	Tulsa	6-7
110.	Milwaukee	Brian Vaughns	Cal-Santa Barbara	6-7½
111.	Detroit	Gerry Wright	Iowa	6-8
112.	Dallas	Sam Hill	Iowa State	6-9
113.	Atlanta	Jose Antonio Montero	Barcelona	6-4½
114.	Boston	Dave Butler	California	6-3

North Carolina's Kenny Smith, No. 5, is a King.

Warriors chose Western Kentucky's Tellis Frank No. 14.

Sel. No.	Team	Name	College	Ht.
	SIXTH ROUND			
115.	LA Lakers	Kenny Travis	New Mexico State	6-3
116.	LA Clippers	Martin Nessley	Duke	7-2
117.	New York	Howard Triche	Syracuse	6-5
118.	New Jersey	Perry Bromwell	Penn	6-1
119.	San Antonio	Ricky Brown	South Alabama	6-8
120.	Sacramento	Darryl Thomas	Indiana	6-7
121.	Cleveland	Harold Jensen	Villanova	6-5
122.	Phoenix	Marcel Boyce	Akron	6-6
123.	Denver	Kelvin Scarborough	New Mexico	6-1
124.	Seattle	Tom Gneiting	Brigham Young	6-10
125.	Chicago	Doug Altenberger	Illinois	6-4
126.	Indiana	Gery Graham	Nevada-Las Vegas	6-4
127.	Golden State	Charunas Marchulenis	Soviet Union	6-3
128.	Washington	Dwayne Scholten	Washington State	6-7
129.	Houston	Fred Jenkins	Tennessee	6-4
130.	Utah	Art Sabb	Bloomfield	6-4
131.	Philadelphia	Tracy Foster	Alabama-Birmingham	6-4
132.	Portland	Bernard Johnson	Loyola-Chicago	6-3
133.	Milwaukee	Gay Elmore	VMI	6-5
134.	Detroit	Antoine Joubert	Michigan	6-5
135.	Dallas	Quintan Gates	Texas-El Paso	6-7
136.	Atlanta	Riccardo Morandoti	Turino (Italy)	6-6
137.	Boston	Tim Naegeli	Wisconsin-Stevens Point	6-7
138.	LA Lakers	Frank Ford	Auburn	6-4

Jazz trumpeted Oregon State's Jose Ortiz as No. 15.

Knicks' first pick was St. John's Mark Jackson.

Clippers took Georgetown's Reggie Williams as No. 4.

Sel. No.	Team	Name	College	Ht.
	SEVENTH ROUND			
139.	LA Clippers	Henry Carr	Wichita State	6-9
140.	New Jersey	Frank Booker	Bowling Green	6-2
141.	New York	Wayne Williams	St. Joseph's	6-3
142.	San Antonio	Raynard Davis	Texas	6-9
143.	Sacramento	Scott Adubato	Upsala	6-2
144.	Cleveland	Michael Foster	South Carolina	6-2
145.	Phoenix	Ron Singleton	Grand Canyon	6-0
146.	Denver	Rowan Gomes	Hampton Institute	6-10
147.	Seattle	Mike Giomi	North Carolina State	6-8
148.	Chicago	Earvin Leavy	Central Michigan	6-3
149.	Indiana	Montel Hatcher	UCLA	6-1
150.	Washington	Jamie Dixon	TCU	6-4
151.	Houston	Clarence Grier	Campbell	6-7
152.	Golden State	Ronnie Leggette	West Virginia State	6-0
153.	Utah	Keith Webster	Harvard	5-11
154.	Philadelphia	Eric Semisch	West Virginia	6-8
155.	Portland	Kenny Stone	George Fox	6-7
156.	Denver (from Milwaukee)	Curtis Hunter	North Carolina	6-4
157.	Detroit	Mark Gottfried	Alabama	6-2
158.	Dallas	Gerald White	Auburn	6-1
159.	Atlanta	Franjo Arapovic	Yugoslavia	7-1
160.	Boston	Jerry Corcoran	Northeastern	6-2

1986-87
NATIONAL BASKETBALL ASSOCIATION

FINAL STANDINGS

EASTERN CONFERENCE

Atlantic Division	Won	Lost	Pct.
Boston	59	23	.720
Philadelphia	45	37	.549
Washington	42	40	.512
New Jersey	24	58	.293
New York	24	58	.293

Central Division	Won	Lost	Pct.
Atlanta	57	25	.695
Detroit	52	30	.634
Milwaukee	50	32	.610
Indiana	41	41	.500
Chicago	40	42	.488
Cleveland	31	51	.378

WESTERN CONFERENCE

Midwest Division	Won	Lost	Pct.
Dallas	55	27	.671
Utah	44	38	.537
Houston	42	40	.512
Denver	37	45	.451
Sacramento	29	53	.354
San Antonio	28	54	.341

Pacific Division	Won	Lost	Pct.
LA Lakers	65	17	.793
Portland	49	33	.598
Golden State	42	40	.512
Seattle	39	43	.476
Phoenix	36	46	.439
LA Clippers	12	70	.146

CHAMPION: LA Lakers

PLAYOFFS

EASTERN CONFERENCE

First Round
Boston defeated Chicago (3-0)
Milwaukee defeated Philadelphia (3-2)
Detroit defeated Washington (3-0)
Atlanta defeated Indiana (3-1)
Semifinals
Boston defeated Milwaukee (4-3)
Detroit defeated Atlanta (4-1)
Final
Boston defeated Detroit (4-3)

WESTERN CONFERENCE

First Round
LA Lakers defeated Denver (3-0)
Golden State defeated Utah (3-2)
Houston defeated Portland (3-1)
Seattle defeated Dallas (3-1)
Semifinals
LA Lakers defeated Golden State (4-1)
Seattle defeated Houston (4-2)
Final
LA Lakers defeated Seattle (4-0)

CHAMPIONSHIP
LA Lakers defeated Boston (4-2)

1986-87 INDIVIDUAL HIGHS

Most Minutes Played, Season: 3281, Jordan, Chicago
Most Minutes Played, Game: 64, Floyd, Golden State, vs. New Jersey, 2/1 (4 OT)
Most Points, Game: 61, Jordan, Chicago, vs. Detroit, 3/4 (OT);
Jordan, Chicago, vs. Atlanta 4/16
Most Field Goals, Made, Game: 22, Jordan, Chicago, vs. Detroit, 3/4 (OT);
Jordan, Chicago, vs. Philadelphia, 3/24;
Bird, Boston, vs. New York, 4/12;
Jordan, Chicago, vs. Atlanta, 4/16
Most Field Goal Attempts, Game: 43, Jordan, Chicago, vs. LA Lakers, 11/28;
Jordan, Chicago, vs. Houston, 1/15
Most 3-Point Field Goals Made, Game: 6, Person, Indiana, vs. Phoenix, 2/11
Most 3-Point Field Goal Attempts, Game: 10, Wood, New Jersey, vs. Portland, 1/9
(OT);
Aguirre, Dallas, vs. San Antonio, 2/20
Most Free Throws Made, Game: 26, Jordan, Chicago, vs. New Jersey, 2/26
Most Free Throw Attempts, Game: 27, Jordan, Chicago, vs. New Jersey, 2/26
Most Rebounds, Game: 27, Williams, New Jersey, vs. Golden State, 2/1 (4OT)
Most Offensive Rebounds, Game: 16, Barkley, Philadelphia, vs. New York, 3/4;
Barkley, Philadelphia, vs. Denver, 3/20
Most Defensive Rebounds, Game: 22, Williams, New Jersey, vs. Golden State, 2/1 (4
OT)
Most Offensive Rebounds, Season: 390, Barkley, Philadelphia
Most Defensive Rebounds, Season: 775, Oakley, Chicago
Most Assists, Game: 25, McMillan, Seattle, vs. LA Clippers, 2/23
Most Blocked Shots, Game: 15, Bol, Washington, vs. Indiana, 2/26
Most Steals, Game: 10, Robertson, San Antonio, vs. LA Clippers, 11/22
Harper, Cleveland, vs. Philadelphia, 3/10
Most Personal Fouls, Season: 340, Johnson, Portland
Most Games Disqualified, Season: 16, Johnson, Portland

INDIVIDUAL SCORING LEADERS
Minimum 70 games or 1,400 ponts

	G	FG	FT	Pts.	Avg.
Jordan, Chicago	82	1098	833	3041	37.1
Wilkins, Atlanta	79	828	607	2294	29.0
English, Denver	82	965	411	2345	28.6
Bird, Boston	74	786	414	2076	28.1
Vandeweghe, Portland	79	808	467	2122	26.9
McHale, Boston	77	790	428	2088	26.1
Aguirre, Dallas	80	787	429	2056	25.7
Ellis, Seattle	82	785	385	2041	24.9
M. Malone, Washington	73	595	570	1760	24.1
Johnson, LA Lakers	80	683	535	1909	23.9
Davis, Phoenix	79	779	288	1867	23.6
Olajuwon, Houston	75	677	400	1755	23.4
Chambers, Seattle	82	660	535	1909	23.3
McDaniel, Seattle	82	806	275	1890	23.0
Barkley, Philadelphia	68	557	429	1564	23.0
Harper, Cleveland	82	734	386	1874	22.9
Nance, Phoenix	69	585	381	1552	22.5
J. Malone, Washington	80	689	376	1758	22.0
Drexler, Portland	82	707	357	1782	21.7
Malone, Utah	82	728	323	1779	21.7

REBOUND LEADERS
Minimum 70 games or 800 rebounds

	G	Off.	Def.	Tot.	Avg.
Barkley, Philadelphia	68	390	604	994	14.6
Oakley, Chicago	82	299	775	1074	13.1
B. Williams, New Jersey	82	322	701	1023	12.5
Donaldson, Dallas	82	295	678	973	11.9
Laimbeer, Detroit	82	243	712	955	11.6
Cage, LA Clippers	80	354	568	922	11.5
L. Smith, Golden State	80	366	551	917	11.5
Olajuwon, Houston	75	315	543	858	11.4
M. Malone, Washington	73	340	484	824	11.3
Parish, Boston	80	254	597	851	10.6

FIELD-GOAL LEADERS
Minimum 300 FG Made

	FG	FGA	Pct.
McHale, Bos.	790	1307	.604
Gilmore, S.A.	346	580	.597
Barkley, Phil.	557	937	.594
Donaldson, Dall.	311	531	.586
Abdul-Jabbar, LAL	560	993	.564
B. Williams, N.J.	521	936	.557
Parish, Bos.	588	1057	.556
Johnson, Port.	494	889	.556
McCray, Hou.	432	783	.552
Nance, Phoe.	585	1062	.551

3-POINT FIELD-GOAL LEADERS
Minimum 25 Made

	FG	FGA	Pct.
Vandeweghe, Port.	39	81	.481
Schrempf, Dall.	33	69	.478
Ainge, Bos.	85	192	.443
Scott, LAL	65	149	.436
Tucker, N.Y.	68	161	.422
McKenna, N.J.	52	124	.419
Bird, Bos.	90	225	.400
Cooper, LAL	89	231	.385
Floyd, G.S.	73	190	.384
McGee, Atl.	86	229	.376

STEALS LEADERS
Minimum 70 games or 125 steals

	G	St.	Avg.
Robertson, S.A.	81	260	3.21
Jordan, Chi.	82	236	2.88
Cheeks, Phil.	68	180	2.65
Harper, Clev.	82	209	2.55
Drexler, Port.	82	204	2.49
Lever, Den.	82	201	2.45
Harper, Dall.	77	167	2.17
Stockton, Utah	82	177	2.16
Rivers, Atl.	82	171	2.09
Porter, Port.	80	159	1.99

BLOCKED-SHOTS LEADERS
Minimum 70 games or 100 blocked shots

	G	Blk.	Avg.
Eaton, Utah	79	321	4.06
Bol, Wash.	82	302	3.68
Olajuwon, Hou.	75	254	3.39
Benjamin, LAC	72	187	2.60
Lister, Sea.	75	180	2.40
Ewing, N.Y.	63	147	2.33
McHale, Bos.	77	172	2.23
Nance, Phoe.	69	148	2.14
Hinson, Phil.	76	161	2.12
C. Jones, Wash.	79	165	2.09

FREE-THROW LEADERS
Minimum 125 FT Made

	Ft	FTA	Pct.
Bird, Bos.	414	455	.910
Ainge, Bos.	148	165	.897
Laimbeer, Det.	245	274	.894
Scott, LA Lakers	224	251	.892
Hodges, Mil.	131	147	.891
Long, Ind.	219	246	.890
Vandeweghe, Port.	467	527	.886
J. Malone, Wash.	376	425	.885
Blackman, Dall.	419	474	.884
Pierce, Mil.	387	440	.880

ASSISTS LEADERS
70 Games or 400 Assists

	G	A	Avg.
Johnson, LA Lakers	80	977	12.2
Floyd, Golden State	82	848	10.3
Thomas, Det.	81	813	10.0
Rivers, Atl.	82	823	10.0
Porter, Port.	80	715	8.9
Theus, Sac.	79	692	8.8
McMillan, Sea.	71	583	8.2
Stockton, Utah	82	670	8.2
Lever, Den.	82	654	8.0
Cheeks, Phil.	68	538	7.9

ALL-TIME NBA RECORDS

INDIVIDUAL
Single Game
Most Points: 100, Wilt Chamberlain, Philadelphia vs New York, at Hershey, Pa., Mar. 2, 1962

Most FG Attempted: 63, Wilt Chamberlain, Philadelphia vs New York, at Hershey, Pa., Mar. 2, 1962

Most FG Made: 36, Wilt Chamberlain, Philadelphia vs New York, at Hershey, Pa., Mar. 2, 1962

Most Consecutive FG Made: 18, Wilt Chamberlain, San Francisco vs New York, at Boston, Nov. 27, 1963; Wilt Chamberlain, Philadelphia vs Baltimore, at Pittsburgh, Feb. 24, 1967

Most FT Attempted: 34, Wilt Chamberlain, Philadelphia vs St. Louis, at Philadelphia, Feb. 22, 1962

Most FT Made: 28, Wilt Chamberlain, Philadelphia vs New York, at Hershey, Pa., Mar. 2, 1962; Adrian Dantley, Utah vs Houston at Las Vegas, Nev., Jan. 4, 1984

Most Consecutive FT Made: 19, Bob Pettit, St. Louis vs Boston, at Boston, Nov. 22, 1961; Bill Cartwright, New York vs Kansas City, at N.Y., Nov. 17, 1981

Most FT Missed: 22, Wilt Chamberlain, Philadelphia vs Seattle, at Boston, Dec. 1, 1967

Most Assists: 29, Kevin Porter, New Jersey vs Houston at N.J., Feb. 24, 1978

Most Personal Fouls: 8, Don Otten, Tri-Cities at Sheboygan, Nov. 24, 1949

Season
Most Points: 4,029, Wilt Chamberlain, Philadelphia, 1961-62

Highest Average: 50.4, Wilt Chamberlain, Philadelphia, 1961-62

Most FG Attempted: 3,159, Wilt Chamberlain, Philadelphia, 1961-62

Most FG Made: 1,597, Wilt Chamberlain, Philadelphia, 1961-62

Highest FG Percentage: .727, Wilt Chamberlain, Los Angeles, 1972-73

Most 3-Pt. FG Attempted: 257, Darrell Griffith, Utah, 1984-85

Most 3-Pt. FG Made: 92, Darrell Griffith, Utah, 1984-85

Highest 3-Pt. FG Percentage: .481, Ernie Vandeweghe, Portland, 1986-87

Most FT Attempted: 1,363, Wilt Chamberlain, Philadelphia, 1961-62

Most FT Made: 840, Jerry West, Los Angeles, 1965-66

Kareem Abdul-Jabbar will add to records in 19th season.

Highest FT Percentage: .958, Calvin Murphy, Houston, 1980-81
Most Rebounds: 2,149, Wilt Chamberlain, Philadelphia, 1960-61
Most Assists: 1,123, Isiah Thomas, Detroit, 1984-85
Most Personal Fouls: 386, Darryl Dawkins, New Jersey, 1983-84
Most Disqualifications: 26, Don Meineke, Fort Wayne, 1952-53

Career
Most Points Scored: 36,474, Kareem Abdul-Jabbar, Milwaukee and Los Angeles Lakers, 1970-87
Highest Scoring Average: 30.1, Wilt Chamberlain, Philadelphia/ San Francisco Warriors, Philadelphia 76ers and Los Angeles Lakers, 1960-73
Most FG Attempted: 26,745, Kareem Abdul-Jabbar, Milwaukee and Los Angeles Lakers, 1970-87
Most FG Made: 15,044, Kareem Abdul-Jabbar, 1970-87
Highest FG Percentage: .582, Artis Gilmore, Chicago and San Antonio, 1976-87
Most FT Attempted: 11,862, Wilt Chamberlain, 1960-73
Most FT Made: 7,694, Oscar Robertson, Cincinnati and Milwaukee, 1961-74
Highest FT Percentage: .900, Rick Barry, San Francisco/Golden State Warriors, Houston, 1965-67, 1972-80
Most Rebounds: 23,924, Wilt Chamberlain, 1960-73
Most Assists: 9,887, Oscar Robertson, 1961-74
Most Minutes: 53,443, Kareem Abdul-Jabbar, Milwaukee and Los Angeles Lakers, 1970-87
Most Games: 1,406, Kareem Abdul-Jabbar, Milwaukee and Los Angeles Lakers, 1970-87
Most Personal Fouls: 4,193, Elvin Hayes, 1969-84
Most Times Disqualified: 127, Vern Mikkelsen, Minneapolis, 1950-59

TEAM RECORDS
Single Game
Most Points, One Team: 173, Boston, vs Minneapolis at Boston, Feb. 27, 1959; 186, Detroit, vs Denver at Denver, Dec. 13, 1983 (3 overtimes)
Most Points, Two Teams: 318, Denver 163 vs San Antonio 155 at Denver, Jan. 11, 1984; 370, Detroit 186 vs Denver 184 at Denver, Dec. 13, 1983 (3 overtimes)
Most FG Attempted, One Team: 153, Philadelphia, vs Los Angeles at Philadelphia (3 overtimes), Dec. 8, 1961
Most FG Attempted, Two Teams: 291, Philadelphia 153 vs Los Angeles 138 at Philadelphia (3 overtimes), Dec. 8, 1961

Most FG Made, One Team: 72, Boston, vs Minneapolis at Boston, Feb. 27, 1959; 74, Denver, vs Detroit at Denver, Dec. 13, 1983 (3 overtimes)

Most FG Made, Two Teams: 142, Detroit 74 vs Denver 68 at Denver, Dec. 13, 1983 (3 overtimes)

Most FT Attempted, One Team: 86, Syracuse, vs Anderson at Syracuse (5 overtimes), Nov. 24, 1949

Most FT Attempted, Two Teams: 160, Syracuse 86 vs Anderson 74 at Syracuse (5 overtimes), Nov. 24, 1949

Most FT Made, One Team: 59, Syracuse, vs Anderson at Syracuse (5 overtimes), Nov. 24, 1949

Most FT Made, Two Teams: 116, Syracuse 59 vs Anderson 57 at Syracuse (5 overtimes), Nov. 24, 1949

Most Rebounds, One Team: 109, Boston, vs Detroit at Boston, Dec. 24, 1960

Most Rebounds, Two Teams: 188, Philadelphia 98 vs Los Angeles 90 at Philadelphia, Dec. 8, 1961 (3 overtimes)

Most Assists, One Team: 53, Milwaukee, vs Detroit at Detroit, Dec. 26, 1978

Most Assists, Two Teams: 88, Phoenix 47 vs San Diego 41 at Tucson, Ariz., Mar. 15, 1969

Most Assists, Two Teams, OT: 89, Detroit 48 vs Cleveland 41 at Cleveland, Mar. 28, 1973

Most Personal Fouls, One Team: 66, Anderson, at Syracuse (5 overtimes), Nov. 24, 1949

Most Personal Fouls, Two Teams: 122, Anderson 66 vs Syracuse 56 at Syracuse (5 overtimes), Nov. 24, 1949

Most Disqualifications, One Team: 8, Syracuse, vs Baltimore at Syracuse (1 overtime), Nov. 15, 1952

Most Disqualifications, Two Teams: 13, Syracuse 8 vs Baltimore 5 at Syracuse (1 overtime), Nov. 15 1952

Most Points in a Losing Game: 184, Denver, vs Detroit at Denver Dec. 13, 1983 (3 overtimes)

Widest Point Spread: 63, Los Angeles 162 vs Golden State 99 at Los Angeles, Mar. 19, 1972

Most Consecutive Points in a Game: 24, Philadelphia, vs Baltimore at Baltimore, Mar. 20, 1966

Season

Most Games Won: 69, Los Angeles, 1971-72

Most Games Lost: 73, Philadelphia, 1972-73

Longest Winning Streak: 33, Los Angeles, Nov. 5, 1971 to Jan. 7, 1972

Longest Losing Streak: 20, Philadelphia, Jan. 9, 1973 to Feb. 11, 1973

Most Points Scored: 10,731, Denver, 1981-82
Most Points Allowed 10,328, Denver, 1981-82
Highest Scoring Average: 126.5, Denver, 1981-82
Highest Average, Points Allowed: 126.0, Denver, 1981-82
Most FG Attempted: 9,295, Boston, 1960-61
Most FG Made: 3,980, Denver, 1981-82
Highest FG Percentage: .545, Los Angeles, 1984-85
Most FT Attempted: 3,411, Philadelphia, 1966-67
Most FT Made: 2,434, Phoenix, 1969-70
Highest FT Percentage: .821, KC-Omaha, 1974-75
Most Rebounds: 6,131, Boston, 1960-61
Most Assists: 2,575, L.A. Lakers, 1984-85

MOST VALUABLE PLAYER

1955-56 Bob Pettit, St. Louis	1971-72 Kareem Abdul-Jabbar, Milwaukee
1956-57 Bob Cousy, Boston	1972-73 Dave Cowens, Boston
1957-58 Bill Russell, Boston	1973-74 Kareem Abdul-Jabbar, Milwaukee
1958-59 Bob Pettit, St. Louis	1974-75 Bob McAdoo, Buffalo
1970-71 Wilt Chamberlain, Philadelphia	1975-76 Kareem Abdul-Jabbar, L.A.
1960-61 Bill Russell, Boston	1976-77 Kareem Abdul-Jabbar, L.A.
1961-62 Bill Russell, Boston	1977-78 Bill Walton, Portland
1962-63 Bill Russell, Boston	1978-79 Moses Malone, Houston
1963-64 Oscar Robertson, Cincinnati	1979-80 Kareem Abdul-Jabbar, L.A.
1964-65 Bill Russell, Boston	1980-81 Julius Erving, Philadelphia
1965-66 Wilt Chamberlain, Philadelphia	1981-82 Moses Malone, Houston
1966-67 Wilt Chamberlain, Philadelphia	1982-83 Moses Malone, Philadelphia
1967-68 Wilt Chamberlain, Philadelphia	1983-84 Larry Bird, Boston
1968-69 Wes Unseld, Baltimore	1984-85 Larry Bird, Boston
1969-70 Willis Reed, New York	1985-86 Larry Bird, Boston
1970-71 Lew Alcindor, Milwaukee	1986-87 Magic Johnson, L.A. Lakers

ROOKIE OF THE YEAR

1952-53	Don Meineke, Fort Wayne
1953-54	Ray Felix, Baltimore
1954-55	Bob Pettit, Milwaukee
1955-56	Maurice Stokes, Rochester
1956-57	Tom Heinsohn, Boston
1957-58	Woody Sauldsberry, Philadelphia
1958-59	Elgin Baylor, Minneapolis
1959-60	Wilt Chamberlain, Philadelphia
1960-61	Oscar Robertson, Cincinnati
1961-62	Walt Bellamy, Chicago
1962-63	Terry Dischinger, Chicago
1963-64	Jerry Lucas, Cincinnati
1964-65	Willis Reed, New York
1965-66	Rick Barry, San Francisco
1966-67	Dave Bing, Detroit
1967-68	Earl Monroe, Baltimore
1968-69	Wes Unseld, Baltimore
1969-70	Lew Alcindor, Milwaukee
1970-71	Dave Cowens, Boston
	Geoff Petrie, Portland
1971-72	Sidney Wicks, Portland
1972-73	Bob McAdoo, Buffalo
1973-74	Ernie DiGregorio, Buffalo
1974-75	Keith Wilkes, Golden State
1975-76	Alvan Adams, Phoenix
1976-77	Adrian Dantley, Buffalo
1977-78	Walter Davis, Phoenix
1978-79	Phil Ford, Kansas City
1979-80	Larry Bird, Boston
1980-81	Darrell Griffith, Utah
1981-82	Buck Williams, New Jersey
1982-83	Terry Cummings, San Diego
1983-84	Ralph Sampson, Houston
1984-85	Michael Jordan, Chicago
1985-86	Patrick Ewing, New York
1986-87	Chuck Person, Indiana

COACH OF THE YEAR

1962-63	Harry Gallatin, St. Louis
1963-64	Alex Hannum, San Francisco
1964-65	Red Auerbach, Boston
1965-66	Dolph Schayes, Philadelphia
1966-67	Johnny Kerr, Chicago
1967-68	Richie Guerin, St. Louis
1968-69	Gene Shue, Baltimore
1969-70	Red Holzman, New York
1970-71	Dick Motta, Chicago
1971-72	Bill Sharman, Los Angeles
1972-73	Tom Heinsohn, Boston
1973-74	Ray Scott, Detroit
1974-75	Phil Johnson, Kansas City-Omaha
1975-76	Bill Fitch, Cleveland
1976-77	Tom Nissalke, Houston
1977-78	Hubie Brown, Atlanta
1978-79	Cotton Fitzsimmons, Kansas City
1979-80	Bill Fitch, Boston
1980-81	Jack McKinney, Indiana
1981-82	Gene Shue, Washington
1982-83	Don Nelson, Milwaukee
1983-84	Frank Layden, Utah
1984-85	Don Nelson, Milwaukee
1985-86	Mike Fratello, Atlanta
1986-87	Mike Schuler, Portland

NBA CHAMPIONS

Season	Champion	Eastern Division			Western Division		
		W.	L.		W.	L.	
1946-47	Philadelphia	49	11	Washington	39	22	Chicago
1947-48	Baltimore	27	21	Philadelphia	29	19	St. Louis
1948-49	Minneapolis	38	22	Washington	45	15	Rochester
1949-50	Minneapolis	51	13	Syracuse	39	25	Indianap.*
1950-51	Rochester	40	26	Philadelphia	44	24	Minneapolis
1951-52	Minneapolis	40	26	Syracuse	41	25	Rochester
1952-53	Minneapolis	47	23	New York	48	22	Minneapolis
1953-54	Minneapolis	44	28	New York	46	26	Minneapolis
1954-55	Syracuse	43	29	Syracuse	43	29	Ft. Wayne
1955-56	Philadelphia	45	27	Philadelphia	37	35	Ft. Wayne
1956-57	Boston	44	28	Boston	34	38	StL-Mpl-FtW
1957-58	St. Louis	49	23	Boston	41	31	St. Louis
1958-59	Boston	52	20	Boston	49	23	St. Louis
1959-60	Boston	59	16	Boston	46	29	St. Louis
1960-61	Boston	57	22	Boston	51	28	St. Louis
1961-62	Boston	60	20	Boston	54	26	Los Angeles
1962-63	Boston	58	22	Boston	53	27	Los Angeles
1963-64	Boston	59	21	Boston	48	32	San Fran.
1964-65	Boston	62	18	Boston	49	31	Los Angeles
1965-66	Boston	54	26	Boston	45	35	Los Angeles
1966-67	Philadelphia	68	13	Philadelphia	44	37	San Fran.
1967-68	Boston	54	28	Boston	52	30	Los Angeles
1968-69	Boston	48	34	Boston	55	27	Los Angeles
1969-70	New York	60	22	New York	46	36	Los Angeles
1970-71	Milwaukee	42	40	Baltimore	66	16	Milwaukee
1971-72	Los Angeles	48	34	New York	69	13	Los Angeles
1972-73	New York	57	25	New York	60	22	Los Angeles
1973-74	Boston	56	26	Boston	59	23	Milwaukee
1974-75	Golden State	60	22	Washington	48	34	Golden State
1975-76	Boston	54	28	Boston	42	40	Phoenix
1976-77	Portland	50	32	Philadelphia	49	33	Portland
1977-78	Washington	44	38	Washington	47	35	Seattle
1978-79	Seattle	54	28	Washington	52	30	Seattle
1979-80	Los Angeles	59	23	Philadelphia	60	22	Los Angeles
1980-81	Boston	62	20	Boston	40	42	Houston
1981-82	Los Angeles	58	24	Philadelphia	57	25	Los Angeles
1982-83	Philadelphia	65	17	Philadelphia	58	24	Los Angeles
1983-84	Boston	62	20	Boston	54	28	Los Angeles
1984-85	L.A. Lakers	63	19	Boston	62	20	L.A. Lakers
1985-86	Boston	67	15	Boston	51	31	Houston
1986-87	L.A. Lakers	59	23	Boston	65	17	L.A. Lakers

*1949-50 Central Division Champion: Minneapolis and Rochester tied 51-17.

NBA SCORING CHAMPIONS

Season	Pts./Avg.	Top Scorer	Team
1946-47	1389	Joe Fulks	Philadelphia
1947-48	1007	Max Zaslofsky	Chicago
1948-49	1698	George Mikan	Minneapolis
1949-50	1865	George Mikan	Minneapolis
1950-51	1932	George Mikan	Minneapolis
1951-52	1674	Paul Arizin	Philadelphia
1952-53	1564	Neil Johnston	Philadelphia
1953-54	1759	Neil Johnston	Philadelphia
1954-55	1631	Neil Johnston	Philadelphia
1955-56	1849	Bob Pettit	St. Louis
1956-57	1817	Paul Arizin	Philadelphia
1957-58	2001	George Yardley	Detroit
1958-59	2105	Bob Pettit	St. Louis
1959-60	2707	Wilt Chamberlain	Philadelphia
1960-61	3033	Wilt Chamberlain	Philadelphia
1961-62	4029	Wilt Chamberlain	Philadelphia
1962-63	3586	Wilt Chamberlain	San Francisco
1963-64	2948	Wilt Chamberlain	San Francisco
1964-65	2534	Wilt Chamberlain	San Fran.-Phila.
1965-66	2649	Wilt Chamberlain	Philadelphia
1966-67	2775	Rick Barry	San Francisco
1967-68	2142	Dave Bing	Detroit
1968-69	2327	Elvin Hayes	San Diego
1969-70	*31.2	Jerry West	Los Angeles
1970-71	*31.7	Lew Alcindor	Milwaukee
1971-72	*34.8	K. Abdul-Jabbar	Milwaukee
1972-73	*34.0	Nate Archibald	K.C.-Omaha
1973-74	*30.6	Bob McAdoo	Buffalo
1974-75	*34.5	Bob McAdoo	Buffalo
1975-76	*31.1	Bob McAdoo	Buffalo
1976-77	*31.1	Pete Maravich	New Orleans
1977-78	*27.2	George Gervin	San Antonio
1978-79	*29.6	George Gervin	San Antonio
1979-80	*33.1	George Gervin	San Antonio
1980-81	*30.7	Adrian Dantley	Utah
1981-82	*32.3	George Gervin	San Antonio
1982-83	*28.4	Alex English	Denver
1983-84	*30.6	Adrian Dantley	Utah
1984-85	*32.9	Bernard King	New York
1985-86	*30.3	Dominique Wilkins	Atlanta
1986-87	*37.1	Michael Jordan	Chicago

*Scoring title based on best average with at least 70 games played

Official 1987-88 NBA Schedule

*Afternoon Game

Fri Nov 6
Mil at Bos
Cle at NJ
Ind at Phil
Wash at Atl
NY at Det
Utah at Dal
SA at Hou
LAC at Den
Sea at LAL
GS at Sac
Phoe at Port

Sat Nov 7
Bos at Wash
Cle at Atl
NY at Ind
Phil at Chi
Det at Mil
Dal at SA
Sac at Utah
Port at LAC
Denver at GS
Phoe at Sea

Sun Nov 8
Hou at LAL

Mon Nov 9
Bos at NY

Tue Nov 10
Chi at Atl
Det at Ind
Wash at Mil
LAL at SA
GS at Phoe
Utah at LAC
Den at Sac
Hou at Port
Dal at Sea

Wed Nov 11
Ind at Bos
Chi at NJ
Atl at NY
Phil at Wash
Mil at Cle
Dal at Utah
Phoe at GS

Thu Nov 12
Sea at SA
Port at Den
LAC at LAL
Hou at Sac

Fri Nov 13
Cle at Bos
Det at Phil

NY at Wash
NJ at Chi
Sea at Dal
Phoe at Utah
GS at LAC

Sat Nov 14
Mil at NY
Phil at Atl
Det at Cle
Ind at Chi
Port at Dal
Utah at Hou
Sac at Den
SA at Phoe
LAL at GS

Sun Nov 15
Wash at NJ
Bos at Ind
Atl at Mil
Sea at Hou
SA at LAL

Tue Nov 17
Hou at NJ
Bos at Cle
Wash at Chi
GS at Mil
LAC at SA
Den at Utah
Port at LAL
Ind at Sac

Wed Nov 18
NY at Bos
Chi at Wash
GS at Atl
Phil at Det
LAC at Dal
Ind at Den
Utah at Phoe
Port at Sea

Thu Nov 19
NY at NJ
Hou at Cle
Mil at Sac

Fri Nov 20
Bos at Phil
GS at Det
Atl at Chi
SA at Den
Ind at Utah
LAC at Phoe
Dal at LAL
Wash at Port
Mil at Sea

Sat Nov 21
Bos at NJ
GS at NY
Hou at Atl
Phil at Cle
Det at Chi
Utah at SA
Den at LAC
Dal at Sac
Wash at Sea

Sun Nov 22
Mil at LAL
Ind at Port

Mon Nov 23
Chi at Bos (Hart)
SA at NY

Tue Nov 24
Cle at Phil
Det at Hou
NJ at Den
Wash at Utah
LAC at GS
Sac at Port
LAL at Sea

Wed Nov 25
Atl at Bos
NY at Cle
SA at Ind
Chi at Mil
Det at Dal
Hou at Phoe
Wash at LAC

Thu Nov 26
NJ at Sac

Fri Nov 27
Sea at Bos
SA at Det
Atl at Ind
Chi at Dal
Hou at Utah
NJ at Phoe
Den at LAL
Phil at GS
LAC at Port

Sat Nov 28
* Cle at NY
Det at Wash
SA at Atl
Sea at Ind
Bos at Mil
Chi at Hou

Dal at Den
Phil at Sac

Sun Nov 29
* NJ at Port

Mon Nov 30
Ind at Mil
Phil at Utah

Tue Dec 1
Det at NJ
Sea at NY
Bos at Atl
Den at Hou
Chi at GS
LAL at Sac
Phoe at Port

Wed Dec 2
NJ at Bos
Sea at Cle
Mil at Det
Wash at Ind
Hou at SA
Sac at Den
Chi at Utah
Phil at LAC
Port at LAL

Thu Dec 3
Atl at Wash
NY at Phoe

Fri Dec 4
Sea at Phil
NJ at Atl
Bos at Det
Cle at Ind
LAL at Mil
GS at Dal
Chi at Den
NY at Utah
Sac at LAC

Sat Dec 5
Sea at Wash
LAL at Cle
Den at Dal
GS at Hou
Chi at SA
Port at Phoe
Utah at Sac

Sun Dec 6
Phoe at LAC
NY at Port

Tue Dec 8
LAL at NJ

Wash at NY
Port at Det
Mil at Ind
Phil at Chi
Sac at Hou
Utah at SA
Atl at LAC
Cle at Sea

Wed Dec 9
Den at Bos
Port at Phil
LAL at Wash
Sac at Dal
Atl at Phoe
Cle at GS

Thu Dec 10
Ind at NJ
Den at NY
Mil at Chi
Utah at Hou
Sea at LAC

Fri Dec 11
LAL at Bos
Wash at Det
Port at Mil
Phoe at Dal
Atl at GS
Cle at Sac

Sat Dec 12
Wash at NJ
* Den at Phil
NY at Det
Port at Ind
* Hou at Chi
Phoe at SA
GS at Utah
LAC at Sea

Sun Dec 13
Dal at Mil
Cle at LAL
Atl at Sac

Mon Dec 14
Sea at Utah

Tue Dec 15
SA at NJ
Mil at NY
Bos at Wash
Ind at Atl
Dal at Cle
Chi at Det
Phoe at LAL
LAC at Sac
Sea at Port

Wed Dec 16
Utah at Bos
Dal at NJ
SA at Phil
Hou at Den

Thu Dec 17
Phil at NY
Ind at Wash
Cle at Chi
Hou at LAC
LAL at GS
Sac at Sea

Fri Dec 18
NJ at Cle
Dal at Det
Utah at Ind
Atl at Mil
Den at SA
Port at Phoe

Sat Dec 19
NJ at NY
Dal at Phil
Chi at Wash
Utah at Atl
Den at Hou
LAL at LAC
Sea at GS

Sun Dec 20
Phil at Bos
Ind at Cle
Sea at LAL
Phoe at Sac
SA at Port

Mon Dec 21
Utah at NJ

Tues Dec 22
Bos at Phil
Cle at Wash
Dal at Chi
NY at Mil
Atl at Hou
Phoe at Den
SA at Sac
GS at Port

Wed Dec 23
Phil at NJ
Chi at NY
Utah at Cle
Dal at Ind
Sea at Phoe
SA at LAC
Sac at LAL
Den at GS

Fri Dec 25
Det at NY
Atl at Phil

Sat Dec 26
NY at Atl

Port at Cle
NJ at Det
Chi at Ind
Wash at Mil
Hou at Dal
GS at SA
Sea at Den
* LAL at Utah
Sac at Phoe
Bos at LAC

Sun Dec 27
Cle at NJ
Bos at Sac

Mon Dec 28
Phil at Phoe
Den at Sea

Tue Dec 29
Mil at NJ
Port at NY
Hou at Det
Atl at Chi
Sac at Dal
Utah at Den
Phil at LAL

Wed Dec 30
Port at Wash
Atl at Cle
Det at Ind
Hou at Mil
Sac at SA
GS at Utah
Phoe at LAC
Bos at Sea

Fri Jan 1
LAC at NY
Den at Wash
Phil at Port

Sat Jan 2
Hou at Wash
* Phoe at Cle
Den at Det
NJ at Chi
Ind at Mil
Dal at SA
Bos at GS
Utah at Sac
Phil at Sea

Sun Jan 3
LAC at Atl
* LAL at Port

Mon Jan 4
Phoe at Phil
Den at Cle
Dal at Hou
Bos at Utah
SA at LAL

Tue Jan 5
Phoe at NY

NJ at Wash
Det at Atl
Ind at Chi
LAC at Mil
SA at GS
Sea at Port

Wed Jan 6
NY at Bos
Den at NJ
Utah at Phil
LAC at Cle
Atl at Det
Dal at LAL
Hou at Sea

Thu Jan 7
Mil at Ind
Den at Chi
Dal at Phoe
Hou at GS
SA at Sac

Fri Jan 8
Wash at Bos
NY at NJ
LAC at Phil
Cle at Atl
LAL at Det
Utah at Mil
Sac at Port

Sat Jan 9
Bos at NY
Cle at Phil
LAC at Wash
Den at Atl
LAL at Ind
Utah at Chi
Phoe at Hou
Dal at GS
SA at Sea

Sun Jan 10
* NJ at Mil
Sea at Sac

Mon Jan 11
LAC at Ind
Den at Phoe

Tue Jan 12
NY at Cle
Bos at Mil
Phil at Mil
GS at LAL

Wed Jan 13
Det at Bos
NJ at Phil
Ind at Dal
Atl at SA
Port at Utah
Hou at Phoe
LAL at LAC
GS at Sea

Thu Jan 14
Sac at NJ
Mil at Wash
Chi at Cle
Port at Hou
Atl at Den

Fri Jan 15
Sac at Bos
NY at Phil
Cle at Det
Ind at SA
LAC at GS
Utah at Sea

Sat Jan 16
Bos at NJ
Phil at NY
Det at Chi
* Atl at Dal
Ind at Hou
Port at SA
GS at Den
LAL at Phoe
Sea at LAC

Sun Jan 17
* Sac at Wash
* Cle at Mil

Mon Jan 18
* GS at Bos
Phoe at NJ
* Atl at NY
Wash at Chi
* Det at Den
Dal at LAC
* Hou at LAL
* Ind at Sea

Tue Jan 19
Chi at Atl
Mil at SA
Hou at Sac
Dal at Port

Wed Jan 20
Phoe at Bos
GS at NJ
Wash at Phil
Det at Utah
Ind at LAC
NY at Sea

Thu Jan 21
Atl at Cle
Mil at Hou
LAL at Den

Fri Jan 22
Atl at Bos
GS at Wash
NJ at Ind
Phoe at Chi
LAC at Dal
SA at Utah
NY at LAL

Thu Jan 14
Den at Port
Det at Sea

Sat Jan 23
Bos at Cle
GS at Chi
Mil at Dal
LAC at SA
NY at Sac

Sun Jan 24
* Phil at Wash
* NJ at Atl
* Phoe at Ind
Det at Port
* LAL at Sea

Mon Jan 25
Cle at Utah
Mil at GS

Tue Jan 26
NJ at NY
Bos at Atl
Chi at Ind
SA at Dal
LAC at Hou
Utah at LAL
Sea at Sac
Mil at Port

Wed Jan 27
Wash at Bos
Chi at Phil
Ind at Det
Cle at SA
Dal at Phoe
Port at GS

Thu Jan 28
NY at Wash
Cle at Hou
Mil at Den
LAL at Sac

Fri Jan 29
Ind at Phil
Bos at Det
NJ at Chi
Sea at Dal
Mil at LAC
Atl at LAL
Utah at GS
Phoe at Port

Sat Jan 30
Det at NJ
Wash at Cle
NY at Chi
Hou at Dal
Sea at SA
LAC at Den
Atl at Utah
Sac at Phoe

Sun Jan 31
* Phil at Bos

Mon Feb 1
Det at Cle
GS at Ind
NJ at Dal
Sea at Utah
Chi at Sac

Tue Feb 2
Wash at NY
Det at Mil
Phoe at Hou
NJ at SA
Atl at Port

Wed Feb 3
Ind at Bos
GS at Phil
Cle at Wash
Dal at Den
Sac at Utah

Thu Feb 4
Det at NY
GS at Cle
Phil at Ind
Bos at Mil
NJ at Hou
Den at SA
Chi at Phoe
* LAL at LAC
Dal at Sac
Utah at Port
Atl at Sea

Sun Feb 7
* All-Star Game
at Chi

Tue Feb 9
NJ at Wash
Phil at Atl
Det at Chi
Cle at Mil
Utah at Dal
Bos at Hou
SA at Den
LAC at Phoe
Ind at LAL
Sac at GS
Sea at Port

Wed Feb 10
Chi at NJ
Wash at Cle
NY at Det
Bos at SA
Dal at Utah
Phoe at LAC

Thu Feb 11
Mil at Phil
LAL at Den
Ind at GS
Port at Sac
Hou at Sea

Fri Feb 12
NJ at Cle
Atl at Det
Chi at Mil
Bos at Dal
LAL at SA
Ind at Phoe
Hou at LAC
Den at Port

Sat Feb 13
Cle at NY
Wash at Atl
Chi at Det
Sea at GS
Phoe at Sac

Sun Feb 14
* Phil at NJ
Utah at Den
Dal at LAC
* Bos at LAL
* Hou at Port

Mon Feb 15
NJ at NY
* Mil at Wash
* Sac at Cle
Phil at Det
* Atl at Chi
GS at SA
Port at Utah
Bos at Phoe
Dal at Sea

Tue Feb 16
Sac at Atl
NY at Ind
GS at Hou
LAC at LAL

Wed Feb 17
Cle at Phil
Sea at Mil
Wash at Dal
Bos at Den
Phoe at Utah
Port at LAC

Thu Feb 18
Sac at NY
Sea at Det
Cle at Ind
LAL at Hou
* SA at Phoe

Fri Feb 19
NJ at Phil
LAL at Atl
Sac at Chi
Det at Mil
GS at Dal
Wash at SA
Utah at LAC
Bos at Port

Sat Feb 20
Sea at NJ

Wash at Hou
LAC at Utah
Den at Phoe

Sun Feb 21
Sea at Atl
* Chi at Cle
Sac at Ind
* Phil at Mil
* Det at LAL
* SA at Port

Mon Feb 22
NY at Bos (Hart)
Phoe at Dal
Phil at Hou
Wash at Den
SA at GS

Tue Feb 23
Port at NJ
Mil at NY
Ind at Atl
Sea at Chi
Wash at LAL
Det at Sac

Wed Feb 24
Port at Bos
Mil at Ind
Cle at Dal
Phil at SA
Den at Utah
Det at GS

Thu Feb 25
Dal at Hou
Cle at Phoe
NY at LAC
Wash at Sac

Fri Feb 26
Mil at Bos
NJ at Det
Atl at Ind
Port at Chi
Hou at SA
Phil at Den
Utah at LAL
NY at GS
Sac at Sea

Sat Feb 27
Ind at NJ
Port at Atl
Mil at Chi
Phil at Dal
Wash at Phoe
Cle at LAC
GS at Sea

Sun Feb 28
* Bos at Det
SA at Hou
* NY at Den
Phoe at LAL

Mon Feb 29
Chi at Phil
Den at Dal
Wash at GS
Utah at Sac
Cle at Port

Tue Mar 1
LAC at NJ
Ind at NY
Det at Atl
Bos at Mil
Phoe at SA
Hou at Utah
LAL at Sea

Wed Mar 2
NJ at Bos
Ind at Wash
LAC at Det
Sac at Dal
Cle at Den
Hou at GS

Thu Mar 3
Phil at Chi
Port at Phoe

Fri Mar 4
LAC at Bos
Phil at NY
Wash at Ind
Hou at Dal
Sac at SA
Phoe at Den
GS at LAL
Utah at Sea

Sat Mar 5
NY at NJ
Det at Wash
Mil at Atl
LAC at Chi
Sac at Hou
SA at Utah
GS at Port
Den at Sea

Sun Mar 6
* Cle at Bos
Mil at Det
Phil at Ind
* LAL at Dal

Mon Mar 7
Chi at NY
LAL at Phil
NJ at Utah
Den at Sac

Tue Mar 8
Phoe at Atl
Det at Ind
SA at Mil
Port at Dal
Hou at Den
Sea at GS

Wed Mar 9
SA at Bos
LAL at NY
Phoe at Wash
Mil at Det
Utah at Det
NJ at LAC
Sea at Sac

Thu Mar 10
LAL at Chi
Port at Hou
NJ at GS

Fri Mar 11
Ind at Bos (Hart)
Sac at Phil
Utah at Wash
NY at Atl
SA at Cle
Phoe at Det
Den at Mil
GS at LAC

Sat Mar 12
Utah at NY
Cle at Det
SA at Chi
Dal at LAL

Sun Mar 13
* Atl at Bos
* Wash at Phil
* Den at Ind
* Phoe at Mil
GS at Hou
* LAC at Port
NJ at Sea

Mon Mar 14
Cle at NY
SA at Wash
Sac at Det
GS at Dal
Utah at Phoe
NJ at LAL

Tue Mar 15
Phil at Atl
Bos at Ind
Cle at Chi
Sac at Mil
LAC at Hou
Sea at Phoe
LAL at Port

Wed Mar 16
Mil at NJ
NY at Phil
Chi at Wash
LAC at SA
Dal at Utah
Phoe at GS

Thu Mar 17
Det at Cle
Wash at Ind

Sea at Hou
Port at Den

Fri Mar 18
Atl at NJ
Ind at Phil
Bos at Chi
Sea at SA
Den at Utah
Dal at LAC
Port at GS

Sat Mar 19
Atl at NY
Phil at Wash
Cle at Mil
Utah at SA
LAL at Phoe
Hou at Sac

Sun Mar 20
* Chi at Bos
* Ind at NJ
Wash at Det
* Sea at Den
Sac at LAC
LAL at GS
* Dal at Port

Mon Mar 21
Mil at Atl
NY at SA
LAC at Phoe

Tue Mar 22
Phil at NJ
Ind at Det
Atl at Mil
NY at Dal
SA at Den
Phoe at Utah
Hou at LAL

Wed Mar 23
Wash at Bos
Chi at Phil
NJ at Cle
Den at LAC
Sac at GS
Port at Sea

Thu Mar 24
Atl at Wash
NY at Hou
Sac at Utah
Mil at Phoe

Fri Mar 25
Phil at Bos
Chi at Cle
NJ at Ind
Port at Dal
Det at SA
GS at LAC
Den at LAL

Sat Mar 26
Bos at NY
NJ at Wash
Cle at Atl
Ind at Chi
SA at Dal
Port at Hou
Mil at Utah
Det at Phoe
Den at GS
LAL at Sac
LAC at Sea

Mon Mar 28
Bos at NJ
Dal at NY
Hou at Phil
Det at LAC

Tue Mar 29
Dal at Atl
NY at Cle
Port at SA
Utah at LAL
Den at Sac
Chi at Sea

Wed Mar 30
Hou at Bos
Mil at Phil
Cle at Wash
Atl at Det
GS at Phoe
Chi at LAC

Thu Mar 31
Hou at Ind
NY at Mil
Sac at Den
GS at Utah
SA at Sea

Fri Apr 1
Det at Bos
Atl at Phil
Dal at Wash
SA at LAC
Chi at Port

Sat Apr 2
Hou at NY
* Ind at Cle
NJ at Mil
GS at Den
LAL at Utah
LAC at Sac
Phoe at Sea

Sun Apr 3
* Dal at Bos
Wash at NJ
* Chi at Det
* Atl at Ind
Sac at LAL
* SA at Port

Tue Apr 5
Det at NJ
NY at Phil
Mil at Atl
Cle at Ind
Wash at Chi
Den at Hou
Utah at Phoe
Sea at LAL
SA at GS
LAC at Cle

Wed Apr 6
Wash at Cle
Chi at Mil
Phoe at Dal
Port at LAC
SA at Sac
GS at Sea

Thu Apr 7
NJ at Atl
Utah at Hou

Fri Apr 8
NJ at Bos
Det at NY
Ind at Wash
Mil at Cle
NY at Chi
Utah at Dal
Den at SA
LAC at LAL
Phoe at GS
Port at Sea

Sat Apr 9
Det at Atl
Ind at Mil
Den at Dal
Sac at Phoe
LAL at Port
Hou at Sea

Sun Apr 10
* Cle at NJ
* Bos at Phil
* NY at Wash
Hou at LAC
GS at Sac

Mon Apr 11
Det at NY
Wash at Atl
NJ at Ind
Phil at Mil
Den at Phoe
Utah at GS

Tue Apr 12
Atl at Cle
Hou at SA
LAC at Utah
Port at LAL
Dal at Sac

Wed Apr 13
Mil at Bos
Ind at NY
Wash at Phil
Cle at Det
LAL at Den
SA at Phoe
Dal at GS
LAC at Sea

Thu Apr 14
Chi at Ind
Sac at Hou
Port at Utah

Fri Apr 15
Chi at NJ
Wash at NY
Atl at Phil
Bos at Cle
Mil at Det
Sac at SA
Hou at Den
Phoe at LAL
GS at Port
Dal at Sea

Sat Apr 16
NY at Atl
NJ at Det
Phil at Ind
SA at Utah
Sea at Phoe
LAC at GS

Sun Apr 17
* Bos at Wash
* Mil at Chi
* LAL at Hou
* Dal at Den
* Sac at Port

Mon Apr 18
Ind at Cle

Tue Apr 19
Det at NY
Atl at NJ
Chi at NY
Mil at Phil
Dal at Hou
LAL at SA
Sea at Den
GS at Phoe
LAC at Sac
Utah at Port

Wed Apr 20
Ind at Atl
Wash at Mil
LAL at Dal
Utah at LAC
Port at GS
Phoe at Sea

Thu Apr 21
Chi at Bos

NJ at Phil
Det at Wash
SA at Hou

Fri Apr 22
Bos at Atl
Ind at Det
Cle at Chi
NY at Mil
SA at Dal
LAL at Phoe
Sac at GS
Den at Port
Utah at Sea

Sat Apr 23
Mil at NJ
Atl at Wash
Phil at Cle
NY at Ind
LAC at Den
Hou at Utah
Port at Sac

Sun Apr 24
Phil at Det
* Bos at Chi
Phoe at Hou
* Dal at SA
Sea at LAC
* GS at LAL

Revised and updated with over 75 all
new sports records and photographs!

THE ILLUSTRATED
SPORTS RECORD BOOK
Zander Hollander and David Schulz

Here in a single book are more than 350
all-time sports records with stories and
photos so vivid it's like "being there." All the
sports classics are here: Babe Ruth, Wilt
Chamberlain, Muhammad Ali ... plus the
stories of such active stars as Dwight Gooden
and Wayne Gretzky. This is the authoritative
book on what the great records are, and
who set them—an engrossing, fun-filled
reference guide filled with anecdotes of
hundreds of renowned athletes whose
remarkable records remain as fresh as when
they were set.
